W9-BVH-860

THE
HARDING
AFFAIR

THE
HARDING
AFFAIR

LOVE AND
ESPIONAGE
DURING THE
GREAT WAR

JAMES DAVID
ROBENALT

palgrave
macmillan

THE HARDING AFFAIR
Copyright © James David Robenalt, 2009.
All rights reserved.

First published in hardcover in 2009 by PALGRAVE MACMILLAN® in the US—
a division of St. Martin's Press LLC, 175 Fifth Avenue, New York, NY 10010.

Where this book is distributed in the UK, Europe and the rest of the world, this is by
Palgrave Macmillan, a division of Macmillan Publishers Limited, registered in
England, company number 785998, of Houndmills, Basingstoke, Hampshire
RG21 6XS.

Palgrave Macmillan is the global academic imprint of the above companies and has
companies and representatives throughout the world.

Palgrave® and Macmillan® are registered trademarks in the United States, the United
Kingdom, Europe and other countries.

ISBN: 978-0-230-10695-6

Library of Congress Cataloging-in-Publication Data
Robenalt, James D., 1956–
   The Harding affair : love and espionage during the Great War / James David
Robenalt.
      p.   cm.
   Includes bibliographical references and index.
   ISBN-13: 978-0-230-60964-8 (hardcover)
   ISBN-10: 0-230-60964-3 (hardcover)
   (paperback ISBN: 978-0-230-10695-6)
   1. Harding, Warren G. (Warren Gamaliel), 1865–1923—Relations with women.
2. Phillips, Carrie Fulton, 1873–1960.   3. Presidents—United States—Biography.
4. World War, 1914–1918—United States.   5. Espionage—United States—
History—20th century.   6. Harding, Warren G. (Warren Gamaliel),
1865–1923—Correspondence.   7. Phillips, Carrie Fulton, 1873–1960—
Correspondence.   8. United States—History—1913–1921.   I. Title.
E786.R63   2009
973.91'4092—dc22

2009015910

A catalogue record of the book is available from the British Library.

Design by Letra Libre, Inc.

First PALGRAVE MACMILLAN paperback edition: May 2011

10   9   8   7   6   5   4   3   2   1

Printed in the United States of America.

CONTENTS

FOREWORD

John W. Dean

his is a truly unique and historic book because of the truly
unique and historic material upon which it is based: A treasure trove of love letters—"PG–13" or "R" rated by today's
standards because some of the material is remarkably explicit—
written by Warren G. Harding to Mrs. Carrie Phillips, his
longtime lover, who saved the future president's letters and occasionally added
her own notes and drafts to the collection. There are in existence roughly 788
handwritten pages by Harding found in the form of 106 letters, which include
poetry and other materials he sent to Carrie over the years. In addition, there
are approximately 138 pages written by Carrie, which include her notes along
with what appear to be drafts of letters she prepared, if not unsent letters.* The
longer Harding letters run between 20 to 30 pages, but these were composed
of multiple letters written over several days. Some letters were written on the
pages of a reporter's stenographic-type notebook from Harding's old newspaper days, many are on U.S. Senate Chamber stationery, while others are
on hotel stationery, sent while he was traveling.

This collection of writings amounts to much more than old love letters;
rather, they result in a strikingly intimate self-portrait unlike any other of the
often-maligned twenty-ninth president of the United States. While Harding
holds no unique presidential distinction by having had an extramarital affair,

---

* In addition, Carrie also saved telegrams from Harding; two letters from her brother Chester relaying information from Harding while he was president; twelve pages of a draft letter from her to Dr. Carl Sawyer
about Harding's memorial following his death in 1923; fifty-four envelopes; an invitation to Harding's inauguration; photos; and other miscellaneous items.

these letters reveal how truly complex his affair became, given the fact that Carrie Phillips, Senator Harding's (soon to be President Harding's) lover, was likely a German spy and the United States was heading into the Great War: World War I.

Many will wonder how these letters ended up in the possession of James D. Robenalt, the author of this book, *The Harding Affair*. Given the fact that these letters were almost destroyed—and the original copies have been sealed since the middle of the 1960s—it is a story that should be told.* To anyone aware of the compelling history behind these letters and Harding's papers, as I am, I must also state that it is fortuitous that Jim Robenalt is the first to dig into them, not because he will have the last word on the letters but rather because there will not be much to add to the remarkable job he has done in analyzing them and showing their significance. Jim's "day job" is working as a high-powered, extremely able, big-case, Cleveland-based trial and appellate attorney, which does not fully explain his credentials for this project. Rather, one must know Jim, and of his deep family roots in Ohio, to appreciate his fascination with, and understanding of, the history of his state and its political figures. His skills for handling this project will become evident in the pages that follow, especially his probing research and evenhanded analysis. He has carefully translated not-always-legible handwritten material, dated the letters (which was extremely difficult when they were undated, commingled, or identified with only a month and day but no year). Most important, he has placed the letters in their full historical context. Given the fact these letters were never written for public consumption, and many of them are highly sensational, it is a credit to him that while Jim has withheld nothing, he has treated the material fairly and squarely.

These remarkable letters first surfaced at a very awkward time, back in the fall of 1963, just when the Harding Memorial Association in Marion, Ohio, had finally agreed, after years of resistance, to provide Harding's presidential papers to the Ohio Historical Society (OHS) in Columbus. Contrary to the long-held impression that former First Lady Florence Harding had destroyed all Harding's records, substantial materials had been found after Harding's death in office in 1923, only to be stored in the basement of the White House

---

* This foreword is based on material that Jim and I gathered to offer a book about the letters to a publisher. Initially, we planned to do this as a joint project. But my own schedule precluded my coauthoring; nonetheless, I have been involved in the project from the sidelines since the outset to its completion. In fact, after I published *Pure Goldwater* (2008) with Palgrave Macmillan, I realized this book would be perfect for their list, so I sent Jim to Airié Stuart, Palgrave's publisher, and she agreed.

and then years later sent to the Harding Memorial Association, which had not seriously looked at them.

The transfer and unpacking of Harding's presidential papers at OHS prompted Francis Russell, a Harvard-educated author and a contributing editor of the *American Heritage* magazine, to travel to Columbus to look at the material when he was working on a new biography of Harding. There Russell and other historians were greeted by Kenneth Duckett, a professional archivist, who had joined the OHS a few years earlier and had successfully negotiated the transfer of Harding's material. While the unpacking of the Harding papers was under way, Russell traveled to nearby Marion, Ohio, Harding's home, to talk to locals and chase rumors. In Marion, Russell quickly picked up the well-known local story that Carrie Phillips's court-appointed guardian attorney had, following her death in 1960, retained possession of a box filled with love letters from Warren Harding. Disregarding any fiduciary responsibility to Carrie or her estate, the attorney agreed to show the letters to Russell when he called. He immediately realized their potential value to his project. Upon initial inspection, Russell convinced Carrie's attorney that it would be best to give the letters to the OHS, mostly to safeguard them from the clutches of the Harding Memorial Association, from whence it had taken a half century to extract Harding's presidential papers.

Russell called Ken Duckett and told him of the find, and arranged to bring Duckett back to Marion. Initially, Duckett was thrilled, for as the curator of manuscripts at the OHS, he would be delighted to add the material to the Harding collection. But quickly he had second thoughts, based on his years of experience in dealing with the Harding Memorial Association. Duckett realized that the letters would be a big problem. If OHS acquired the letters, and this fact came to light, he was worried the Harding Memorial Association would end its dealings with OHS. In addition, Duckett was concerned that the Republican-controlled Ohio legislature that funded OHS, and Republican governor James Rhodes, would likely want the letters to disappear because they would not want the shadow of President Harding to fall on them. Accordingly, within a few days, Russell and Duckett became collaborators in a plan to keep the letters secret until Russell published his book. Russell wanted to be in control of the letters so they would first appear in his book; Duckett, realizing their historical importance, wanted to preserve them.

Russell seemingly had an agenda for his Harding biography. It appeared that he wanted to prove—notwithstanding evidence to the contrary—that Harding's family included African ancestors. This goal is well documented in Russell's letters to Duckett and is supported by Duckett's diary. For example, Russell's mind-set could not be more plainly on display than in a letter he wrote to Duckett in 1966: "I want the title [of my book] to be The Shadow of Blooming Grove—The Life and Times of Warren Gamaliel Harding. Mc-Graw-Hill disapproves of From Whore House to White House, although I still think it would sell better. The Nigger in the Woodpile was another rejected title." The book would, in fact, ultimately be titled *The Shadow of Blooming Grove.*

Based on his later writing, it is clear that Russell's quick scan of Harding's letters convinced him that all the scandalous rumors he had heard or read about Harding were true. In fact, however, Russell could not have any idea what was actually contained in the letters from the time he spent with them. He reviewed the letters in Carrie's former attorney's office, where he took a few hurried notes and focused almost exclusively on sexual material. Duckett gave him another fleeting look at the letters later in Columbus, but Russell had less than a day's worth of time to review over 900 pages of difficult, handwritten material that had not been cataloged or organized. He could not have begun to understand the material, which has taken others years to assemble and reconstruct. Still, Russell produced a 700-page Harding biography largely based on his limited, arguably myopic, review.

Duckett, a trained historian, quickly became unimpressed with Russell's scholarship, as he wrote in his diary after their first meeting: "The man is no historian: he is a professional writer with a nose for the scandalous, and he found it about Harding." Circumstances forced Duckett to become increasingly entwined with Russell. Years later, Duckett realized he had overreacted at the potential of crossing swords with the Harding Memorial Association and Ohio Republican politicians. Nonetheless, his concern for the letters and for keeping their existence unknown to others at OHS was well placed. Destruction remained a real threat. For this reason, it is understandable that he believed he had no choice but to enter a secret pact with Russell to preserve the letters.

Accordingly, Duckett and Russell typed out a convoluted confidential agreement that would enable Russell to have his second brief look at the letters, before Duckett secured them by hiding them in an OHS vault. In addition, Duckett agreed to secretly microfilm the letters (Xerox and other such copying was yet to become commercially available) and to send microfilmed copies to trusted custodians, both inside and outside the state. According to this secret agreement, when Russell was ready to release his book, Duckett would anonymously mail microfilmed copies to important libraries, such as Yale and the New York Public Library, and he would profess ignorance of any involvement with Russell, saying only that Russell had delivered a sealed box to the OHS that had never been opened or inspected. "I will be properly amazed," Duckett wrote in their secret plan, when the OHS was presented with its own anonymous copy of the microfilm.*

The Russell and Duckett secret plan was quite amateurish. To hide his activities, Duckett even got into a fistfight with the director of the OHS one evening, when he was busy secretly microfilming the Harding letters in a vault in the basement. By the spring of 1964, however, the existence of the letters in the OHS vault became known to Duckett's superiors, just as the official Harding papers were being released for public use. This should have been a joyous occasion for Duckett. In fact, it was overshadowed by a looming showdown with his superiors and the OHS board, who were trying to undercut his effort to protect the letters. Duckett reported in his diary of a "long session in which I was hit from all sides" on April 20, 1964. Just as he had worried, the OHS board wanted either to destroy the letters or to return them to Marion so the locals could dispose of them. With pressure building, Duckett wrote Russell that a Marion judge had told the OHS officials: "You have a problem, we have a solution. You want to get rid of those letters, bring 'em back to Marion and we'll take care of them."

The internal fight over the letters soon seeped out of the confines of the OHS leadership, and several Harding biographers (working at the OHS on the Harding papers) got wind of existence of the letters, which, pursuant to a court order, had been returned to Marion. When Duckett had been asked by his superiors if he had made copies—he had been seen with a microfilm camera in the vault—he ducked the question. He recorded feeling that these were "the gloomiest days of my life." While he had backup copies, microfilm is not the best copying method, so he worried about the originals being destroyed in Marion.

It was at this time that Duckett mailed microfilmed copies of the letters to personal friends in Dayton, Denver, and San Francisco. Soon the news media picked up word of the letters. On July 7, 1964, the *Toledo Blade* called Duckett to inquire about the Harding letters. Duckett was less than forthcoming but immediately advised Russell of the inquiry, who soon called him back to say that the *New York Times* was going to break the story the next day. "Very nervous evening," Duckett wrote in his diary.

---

* Russell, ignoring the existence of the written agreement, would later deny having any involvement with Duckett regarding any of this. In 1978, for example, when he wrote an article about the Harding letters in *The Antioch Review*, he protested the limited time Duckett gave him to review the letters, yet it was the time that he and Duckett had secretly agreed upon: "But to this day I have never been able to understand Duckett," Russell questioned, "Why an hour? Why not two hours? A day? Any time at all?"

The *Toledo Blade* story on July 8 was mild, referring to "personal letters" of Harding's that were "once in the possession of Mrs. Carrie Phillips." The *New York Times* story, written by R. W. Apple, appeared on July 10, and it was sensational. A front-page headline (inaccurately) proclaimed: "250 Love Letters From Harding to Ohio Merchant's Wife Found." Francis Russell was identified as the source, and he described the letters and their content. Quotes from Harding's letters, taken from Russell's notes, were included in the *Times* story, and Russell told Apple that the letters "gave credence to charges made by Nan Britton in a book she published in 1927" about her purported affair and love child with Harding. (In fact, close study of the letters tends to discredit Ms. Britton's story.) News of the letters flashed around the world. Francis Russell had effectively made his preemptive strike to further trash the former president's reputation.

Following the national attention to the letters, Duckett wrote to Oliver Jensen, founder and editor of *American Heritage,* that: "I have heard the words 'burn, destroy and suppress' so many times since I acquired the papers, that I have determined that extraordinary precautions must be taken to insure their preservation and their use by historians." Accordingly, Duckett enclosed with his letter a microfilm of the letters. "Without these letters the truth will never be known about Warren G. Harding and his times," Duckett explained. Two days later, the head of the OHS called Duckett and ordered him to turn over all the microfilmed copies he had of the Harding letters. Duckett contacted Russell and Jensen. *American Heritage* offered Duckett a place on the payroll until he could find a job. Duckett turned them down, but he had hired attorney, Norton Webster, who also feared destruction of the material, and who told his client that he should not surrender the letters and that they "must prepare to fight."

On July 29, 1964, things came to a head. The associate director of OHS, Daniel Porter, made a last demand. "Then at 2:30 [in the afternoon] they came, the attorney from Harding's [lawsuit] and a man from the sheriff's office with Porter and they served me a suit for a million dollars," Duckett wrote, and added that he casually tucked the lawsuit papers in his desk and continued to type a letter. After a call to his attorney, he went home and recorded in his diary: "Bought a fifth of champagne and Alma [his wife] and I celebrated being sued. The kids think I'm crazy."

Not surprisingly, and no doubt prompted by the *New York Times* story, the Harding family decided to sue Russell, Duckett, *American Heritage,* and McGraw-Hill, Russell's publisher, to exercise Harding's copyright interest (then belonging to his heirs) in the private letters to prevent their exploitation. An Ohio state court in Columbus issued a temporary injunction forbidding further the publication of any of the letters until the copyright matters were resolved. *American Heritage* agreed to pay Duckett's defense costs. When Duckett was deposed, his attorney seriously considered whether he should invoke the Fifth Amendment, but decided his client must testify, so on August 10, Duckett admitted to making only four microfilmed copies of the letters. "Very depressed," he wrote of his deposition. After the deposition, the Harding family's attorney informed the press that "the Harding heirs wanted the letters—at least the sensational ones—suppressed forever." This comment sparked something of a national debate on the subject.

All the while, Francis Russell was working on his Harding biography. Once further use of the letters had been enjoined, he completed his research in Ohio, packed up, and returned to New England to write his book. The Harding family's lawsuit annoyed Russell greatly, for it spoiled his project and put him into a fighting mood. In August 1964, he wrote Duckett that the *American Heritage* lawyers were talking about settlement, since the letters were currently preserved and the objective of protecting them had been accomplished. Russell, however, was against settling. "For myself," he protested, "I am not going to surrender my notes to anybody, and if in the end I have to paraphrase rather than quote I'm sure I can denigrate our Hero quite as effectively even so." Of course, the *American Heritage* magazine loved the attention the dustup over the letters had created, and to keep the debate alive, it issued a press release entitled "Should Presidential Papers Be Destroyed?" The magazine announced that, in order to avoid disasters of the past, including the destruction of some of Lincoln's papers, "it had sequestered a complete set of photographic copies of the Harding-Phillips letters for their historic safekeeping."

The lawsuit was not resolved by the time Russell completed his book, so he still could not use the letters. When he published his book—the diatribe against Harding he had promised from the outset—he relied on the material in his notes and what he could recall about the letters but left blank white spaces on the pages where he had made his own hand-copy of contents of the few letters he had seen. Nonetheless, he remained cheerful. "Beyond that I ride round the countryside afternoons on my bicycle," he wrote Duckett, "and that is my idea of fun." Duckett, however, was hardly having fun. He was bearing the brunt of the lawsuit. He had been publicly reprimanded by the OHS, and although he had not been fired, he left OHS under pressure and found another archival post in Illinois.

When the suit was finally settled, the Harding family (who had the copyright to the contents of the letters) purchased the possessory rights to the letters from Carrie Phillips's estate, *American Heritage* paid some money in the settlement, and the original letters themselves were sent off to the Library of Congress for fifty years, where they remain sealed until 2014. The microfilms Duckett admitted he made were placed under similar seal in the OHS. (The Harding family kept a copy, and over the years, they have allowed only a very select number of scholars to look at the letters.) Everything was confirmed in a stipulated settlement order of the court. However, the settlement was very loosely drawn, and it failed to account for all the microfilmed copies that Duckett had prepared and squirreled away.

After the dust settled, Duckett recovered one of the sets of the letters that appears to have gone unaccounted for. He began the tedious task of deciphering their contents and doing the necessary background research to date the letters and place them in context. Duckett's years of research provided a foundation upon which Jim has built and constructed his narrative. As Ken Duckett grew older, he gifted his papers to the Cleveland-based Western Reserve Historical Society. Unbeknownst to that institution, these papers included the microfilmed Harding letters.

Knowing Jim Robenalt's credentials as a top Cleveland attorney, and that he had a deep interest in the period, since he had then recently published a book on Ohio politics of the Harding era (his great-grandfather had headed the Democratic Party in Ohio and knew Harding as a personal friend but political opponent), the Western Reserve Historical Society sought his advice. Jim found that the copyright in the letters had long expired.

On October 5, 2004, Case Western Reserve University in Cleveland hosted the Vice Presidential Debate between Vice President Dick Cheney and Senator John Edwards. As part of that event, Jim organized a symposium on Ohio presidents—William Henry Harrison, Ulysses Grant, Rutherford Hayes, James Garfield, Benjamin Harrison, William McKinley, William Howard Taft, and Warren Harding—inviting scholars and family of those presidents to participate. Because I had done a biography of Harding for Arthur Schlesinger Jr.'s American Presidents Series, Jim invited me and Dr. Warren G. Harding III, the great-grandnephew of the president, to discuss the Harding presidency. I was pleased to learn from Dr. Harding that the family enjoyed my book, *Harding* (Times Books, 2004), but even more pleased to discover, during informal meetings before and after the symposium, that the Harding family recognized that mistakes had been made by the Harding Memorial Foundation in suppressing information about the Harding presidency. This suppression often gave the false impression that there was something to be hidden, when, in fact, there was much to be revealed that showed what a fine man, and able president, Harding had been a far better president than history has ranked him.

About a year after the symposium, Jim joined me when I gave a speech at the College of Wooster, a short drive south of Cleveland, and where I had completed my undergraduate work. Jim was interested because William Estabrook Chancellor, author of an infamously racist book about Harding, had been on the faculty at Wooster in the 1920s at the time of publication. When we returned to Cleveland, Jim and I visited the historical society and Duckett's material, where I had a brief look at a few of the microfilmed Harding letters. Having gotten to know Jim, I recognized immediately what should be done with the letters: Jim should write the book he has now written.

THE
HARDING
AFFAIR

PROLOGUE

"'Twas a Search in Vain"

O n Sunday, May 27, 1917, a train pulled into Penn Station in New York City at nine o'clock at night. Among those on board was Warren G. Harding, a U.S. senator from Ohio. He was recognized by some, but most people drifted past him. He traveled alone, not an uncommon thing even for a man of his status.

Senator Harding was a distinguished-looking man, with finely combed white hair, offset by thick dark eyebrows and a kind face. As usual, he was nicely turned out, his tailored suits hiding an acceptable midlife paunch. "He looks like a president" was something often said of him, but in person he was even more striking and magnetic than the usual high-ranking statesman. Although moving pictures were in their infancy at the time, it could be said that he had an early movie star quality about him: something deep, ineffable, and melancholy.

In photos, he looked too serious, and he knew it, for that was not who he really was. "So my portrait looks, as you stated, solemn and forbidding?" he once wrote to his neighbor, Carrie Phillips, of a photograph she kept on her wall when she was living abroad in Berlin. "Well, all my pictures have that sad and solemn look," he confessed. "Can't be otherwise, I guess, so long as I look that way. That *sober, distressed look is inherited,* so I can't help it," he wrote underlining the words for emphasis.

"I get it from my mother, who was careful and contented, and it comes from her father," he wrote of his stern appearance. "I never saw him, but have seen his pictures, and that *same solemn look* that clouds your room is in his face. Some day I'll pose for a laughing picture, and send you a copy," he added.

"I do laugh sometimes."

He missed Carrie terribly, back when she was an ocean away, and dreamed of what it would be like to trade places with his portrait in that Berlin pension. "I know I should smile if I could take the picture's place," he wrote. "You could put a different light in my eyes."[1]

In person, he had an intimate manner, an easy smile, a honeyed, baritone voice. He liked people. Women found him unusually attractive. After he died, his secretary of state, Charles Evans Hughes, bestowed upon him the greatest compliment one American can pay to another. "He belonged to the aristocracy of the plain people of this country," Hughes said.[2]

In May 1917, Carrie Phillips was back in the United States, and Warren Harding was looking for her in the New York train station. He took a rushed glance around and then he hurried over to Grand Central, where he checked his luggage. From there he made haste to the Biltmore Hotel. "I searched the lobby and parlors, then enquired at the desk," he later wrote to Carrie.[3] "Failing in that I went to the Manhattan [Hotel] expecting to find you or a note or telegram," he wrote, "and was again disappointed."

He returned to Penn Station to look again. No luck.

"'Twas a search in vain. So back to the Biltmore and Manhattan till 11:30, then a twenty minute vigil at the Grand Central and finally to bed in my midnight train for Boston, tired and disappointed."

He had known Carrie Fulton Phillips for a long time. She was from his hometown in Ohio, married to one of his best friends. She was beautiful, ample and fleshy, strong-willed, and the mother of one child, a daughter named Isabelle. Harding was childless, stuck in a complicated and sexually arid marriage to a woman five years his senior. The Harding marriage had become a business relationship, lacking the deep affection Warren needed. By 1917, Carrie and Warren had been in an intimate and stormy love affair for twelve years. Theirs was no short-term tryst.

The world was at war, an appalling conflagration, and the United States had just joined in, officially taking sides after nearly three years of neutrality while vicious warfare among the combatants had led to a virtual stalemate and had brought the civilized world to its knees. Harding was quietly leading the opposition to Woodrow Wilson and his expansive goals in calling the country to a war. Harding was worried more about protecting America—he was not particularly concerned about Wilson's crusade to save the world, and he was apprehensive that the strains of the war within the country were dividing the loyalties of its citizens, one against the other. The war in Europe had taken the country to the brink of another civil war, Harding thought. But this time, the division was along ethnic and national heritage lines.

Fear, paranoia, and outrage spilled over into every town, small or large. Those who considered themselves patriots began to spy on their neighbors. German Americans and recent German immigrants were vilified. Vigilante groups sprang up. Mail was searched, comings and goings watched. Quiet arrests were made. Labor leaders were rounded up. Free speech, especially any criticism of the war or its conduct, could become the reason for a ten-year jail sentence.

Harding was morose. He was not only vexed about the stability of his country, but he thought his relationship with Carrie was finally at its end. "I can't quite explain," he wrote to her. "I guess my spirit is broken, or my nerves gone, or both. I am in a half hopeless state. The light has gone out, and I am wearied. One thought insists—I loved you all that I ever said or acted—which was not a little—and I do know, and in that love and the full consciousness of having lost yours, I mean to do all in my poor way to make amends, to pay in contrition and in such poor service and tribute as I may render."[4]

Three years after his unsuccessful search in New York City for the woman he loved, Warren Harding was president of the United States. And three years after that, he was dead. He was fifty-eight years old.

One thing is sure: It is hard to defend yourself once you are dead.

When he died unexpectedly in San Francisco's Palace Hotel in August 1923, Warren G. Harding was one of the most beloved men in the country. He was kind, decent, handsome, a man of eminent reason. He also had a rare political attribute: courage. In his first address to Congress he asked for the passage of an antilynching law.[5] Six months after taking office, he was the first sitting president to travel into the deep South to make a bold civil rights speech. Democracy was a lie if blacks were denied political equality, he told an enormous crowd separated by color and a chain-link fence in Birmingham, Alabama.[6] A few months later, on his first Christmas in the White House, he pardoned Socialist leader Eugene Debs, who was rotting away in an Atlanta prison. Debs's crime? He spoke out against the draft and the war after America entered the conflict. "I have heard so damn much about you, Mr. Debs," Harding said when Debs arrived in the Oval Office to personally receive his pardon without conditions attached.[7]

Warren Harding brought the world together in the first arms limitation treaty. He also signed the peace treaty that ended the war with Germany. He established the first Office of the Budget. He supported the concept of a world court, and he opened the White House to the people after years of closure by the reclusive President Wilson, who tried to hide the ravages of a massive stroke. Harding was a breath of fresh air to a war-weary nation, a pillar of steadiness in a world staggering from economic and political instability. While Germany would sink into economic and political chaos, giving rise to the Nazi movement, the United States survived World War I with a secure government.

As a senator, Harding challenged Woodrow Wilson's policy to go to war "to make the world safe for democracy." Wilson wanted Germany to be a democracy, by force if necessary. Harding thought it was "none of our business what type of government any nation on this earth may choose to have."[8] He privately wrote to former president Theodore Roosevelt just after war was declared: "It has seemed to me that one of the great essentials in this serious time is to commit our foreign born citizenship to the American cause, and I have not thought it helpful to magnify the American purpose to force democracy upon the world. I do think it mightily essential that we establish the fact that democracy can well defend itself."[9]

Despite his limited time in office, Harding's record is remarkable in so many respects, now long forgotten. Teapot Dome, the scandal involving the sale of federal lands rich in oil reserves by Harding administration officials, erupted after his death, and it has never been shown that he knew anything about it. John Kennedy (the only other senator until President Obama to ascend directly from the Senate to the White House) was president for almost the same length of time as Warren Harding, but his record was decidedly mixed: Disasters such as the Bay of Pigs and involvement in Vietnam weigh against successes such as the handling of the Cuban missile crisis and the nuclear test ban treaty. Yet history could not have treated these two men more differently. Kennedy became an icon; Harding was deemed a failure.

What happened?

Ironically, letters showing his adultery, and the story surrounding their discovery, may be Warren Harding's salvation.

In October 1963, a month before Kennedy's assassination, a box filled with letters was placed on a kitchen table in a lawyer's home in Marion, Ohio, for inspection by Francis Russell, a respected author.[10] Russell was astounded by what he saw: almost nine hundred pages of handwriting—long, sprawling missives of love, some forty pages in length, some on United

States Senate Chamber stationery. They were in disorder. A few of them were attached to envelopes with postmarks; most had no date identification other than "Easter morning" or "January 8."

Russell had credentials. He was Harvard educated, a contributing editor to the *American Heritage* magazine, and author of dozens of books that had received critical acclaim. But the Harding letters could not have fallen into more dangerous hands. Privately, Russell loathed Warren Harding. He believed the long-standing but mostly unspoken rumor that Harding came from mixed blood. His book, *The Shadow of Blooming Grove*, the title itself referencing the race rumor, would become a bestseller and deeply influence, and in many ways help form and solidify, the modern perception of Harding as a failure.

Russell was not interested in mining the full content of the letters Warren Harding wrote to Carrie Phillips. Russell, it appeared, sought scandal. He focused on titillating passages, skipping over the more profound parts and the real story of a forbidden but passionate love. "Compared to what is available today in any drugstore bookrack," Russell would later tell the press, "Harding's eroticism is naive and even pathetic as the quality of his mind peeps through the boudoir phrases."[11] Russell's obsession with sex and race caused him to miss the most important story in the letters. Warren Harding's love for Carrie Phillips was set against one of the greatest man-made disasters of all time: the Great War. At the time Harding and Phillips began their love affair in 1905, neither of them could have imagined how this world calamity would intersect with their lives: he a U.S. senator with the power to vote on war, and she an uncompromising pro-German advocate.

Would he follow his conscience and vote for war? Did Carrie Phillips become a German spy? And who really was this man from Marion, Ohio, born in a crude farmhouse at the conclusion of the Civil War, who would become the twenty-ninth president of the United States? The masthead to the newspaper he founded and edited for most of his adult life, the *Marion Star*, carried this admonition: "Remember there are two sides to every question. Get them both. Be truthful. Get the facts. Be decent, be fair, be generous."[12]

The story that begins to unravel these mysteries begins in a hotel in Chattanooga, Tennessee, at the height of World War I.

CHAPTER 1

Espionage in Chattanooga

The Baroness

The plainclothes night watchman for the hotel, Thomas Stiff, knocked on the door.

He heard shuffling inside, and then it grew quiet. The door slowly opened and a woman in her middle years with thick auburn hair, swept back, gave him an imperious stare. Her eyes were piercing, and her manner suggested irritation. She was full figured and only partly dressed. Stiff considered her "disrobed."[1] He knew from hotel records that she claimed the title baroness.

Stiff was accompanied by Officer D. G. Grant of the Chattanooga police department. Stiff called Grant to join his investigation when he found that an army lieutenant was not in the room in which he was registered for a second night in a row. Suspicious, Stiff and Grant stood outside the baroness's room, looking past her to try to see what was going on inside. The time was just after one in the morning, on December 13, 1917. Stiff had seen the lieutenant leaving the baroness's room the night before. "At least I thought it was him," Stiff would later testify. When he checked the lieutenant's room between nine and ten o'clock that evening, the lieutenant was there, but when he returned after midnight, he could not raise the man. He entered his room and discovered his army overcoat, but there was no sign of the lieutenant.[2]

Although they lacked a warrant, Stiff and Grant brushed past the baroness and spotted the lieutenant under the bed, wearing his one-piece underwear. Slowly he emerged. He was young looking and could have been the baroness's son. Either the baroness or the lieutenant said they wanted to keep this thing quiet. Stiff asked the lieutenant who he was and what he was doing in the baroness's room. "This is my brother," she interrupted, shushing the young man.

"Funny your brother is in your room at this time of night," Stiff said with a sneer. Grant sniggered. Then Stiff grew serious. "You should consider yourself under arrest."

The lieutenant confessed he was not her brother. He did expect to marry the baroness, though, as soon as she received her divorce from her third husband. Stiff looked at them: The lieutenant was clearly half her age, and although she appeared in her early forties, she exuded a powerful sexual attractiveness. The lieutenant, however, looked like a boy off a Kansas farm. The young man asked Stiff if there was anything he could do to avoid going down to police headquarters. The night watchman said there was nothing he could do and told them to get dressed. The next morning, the baroness and the lieutenant were arraigned on charges of vagrancy.

She should have left town, but a local lawyer encouraged her to stay to try to control any newspaper story that might appear and to help the lieutenant fight any repercussions at the army base where he was stationed.[3] In hindsight, it was some of the worst legal advice given in the history of Chattanooga because another arrest awaited the baroness. This time the charge would be espionage.

CHAPTER 2

The American Protective League and Love Tricks of Women Spies

The arrest of Baroness Iona Zollner on charges that she was aiding and abetting the enemy in a time of war by extracting classified military information from an unsuspecting army lieutenant made national headlines. "Baroness Iona Zollner of New York, wife of a German army officer serving on the Flanders front, was held without bail for the Federal Grand Jury here today on the charge of violating the espionage act," the *New York Times* reported on December 25, 1917.[1]

A month and a half later, the *Cleveland Plain Dealer* ran an article in its Sunday magazine entitled "Love Tricks of a Woman Spy."[2] A fetching photo of the baroness appeared above the caption "Baroness Iona Zollner, arrested in the presence of an Army officer, and interned after the discovery of a secret code book and letters." She was described physically as "a beautiful brunette, at the most dangerous age in life—the ripe, full-blown era of 35, when women no longer wonder at the mysteries of life, and only long to defer the inevitable day when they will become memories." Her story was used as an example of how women spies had become an alarming force in a war where American loyalties were sharply divided. German Americans in particular were torn between love of their native homeland and loyalty to their adopted country. "In every great hotel in America, where the wealth, the fashion and the soldier blood of the particular locality come for display and for recreation, the great secret force of Wilhelmstrasse has its woman on guard."

"In war," the article warned, "the female of the species is more deadly than the male."

The baroness had been arrested near a sprawling army mobilization camp named Fort Oglethorpe just outside Chattanooga. She was not a German by birth but the daughter of a German American, described in the paper as Wilhelm Pickhardt, a New York millionaire. The paper reported that the baroness, a woman of multiple marriages, "by the travesty of fate" had a son by her first husband who was a cadet at the United States Naval Academy.

Wilhelm Pickhardt? That name sounded familiar to the postmaster in Marion, Ohio, a man named Frank Campbell, and he began to put things together.[3] Pickhardt was an unusual name and Campbell had been intercepting and tracking mail between a Navy lieutenant named Adolf Pickhardt and a young woman in Marion named Isabelle Phillips, the daughter of Carrie and Jim Phillips, prominent Marion residents. "We have in our files tracings of his hand-writing secured from envelopes of the numerous letters received from him by Miss Phillips," Campbell wrote.[4] Perhaps this Lieutenant Pickhardt was related to the baroness: a brother, a son, or a cousin?

It all seemed to fit. The Phillipses were known to be thoroughly pro-German. Carrie and Isabelle had spent a number of years living in Berlin just before the outbreak of hostilities. And Frank Campbell knew that Carrie Phillips had a secret connection to Marion's most prominent citizen, Senator Warren G. Harding. Campbell's antennae were up.

Campbell reported his suspicions of the connection between the baroness and the Phillipses to federal authorities and to a man named Asa Queen, the local chief of the American Protective League (APL) in Marion. The APL was a vigilante group of men who were leading citizens in their cities and towns across the United States, organized to support the Department of Justice and its understaffed Bureau of Investigation (later known as the Federal Bureau of Investigation) when the nation was drawn into the war in the spring of 1917.[5] At the end of 1914, the Bureau of Investigation had only 122 agents and the Secret Service had just 50. The APL was a volunteer police force that sprang up literally overnight just after war was declared, made up of patriotic citizens, mostly entrenched businessmen who did not serve in the military. "They were the best men of the city," Emerson Hough, the official biographer and apologist of the APL, wrote in 1919 at war's end. "They worked for principle, not for any excitement, nor in any vanity, not for any pay. . . . They were all good men, big men, brave and able, else they would have failed, and else this organization never could have grown."[6] They carried badges. The official letterhead of the APL stated: "Organized with the Approval and Operating under the Direction of the United States Department of Justice, Bureau of Investigation." The APL started with one purpose: to ferret out German spies and saboteurs and those who would commit treason. "League members liked to refer to their organization as a web spun to entrap German spies," one historian has written.[7]

At its peak, the APL had over 250,000 members in 600 cities. The fact that Marion, Ohio, a town of 12,000, had a branch of the APL, and a "chief" of that branch, attests to its pervasiveness. APL agents were officially prohibited by the Department of Justice and the Bureau of Investigation from exercising police power, but they routinely stopped, questioned, and frequently arrested fellow citizens suspected of disloyalty. They broke into homes, offices, and hotels; intercepted mail; and listened in on telephone calls. As with any such loosely defined group, their mission was murky and at times the goals shifted. They began to harass labor organizations, such as the International Workers of the World (the Wobblies). Leaguers illegally detained "slackers" (draft dodgers), assisting in the arrest of an estimated 50,000 men from the streets of New York City and nearby communities over a couple of days in September 1918.[8]

Postmaster Campbell placed a call to the Post Office Inspector in Cincinnati on the afternoon of Wednesday, February 13, 1918. He told the inspector that he had uncovered a hastily planned trip by Jim Phillips and his daughter, Isabelle, to travel by train that afternoon south to Cincinnati and then to Lexington, Kentucky. Campbell thought the two were en route to Chattanooga to see Baroness Zollner in her jail cell and asked that they be followed. The Post Office Inspector brought in the local office of the Bureau of Investigation. What was the reason for Campbell's communication? Due to concerns that had been circulating since the summer of 1917, the Phillipses were already on a watch list maintained by the APL's national office in Washington, D.C.[9] The Marion division of the APL had conducted its initial investigation into the family after a request, dated January 14, 1918, from Charles D. Frey, the APL's national director. The preliminary finding of the Marion APL branch was shocking:

> Since [Frey's January 14 letter] we have concentrated considerable effort toward securing evidence against these parties. The Captain of the Merchants Division in our organization was detailed on the case and we are now convinced that these parties are German spies and they are receiving money from the German Government. We believe this to be an extremely serious case, and one that demands the services of the strongest secret services detective you have to wind it up.[10]

It would take a few more reports, but eventually cooperating agents of the Bureau of Investigation would uncover what they believed to be an even greater threat to national security. It was common gossip in Marion, Bureau Agent Howard Stern found out in detailed interviews in Marion in March 1918, that Senator Warren G. Harding was having an affair with Carrie Phillips, Isabelle's mother. "In fact, it seems to be open and notoriously known, as stated by different citizens of Marion, that whenever Mr. Phillips leaves town that Senator Harding is always in Marion," Stern wrote.[11]

How had this state of affairs arisen? What was the relationship between the senator from Ohio, a man who would be elected president of the United States, and his neighbor, whom fellow citizens had concluded was a German spy?

Letters discovered in October 1963 but placed under seal in the Library of Congress provide many of the answers.

CHAPTER 3

"The Sweetest, Dearest Little Brother You Ever Saw"

In some ways, Warren G. Harding seemed like the most unlikely person to become enmeshed in an extramarital relationship. Certainly there was little in his background to foreshadow it.

Harding came from a big family, stable and loving, one that was strongly grounded in an evangelical Christian faith. His mother and father were a good match. Warren was the oldest of eight children (two of his siblings would die on the same day in childhood), and he was so close to his mother that, even as an adult, he delivered flowers to her every Sunday, whether or not he was in town.[1]

His parents, George and Phoebe, met as children and fell in love as teenagers. In May 1864, at the height of the Civil War, they eloped when they were not yet in their twenties. Just before George Tryon Harding enlisted in the Army as a musician drummer boy, he and Phoebe Dickerson, the youngest of nine children (eight of them girls), hitched up horses to his wagon and drove to nearby Galion, Ohio, with one of Phoebe's older sisters as a witness, and secretly married. No one told their parents. At nineteen, Tryon, or Try as he liked to be called, joined the 136th Ohio National Guard Infantry under a three-month enlistment and went off to war. Phoebe returned to her parents. The marriage came to light several months later, when Try contracted typhoid fever just as his regiment was returning to Ohio. When Phoebe demanded to be by his side, her father insisted on an explanation, and she told the truth.[2]

According to a story he often repeated, Try met Abraham Lincoln in the White House before returning to Ohio, calling on the president with a few fellow soldiers to pay their respects. As Try recalled it, after an hour wait, Lincoln appeared. Try announced that he and his friends were boys from the Buckeye State who wanted a glimpse of him so they could tell the folks back home they had seen the president of the United States. Lincoln thanked them for their service and said, "The Buckeye State has been loyal to me, and I certainly appreciate it." Try noticed the enormity of Lincoln's hands. "The President took the right hand of each of [us] in turn between his two hands in greeting [us]," he told the editor of the *Ohio History* journal years later. Lincoln excused himself due to the press of business but said as he departed, "And now you can tell your people at home that you have seen the handsomest man in the United States."[3]

Although he eventually recovered from typhoid, Try was discharged as a convalescent with a certificate of disability. He took Phoebe to a rough five-room frontier farmhouse that had been built by his great-great-grandfather in Blooming Grove, Ohio, some miles outside Marion. Blooming Grove is the locale where one of Harding's ancestors allegedly married an African American woman. The rumors never could be substantiated.

Try Harding was a complex but contented man. He would say that the family's homes, though humble, were always "full of love, sunshine and gladness."[4]

Warren Gamaliel Harding was born to Try and Phoebe on November 2, 1865. Phoebe was a proud but anxious mother. She wrote her brother and one of her sisters a year or so after Warren's birth (referring to him by his pet name, "Winnie"):

> I have plenty of housework sewing, knitting to do besides taking care of the sweetest, dearest little brother you ever saw, and I bet you would say so if you could be with him awhile. But I tell you, Clara, they are a troublesome comfort, when I think of the great charge that is upon my shoulders, the responsibility of training as he should be, and the care and anxiety I feel about his future; but still I would not part with him for anything in the world. I think if every child just knew the love a parent had for his child, they would never wound their feelings or do anything contrary to their wishes; but that they will never know until they see their own offspring figuring on the stage of this life. Winnie is always walking, he will walk all along the walls, but don't go alone. He has a head as large as [sister] Lo Flack and a beautiful shaped one too. It attracts a great deal of attention. Oh, we think he is all right, but it is an impossibility to get his picture taken. We have tried several times but to no effect—he won't sit still.[5]

Try was the entrepreneur in the family, the self-taught country doctor who read medicine and took courses in a Cleveland homeopathic medical school before getting his degree. He was sentimental, full of energy and vigor, constantly on the move, speculating, trading services for goods, and taking up risky and often losing business opportunities, including a small newspaper, the *Caledonia Argus*. It was there that Warren got his first taste of the newspaper business, working as a printer's devil. Phoebe Harding was more serious in demeanor, a midwife (she too would take courses at the Cleveland homeopathic hospital college), and a deeply religious woman. Not long after two of their children died on the same day in March 1878 of a severe form of jaundice, she became a Seventh-day Adventist.

Several of Warren Harding's younger siblings became active believers in the teachings of the Adventists, and evangelism, prophesy, and physical healing became especially prominent in the Harding family. When Harding was president, his younger brother George, a physician, was widely quoted at a World Conference of the Seventh-day Adventists in San Francisco in May 1922, as predicting that the end of the world was close at hand. [6]

Warren's youngest sister, Carolyn, along with her husband, Heber Votaw, became the first Seventh-day Adventist missionaries in Burma, arriving in 1905. Though away for long periods of her life, Carolyn regularly proselytized with Warren as only a family member could do. "Dear boy," she wrote him from Kemmendine in 1912, "there is no one who will care for you like your own blood. Just write that down. We love as water can never do. *I do*." [7] She prodded him to take religion more seriously, believing time was running short:

Never mind, you are my big brother and must listen. Dear me, Warren, sometimes when I think of you and what a power you'd be for God if consecrated to Him—I can't forbear thinking that down in your heart you are only putting it off. I am sure that both you and [spouse] Florence are the type that if you would investigate this message you'd see how reasonable is the real truth of God. It is a living thing, not a dead forum. A thing must have life to transform characters as it does. Surely Warren you can see the strides the world is taking toward the end. The prophesies have become present history.

As a teenager, Warren grew rapidly. His sister closest in age, Charity, or Chat, always believed that the difficult work he was asked to do as a child contributed to his frequent illnesses as a young adult and perhaps even to his premature death. "I have often thot, and *so did he* after he was older, that such heavy work (when he was so young and developing rapidly) was not conducive to a strong physical foundation for later life." [8] She remembered how his day of work was so strenuous that he had trouble turning it off. "He was too tired to rest and sleep at night," she wrote. "He would drive those horses all night long, for we could hear him in his slumbers."

As a young man, Warren looked to Adventist health institutions when he was ill, choosing as his refuge the most famous of the Seventh-day Adventist institutions: the Battle Creek Sanitarium in Battle Creek, Michigan.

The founder of the Battle Creek Sanitarium, Dr. John Harvey Kellogg, was a pioneer in introducing cereals into the Western diet as one of the original health foods. He prescribed a low-fat, low-protein diet with an emphasis on nuts, whole grains, and fiber-rich foods. The Postum Cereal Co., with its Grape-Nuts and Post Toasties, all came out of the Battle Creek Sanitarium. "It makes Red Blood" was the original slogan of Postum Cereals.[9]

The records of the Battle Creek Sanitarium show that Harding visited there in 1889, when he was twenty-four; twice for extended stays in 1894, when he was twenty-nine; once in 1897, when he was thirty-two; and for a week in 1903, when he was thirty-eight.[10] His sister Charity said he had "a nervous breakdown" before he was married and that this was the reason for his first stay in the sanitarium.[11] The last visit came after he was elected lieutenant governor of Ohio, when he "had a severe sick spell" resulting from a serious inner ear infection (mastoid). There were no visits after his relationship with Carrie started.

In 1905, Florence Harding, then forty-four, suffered a serious illness related to a diseased kidney, a defect she had from birth. In February, she underwent risky surgery at Grant Hospital in Columbus and had a long recovery after returning to Marion. Harding had hoped to run for governor that year but bowed out when it was clear that the Republican governor, an unpopular man named Myron Herrick, decided to run for reelection.[12]

That same year, Warren Harding had a friend who was in need of the services of the Battle Creek Sanitarium. Jim Phillips, whom Harding knew from business associations in Marion (Jim owned a dry goods store and Warren was the editor of the town's most important newspaper), was suffering from some illness or depression. There are no records to describe the nature of his malady, but it may have been brought on by the death of his child, a son, in 1904. "Your kind note introducing Mr. Jas. Phillips reached me some days ago," one of the treating physicians from the sanitarium wrote to Harding on May 2, 1905.[13] "I am pleased to report that Mr. Phillips is getting along nicely and seems to be enjoying himself here at the Sanitarium. We will be pleased of course to do everything possible to make Mr. Phillip's stay here pleasant and profitable for him."

During the summer of 1905—there are few hints why or what led up to it—Warren Harding declared his love for Jim Phillips's wife, Carrie Fulton Phillips.

In his letters to her, he consistently celebrated August 23, 1905, a Wednesday, as the anniversary date for the start of the relationship. Whether she reciprocated immediately is not clear. Since the letters Carrie kept date only from Christmas Eve 1910, anything about the relationship and its start in 1905 can be based only on retrospective comments that do not tell the full story.

But the letters do disclose a period of courtship or moral searching, perhaps both, in the face of an overwhelming attraction. The relationship became a sexual one, but apparently only after three years.[14]

Warren would always feel the pull of the gravitas of his religious mother throughout his life. After he died, his sister Charity wrote about her mother's hopes for Warren: "My mother was a devout Christian and to be real honest I do think her first objective for Warren was to be in service for the Lord. I believe she thought his service higher than to be President of his country."[15]

CHAPTER 4

Saturday,
December 22, 1917

An Espionage Hearing Begins

"The baroness came into the courtroom Saturday morning vividly painted, wearing a heavy veil, her hair richly red beneath a large black hat," a reporter for the Chattanooga *Daily Times* wrote.[1] Baroness Iona Zollner was described as "a striking personage . . . of winning manner and voluptuous figure."[2] She was no shrinking violet, despite her exhaustion due to her ten-day incarceration in a city jail. "She is vivacious," the reporter noted, "a characteristic that evidenced itself even while under the fire of examination." Another reporter studied the baroness and thought that she "would be able to charm secrets out of army officers or others she might get under her spell." If she had not wrung information from any young officer, it was only because "they knew nothing . . . or because she does not want to learn them."[3] Certainly this was a dangerous woman. The courtroom was crowded, with many of the men dressed in Army uniforms.[4]

The man there to preside over the preliminary hearing was a U.S. commissioner, Samuel J. McAllester, a straitlaced and seasoned lawyer. The hearing was to determine if probable cause existed to hold her for a trial on the charge of espionage. McAllester banged the proceeding to order in the federal courtroom in Chattanooga, commencing precisely as scheduled at 10:30, Saturday morning, December 22, 1917.[5] He read aloud the complaint containing the charges. The baroness listened and, through her attorney, the Honorable C. C. Abernathy, pled not guilty. The U.S. district attorney, Wesley T. Kennerly, expected her plea of innocence, but he did not buy it. He was ready to put forth substantial evidence against the baroness.

Kennerly called as his first witness, John R. "Jack" Thompson, the U.S. marshal for the district. Thompson had collected his evidence and was prepared for his direct examination. Kennerly fired his opening questions in staccato fashion:

"Were you in Chattanooga about the 12th or 13th of this month?" he asked.

"I was on the 13th. I came here on the evening of the 13th," Thompson said.

Kennerly followed: "After you came to Chattanooga did you enter upon the investigation of the charges now pending against this defendant?"

"I did," Thompson replied.

"Where did you first see her?"

"At the Park Hotel," was the response.[6]

Thompson had been waiting for her. The baroness entered the lobby of the hotel, he said, with an Army officer whom he later identified as Lieutenant John William Spalding of the Sixth United States Infantry, stationed at Fort Oglethorpe. They walked to the elevator, talked some, and then she got in the elevator and went upstairs by herself, while the lieutenant started back out through the front doors of the hotel. Thompson and his associate, Deputy Marshal T. F. McMahon, followed Spalding out of the hotel onto the street.

Thompson recognized that the lieutenant sensed the attention and acted in an uneasy manner. "He rather turned quickly," Thompson said, "and started out the folding doors there and I followed him out the door and just about the time he was going to step on the street I laid my hand on his shoulder. I said, 'pardon me sir would you care to tell me what your name is?'" The lieutenant twisted abruptly and said his name was Spalding, and then Thompson asked him the name of the lady he had just escorted into the hotel. This put Spalding was in a fighting mood. "What is that to you, sir?" Thompson replied, "I am here on an investigation for the Government."

"Well, I am getting all fired tired of having you all around after me on the street and spying about in my private business," Spalding shot back. "He was coming at me pretty rough," Thompson told the crowd in the courtroom, "and I went back at him in the same way." Thompson and McMahon next took the elevator to the floor where the baroness kept a room, knocked on the door, told her they were U.S. marshals and that they wanted to speak with her. She said she would not submit to an interview without a lawyer. She was allowed to call a local lawyer, Mr. Abernathy, and since his office was across the street from the hotel, he said he would come right over. While the two marshals waited downstairs in the hotel parlor for the baroness and her attorney, Spalding, irate, returned with two of his fellow officers from the Army base who had come with him to town for the evening. The men were prepared for a brawl. Spalding told his friends that he had been insulted by two men at the hotel. One of the friends would testify: "[T]hese men had approached him in an ungentlemanly manner," and one of them had shaken his fist in Spalding's face, saying "I have your number, I am on your track, I know you and I am wise to you."[7]

Tensions escalated in the hotel lobby. A row between the Army officers and the federal marshals appeared likely. Deputy Marshal McMahon was a pugilist, ready, he said, to take up fisticuffs. "He was going to start more of his fuss," McMahon testified, "and I made the remark that we didn't want him around and told them if they came for a roughhouse we would accommodate them."[8] But when the officers with Lieutenant Spalding realized the men they were assailing were U.S. marshals, they backed down and apologized, leaving a fuming but rebuked Spalding. The baroness, the investigators, and Attorney Abernathy all met in the hotel parlor. Of the two investigators, McMahon was the more aggressive. When he was on the stand, the baroness's attorney, Mr. Abernathy, cross-examined him on his rough interrogation tactics. McMahon was in her face, shaking his fist at her.[9]

The baroness denied being of German heritage, the investigators both testified, but then she admitted it. Abernathy and the baroness both said she was divorced from the German officer, William Zollner, her third husband. She then had to admit that she had only filed a bill for divorce. These were two strikes, from the investigators' viewpoint. She was not being truthful.

"I said," Jack Thompson testified, "'you have made misstatements to me as to being divorced.'" He was not impressed, he told the commissioner. He recounted what he told her: "At first you said you was divorced, now you say you ain't divorced.'" Worse, she could not get her ancestry straight. "'Now you have made misstatements as to that,'" he testified he said to her. "'The first question I asked you when I commenced interrogating you, I asked if you were a German, and you said you was not.'"

It was not a good beginning for the baroness, nor was it clear what benefit Abernathy was providing as her counsel.

CHAPTER 5

Carrie

She is a mystery.

Warren Harding thought that Carrie Phillips was one of the most beautiful women he had ever known. "Someday, whatever the fates may be," he wrote to her in 1913, "there will come to you a conviction that I bestowed on you an admiration that had no alloy of flattery. You are as physically beautiful as you are noble in character; exquisite face, superb form, a surpassing girl, an adorable tenement of a loving heart, precious passion and an ennobling soul. I wouldn't change a feature or proportion, and mighty few attributes."[1] She evoked in him a powerful sexual desire. Writing of a weekend they shared in New York, he remembered:

At New York, I had given you all—the very last passions, I thought, in a perfectly ecstatic loving, and I was prostrate from the excessive joy of it, dead from rapture. I was faintly able to admire you, and was indulging my eyes on a mirrored picture of you grander than any artist ever painted, when you were somehow inspired to love again—to make the most of a few remaining precious hours. I do not know what inspired you, but you were moved to love, and resurrected me, and set me aflame with the fullness of your beauty and the fire of your desire, and you loved me, gave me your unfailing kisses, and intoxicated me with your breasts, and then imprisoned me in your embrace and gave me transport—God! My breath quickens to recall it.[2]

It is hard, though, to attain a full picture of her. Aside from some of her own isolated jottings and notes, the material in her collection consists mainly of his letters and writings. Rarely is she available in the first person, and what can be known of her is generally in reflection through his words, his views and observations of her. Even though she is the prime actor in Harding's letters, so much of what he wrote about her concerned the emotions she stirred in him; he wrote less about who she was, or what she thought or believed, though her political views during the war were the subject of much comment and consternation. The few notes of her own that she kept are difficult to read (her handwriting could be indecipherable) and reflect random, scattered, and sometimes completely jumbled thoughts. Some of these notes seem to be her way of mapping out thoughts to use in letters back to him. She poured out her thoughts in these notes, emoting and reacting to his letters. Some of her notes were dangerously slanderous, especially when she was in high froth over the war or Florence Harding.

She was born eight years after Harding, on September 22, 1873, in Bucyrus, Ohio, a town of about three thousand then, the daughter of Matt and Kate Fulton. Matthew H. Fulton was a native of Pennsylvania and a Union soldier in the Civil War. According to his obituary he served in the battle of the Wilderness and was wounded and taken prisoner at Gaines Mills.[3] Some biographers have asserted that Matthew Fulton came from the same family as the inventor of the steam engine, Robert Fulton, though little direct proof exists.[4] Matt moved to Bucyrus in the middle of Ohio a few years after the war ended and took a job as a telegraph operator for a railroad. There he met Kate Nessie Swingley, the daughter of a local physician, purportedly a descendant of Ulrich Zwingli, the sixteenth-century Swiss theologian who was one of the leaders of Protestant Reformation.[5] Matt and Kate were married in November 1871.

Matt became a leading citizen of Bucyrus. Though a Republican in a strongly Democratic district, his "attractive and amiable personality" made him popular and "highly esteemed by everybody." He was appointed postmaster during the administration of Chester Arthur and was twice elected mayor. He worked as an agent for several railroads and for two years was a train dispatcher. The Fultons had four sons and one daughter, Carrie. Matt Fulton died suddenly in 1906, a year after the relationship between Carrie and Warren Harding began. At sixty-six, he was a sufferer of "organic heart trouble," perhaps a consequence of his long imprisonment during the war.[6]

Carrie married Jim Phillips on June 10, 1896.[7] She was twenty-three years old and a schoolteacher. Jim was nine years older, Warren Harding's contemporary, and a prosperous merchant. He became one of the owners of Uhler & Phillips, a flourishing dry goods store (the letterhead read: "Uhler & Phillips, Foreign and Domestic, Dry Goods, Fancy and Staple Notions, Cloaks, Suits and Infants' Wear").[8] He came to Marion in 1891, the year Warren and Florence Kling were married, from nearby Kenton, Ohio. Jim had grown up in Wyandot County, one of ten children.

Like many merchants of the day, Jim joined clubs and organizations that promoted city expansion and development. He was a charter member of the Marion Commercial Club, where he met and befriended the newspaper editor, Warren Harding. Jim also was one of the organizers and a member of the board of directors of the Marion Savings Bank. Like Harding, he was a Mason and an Elk, and he belonged to other fraternal organizations such as the Modern Woodmen of America and the Royal Arcanum.

Carrie gave birth to a daughter, Isabelle, on March 25, 1897, nine months after her marriage to Jim. Years later, Harding used the occasion of Isabelle's birthday to muse about how women in his time commonly married at a very young age. "This is I's birthday," Harding wrote to Carrie on March 25, 1913, when she and Isabelle were in Berlin. "So Isabelle is 16?" he wrote. "I know a dozen women who were married at that age. I have an aunt who was married at 17, and I know a very handsome woman in Washington who was married at 15, divorced at 26, married again at 28 and cutting capers with men's hearts at 30."[9] In 1902, a son was born to Jim and Carrie, named James in honor of his father. Two years later, in 1904, the boy died. His death and their deep grief cast a darkness over the marriage. Within a year, Jim was a patient at the Battle Creek Sanitarium and Carrie was starting her affair with Warren Harding.

Jim Phillips left few documents but enough to demonstrate that he and Harding were good friends. One letter in the Harding papers shows that the two men invested money in businesses together.[10] They occasionally loaned each other money. Jim even consulted with Warren about Carrie when she was in Europe, seeking his advice on how to get her to come home. At times, Jim considered Warren a confidant.

Two years after the relationship between Warren and Carrie had begun, Warren took a trip to Europe. This journey would come to have a profound impact on their secret relationship as it started the chain of events that led to

Carrie's move to Berlin in 1911. The idea of a European excursion came up out of the blue in July 1907, when Florence Harding's father, Amos Kling, shaken by his daughter's precarious health, asked the couple to join him and his second wife (Florence's mother had died years earlier) on the extended tour.[11] A long vacation had become a possibility for the Hardings since the *Marion Star* was up and running, thriving and profitable. Moreover, nothing was happening on the political horizon. Harding had served two terms in the Ohio State Senate and one term as lieutenant governor. After his election as lieutenant governor many of his friends, including Carrie and Jim, began a lifelong habit of calling him, affectionately, "Gov." In 1907, though, he was out of office.

Florence Harding's father, Amos Kling, a wealthy autocrat and curmudgeon, hated Warren when his daughter married him in 1891. Amos refused to attend the wedding ceremony at the house the couple had built on Mount Vernon Avenue. Florence's previous marriage to Henry "Pete" De-Wolfe, an immature, ne'er-do-well, alcoholic from an prosperous Marion family, had been a disaster (there is some speculation the two were never married, but they clearly received a decree of divorce). Florence and Henry had one child, a son they named Marshall, and were separated almost immediately after Marshall's birth. Henry lived a short and tragic life, losing one of his arms in a railroad accident and dying at thirty-six of alcoholism. Marshall was adopted by Amos Kling and raised in his home.[12] Florence taught piano to make a living, residing on her own in quiet disgrace in the small town.

Kling's hostility to Warren arose in part from his belief that his daughter was again throwing herself away to a man who would amount to nothing. Much has been written that Amos believed the rumors of mixed blood in the Harding line and objected to Warren for this reason, but none of this is very well substantiated. Clearly, though, there was ill feeling between the two. Kling seemed to get over it, but Harding privately held on to his bitterness for the rest of his life. When Amos was in his last illness and finally died in the fall of 1913, Harding wrote to Carrie of his deep enmity toward his father-in-law, saying he cared for him "less than any man living."[13]

But in July 1907, things had been patched up sufficiently between father, daughter, and son-in-law so that Warren and Florence considered and then accepted the last-minute offer for the European trip.[14] On the ocean liner over, the SS *Arabic,* Harding recorded aspects of the trip in a series of letters to his sister Carolyn and some that he sent back to his next-door neighbors, the Christians. He and Florence left Marion on July 30 and reached New York in time to sail on August 1.[15] Harding wrote his sister that when he told their mother of the trip, she was surprised, knowing of the strained relationship with Florence's father. "Our going was quite unexpected," he wrote. "We decided it one day very suddenly, half in jest, and were really not sure we would go until the ship left New York."[16]

Florence's father proved to be a source of a good deal of unintended humor on the voyage over. He ate so much that the ship's steward "threatened to charge him double fare the next time he books passage," Warren wrote his neighbor, Mildred Christian.[17] In the ship's spacious library, as Warren and Florence read or wrote letters, Amos would nod off, making alarming noises. "Florence and I are writing in the library and lounging room, as large as the Sawyer Sanitarium dining room," Harding wrote Mildred. "Her father is sleeping just by, and Florence had to awaken him because a group of passengers were gambling whether it was the fog horn or a man snoring which they heard. It was not the fog horn, though it might thus have deceived the average hearer."

Describing the trip to a gathering of Kansas farmers when he was speaking on behalf of William Howard Taft during his run for the presidency in 1908, Harding entertained with one of his homey stories that made him such a popular speaker:

> This is a fast and wonderful age. I spoke of being abroad last year, a trip every American ought to take. One ought to see the wonders of his own land first, then go abroad, and he will return with a heart swelling with pride in this glorious land of ours. Like all travelling Americans, when in London, I visited the great British museum. One could profitably spend a week there. While we were gazing on a notable Egyptian mummy, placarded B.C. 421, two countrymen from Shropshire, England, came up. They were a little lame in archaeology and anthropology but gazed in natural wonder at that dried and speechless form, evidently a man—speechless for two thousand years. Finally Hiram said to Henry, "I wonder what them figures mean [referring to placard of B.C. 421]?" "I am not sure," said Henry, "but I think it's the number of the automobile that run over him."[18]

Later in the same speech, though, he spoke movingly about his feelings upon his return to the United States:

> One beautiful autumn morning, in October, when the sea and sky were a blended blue, and the morning sun emblazoned a path like of sapphires and emeralds, I stood on the forward promenade deck of a great ocean liner moving up to anchor at quarantine off New York. It was at that moment of indescribable satisfaction that comes of gratitude and love of country and makes one forget all else while the heart palpitates in eagerness to gaze again on the shores of home and native land. We had outridden the storms, we had passed through seemingly unending fog, with a blind faith in the sturdy men of the

sea and the kindliness of fate, and the sunshine and the glistening Jersey hills seemed to be the outward manifestation of the inward rejoicing of the three thousand souls. The stage setting was complete when the German military band, which had caught the home-coming emotions a hundred times before, set vibrant the stirring strains of "My Country, 'Tis of Thee, Sweet Land of Liberty." The climax was reached. Of a thousand sensations experienced in a trip to Europe and her accumulated art and civilization, there is nothing to compare with reaching hailing distance of the great Statute of Liberty again.[19]

When they did return to Marion, Warren depicted his experiences to Carrie and Jim Phillips in a way that must have inspired the idea that the couples should travel together to the European continent. This trip, the second for Warren and Florence in just two years, came to fruition beginning on February 4, 1909, when the Phillipses and Hardings boarded the SS *Deutschland,* a German speedster of the Hamburg-American line. The trip had a slow start. Harding wrote to Mildred Christian that they were fifteen hours late getting off and a day behind schedule because "our good ship dragged her bottom in the mud of the Hudson for a couple of hours and we couldn't get out to Sandy Hook before dark, so we lay in quarantine all night."[20] The delay, however, did not dampen the disposition of the travelers. Warren joked to his neighbors back home of the shopping frenzy Florence and Carrie set off in New York before they boarded the *Deutschland:* "The Duchess [his nickname for Florence] and Mrs. Phillips wanted to leave enough money in the shops so they could do business until we get back and scatter more."

The crossing was much rougher than the 1907 voyage. Taking a southern route on the way to Madeira Island off the coast of Portugal, the "big vessel tossed and rolled, until our trunks waltzed about our stateroom," Harding wrote, "but we never surrendered and we stayed on deck with our deck chairs lashed to keep them from dancing across the decks." The weather was cooler, requiring the use of heavy wraps and blankets on deck, leaving Harding unable to participate in a ship dance. "[T]oo rheumatic to kick about in gaiety," he wrote. Harding could not help but notice that the ship's captain paid special consideration to his party, inviting them for coffee and cigars in his cabin. Warren speculated that the captain's attention was "because of our good looking women." When they stopped at Madeira to sample its famous wines, he joked that spending by the two couples "sent a wave of prosperity over the island."[21]

The Hardings and Phillipses visited Italy, Spain, Switzerland, France, and, most significantly for Carrie, Germany. Two months later, at the end of April, they returned to the United States on the *President Lincoln,* a German liner with its distinctive six masts. Harding's letters to Carrie Phillips years later attribute a special significance to this return trip and confirm that by this time the affair had grown intimate. Referring to all of Carrie's experiences on the great ocean liners of the day, he wrote: "I hope you liked the Lincoln best of all."[22] He said that he "experienced delights on the Lincoln that I never knew on any other—so good to cruise in the morning, the grandest baths, the Lincoln's for me." He remembered their stolen moments on the ship as it steamed to New York. "It was so grand to begin the day with glorious kisses and fond caresses, and you were so superb. Oh, dearie, I am always admiring." Thinking about it all several years later when she had moved to Berlin, he still was moved by his desire for her. "Honestly, I hurt with the insatiate longing, until I feel that there will never be any relief until I take a long, deep, wild draught on your lips and then bury my face on your pillowing breasts."

With their homecoming to Ohio, Warren found that his political career was reviving despite his long absence. The Republicans needed a candidate for governor in 1910, and his name was mentioned across the state. He resumed an active role on the speaking circuits, giving some of his favorite speeches on Alexander Hamilton, America's destiny, and the gospel of American optimism. His excellent speaking voice gave him an added charm on the speaker's platform, and his self-deprecating humor played well with his conservative, mostly rural audiences. "It is not bad stuff," he wrote one promoter of his Hamilton speech, "but I never try to sell to my friends for fear I [will] cheat them."[23]

For her part, Carrie had seen enough to know she wanted to spend more time than a vacation in Germany. She had wanted to learn German since she was a child. Harding even counseled her when she was in Berlin to be patient: "Don't be discouraged about your German," he wrote to her. "It is coming, and all the while will grow more easily. I have no experience, yet I am sure of this. It has been a lifelong ambition with you to know it, and that kind of desire and persistent pursuit can not fail."[24]

His 1910 race for governor was a problem. Carrie never reacted well when Harding wandered back into politics, and 1910 would be no exception. His run would open a rift that would leave her packing for Berlin, just in time for her to witness firsthand the events that would lead up to the First World War.

CHAPTER 6

Baron Kurt Loeffelholz von Colberg

The witnesses at the preliminary hearing testified against the baroness one after the other: the U.S. marshals who arrested her, the Army officers who had come to town with Lieutenant Spalding that night, the Chattanooga police officer and the hotel detective who caught the lieutenant under the bed, the manager of the hotel, and even the hotel's headwaiter. What they had to say did not sound good for the baroness. She had arrived in town one day and toured the army camp at Fort Oglethorpe the next, attending a dance with the officers later in the week, and she openly cavorted with an officer who was half her age, paying all his bills, including his transportation expenses to report to the induction camp and his hotel room in town.

The U.S. marshals had a hard time deciphering an odd letter written by the baroness's youngest son, Bedford, sent from New York to her at her hotel. "The letter kind of read funny," Deputy Marshal McMahon testified, "and she said it was from her sixteen year old boy and we thought it was some kind of code."[1]

The most tantalizing piece of information was Lieutenant Spalding's handwriting on a paper in an envelope bearing the name of the Congress Hall Hotel, Washington, D.C., which was found in the purse the baroness had deposited in the hotel safe. It plainly was a code to be used in letters to advise the baroness when troops from Camp Oglethorpe would be sailing for Europe.

After all this accusatory testimony, it was finally the baroness's turn to speak. She took the stand at four-thirty on Saturday afternoon, "in an apparently weak physical condition and for more than an hour her voice was hardly audible," the Chattanooga *Sunday Times* reported.[2] "As the direct examination went on she grew stronger, and when U.S. District Attorney Kennerly started his grueling cross-examination, she had herself well in hand and did not falter." Kennerly would later call her a fraud. "Why your honor," Kennerly said to the judge in closing argument, "this is the most extraordinary woman. She is the most consummate actress I have ever seen on the witness stand."[3]

On direct examination, she was ready to explain everything, starting with a careful telling of her life story, trying somehow to make sense out of her multiple marriages, the strange messages she brought with her to Chattanooga, and her deep German connections. "You go ahead in your best way Mrs. Zollner," her attorney instructed her early in her examination, "and just detail to the Court everything."[4]

It is true, she said, her father, Wilhelm Pickhardt, was a German native who had come to New York when he was twenty-one years old. His family was from Berghausen, Germany, where they had lived for many generations. He studied architecture, intending to follow in his father's footsteps, but he became interested in the dyestuffs business and formed an importing business with Adolf Kuttroff in New York City in 1870, the firm of Pickhardt & Kuttroff.[5] Wilhelm Pickhardt became somewhat famous in New York City in his lifetime. He made enough money to be considered part of "society." His marriage to Beresford Strong solidified his claim to higher social standing in New York. Her family included Irish and English nobility—she was a direct descendant of Dudley Sutton, the youngest son on the Earl of Northumberland, and Lady Elizabeth Beresford, a descendant of George Beresford, the Marquis of Waterford and Marcus Beresford, the Earl of Tyrone. The baroness's grandmother, Anne Sutton, came to the United States from Dublin in 1863 and married Henry Strong.[6]

Pickhardt purchased 25,000 acres in the Adirondacks, bred and raced trotters, owned and ran Wildbrook Stud Farms, and even undertook to cross the American deer with the German deer. "In Mr. Pickhardt's opinion," the *New York Times* reported, "the quality of the American venison is far superior to any other in the world, while the horns and coats of the German deer are better than those of the American breed."[7]

Pickhardt made some odd financial decisions. By 1895, he overextended himself in the construction of a huge mansion at the southern corner of Fifth Avenue and Seventy-fourth Street. "The mansion is of brownstone, four stories high, and is one of the largest dwellings in the city," according to the *New York Times.* "In building it, Mr. Pickhardt was rather finicky, changing his plans and his builder from time to time, and expending vast sums to suit his varying whims." He imported an organ for the house at a cost of $50,000, then altered his plans and hired new architects. "He did this several times and finally completed the house in 1889 at an expense of $1,000,000."[8] But the Pickhardts never moved into the house. The mansion had to be sold at auction when the mortgage went into serious arrears in 1895. It was purchased for $472,500 by Albert Duane Pell, a wealthy collector of china and old silver. Around the city, the mansion became known as "Pickhardt's folly."[9]

Pickhardt spoke German at home, so the language came naturally to Iona. He continued to maintain a fine estate in Berghausen and visited his homeland often. Becoming ill in 1894—"a bad attack of the grip"—he moved back to Germany in search of better health. At sixty-one, he died suddenly at the Hotel du Nord in Cologne in June 1895, a few months after his New York mansion was sold at auction. Pickhardt was buried in a family plot in Berghausen, and services were held at the same hour at the homestead in Germany and in his New York residence at 13 West Eighty-second Street.[10] His estate, estimated in the newspapers as $10 million but likely much more, was to be divided among his wife and five children, including Iona, who at the time was in boarding school.[11] The family chemical and dye business was thereafter run by Wilhelm's brother, Iona's uncle, Carl Pickhardt. Carl would become the father of Adolf V. S. Pickhardt, who, according to the postmaster of Marion, Ohio, would become engaged to Isabelle Phillips.

Iona's four brothers—Emile, Sydney, Adrian, and Ernest— all traveled different paths. Emile spent much of his time in the Adirondacks at the family estate. Sydney secretly married Lillian Clower Kelsey, a stage actress who appeared in plays with John Wilkes Booth's father, Junius Brutus Booth, Kate Claxton, and Charles Stevenson.[12] Mrs. Pickhardt "did not fancy the marriage," according to the *New York Times,* believing Miss Kelsey was below the family's social status. When a *Times* reporter was tipped off about the clandestine marriage (Sydney's whereabouts were determined when he began cashing checks from his mother at a local grocery store), the newspaper predicted that the young man would be disowned when his mother read about the marriage. "As she makes out the checks for all the children and controls the money, it was thought that she might use the privilege to cut off her son in his allowance, and possibly try to annul the marriage." Sydney was described at twenty-eight as a man who "lives a life of leisure." Like his father, he was "well known at several clubs, where he spends much of his time." Within six months, however, Sydney would die suddenly in Glasgow, Scotland, the newspaper reporting only that he "was not engaged in any business" and that he had been "married less than a year ago."[13]

Iona's brother Adrian, according to her testimony in the espionage trial, became an alcoholic squanderer, but her portrayal of him may have been influenced by the fact that Addie's spouse cooperated with investigators after Iona was arrested. "My brother made a certain income," Iona testified, "and he took a place at Hampstead, Long Island, where he kept dogs and he mingled in with different people down there and it seems that he ran himself into debt with dogs, and I think horses, too—horse racing and different things."[14] Her younger brother, Ernest, would attend Harvard and become a poet and writer and move to London. Considered brilliant by Iona, he would marry into the Theodore Roosevelt family.

Iona Wilhelmina Sutton Pickhardt was born in New York in 1873. She married Charles Warner Shope, a New Yorker whose family was from good society, at the Church of Heavenly Rest on Fifth Avenue in New York on April 19, 1897.[15] They had two sons, Beresford and Bedford, before Shope died of cancer in January 1902. Iona moved to Paris the following October to live with Shope relatives and spent the winter of 1903 with them.[16] In Europe, Iona suffered a "breakdown with nervous prostration" and recovered by taking a cure at an exclusive resort in the "high climate" at St. Moritz in Switzerland. She then moved to England, taking up residence in fashionable Sunningdale district with her mother, commuting to London to attend the season. She and some American friends visiting London traveled to the continent and found their way to a German spa.

"It was at Bad Homburg that I met the Baron," Iona testified, "right outside Frankfort." Kurt Loeffelholz von Colberg was from a Nuremburg family that carried a Bavarian title of Frieherr (baron). Iona apparently caught the eye of the baron, a man six years her senior. He wrote to her when she visited Baron and Baroness Oppenheim in Cologne on her way back to London.[17] The Oppenheims were of the famous German banking house, Sal Oppenheim Jr. & Cie, and the Baroness Oppenheim was an American who had married into the German family. The Oppenhiems encouraged Iona to return to Frankfort to pursue a relationship with Loeffelholz von Colberg. A courtship followed, and Iona and the baron were married in London in 1906.[18]

They lived in an apartment in Frankfurt. Although he was a Bavarian nobleman, the baron was accepted into the Prussian army—a high honor—

and he sat for the examination to join the German General Staff, which he passed, so he and Iona moved to Berlin not long after their marriage. There the baroness traveled in the circle of the Imperial Court and met many of the members of the royal family, the Hollenzollerns. "The person who introduced me to the Kaiser was the Countess Breston," Iona testified, "the Lady in Waiting." Iona became especially friendly with the kaiser's youngest sister, Princess Margaret of Prussia. According to her testimony, the princess and her children attended a birthday party for Iona's second son, Bedford, in Frankfurt.[19]

Baron Loeffelholz von Colberg and his wife entered life in Berlin at a heady time. The German Empire was quickly becoming a world power. Something, though, was amiss between Iona and her husband. In March 1907, she returned to New York to deal with some issues related to her father's estate. On the way over, she sailed with Alfred von Lowenfeld, adjutant to the kaiser. He was traveling as part of peace exchange that had been sponsored by philanthropist Andrew Carnegie. By 1908, after two years of marriage, Iona and the baron were separated. She moved to London to live with her mother and brother Ernest. Iona charged her husband, the baron, with "brutality" and filed for divorce in a Frankfurt court, which was granted in 1909. The baron "lost his uniform" and was kicked out of the army.

Five years later, when she was arrested in Tennessee, she had wed yet another German soldier, a man named Zollner.

CHAPTER 7

"It Flames Like the Fire and Consumes"

In 1910, Ohioan William Howard Taft was in the White House, but Ohio Republicans were split into factions and still dominated by bossism. Taft had succeeded Theodore Roosevelt when Roosevelt decided not to run for another term in 1908. Three weeks after leaving the White House in March 1909, Roosevelt went on a safari for almost a year, shooting lions and elephants in central Africa, and then he toured European capitals, where he was received like a head of state in a meeting with Kaiser Wilhelm II in Berlin. The kaiser told him he was the only private citizen ever to review the troops of Germany. On the back of a photograph taken of the two men shaking hands, Kaiser Wilhelm wrote: "When we shake hands we shake the world."[1] While in England, Roosevelt attended the funeral of the kaiser's uncle, King Edward VII, who had succeeded Queen Victoria when she died in 1901. Edward, known as the Uncle of Europe because he was related to nearly every monarch on the continent, died on May 6, 1910. With him, the prospects for continuing peace in Europe died as well.

When Roosevelt arrived home in New York on June 18, 1910, he was greeted as a conquering hero. Trouble was brewing, though, between the supporters of the ex-president and President Taft. The rift would boil over in the presidential election of 1912 and have a direct impact on the destiny of Warren Harding.

A foreshadowing of the danger to come would play out in the governor's race in Ohio in 1910. In the special brew that has always boiled in Ohio's cauldron of politics, Harding made the ill-considered decision to run for governor. He would regret it. In Ohio, he was considered the friend of the party conservatives and a devotee of the disfavored President Taft. True Progressive Republicans were still drawn to Theodore Roosevelt and did not like the uncharismatic Taft. Harding carried additional baggage: his previous support of Joseph Foraker, a past governor of Ohio and U.S. senator who left the Senate under a cloud of scandal in 1909. (William Randolph Hearst published letters showing that Foraker had accepted a large retainer from the Standard Oil Company while in the Senate.)

In order to have any chance of success, Harding had to appear to be an "unbossed" candidate, distancing himself from Foraker and other party power brokers. "I will conduct no campaign for the nomination nor organize any machine to promote my candidacy," Harding wrote in a June 1 letter to delegates to the state convention.[2] He won the nomination but faced long odds in the general election. Too many years of Republican rule in the state following the Civil War had left the party subject to charges of complacency and corruption. Support had turned strongly to the Democratic Party in Ohio, and a popular lawyer and judge from Cincinnati, Judson Harmon, sat in the governor's office, to which he had been elected in 1908. (The governor's term was two years at the time.)

Harmon had been the attorney general of the United States in the Grover Cleveland administration and was known as a reformer and trust buster. "Guilt is always personal," he said about those who ran the great trusts, railroads, and corporations. He was not much of a Democrat, though. A conservative at heart, he eventually opposed many of the highly popular programs of the Progressives to make democracy more direct. His opposition would cost him a shot at the Democratic nomination for president in 1912. William Jennings Bryan denounced him as a reactionary.[3] But in 1910, Harmon's reputation in Ohio was that of an avenging prosecutor who relentlessly pursued and exposed Republican corruption, especially the bribery and perfidy of local party boss George Barnesdale Cox of Cincinnati. The deck was stacked against any Republican challenger.

Harmon was assisted in his reelection in 1910 by a lackluster and uninspired performance by Warren Harding and his campaign manager, Malcolm Jennings, one of Harding's associates at the *Marion Star*. After Warren secured the Republican nomination at the end of July, he and Florence, in response to an invitation from President Taft, took a long motor trip to the East Coast and visited with Taft and his wife, Nellie, at the summer White House in Beverly, Massachusetts.[4] "I shall be more than pleased to call and pay my respects," Harding wrote to the president's secretary, "and receive his advice on matters relating to the coming campaign in Ohio." Warren persuaded Jim Phillips that he and Carrie should join them on the excursion to meet the president. Jim found the tour exhilarating. Writing Harding afterward about a true-up of expenses, he added: "I never had a better trip."[5]

Malcolm Jennings was clearly frustrated by Harding's cavalier, almost fatalist attitude toward the campaign. "Do you realize," he wired Harding in mid-August, while he was with Taft at his summer cottage, "that the delay in organizing may be costly? With the election only two months away not a wheel has been turned, no committee selected, not a dollar of funds raised, no headquarters engaged, no poll ordered, not a speaker invited—nothing done except to nominate a ticket," Jennings moaned.[6]

Even Harding's closest friends felt glum about his prospects. His best pal from his days in the Ohio Senate, Ed Scobey, warned Harding after his nomination that he had been "feeling out the situation" and found "conditions bad." Scobey assured him that the electorate had nothing against him personally, "but are sore over the Republican Party, especially the Taft administration."[7] Another supporter was blunter: "Permit me to say that you are unfortunate in having received the nomination for governor, as I believe you will be the worst defeated republican candidate that ever ran for governor in Ohio."

The predictions of doom turned out to be correct. Governor Harmon won by over 100,000 votes. It was a confounding defeat for Harding, and a warning of the approaching storm for the Republicans nationally. Harding felt the sting of the rout, even losing in his own county. He told most people he was through with politics. "I did the best I could in view of the conditions," he wrote to President Taft's secretary on November 15, "and I am cured of any attack of ambition along political lines which may have troubled me."[8]

Perhaps his mother's passing in the spring of 1910 helps to account, in part, for Warren's disorganized, even dispirited campaign. He seemed adrift, at loose ends, after her death. "Dear good Mother died this Sunday morning at seven o'clock," he wrote with high emotion to his sister Carolyn in Burma. "Father, Deacon [the family's nickname for Harding's younger brother, George], Mary, Florence, and I were at her bedside when the end came. . . . Before she lost consciousness, Deacon asked her if she was praying. 'No, I am only trusting,' she replied."[9]

Freed from politics, Harding renewed his relationship with Carrie. On December 7, 1910, a month after his election defeat, he ordered six books from Charles Scribner's Sons; their titles suggest he was turning over in his mind the meaning and mystery of his relationship with Carrie. The books all had common themes of love, scandal, mystery, poetry, and passion, and included: *Love Affairs of Lord Byron,* by Francis Gribble; *Eugene Field's Poems;*

Rest Harrow, a novel by Maurice Hewlett about a "difficult" girl and her love affair; *At the Villa Rose,* a mystery by British author A. E. W. Mason; *Married Life of F. Carrols;* and *Cupid's Cyclopedia,* by Oliver Herford with John Cecil Clay.[10]

If Harding read about the love affairs of Lord Byron during December 1910, he may have compared the fire he felt for Carrie to the mad ardor Byron expressed for one of his most scandalous lovers, Lady Caroline, a married and troubled noblewoman. He would have noted one difference, though. After the conquest, Byron quickly grew tired of Lady Caroline, something that did not happen in Harding's relationship with Carrie. In December 1910, five years after the start of their affair, she still moved him to write of a love that possessed him entirely.

On Christmas Eve, he wrote a long love note on the back of a photo taken of him for the campaign. It is the first writing of the collection that Carrie saved. Of his love for her, he wrote: "It flames like the fire and consumes."

CHAPTER 8

Christmas Eve, 1910

$\mathcal{M}$y Darling:
There are no words, at my command, sufficient to say the full extent of my love for you—a mad, tender, devoted, ardent, eager, passion-wild, jealous, reverent, wistful, hungry, happy love—unspeakably encompassing, immeasurably absorbing, unendingly worshipping, unconsciously exalting, unwillingly exacting, involuntarily expounding, everlastingly compensating. All the love a man can know and feel and endure, and gladly, oh, so gladly give. It flames like the fire and consumes; then cools to sweet nepenthe[1] and soothes in blessedness. It racks in the tortures of aching hunger, and glows in bliss ineffable—bliss you only can give. It is the prayer and benediction of my heart; the surpassing passion of my body, the conviction and consecration of my mind, and the hope and heaven of my soul. I love you thus, and more. I love you more than all the world, and have no hope of reward on earth or hereafter, so precious as that in your dear arms, in your thrilling lips, in your matchless breasts, in your incomparable embrace. To have and to hold you, in happiness to you, [here it begins to go up the side of the page] exclusively, in satisfying and satisfied love, would be the triumph of living and loving.[2]

CHAPTER 9

A German Cavalry Officer Named Zollner

fter her divorce was complete, the baroness took a trip to Italy. She traveled with her mother and brother, Ernst Wilhelm Sutton Pickhardt, who purportedly was sick and wanted to investigate the site where the poet Shelley was buried. The baroness said that her brother always "wanted to be buried in Rome by the side of Shelley."[1]

E. W. Pickhardt was a scholar in Greek mythology. Iona said he was "a great genius" who had been accepted at Harvard when he was just seventeen. By the time he was twenty-six, she said, he had been awarded multiple academic degrees and distinctions from Harvard, including a PhD and a Doctor of Laws.

E. W. was married for a time to Theodore Roosevelt's first cousin, Maude Fortescue. Maude was the illegitimate daughter of T.R.'s uncle and idol, Robert Barnwell Roosevelt. Robert was a congressman from New York, an author and naturalist, who had fathered several children with his wife, Elizabeth Ellis Roosevelt, and had three children with an Irish immigrant by the name of Marion Theresa ("Minnie") O'Shea. For a time, Robert kept both families in different homes on the same street (Twentieth Street in Manhattan), and he listed himself in the New York City Directory as a lawyer under the fictitious name "Robert F. Fortescue" with respect to his illicit family. Robert and Minnie O'Shea eventually married in London after his first wife died, but their children kept the Fortescue name. In newspaper accounts, they were referred to as

Robert's "stepchildren" after his marriage to Minnie, though they were in fact Robert and Minnie's full children. Thus, Maude Fortescue, Robert's only daughter with Minnie, was Theodore Roosevelt's first cousin.[2]

Maude and E. W. Pickhardt were married in Grace Church in New York on June 20, 1900, three weeks before Theodore Roosevelt was nominated for the vice-presidency on a ticket with Ohioan William McKinley, who was running for a second term.[3] A year later, in September 1901, McKinley was assassinated in Buffalo at the Pan-American Exposition and Roosevelt, at forty-two, became president of the United States.

Maude and E. W. moved to London after their marriage. He became a poet of some note, issuing a book of his poems in 1908 in London through Elkin Mathews, the avant-garde publisher of William Butler Yeats, James Joyce, and Ezra Pound. E. W.'s book included his major work, the tragedy "Ariadne Diainomene," about the mythical daughter of the Greek king Minos of Crete who became the consort of the god Dionysus. The poem is said to have been the source of inspiration and information of later works by William Carlos Williams.[4]

During her testimony, the baroness clearly wanted to leave the impression that her heroic brother tragically succumbed to tuberculosis and that, like Shelley, he was a luminous poet who died young. In fact, E. W. died from an overdose of drugs in a London hotel in July 1909, six months after Iona divorced her husband. "Drug Kills E. W. S. Pickhardt" was the obituary headline in the *New York Times* on July 8, 1909. "Ernest W. S. Pickhardt of New York died in a hotel in London on July 4 of an overdose of a drug taken to induce sleep," the newspaper reported. An inquest followed, with Iona as one of the central witnesses. "Baroness Irene von Colberg [*sic*], the dead man's sister, testified that he was in the habit of taking drugs in large quantities to relieve his insomnia."[5] The coroner's verdict was "death by misadventure." The newspaper reported that E. W. was "the divorced husband of the stepdaughter of the late Robert B. Roosevelt, uncle of Theodore Roosevelt."

It was on the ship to Italy before E. W.'s death that the baroness met a young German cavalry officer named Wilhelm Martin Zollner. Lieutenant Zollner, later Captain, was on leave from his unit as a result of a slight heart problem, and he had been given permission to take a year off. He chose to restore himself by going tiger hunting in India. On the ship to Italy Zollner apparently fell instantly in love with the baroness. According to her testimony, he "expressed his sentiments" to her, but she did not encourage him "because of my past experience and I felt that I owed a duty to my boys and he was young and he had not had the responsibilities of life that I had and told him to re-consider it and he left me in Genoa."[6]

Zollner departed for his tiger-hunting trip but returned determined to win the baroness. He found Iona in Rome. "My mother joined me and after that winter, Mr. Zollner, my mother and I went to London," Iona testified. "You see in Germany it is this way, if an officer becomes engaged he has to ask permission of his Colonel and the Colonel has to look up his wife's family history and if she is not all right the Colonel can simply veto that engagement, so Mr. Zollner went back to tell his Colonel and everything was all right."[7]

Her story about the beginning of her relationship with Zollner was slightly different when she spoke with a reporter for the *New York Times* when she and Zollner came to the United States to be married in 1910. Holding court in a hotel in New York in April, Iona gave this account of their engagement:

> At the Oxford Hotel last night Baroness von Colberg was willing to talk about her third romance, and to refer casually to the others.
>
> "Lieut. Zollner," she said, "was visiting in London, where I met him socially. Really, I am not at liberty to mention the names of the people in whose home I met him, but it was in society, that is definite enough.
>
> "He was contemplating a tour of the world you know, and I just delight in touring. We announced our engagement in London and Munich, where his relatives reside, and made an appointment to meet in this city for the ceremony and then make the trip around the world together."[8]

The press seemed more amused than anything else about her third marriage. "Because she left her divorce papers behind in her hurry to leave London to keep an appointment in this city with her prospective bridegroom," the *New York Times* chortled, "it was necessary for the Baroness Ione Loeffelholz von Colburg [sic] to make an affidavit before City Clerk Scully yesterday afternoon that she was at liberty to wed." The city clerk sarcastically noted that the baroness seemed to have lost her American accent, given the ease with which she conversed in German with her fiancé. She responded that she never had an American accent on account of her father being a native German and that to her "German came naturally."

The lieutenant also came in for some poking by the *Times*. "Zollner has already figured in the daily news," it sardonically noted, "although he has been in this country only since Monday." The paper described how Zollner, on his voyage over on the *Kaiserin Augusta Victoria,* had become engaged in what he thought was a friendly game of bridge with two American men but soon found himself beaten out of $750. He complained to the captain of the ship that he had been taken by "sure thing" men, and although the captain agreed, Zollner decided not to press charges. "To reporters who met him at the dock," the *Times* recited, "he said that his experience disgusted him with Americans."

Though she claimed her wedding was long planned, Iona and Zollner scrambled to find a best man, a minister, and a church for their nuptials, finally settling on the Holy Trinity Methodist Episcopal Church at Central Park West and Sixty-fifth Street. According to the newspaper, the honeymoon was to start in Niagara Falls, from where the pair intended to travel to Chicago and San Francisco. From California Zollner and the baroness were scheduled to go aboard on their world tour, sailing first for Japan.

Though Iona became ill in San Francisco, she recovered, and things seemed to be going well until the couple reached the Far East. From Japan, they traveled to China, and then Singapore, where, to the baroness's surprise, Zollner decided it was a good idea to purchase, with her money, a rubber plantation. In her espionage hearing, she said his brash act was not what they had agreed upon when they were married. She testified that Zollner had agreed to give up his military career and buy an estate in Germany, becoming a gentleman farmer once they returned from their extended honeymoon.

But instead, in the fall of 1910, the baroness found herself in the jungle outside Singapore, clearing brush and planting rubber trees. This part of the world tour, at least, did not seem to delight her.

CHAPTER 10

"Constant"

Few of the letters Carrie kept tell the story of exactly what happened in 1911 that led to her decision to leave her husband in Ohio and take their daughter, Isabelle, to Berlin to be educated. Harding called this a period of "exile" for Carrie, and he seemed to suggest in letters to her that he was to blame, at least in part, for her leaving the country. "I'm more sorry that I can write that your exile is so oppressing," he wrote her.[1] "I fear that it is the *yoke* that I have imposed."

Gossip in Marion also may have played a role in her decision to leave. In one letter, Harding identifies Carrie's detractors in Marion as "knockers," implying that they were behind her banishment. "How often do I wish I could have you, openly and honored, and have this pleasing and profitable business," he wrote to her in January 1913, referring to the success of his newspaper.[2] "I could do for you, and have you dwell where the knockers here could never reach you, and we could do the things we should mutually, visit, and travel all we craved, without worry about material things. Wouldn't such a fate be kind, for we would only need to be here [in Marion] as we ourselves would choose."

Another letter contains a more direct mention of his role and that of local gossip in her going to Germany:

You have written me a dozen times that all your unhappiness has dated from 1905. You haven't expressly blamed me for it, but I can make my own application. I declared my love that year, and pursued you ever after, until you found peace in going away. I suspect when you soberly cast [indecipherable] you will not wish those unhappy times returned. I rather think you will enjoy your return next year. Conditions will have changed, the old knocking will have ceased, the gossip been largely forgotten, and you will readily command your all, in every way.[3]

But there certainly could have been other motivations for her move abroad. She had a love of the German language and always wanted to learn it. Nor was it entirely unusual for Ohioans of German descent to send family members to Germany for a more formal, and what many believed would be a more rigorous, education. There is also the possibility that Carrie lost faith that she and Warren would ever be able to be together in an open relationship together. Both saw impediments: She worried about her daughter; he seemed incapable of really walking away from politics.

The year 1911 began with Warren Harding groping for his place in the world after his devastating election rout. Florence's son from her first marriage, Marshall DeWolfe, who had moved to Colorado in an attempt to treat his tuberculosis, also was struggling to find himself and was becoming more and more of a burden on his mother and his stepfather. Marshall had been sent to the Agnes Memorial Sanatorium in late 1909, a clinic for sufferers of lung problems seven miles east of Denver. The setting of the clinic was spectacular, with uninterrupted views from Pike's Peak to Long's Peak. The clinic's founders meant to provide their patients with an open-air environment, some quiet, medical attention, and an education on how to care for themselves after their release.[4] Marshall apparently recovered enough by 1911 to start up a newspaper in tiny Kersey, Colorado, but he was a spendthrift, unable to support his wife, Esther Neely DeWolfe, and their first child.[5] "Would you please send me forty dollars," Marshall wrote in desperation to Harding on February 1, 1911, "and will repay you just as soon as collections loosen up."[6]

At about this time, Harding's own restlessness led to a spur-of-the-moment suggestion to his friend Jim Phillips that he, Carrie, and Florence take an "economy" vacation to Bermuda. Harding made plans with Jim by telegram, as Jim was in New York at the time with his partner Ed Uhler, probably on a buying trip for their dry goods store. "As I understand it," Jim wrote Harding from the Navarre Hotel in Manhattan, "the slogan on this trip is economy." For some reason, Jim and Harding were concerned about Ed Uhlers finding out about the trip. "I told Carrie," Jim wrote, "that she should not mention going if she accepts, till after the Uhlers are home a few days at least, as I will not tell Ed while he is here as it would spoil his stay."[7] The Hardings and the Phillipses took the two-week holiday to Bermuda in March. It was their third trip together in three years.

Marshall's financial and health problems grew worse that spring. Before Harding left for Bermuda, he received a letter from a man who had leased the newspaper to Marshall in Kersey. "I write this to inform you," the man wrote Harding, "that to all appearances Marshall E. DeWolfe has 'skipped out' from Kersey without notifying anyone of his intention."[8] Marshall was on a tear, showing signs of his father's alcoholism. "He has been neglecting his business lately, going up to Denver about once a week for the past 7 or 8 weeks, and if he has left for good, you can easily see the injury he had done me." When the couples returned from Bermuda, Jim Phillips made plans to visit one of his brothers, John, who also had moved west because of health problems, and he volunteered to look in on Marshall. Upon his arrival in Denver in late April, Jim contacted the man who had leased the newspaper to Marshall. "I told him that I was a personal friend of yours," Jim wrote Harding, "and that I wanted to talk over matters concerning Mr. M. E. DeWolfe."[9]

A few days later, Jim met up with Marshall in Kersey. "A Colorado town of 350 inhabitants don't seem to me to be as good as an Ohio town of the same size [to start up a weekly newspaper]," Jim wrote Harding, "so that you may judge for yourself about what the prospects are." Jim was told by a local banker that Marshall could do well but only if "the Denver trips and the booze was cut out." Jim wrote that he was sorry to render such an unfavorable account of what he found but felt that Harding wanted "the facts only and I have given them as they came to me." He cautioned Warren not to tell Marshall's wife Esther or Florence about his investigation into Marshall's affairs. "Do not think Esther will like it and prefer that the Duchess does not find out that I visited Kersey for the purpose of making a report."

Jim apparently had made a similar trip the year before, and he was concerned by the obviously deteriorated situation he found. "Marshall don't look so well as last year," Jim advised Warren, "he has lost seven pounds since I last saw him and has bad coughs." It is not clear how Warren felt about Marshall DeWolfe, but after years of Marshall's destructive behavior, he had nothing but disdainful things to say when he wrote about him in his letters to Carrie. Writing when Florence Harding was "desperately ill" with her recurring kidney disease, Warren noted harshly: "Another trouble—not yet known here—so you will please not allude to it until you hear it from another source—my worthless, drunken step-son has been cutting [indecipherable], flying checks, borrowing money, boozing awfully, and his wife and children are coming back to her parental home. Isn't it all too bad? I could say 'I told you so,' to both wife and her husband, but what's the use?"[10]

Marshall would die on January 1, 1915, of tuberculosis and alcoholism. He was just thirty-four years old.[11] His widow, Esther, the daughter of a former Democratic mayor of Marion, returned to her hometown with two young children, the only semblance of a family Harding would have outside his father and brothers and sisters. They did not appear to play a large role in either Warren's or Florence's life. Though Marshall tried to pull himself out of his desperate situation before he died, his genetic predisposition to alcoholism and his battle with tuberculosis proved too much. His letters to Warren and Florence took on an almost pathetic quality toward the end of his life. "Dear Folks," he wrote from Denver in March 1914, requesting more money to buy yet another newspaper. "I am out to make good and am going to do so," he wrote. "It is going to be a rustle but I am certain I can do it." He tried to reassure them that he was acting responsibly, but he was clearly sinking. The erratic Denver weather was also taking its toll on his health. "I am home every evening going to bed between 7 and 8 and getting up between 6 and 7," Marshall wrote. "Family all well. I am feeling only fair. Too much weather. Twas 2 below yesterday. Thursday was 68. Today tis very comfortable."[12]

In early June 1911, Harding received a letter from his good friend Ed Scobey responding to yet another proposal of Harding's to travel: this time to Iceland. Harding clearly was restless. Scobey had been living in the Lower Rio Grande Valley outside San Antonio, Texas, since 1907 when he moved South for health reasons. He took up citrus farming and later bought a storage company after leaving Ohio.

Scobey responded to Harding that the prospects for the Iceland trip were not good, as he faced the task of training a new farmer caretaker for his citrus plantation, but the truth was he did not like the idea of the cold weather and he was dreadfully afraid of water. "That Iceland trip doesn't appeal to me," Scobey wrote, "as I talked to some people who had made that trip in July and they said they had to have on all the clothes they had and then almost froze to death."[13] Harding let the matter sit for few weeks, during which time he and Florence attended the celebration of the Tafts' silver wedding anniversary in Washington, a dancing party on the White House lawn on June 19.[14] Harding again revisited the idea of a trip, proposing a vacation in Europe. Scobey liked this idea better but still feared the water. "I like your Switzerland, Italy and Austria trip, and believe I would enjoy it much better than Iceland," he wrote.[15] Scobey insisted that Harding book passage on a major ocean liner. "Be sure and get it on a good boat, because I do not want to sink."

By July things were set. "Be sure and get a good boat," Scobey again reminded Harding, "not too slow a boat because I am not a good sailor."[16] For some reason the Scobeys and Hardings did not travel over together. A nervous Scobey sailed at the end of July across the Atlantic on the White Star Line's SS *Laurentic,* a cousin of the *Olympic* and *Titanic* (which was less than a year away from its tragic maiden voyage). "This boat is a fair sized canoe," Scobey wrote Harding from on board, "[though] not as long as I like." He found the stateroom "all you could ask, everything up to now," but despite the ship's size, his jitters about sailing were not alleviated. "I am told the last trip over they saw one hundred icebergs and was laid up for twelve hours by fog." All this chatter about icebergs did little to settle his nerves. "When they talk of fog and icebergs, you know how cold my feet get," he wrote. The terror Scobey experienced on the trip over, he claimed, brought him to religion. He wrote Harding from the ship that he was turning over a new leaf and that he intended to spend all his time on the voyage "trying to repent for all the bad things I ever did," though he had to concede that the time steaming over "will be too short to accomplish all this."[17]

The Hardings followed the Scobeys, leaving for England in the first week of August.[18] Whether planned or not, Carrie was in London at the same time Warren and Florence arrived. She either was on her way to Berlin with Isabelle or she traveled there from Germany, the letters do not specify. Somehow they arranged to meet secretly on August 18, 1911, a Sunday, at a London tavern and later in the Devonshire Hotel.[19] These encounters were some of the most passionate and amorous experiences of their relationship. The day they stole away in London was typically English—rainy and gloomy, but the fires burned brightly between them, both knowing that they faced a lengthy separation. Writing Carrie on a day of miserable weather a few years later, Warren was reminded of their time in London. "And such abominable a day, dark, sifting rain at times, foggy at others, and gloomy on the whole," he wrote. "Rather such a day as our last in London and such a day as I would rejoice to give up to the solace of gratifying loving."[20] Another letter discussed their rendezvous, weaving it as part of a greater tapestry of memories of such times with her:

You little guess how oft I fashion the picture of you from memories of vivid impressions and then worship—infatuated and fascinated, *even as the real has so oft impelled.* I make a composite—*a picture of the bride of October 17,*

in her matchless flowing hair, the bride who opened my eyes to a new understanding of indescribable beauty; *and touch of shapeliness as I saw it reflected in the mirror of a London tavern, aglow with passion's enraptured
embrace; with a* morning's regalness *when mounting the throne of love and
wielding love's scepter in Richmond; with a breath of the* old year *dying* in love's
fleeting gasps *and the New Year* drowning in ecstasy *in Montreal; with the
glory of the afternoon and the matchless sweetness of the incomparable night at
Le Marquis, when love's universe was there, and there only. I should weary you
inexcusably if I even half tried to give a pencil touch of the* composite *pictures
that make up the mastering vision,* glorifying you *and stirring unlimited praise
and unbounded admiration and such unending worship.*[21]

He always took delight in recalling the Devonshire experience. "Wouldn't you
like me worshipping at Vespers, like at the dear old Devonshire, when from
a jeweled cup was poured the *last precious* drop, literally, and oh, so gladly
and ecstatically, for communion at the consecration eternal," he wrote while
she was still in Europe.[22] So mesmerized was he over the encounter that he immediately wrote a letter burning with passion and sent it to her, either at a
London hotel or to her address in Berlin. The letter did not reach her but
was instead returned to him, where he intercepted it before it could be seen
by his wife. In re-reading it, he was proud of its fervor. "Yet (excuse the ego-
tism)," he wrote Carrie, "nobody ever wrote a page more aflame with love
than the note I penned you after the London meeting, which fortunately
came to *me* after 'Security' returned it. I can feel the glow of that writing yet.
I was enraptured and could be again. There is no limit to the love and ardor
you are capable of inspiring."[23]

Warren was not the only one on the European trip who found a secret
lover. While in Paris for eight days, Scobey met up with a young woman he
knew from Nebraska. Harding did not know it at the time, but Scobey snuck
off to meet with her, as Harding recounted to Carrie in a letter written a few
years later:

> *I think I know the temptations of your dwelling abroad and the dangers to our
> love, in spite of your helpful assurances. Do you recall my referring to Miss
> (can't recall her name) whom the Scobeys knew and whom we met in Paris. She
> is a Nebraska girl, and has been creating quite a furor in concert work in all the
> western cities. She can sing, for I heard her at the Grande Bretagne, and the
> whole house was applauding her little private recital for our benefit. Scobey con-
> fessed to me that he kept six trysts with her in Paris, in the eight days we were
> there—and I never knew it, and thought I was with him every hour. I can re-
> call now that nearly every day he would propose that we go to the Express office
> and write, and that program so suited my plan to write to you that we perfectly*

agreed. I was so absorbed in writing to you or reading your letters that I never sus-pected but once that he was busy when out, and never suspected the soprano.[24]

Once Carrie was in Europe, Harding found that he needed to develop a system to send secret messages to her. At some point after the beginning of 1912, he penned a three-page code that the two could use.[25] Carrie kept a copy with Harding's letters. The code contained sixty-four ordinary words that were given a special meaning and were to be used in public telegrams or in letters that might be read by others.[26] In each case, the special words would be underlined to alert the reader that a coded message was intended. Harding also utilized the method of writing "public" or "open" letters to be sent in the same envelope with love letters.[27] The first five or six pages would be newsy, for public con-sumption (by Isabelle in Berlin, for example), and a love letter would follow, so that the recipient could show the letter without revealing the private love let-ter. At other times, Harding sent entirely open letters to signal the arrival of a love letter to come. In all cases, he warned Carrie to be careful about where she sent her letters and he asked her to tell him how to securely address his letters to her. "Open letters, meant for other eyes can be addressed anywhere and it doesn't matter what happens to them," he wrote her, "but letters like I write to you ought to be safely addressed."[28]

Some of the words were tailored to fit her time in Europe. For example, "Destroy" meant "Grand Hotel, London," "Reflex" meant "N. German Lloyd Streamer (ship name)," and "Deprive" was to be translated as "Mail your next letter to Southern at Columbus [a hotel in Columbus, Ohio]—to W. W. P.," initials for a pseudonym that played on the pet name Pouterson.

Other words were more personalized love messages, and he continued to use them in private letters even after she returned from Europe. "Matrix" was such a word, meaning "I am utterly and gladly all yours—today and al-ways." "Cloudy" was intended to be read as "Message not clear." "Mellow" meant, "I want to come to you in your dreams tonight, oh, so close." He was even comical and ribald with some of the terms: "Sismine" meant "You, my adored," and "Govhard" meant "Hungering me."

In most of his public letters, he addressed her as "Sis" or simply "Carrie" and signed them "Gov" or "W.G.H." But in his private letters, his salutations were "My Darling Carrie," "Sweetheart," "Dearly Beloved Sweetheart," and "My Dear Sis." Sometimes he wrote to her as "F.A.K." and signed himself as "F.H.K." Other times, his signature was "J.V.A." Their correspondence does not reveal the meaning of these initials.

He loved to refer to her as "Mrs. Pouterson," an obvious pun. "Pouterson" or "Mrs. W. W. P." was Carrie in her most sensual mood. Sometimes together they were "the Poutersons," and he occasionally was "Mr. Pouterson." "Still," he wrote her following one of their assignations, "when I saw Mrs. Pouterson, a month ago, she persuaded me you still loved. I had a really happy day with her."[29] Elsewhere he wrote: "Tell Mrs. Pouterson that if she happens to be there at that time at the new William Penn hotel I will look her up and anticipate an agreeable visit."[30] He often called himself "Jerry" when in a particularly sexual, wild, or celebratory frame of mind, though this was a nickname he also used with other Marion friends, probably taken from his sentimental love of Christmastime and the traditional Tom and Jerry drink.[31]

But the word he settled on to sign most of his letters to her was "Constant." According to the code, the word meant "I love you more than the world." It became his most frequent valediction in his letters to her. He used it with ever greater frequency as their relationship became strained, especially during the war.

In October, Warren returned to the United States from his long vacation abroad with the Scobeys, but already plans were in the works for Carrie to secretly return from Berlin to see him in New York. The draw between them was obviously so strong that she was willing to risk a winter voyage across the angry Atlantic to be with him. This covert meeting, straight out of a romance novel, was one of the most frenetic and breathtaking of their relationship.

CHAPTER 11

"I Got the Fever"

Lieutenant Zollner felled trees in virgin area in Singapore and began planting the rubber estate in the fall of 1910, the baroness related from the witness stand. "I think he got the land in September and I left him in October and went back to England and to my mother who was living in Brighton at the time and stayed with my mother."[1] Iona was pregnant with their daughter, whom they would call Nonie, when she left Singapore. Her boys from her first marriage to Shope, Beresford and Bedford, joined her in Brighton from their schools in London because her mother, Beresford Strong Pickhardt, was seriously ill. "My darling mother died in January, 1911," Iona testified, "then I left Brighton and went to London and my husband joined me there in March and my baby was born on the 26th of June, my little girl, and about three or four weeks after that we went to Dover, where he had a little cottage and spent the summer and when baby was three months old we took a ship and went out to Singapore again and remained in Singapore for a couple of months."

The jungle turned out to be a particularly inhospitable environment for a woman with an infant. She said that she quickly "got the fever," as did her husband. She lay ill for some time and finally decided to leave in July 1912. She was told that the best thing for her to do was to get away from Singapore as soon as possible, so she gathered up her baby girl, left Zollner behind, and returned to England, taking a house at 10 Kensington Gate in London. She was so ill, she said, that she nearly died.

Zollner remained in the Far East. The baroness, with her mother, father, and favorite brother all dead, was on her own with her children. Given her inheritance, though, and the fact that the money now belonged to her and her two surviving brothers, she was no doubt comfortable in London.

CHAPTER 12

"Fate Timed that Marvelous Coincidence"

The last moments of the year 1911 were ticking away. The bells began to ring, a few here, a scattering there, and then a grand crescendo, and the two lovers in Montreal found that the climax of their lovemaking, by pure happenstance, matched exactly the uproar all around them. Writing about the experience exactly one year later, Warren Harding could hardly find the superlatives to describe his astonishment. "You can guess where [my thoughts] centered," he wrote Carrie, "—on the New Year's beginning a year before, when the bells rang the chorus while our hearts sang the rapture without words and we greeted the New Year from the hallowed heights of heaven." The timing was astonishing and dreamlike to both of them. "Fate timed that marvelous coincidence," he recalled, "it was impossible for us to have planned, and I count it to be one of the best remembered moments of my existence."[1]

Leading up to this sublime experience, Harding found little to be cheered about on a personal or political front. When he came back to the United States after his third European vacation, he could see the fight forming within his party. President Taft and Theodore Roosevelt were engaged in serious sparring. Taft fired Gifford Pinchot, a conservationist and the head of the U.S. Forest Service, for insubordination in the second year of his presidency and that act started the fissure with the Progressives and Roosevelt supporters. Pinchot, a close ally of Theodore Roosevelt's, openly challenged

Taft by suggesting that the president's secretary of the interior was in league with big-timber interests. After he was let go, Pinchot became a martyr around whom Rooseveltians rallied.

At home, not much other than work at the newspaper and some desultory speaking engagements awaited Harding. Jim Phillips, seemingly oblivious to Harding's ongoing affair with his wife, sent Harding a belated but cheerful birthday greeting and a present on November 22.[2] Harding made plans to deliver a rather mundane speech in Cincinnati at a memorial service for a lodge of Elks on December 3.[3] Nothing on the surface, at least, suggested that he was engaged in anything other than the routine of ordinary life. Yet behind the scenes, he and Carrie were making plans for her to come home, undertaking the treacherous and expensive voyage back across the Atlantic in the middle of December to rendezvous with him in New York. The logistics alone must have been daunting. Carrie had to find some accommodation for Isabelle and make up some excuse for leaving her at the holidays for several weeks. Harding also had to invent some ruse to allow him to travel, though nothing in the record hints at what he told Florence.

His letters to Carrie imply there was some heartbreak between them, a misunderstanding or drama playing out that needed to be addressed. She told him that her love began to change in 1911.[4] After meeting up in New York, the two headed for Boston, and it was there, according to his letters, that they confronted the hurt between them and apparently resolved it (he referred to it as "a buried grief in Boston").[5] Whatever the cause of the pain, Boston was the cure. "If I could only have you," he wrote to her later, "I'd kiss and caress to happiness. I'd turn the tables, reciprocating for that wondrous baptism of kisses in Boston that healed two hurting hearts."[6]

From Boston, they took a train to Montreal. By the time they reached there, the love spell was on, and he would write repeatedly that Montreal was "our best," a "feast," always associating the ethereal experience with New Year's and new beginnings.[7] "Wouldn't you like to hear the New Year bells in Montreal greeting a really new and glad year for us, while we poured a libation like only Gods may pour for the goddesses of their universe?" he wrote to her.[8] "I want to know. I want you to have the same wishes as I do. I want you to suffer the same hunger, the same wild desire."

Despite his claim that he was through with politics after his electoral thrashing in 1910, and perhaps because of his loneliness for Carrie once she returned to Germany, Warren found himself again drawn to the game of politics. The Ohio Society in New York invited him to deliver a toast to "the Buckeye State" at their annual banquet in New York City at the end of January 1912, which he accepted. President Taft was slated to be the guest of honor. The organizer of the event wanted to avoid adding fuel to the growing division in the Republican party. "I have been particularly anxious this year to avoid political speeches and make the occasion a real home affair in honor of the President as an Honorary Member of the Ohio Society," William Hawk wrote Harding. "I am going to try to limit the time of our speakers and avoid epoch-making speeches."[9] Hawk hoped Harding's toast would be "in the lighter, optimistic vein rather than to take up the political question, which seems to be a terrible tangle." A room for Harding was arranged at the Manhattan, one of his favorite hotels.

On Saturday, January 27, 1912, Harding checked into the Manhattan and attended a matinee showing of *The Wedding Trip* at the nearby Shubert Theater. Harding found the musical delightful. One of the songs—likely the duet "A Lesson in Love," sung by the bridegroom and his widowed mother—was so memorable that Harding wrote his own doggerel verse to the tune the next day in a long love letter to Carrie.[10]

Before composing his letter, though, he attended the Ohio Society banquet on Saturday night at the Waldorf-Astoria. Described as a "very formal evening," the twenty-sixth annual meeting of the group saw its biggest attendance in recent years, some 800 Buckeyes and their guests, and although the reception was "noisy and cordial," there was a real tension under the surface.[11] Taft used the occasion to attack Theodore Roosevelt's radical demands for the recall of unpopular judges by a vote of the people and for the reversal of judicial decisions by plebiscites if the electorate disagreed with a decision. Roosevelt's proposal was anathema to a conservative like Taft, who had aspired his whole life to be a judge (he had been a state court judge and a judge on the U.S. Sixth Circuit Court of Appeals, and President Harding would appoint Taft as chief justice of the Supreme Court of the United States in 1922, making him the only person in American history to serve both as president and chief justice).

Taft felt Roosevelt's proposal was nothing short of a reckless, political ploy that threatened the carefully structured separation of powers set forth in the Constitution. Speaking to an audience seated at tables filled with only men (women were relegated to boxes in the galleries surrounding the main floor), Taft was adamant in his opposition to the irresponsible Roosevelt experiment: "To take away from the courts that element of independence, that power to determine right and justice without regard to the vote of the majority of the people is utterly to destroy the administration of justice, and make it as dependent upon despotic rule as if we had one man power in this government rather than popular control."[12]

Harding gave his toast to Ohio before Taft spoke (the newspapers did not record its content) and then the night ended with the president leaving to attend three other functions, including a ball given by the Daughters of Jacob at the Seventy-first Regiment Armory. Harding attended a party of some sort, likely in the Waldorf, where he spoke with some women who flattered and bored him, and then he retreated to his hotel where, the next day, he wrote a love letter to Carrie. The first five pages, which do not survive, were likely a "public" letter. Carrie kept the remaining pages, including Harding's spoof on the song from *The Wedding Trip,* which he could not get out of his head. "It's a darling love song," he wrote to her back in Berlin, "love, love, love, is the inspiration of all, the spirit and soul of life."[13]

A national campaign was underway.

CHAPTER 13

"I'd Rather Be a Licked Warrior and Survive, than a Healthy Coward"

On Monday, May 13, 1912, Warren Harding wrote out a quick letter to Carrie in Berlin. The political season was in full swing, and he was hurried and under pressure. That year for the first time primaries, part of the Progressive movement to make democracy more direct, were widely employed by the states in the presidential contest, but no one knew for sure what to do with the results. Harding was a skeptic, believing that popular government was "made operative through the party."[1] As his biographer Randolph Downes wrote: "Harding engaged in high praise of party loyalty. Party organization and discipline were great virtues, not symptoms of corruption." He believed a candidate should emerge from a party convention, not a primary election. "A man, before he submitted his claims and his ambitions to the electors at a general elections, had to pass through the winnowing process of a party caucus or convention," Harding wrote in an editorial in the *Marion Star* about how American government had always worked before the invention of primaries. "Back of him, when elected, was a party responsibility, and the party was jealous of its [the party's] prestige and standing."[2]

He had written little to Carrie in recent months. On her way back to Europe, she wrote some letters that left him perplexed. After reading them, he tore them "into tiny bits," finding it hard to understand her "note of dissatisfaction" after their unforgettable time together in Boston and Montreal. "It must be a disappointment in me," he concluded after long reflection and debate with himself. "Well, dearie, don't waste precious hours fretting over a flaw in your garnet, when yours is the privilege of a perfect ruby." If she craved the attention of other men, he released her and told her she was free to seek her own happiness. "You see, dearie, the world is full of attractive, worth while people. They are there to be had for the taking, especially for a handsome woman." These are words he would regret.

By May, he felt the distance with her. "Somehow," he wondered, "I have a feeling that you have gotten away from me—and are somewhere beyond my reach." He said he had experienced "moments, now and then, of extreme discouragement." He tried to write what he felt, but nothing seemed to fit. He tore up one forty-page letter that was written like a diary of sorts over several days. He thought the notes would be hopelessly stale by the time they got to her, but he was also in such a state of insecurity that he did not want her to know. "More," he wrote, "I let creep into a page, here and there, a bit of my heart, so I chucked the whole business." Unlike her, he "did not subscribe to the doctrine" of simply writing whatever was on one's mind or what one was feeling. "All right for you to, but I am not agreed. One isn't always happy, nor everlastingly agreeable. Moods change. When I control myself, I reveal only the better side of me. I don't mean by that to fool you, but to spare myself. If one never exposes a sore toe, there will never be any one to know about it."[3]

He wrote that as he was composing his letter, he understood that Carrie would be on a cruise to Venice. She had written that she dreamed of him meeting her there. He said that he would have come had the sale of the *Marion Star* gone through (he had been approached by interested buyers but decided not to sell). Recalling their visit to Venice in 1909, Harding reminisced that "Venice seems a love-land to me," but for him to have come to meet her under the circumstances "would be as decisive as proclaiming my love from the housetops."

Their relationship appears still to have been undiscovered by their spouses. He cautioned her to continue to be careful about addressing her letters to him so they would not be intercepted. "We have done so well thus far that it is a good time to be extra cautious." An overseas postcard had reached his home, causing Florence to suspect Carrie, and he reminded Carrie to say she knew nothing of it when she returned. "My guess is that that card's existence is the only thing in the way of family association [between the Hardings and the Phillipses] this summer," he wrote, showing that he expected her home that summer. "I expect to have an understanding before you arrive."

His strained relations at home and his depression and anxiety over Carrie seemed to cause him to intensify his efforts in the political brawl all around him. But knowing of Carrie's hostility to any political activity, he kept his descriptions limited, making it seem that he was involved only for the passing campaign season. He was a candidate for election as a delegate to the Republican state convention, which in turn would help decide delegates to the national convention. "Gee! I have been busy," he wrote. "We are head over heels in a terrific old political fight, to give Ohio to T[meaning Taft]. The crazy one [meaning Theodore Roosevelt] is stronger than we thought, and it is a battle to the last ditch." Warren wrote to Carrie that much of the "the enemy's energy here is aimed at me personally, and they are ugly, but I do not much care. I am not sure that I'll win, but I am doing my darndest, and if I fail I will be content."

Roosevelt was indeed in the fight. In February 1912, as he left the Ohio Constitutional Convention, he stopped in a Cleveland railway station and was asked his intentions for the upcoming presidential season. He responded: "My hat is in the ring. The fight is on and I am stripped to the waist." Ironically, one of the final straws for Roosevelt had been Taft's institution of a lawsuit in October 1911 against the United States Steel Corporation for violations of the Sherman Antitrust Act. The suit sought to break up a monopoly position U.S. Steel had gained when it acquired the Tennessee Coal and Iron Company several years earlier. President Roosevelt, along with banker J. Pierpont Morgan, had helped to broker that business combination as part of an effort to stem a Wall Street panic. Roosevelt privately was furious over the suit. The great trust buster turned on his successor, who arguably was pursuing more energetically the enforcement of the very antitrust laws that had made Roosevelt so famous.[4]

Despite his declared disdain for direct primaries, Harding did place his name on the primary ballot for election on May 21 as a delegate to the state convention scheduled for June 4–5. "I am not doing one blamed thing this week but work at politics except to write this letter to you," he wrote Carrie. No time, he wrote, to find the breathing space to write her a real love letter. "I would leisure when I write a love letter," he wrote. "I could take [the time] before, but there is no leisure now until after the 21st. Then I'll close the door and write my heart into a grand letter."

He was exhausting himself, not only in Ohio but in trips East. "Oh I was in the dumps," he revealed. "Maybe I was in a bad state. I was ill. I went out to White Oaks [Dr. Sawyer's sanitarium in Marion] and had myself looked over. The New York eats and indulgences and excess of tobacco nearly put me out of commission." He promised that the current political fight was going to be his last. "It is my last one here. I didn't want to get into this one, but I couldn't go back on Taft, and to have declined to make the race would have seemed cowardly. I'd rather be a licked warrior and survive, than a healthy coward," he commented.

"Besides," he wrote, "it is good sport, when one isn't a candidate for office, and I am *not, not* for *any* office."

He had reason to be concerned that his backing of Taft would be a hopeless undertaking. Roosevelt would all but sweep the primaries in Ohio on May 21, resulting in thirty-four delegates to the Chicago convention for Roosevelt against eight pledged for Taft.[5] The state convention would select the six additional delegates-at-large, and Harding would be among them. As the consequence of some questionable deals at the convention in which Harding took a role, all six delegates-at-large were given to Taft. The result was a mixed message from Ohio. Its primary had been decidedly for Roosevelt, but the state convention was for Taft by a slight but tainted margin. The situation was a mess.[6] The Roosevelt forces ridiculed Harding as a puppet of Taft and the Ohio bosses. He was hissed when he spoke to the state convention. According to one witness, the delegates' behavior "would have disgraced a prize fight."[7]

Notwithstanding his protestations to Carrie that his role in the 1912 election would be limited, Harding was positioning himself, with some degree of vigor, for national prominence in this presidential contest. He was intent on rising from the ashes of his failed gubernatorial race in 1910. He worked hard to get the nod from President Taft to deliver his nominating speech at the convention. A *New York Sun* article suggested Harding for the job on May 31. A few days later, President Taft sent a telegram to Harding at the state convention congratulating him on all his good work there. The very next day, once it was clear that Harding would be one of the six delegates-at-large to the national convention, the president wrote out a letter asking him to place his name in nomination:

> *My dear Governor Harding:*
> *I have already sent you by wire my felicitations and my grateful appreciation of your great victory of yesterday, and I write now to ask you as a delegate at large from Ohio to put my name in nomination at the Chicago Convention.*
> *It is a good deal of a task to do this, but I know of your earnest support of me, and I hope that you will feel like assuming the burden. I know you can do it well, and I should be delighted to be able to have it done by a man who represents the state so worthily as you do.*[8]

Harding accepted immediately,[9] working up a draft (he always wrote his own speeches, usually in longhand) and sending it to Taft for review. Taft wired him back, "I do not propose a single change in what you have sent me."[10] In the meantime, both Taft and Roosevelt visited Marion. "Big doings," Harding wrote to Carrie. "All the town and county will be out." He was set for the fight with Roosevelt. "If we do not skin T. R. here in Ohio, I'll feel like wishing the ship to sink."[11]

Harding was so convinced that Carrie was returning to Marion for the summer that he ordered books from Brentano's in New York to be delivered for her to read on her return voyage on the *Kaiserin Augusta Victoria,* which was scheduled to sail from Hamburg on June 13. The order got mixed up and the books were delivered to another passenger named Phillips, but it did not matter because Carrie did not return that summer.[12] His communication with the Hamburg-American line shows he was looking for information about when the ship would arrive in New York (it was expected June 22). No other letters exist between Warren and Carrie for the rest of 1912, so it is impossible to say for sure why she did not return that summer. One letter suggests that Jim Phillips went to Europe to see Carrie and Isabelle rather than having them return.[13]

Harding delivered his speech at Chicago on Saturday evening, June 22, the day Carrie should have returned. Taft's prediction that it would be a burdensome task was an understatement. By the time Harding took the podium, the convention was in near riot. As biographer Downes noted, "Before Harding was introduced, one leather-lunged Roosevelt delegate roamed up and down the aisles bellowing through a megaphone that the next speaker on the program would be 'Funeral orator Warren G. Harding.'"[14] There had been endless fights over the seating of delegates among the Roosevelt and Taft forces in the week leading up to Harding's speech. Taft's people won all of the seating contests, and Roosevelt supporters claimed they were being steamrolled by the Taft machine.

"At 6:15 o'clock Warren G. Harding of Ohio stepped to the speaker's stand to place in renomination President Taft," the *New York Times* reported. "Harding is a big man with broad shoulders, a loud voice, and a convincing manner of saying things."[15] Always the conciliator, Harding started off by trying to remind the delegates that they were still all Republicans:

The first utterance of the first Republican national convention ever assembled, in resolution declared: "That the maintenance of the principles promulgated in the Declaration of Independence and embodied in the federal constitution is essential to the preservation of our republican institutions." Fifty-six years have not altered that truth. Since that seemingly inspired utterance, reflected in both the name and spirit of the party under whose banners we are met today, Republican statesmen, the Republican Party, and a Republican nation have written the most glorious half century of progress and accomplishment ever penned of any national life.[16]

The next portion of his speech was dedicated to the notion that there is such a thing as "too much democracy," as Harding saw the proposals of the radical Progressives. He likened the situation to that which faced the nation just prior to the Civil War. "Until very recently," he proclaimed, "there was never serious question about the wisdom of representative democracy, because surpassing results in human advancement made it unassailable. Only once before was the foundation of the nation attacked, and in that crisis we saw the dross in the misdirected and sectional passion for country burned in the crucible of fire and blood, and the real gold turned to shining stars in dear Old Glory again."

A student and serious reader of history, Harding worried that so-called reforms threatened the republic he so admired. This split in his party and the danger it posed he condemned since "[t]he world has not yet seen the perpetuated republic, but ours gives promise, and it has seemed to me that an infinite hand, in the consciousness of divine strength, wrote hope and faith into our new world beginning."

Harding then took indirect shots at Theodore Roosevelt. He attacked the phrase "Let the people rule," so popular among Progressives, to make his point that in the United States the people have always ruled, through elected officials. "The American people literally began to rule in 1776, and there never has been a suspension of that power," he cried in his stentorian voice. Then in a way that his audience would have understood, he called out T.R. by reminding his listeners that the people "ruled when they assented to Washington's declination of a third term of the presidency." This was an allusion to the fact that T.R. had already served, in effect, two terms as president of the United States: He had ascended to the presidency in 1901, just six months into McKinley's second term, and then won on his own full term in 1904. The *Times* reported that this line drew particular applause. "Next came a reference to Washington's opposition to a third term," the *Times* reported, "and the Taft delegates were on their feet with a real responsive cheer."

Harding finally mentioned Taft's name when he concluded his "Let the People Rule" segment of the speech, asserting: "They are ruling today, shielded by the law's supremacy and safeguarded by understanding. And they are ruling with unwavering faith and increased confidence in that fine embodiment of honesty, that fearless executor of the law, that inspiring personification of courage, that matchless exemplar of justice, that glorious apostle of peace and amity, William Howard Taft!"

Doubtless by prearrangement, the first mention of Taft's name set off a great demonstration. The Roosevelt delegates sat silent during the interruption, which lasted more than fifteen minutes. Ohio congressman Nick Longworth and his wife, Alice Roosevelt Longworth, T.R.'s daughter, "never budged." According to the *Times,* "Never once did they even smile. In fact both looked exceedingly bored." Just when it seemed the demonstration would wane, someone on the speaker's stand thrust a large silk banner bearing the likeness of William Howard Taft into the hands of a white-haired woman, the widow of Civil War general John A. Logan. She began to wave the flag, tentatively at first and then with vigor, bringing the hall to its fullest roar.[17]

The chairman of the convention, Elihu Root, eventually restored order, pounding his gavel several times. Root was an impressive statesman. He had been McKinley's secretary of war, Roosevelt's secretary of state, won the Nobel Peace Prize for 1912, and was at the time of the convention a U.S. senator and the president of the Carnegie Peace Foundation. He would need all his skills to control the disarray in the hall in front of him. Harding tried to resume his speech, but as he began to extol Taft, the convention hall turned ugly. "He started on a eulogy of Mr. Taft," the *Times* reported, "and the rowdiest scenes of the whole convention began. Scarcely a word of what he said could be heard beyond a few feet." His statement that Taft was the greatest Progressive of his time brought "a storm of hisses, hoots, groans, and boos." Fights broke out. "In the South Dakota delegation a Taft and a Roosevelt man got into an argument, and the former landed on the latter's nose." Harding continued to speak in the face of "the wildest disorder."

Root finally intervened, shoving Harding him to one side, pointing his gavel at the mob, and saying: "You delegates who announced your intention of sitting mute to preserve your self-respect, try and preserve it by remaining mute now." For a moment, the scolding worked. Yet Harding had scarcely delivered another sentence when a fight broke out in the Pennsylvania delegation. Root again took the megaphone and admonished the crowds in the galleries. "You up there are abusing the courtesy of the convention. Please try and keep up the good name of Chicago as well as the whole country, and let the speaker continue." The storm receded, and Harding finished his speech, but the atmosphere had turned poisonous. Tempers were high, emotions raw.

Harding had tried to reach out to the Roosevelt forces by offering his support to Nick Longworth in his ambition to run for governor of Ohio.

Harding's tender was greeted with icy disdain by Alice Roosevelt Longworth. She called him a crook to his face, referring to his involvement with the delegates-at-large dispute at the Ohio state convention, and he walked away. Years later, Princess Alice, as she was known, was unrepentant, writing in her autobiography, *Crowded Hours:*

> Earlier in the day, Harding came over to our seats and, standing in front of them in the aisle, told Nick that he would support him for Governor. I interrupted, saying that I did not believe Nick would accept anything at the hands of the Columbus convention, in the light of its action on the delegates-at-large—that one could not accept favors from crooks. I must say it was a little obtuse and raw of Harding to make that offer to Nick in my presence. Insight and taste, however, were not his strong points. At intervals, for the next twenty-four hours, Nick and Julius Fleischmann pleaded with me to see Harding, to say that I was sorry, that I had not meant to say that he was a crook. But that was what I meant to say, so I did not see him. That, I think, was the beginning of my active distaste for Mr. Harding.[18]

Over time, Warren Harding rose above Alice's pettiness. He cultivated a friendship with the Longworths once he was a U.S. senator and then when he became president. Alice never refused his offers of access or friendship, especially once he was in power, and her stinging comments look particularly spiteful, given Harding's long and patient campaign to bring Theodore Roosevelt back into the Republican fold.

But on this night in 1912, the Republican Party was about to splinter. Roosevelt, sensing all along that he would have to leave the party to continue his fight, did not even allow his name to be formally placed in nomination. On the eve of the convention, T.R. spoke to five thousand of his followers at the Chicago Auditorium about his personal war against bossism. He framed his struggle in biblical, end-of-times terms: "We stand at Armageddon, and we battle for the Lord," he said in a stem-winder that left the audience bedazzled. Some journalists were not so impressed.[19] The *New York Times* found the speech impudent, blasphemous, and burdensome. In a "long, long speech," the paper noted, Roosevelt took nine thousand words "to announce, iterate, and reiterate that his is the cause of 'social and industrial justice,' that his opponents are 'burglars' and that he is the only hope of the people."[20] The *Times* called him unfit for the office. "Mr. Roosevelt's notion that he is fighting the final fight for righteousness is grotesque."

After Harding's speech and other nominating speeches the vote was taken. Taft won, receiving 561 votes to 107 for Roosevelt, and 41 for Wisconsin Progressive Robert La Follette. Nearly 350 delegates abstained. In a hall across town, delegates held a rump convention and nominated T.R. "I am in this fight for certain principles," Roosevelt told the crowd assembled in Orchestra Hall, "and first and foremost of these goes back to Sinai and is embodied in the commandment, 'Thou Shalt Not Steal.'" The party would take its name from a throwaway comment Roosevelt made earlier in the week when a reporter asked him how he was holding up. "I'm feeling like a bull moose!" Roosevelt glibly replied. From that point forward, his supporters called themselves Bull Moosers.

In Burma, Harding's sister Carolyn read about her brother's big moment on the national stage. "I read in the news paper out here," Carolyn wrote from Kemmendine, "that Harding of Ohio made the nominating speech for Taft. It was you of course? But I had thought you were done with all politics. Don't get mixed up in it again dear. It is not clean enough for my big brother."[21]

Before taking to the hustings, Harding found some time in July to vacation briefly with William R. Timken of Canton, Ohio, on his yacht, pleasure sailing around the Great Lakes.[22] W. R. Timken was the brother of H. H. ("Henry" or "Harry" to his family) Timken, founder of the Timken Roller Bearing Co., which had patented a tapered roller bearing used in carriages and early automobiles. The company became enormously successful, and the brothers became important patrons of Harding's in his state and national races. In 1912 the relationship appears to have been in its initial phases. Harding introduced W. R. Timken to some of the luminaries of the Republican Party at Chicago. Not only was W. R. pleased to rub shoulders with "the high and mighty," but he was also taken with Harding's oratory skills. "I still think and talk of your glorious speech you made, it was surely the best ever," Timken wrote.[23]

Harding's trip on the Timken yacht was cut short—for reasons that are not clear—but Florence was once again sick that summer. In a letter sent after Harding left the yacht, W. R. told of preliminary plans for a trip that fall to Texas, where his brother Harry had a ranch. "Since you left we have been after Harry to make him take us all down to Texas this fall. You are to be included in that party, you know."[24] At some point, Harding and Harry had bet $1,000 on the outcome of the election. Harding thought that Taft would beat Roosevelt in the popular vote in Ohio; Timken, a diehard T.R. fan, thought Roosevelt would take the state. When the final votes were tallied, the Democrat Woodrow Wilson, of course, won, nationally and in Ohio, but Taft did beat Roosevelt in Ohio, 278,168 to 229,807. Ohio, however, was the exception. Nationally Taft ran a poor third behind Wilson and Roosevelt. Socialist Eugene Debs garnered nearly a million votes (6 percent of the popular vote), representing the high-water mark for any Socialist candidate ever in a presidential contest. Harry Timken paid Warren Harding his $1,000 after the election but reprimanded him for his support of Taft. "I feel sorry for you old stand-patters," H. H. wrote, "—that is, personally—but politically, I am glad you were so badly beaten, because I feel that the Progressive ideas in both the Democratic and Progressive Parties were absolutely necessary to check the cause of socialism in this country."[25]

Harding sought a reward for his service to President Taft. Immediately after the election the ambassador to Japan resigned, and Harding wrote of his interest in the appointment. If he received the post, he would be closer to his sister in Burma. Daisy, another of his sisters, had left in late summer to travel to China and then to visit Carolyn in Burma. "We have not forgotten you are coming for 1913's winter," Carolyn wrote to Warren, encouraging him to keep his promise to visit her. "You will get material here for a lecture that will make folks sit up and take notice."[26]

Taft had already promised the Japanese ambassadorship to someone else. "The President in the strongest terms commended your loyal support and stalwart Republicanism and expressed regrets that these obligations, incurred some time ago, prevented your appointment as Ambassador to Japan," an assistant secretary of the Department of the Interior wrote to Harding. "He wished me, however, to assure you of his cordial appreciation and to suggest that if other vacancies or changes occur in the diplomatic service during his administration, it may be possible to give you some other appointment that would be satisfactory to you."[27]

Meanwhile the Timken trip to Texas turned into a "shooting trip." Harding did not enjoy the idea of hunting. One of the Texas sponsors of the Timken party, a Houston attorney named Henry L. Borden, sent a letter to Harding expressing his concern that Harding would not enjoy the trip: "I recall that at some period during our stay in Chicago last June, you expressed some disposition not to care to take the life of the many harmless creatures known to hunters as wild game."[28] Borden wrote that he was "hopeful that we shall be able to find other forms of amusement that may interest you and I sincerely hope that nothing will intervene to prevent your coming."

Ed Scobey was looking forward to Harding's visit. "I am glad you won your $1000.00," Scobey wrote his friend on November 12. "You better take that money and get the Dutchess [sic] and come down to San Antonio and spend a couple of months."[29] The Timken party expected to leave for Texas on December 3. Harding was to meet the train in Columbus, where he and others would take another train to St. Louis and then transfer to a private car that would take them to Texas.[30] Harding confirmed his acceptance of the invitation and his intention to go to Texas on November 14.[31]

Nothing seemed to be on the horizon that would prevent him from going hunting.

Nothing except an arrangement with Carrie to meet again in the United States. She would secretly sail back from Europe for a second year in a row to rendezvous with him in New York City.

CHAPTER 14

"Everybody Would Be Able to Get the Better of Me"

The folks and soldiers in the courtroom in Chattanooga had heard about the baroness's trips around the world, her forays to Monte Carlo, her tragic first marriage to Charles Warner Shope, her abusive second marriage to the baron, and her third marriage to the German cavalry officer. She had inherited millions, and her family's advisors and counselors were growing concerned that the sprawling land and plantation that Lieutenant Zollner had purchased in Singapore was an investment that could destroy the Pickhardt fortune.

Her lawyer at the espionage hearing, Mr. Abernathy, needed his client to explain to the U.S. commissioner how she had grown apart from her third husband, the German army officer. When she was arrested, the baroness had told the investigators that she was in the midst of obtaining a divorce from Zollner. Attorney Abernathy wanted her to explain how things had gone wrong in their relationship, when the strains had started, that sort of thing.

"Did your husband then come back to London?" he inquired.[1]

"He came to Kensington Gate in June," she answered.

"Was that after war was declared?" Abernathy asked, trying to move the narrative along. She did not take the hint.

"This was a year before," she said "He came to Kensington Gate in June and that summer we spent in London and he spent all that winter in London. He had been trying to form a company there for the rubber estate and he had received several offers, but turned them down because he thought it was not enough. Still I had correspondence from my Trustee, my then Trustee Mr. Crocker of New York, in which he told me that I was not to invest any more money in that rubber estate, also writing to my husband that he thought it a very risky thing for me to do, that if anything happened to him. . . ."

Here Iona trailed off, but she was not finished. She seemed to remember that her aim was to create the impression of a conflict between her and Zollner.

"I wrote him letters to that effect when he was there," she added. "You see that I am a woman with three children and that if anything happened to the rubber estate everybody would be able to get the better of me, so there were a great many disputes and things of that kind but I always gave in and then my husband refused several offers, the one he thought was the best one was from Mr. Neville Seabright, 9 Drapers Garden, London. My husband left me, I think either April or May it must have been, 1914, went to Munich because you see as an officer in the reserve he had to report and ask for another leave of absence and went to Munich and was granted another two years and he sailed for the estate."

She had more to say. "In the meantime, Mr. Seabright had an offer for a firm in London. I don't want to quote figures because I might not be stating the truth but as far as I can remember the offer was this: 20,000 pounds in cash, the rest in stocks and my husband to be made managing director. This is what he told me after he came back, you understand, but I know there was an offer because, I tell you why, Mr. Seabright cabled my husband, but I don't want to give figures for this offer, and my husband cabled back, 'you take first steamer and bring tico [coffee] beans,' or 'am taking first steamer and bringing tico beans.' My husband got on the P&O ship called *Muldavia*."[2]

The level of detail was becoming mind-numbing and confusing. Abernathy finally broke in, doing the one thing a lawyer dreads: admonishing his own witness on direct examination. "Don't go so much into detail," he pleaded.

The baroness was puzzled. "Why Mr. Abernathy?" she replied.

Abernathy was wise enough not to debate his client while she was on the witness stand. Instead, he tried to return to the chronology, hoping to move the topic to when the war was declared. "Did your husband come back to London when the war was declared?" he asked.

"He got back to London after the war was declared. . . ." she began in again.

The baroness was regaining her strength, after appearing so weak when she had first taken the stand. Now she was plainly enjoying the attention of the packed audience, the soldiers, the lawyers, and the magistrate. Mr. Abernathy, however, was likely wondering what his witness would say next. Clearly he was violating the lawyers' time-tested rule of examination: Never ask a witness a question when you do not know already what the answer will be.

CHAPTER 15

"My Carrie, Beloved and Adored"

Just as the presidential contest of 1912 was reaching its climax, a demented man in Milwaukee drew a Colt revolver from his pocket outside the Gilpatrick Hotel and shot Theodore Roosevelt as he was about to enter a car on the way to a speaking engagement. He shot once, hitting Roosevelt in the chest. "They have pinked me," Roosevelt said as he checked himself to see if any blood was coming from his mouth. He was seriously wounded—the bullet lodged near his lung and broke a rib—but not mortally. The bullet was slowed and diverted by a glasses case and a folded speech in T.R.'s vest pocket. The candidate insisted on being taken to his engagement, where he delivered a speech of over fifty minutes, telling the crowd he had been shot but that it would take more than a bullet to bring down a Bull Moose.[1] It seemed that sympathy across the country for Roosevelt might change the outcome of the election. But the tide was running too strongly in favor of the Democrats, and Wilson won.[2] Roosevelt put on a stoic face but privately sank into a depression. The Bull Moose/Progressive Party he founded had shown strength and promise, but the rift had left his former party, the Republicans, in deep trouble. As a consequence, Wilson would be reelected in 1916, and from 1912 on some began to wonder if the Republicans were finished as a major party. Warren Harding would answer that question in 1920, when he won the presidency in one of the greatest landslide victories in the nation's history.

By then, Roosevelt would be dead, Wilson would have suffered a debilitating stroke, and the country would be hungry for peace and stability after a crushing world war. Warren Harding represented those qualities: peace and stability—or "normalcy," as he would say.

In late November 1912, Warren finalized his plans to see Carrie for the second time in two years with her coming back from Germany to meet up with him in New York. Little in their private letters mentions the exact timing or communications of the arrangements between the two but he finally accepted the invitation for the Texas hunting trip around the middle of November, after the election results were known. In October, he had ordered a yearlong subscription to *Vogue* magazine for Carrie to be sent to her Berlin address, which suggests that he understood that she was planning on staying abroad for at least another year.[3] It seems likely that they decided that another year apart would be too painful to contemplate and that they needed to see each other, in person, when the opportunity arose. That opportunity appears to have been the Texas trip, something Harding did not relish in the first place.

The letters do describe what happened. As planned, Harding met up with the Timkens and guests in Columbus on December 3 and traveled to Texas by train. But he absented himself from the hunting party after a week, telling everyone that something had come up and he had to leave.[4] He handed two letters to a porter on the train to be mailed at intervals to Florence from Texas, and he traveled to New York City, to meet the ship *Mauritania,* which arrived from Europe in New York on Friday, December 13, 1912.[5] Given the short time she would be in America and the recent Titanic disaster the previous spring, it is telling that Carrie would make the long voyage a second time to see Warren. When Carrie later became upset over Harding's letters to Florence from Texas, he explained that sending them had nothing to do with Florence but all to do with his secret rendezvous with her:

> *My Texas letters were part of the program to add to the seemliness of Texas, two little nothings that I left with a porter in the car, to be mailed on the first and third day after I left, to strengthen appearances. I wanted to avoid suspicion, so you could return in safety, and so I could be present to see you off. It worked beautifully for the second letter got here on Monday, and I was home on Wednesday, and not a hint of suspicion ever arose. Regard for you wrote these letters, not a regard for the party addressed. See?[6]*

To soothe her feelings and comfort her, he then wrote some of the most revealing lines in his entire correspondence concerning his marriage:

By the way, I note that your only impatience and tendency to irritability (none of us can ever be wholly free from it, while we are human, and I am not finding fault or deploring the tendency in you) is when you speak or write about the Mrs. This doesn't especially annoy me, I rather expect it. I can see your point of view. But it has occurred to me that I might write a line that will help. You know my love is all your very own, that there isn't one iota of affection in my home relationship, that there is not even thoughtfulness, due sympathy or consideration. It is merely existence, necessary for appearance's sake, because of circumstances.[7]

Carrie and Warren likely stayed a night or two in New York but then set out for Richmond, Virginia. They stayed there all day Sunday, December 15, and had one of those experiences that stayed with him for the next decade. "A year of life," he wrote her, "yea five of them for one heavenly day in Richmond."[8] In the cold of the winter of 1913 in Marion, Warren had nothing but memories of Richmond to sustain him. In early January, on a snowy day, he wrote to Carrie from his office at the *Star:*

I went home last night in the rain, in the night it turned to snow, and the surface is covered under six inches of snow and the trees are robed in white—a beautiful winter scene. When I got home I was too tired to sleep, but I rested and you were summoned in finally. And you came—a vision vividly plain, a goddess in human form—and a perfect form—clad only in flowing hair, and you were joyously received, and Jerry came and insisted on staying while we all retrospected in the happiness of a Sunday in Richmond. It was all very sweet and happy, and contentment, in the riches of fancy, made me forget my worries, and I had such a good night. So, you see, you are a ministering angel when you are quite unaware.[9]

Visions of her left him mesmerized and enthralled, absorbed in love and awash in her animal magnetism. He described a scene one Sunday morning not long after their visit, when he put on his bathrobe after a luxurious bath, the same robe she had worn when they last met. "Three weeks ago it [the robe] touched and covered your beautiful form, and that made it hallowed to me, and I wanted to contact with it, to make me seem nearer to you." He sat before his roaring fire and dreamed of her "to alarming release," he wrote. "I called your name aloud thrice, begging you to come, and a voice upstairs responded, wanting to know what I wanted." Jolted, he sobered up from his dream. "Grate fire dreams are favorites with me," he wrote, "but I'll not encourage them during the desert period ahead."[10]

Carrie would spend less than a week in the United States on her frenetic, high-speed trip, which would have been bookended by six to eight days travel across the Atlantic each way, not to mention the several days it would take to get back and forth to the ship in England from Berlin. Carrie complained that they barely had time to visit or talk.[11] They obviously were wild to see each other, and both wondered whether the occupant of an adjacent room in their Richmond hotel overheard their intense lovemaking. "Wouldn't you like to make the suspected occupant of the next room jealous of the joys he could not know, as we did in morning communion at Richmond?" he joked with her months later.[12] So engrossed were they with each other that the hours on the train trips from New York to Richmond and back passed like minutes. "Surely that was a dandy visit when we strolled in R—," he wrote, "and I never knew minutes to fly as they did going and returning to New York."[13]

Warren paid a price for his early exit from the Texas shooting trip. He wrote to Carrie that Ed Scobey told him that he was "in bad with the Timkens" because they believed that he had "cut their hunting party in Texas on a lark" and that he had been seen in Atlantic City with a very handsome woman three days after he left the party. "The truth is I haven't been in Atlantic City in eight years," he reassured Carrie. "Anyhow, if the Timkens are angry, I don't care a rap. They aren't good company anyway, and their stack of money is nothing to me."[14] Harding paid $25 for his share of the tips for the "Mexican servants at the ranch" and the "colored force on the car," which he thought a bit exorbitant, "but I am not kicking." This squared things up with the rest of the hunting party, and Harding had only Scobey to mend fences with for his premature departure.[15] Though Ed was upset, Harding told Carrie that he would come around. "He is all gold," he wrote her, "and will be all right."[16]

The year 1913 would be a desert for Warren, as he had predicted to Carrie. It dawned with him recollecting, longingly, of New Year's Eve the year before when they were in Montreal together. He had his bridge crowd over for a holiday celebration. When the bells and whistles of the New Year of 1913 began to ring in Marion, he halted the game to retrieve some sandwiches and crack a bottle of wine for his guests so he could steal a moment to reflect on the "marvelous coincidence" of the timing of their sexual climax with the sounding of the New Year's bells the previous year. He returned to the tournament with his friends and retired at two in the morning. He went to bed, covered his head, and sent Carrie a "wireless" message of love and fondness across the ocean. He knew from her letters that she was in Russia for the holiday and that as he laid down his head, she would already be awake, up and about. "Perhaps you didn't get [the wireless messages]," he wrote her, "*but I sent them,* and kissed and fondled and possessed in fancy, and did all I could to give you love's glow to begin your new year."

The next morning, he posted two "fat letters" to her and sent a dictionary by the new parcel post to Isabelle. Jim Phillips paid a visit to Harding later in the day to discuss a business matter. "He seems so confidential to me at times," he wrote. "I showed him your Xmas card, told him I thought it stingy and he agreed. Also showed him the letter sent direct [to Florence], which came while I was in Texas, and my freedom pleased him." The *Marion Star* had had a good year in 1912, and Harding wrote that he was branching out in 1913 with a new weekly, the *Ohio Star*, a venture that would fail after a short run. But Harding said the new project carried little risk for him, whether economically or emotionally. "If it falls flat it will be no dream of mine shattered."[17]

Nevertheless, he worked hard to birth the paper. In the midst of a "perfect avalanche of work" created by production of 50,000 copies of the inaugural *Ohio Star*, Harding shut the door to his office in the afternoon and started a letter on Thursday, January 2. "*My Carrie, Beloved and Adored,*" he started. The letter would be composed in segments over the next five days, put under lock and key in his desk drawer in between times, and eventually grow to thirty-four pages. He still felt the glow from their mid-December meeting as he launched into the letter. He joked that he stopped work to write her a line because it was January 2 "and I haven't scratched you a line *this* year." In seriousness, he immediately followed: "Moreover I am loving you so much, and have such a feeling of sweet wistfulness that I just have to give you a few minutes."[18] He told her that he had burned out his pen writing to her and had to get a new point, which he clearly shook over the paper, leaving a big blotch. "Nothing like starting a new pen," he wrote. "*I love you,*" he scribbled with the new instrument, then underlined those words. "There," he exclaimed, "[the new pen] will write that message so often that when it is well broken in it will write it without a guiding hand, but there will always be an impelling heart behind it."

That night, at nine-thirty, he again took a break from his labors to continue his letter. "Gee!" he wrote, "here is a tired kid, more tired than a wearied lecturer was in a hour or more out of Peoria," referring to some earlier tryst. "But I like it, and if I had you I would come to you to be petted and rested and consoled." He said it had been a demanding day, with the dawning of the *Ohio Star* at exactly six o'clock. Partway through the production of the new weekly, a gear whirling at high speed in the press was stripped, sending a couple of the gear teeth through a plate glass window in the front of the building. Fortunately no one was hurt. "One of those gear teeth would have killed or maimed if they had struck anyone," he told her.[19] Had Harding believed in luck or signs, he wrote, this accident would have annoyed him, but unlike his superstitious wife, he did not accept such things.[20]

He wrote that his newspaper associate and political lieutenant, Malcolm "Mack" Jennings—the man who had run his 1910 campaign for governor— was quitting and moving to Columbus to start up a new consulting public relations firm. He had mixed feelings about losing Jennings. He had been a fine editor at the paper but had opened and read some of Carrie's letters, causing a rift between the two men. "You need not worry about inspected mail," Warren wrote Carrie now that Mack was leaving. "He couldn't suppress his curiosity, however, when there was an opportunity to observe."[21] In parting, Jennings chastised Harding for ignoring his friends and avoiding social gatherings. But Harding was in no mood to attend parties. "Shoot!" he wrote. "I don't care a rap for hospitalities and social mingling that doesn't include you, and that is all there is to say." The odd thing was that Florence didn't seem to care that he had become a hermit. "She pens regret after regret," he wrote, "and never asks me, just takes it for granted." She even declined an invitation from the Tafts at Columbus "who have a prosy, little Presbyterian card party once a year."[22]

He told her of his New Year's resolutions for 1913. "I cut out tobacco in all forms," he wrote, "*before lunch*." He also said he "cut out cuss words, except in great need of them." That day he had come close to blaspheming, he wrote, when "the Mrs. came in to call me downstairs to see where the car had been hit by a street car." He promised not to curse as long as the railway people paid for a new rear wheel.[23]

He was chatty with her about the latest books he was reading. One in particular, a biography of Marshall Ney, one of Napoleon's most trusted generals, known as the "bravest of the brave," caught his attention, and as usual, he was most interested in his subject's love life. "Haven't gotten into his love affairs yet—maybe such a warrior was too busy to love."[24]

He turned fussy about her being too flirty and her engagement in Berlin nightlife, which he had recently read about in dispatches on the newswire at the *Star*. He said that he had seen a bit of the debauchery of Berlin life when he had last visited Europe and that he hoped Carrie was not a part of that scene. "The best things in life do not thrive in such night culture," he warned her.[25]

He asked her to destroy his letters and pictures of himself that he had sent her. This request was nothing new; he would make the same request regularly over the course of their affair. "I think you should have a fire, chuck 'em! Do. *You must.*" He told her she would have to do so when Jim came to Berlin in the summer in any event. In one of his self-deprecating moments, he told her that to destroy his letters would be no true loss, since his messages of love, he understood, could seem repetitive and tiresome. "*It is an old, a darling* old story," he wrote about his letters, "but what I write will seem less thread-worn if you wouldn't keep forty-seven copies on hand."[26]

He related an amusing story of how people in Marion still buzzed about their relationship. Speaking of a woman who was a known gossip, he asked, "Did you hear the one she used to tell about you and me, or *me* rather?" Anticipating she had not heard it, he described the rumor. "She said I bought records for the Victrola with a special view to making love to you by playing them, and never played these certain pieces except when you were there, and in the summer the neighbors could always tell when you were over there by the numbers I put in the machine." Not true, of course, but he said "if I played you one like that tonight it would be Creole Sue—'I sigh for you, I cry for you, I die for you.'"[27]

He continued to plainly state that he was ready to give up his marriage for her and that she was the one who was not ready. His writing also shows their discussion of the dream of becoming parents together. "You write and say you are not ready. For I's sake [meaning Isabelle] and for the sake of the one we hope for, you do not wish to be mine until you can be in the acceptance of the world's requirements. You have said we must wait and hope, and trust a favoring fate. Your utterance of this doctrine has helped me all that any thing can when I am rebellious and blue. . . . Until you are ready, I can't have you." But the contrary was true for him. "If you said you could and would be ready, I would cast the die. I have said it before and will *repeat it now.* It is less cost to me than you, for you are not quite so alone as I am."[28]

While it is not entirely clear what he meant by the reference to a "favoring fate," it could have been related to Florence's precarious health, with her chronic kidney condition, and the fact that he was regularly told that she was likely to die from her condition sooner rather than later. In 1913, Florence would face another relapse, one so serious that her doctor would all but give up hope.

At the beginning of the new year, though, Warren was more concerned with something Carrie had said to him during their rendezvous. She told him in person and then reiterated in a letter she would compose on her voyage back to Germany that she was attracted to another man. While he tried to take the news nonchalantly, he was deeply affected, so much so that his dreams reflected his inner conflict. "A few nights ago I dreamed I was on a train with you," he revealed to her, "and we were quite absorbed, and you would allow me the tiniest, platonic kisses, but never a touch or embrace. I was so annoyed that I woke up in clear rebellion."[29]

He also was becoming more troubled in his relationship with Jim Phillips. When Jim came over for a "long, confidential call" about Carrie and what he might do to convince her to come back from Berlin, Harding wrote that he had a "terribly smitten conscience."[30] Jim thrashed out a business proposition that would involve him selling his interest in the Marion dry goods department store and moving to Cleveland to buy a store there. Harding tried to talk him out of it, arguing that the new venture would be a heavy load and that Jim should be "throwing off burdens instead of adding to them."[31]

Why take it all on? Warren asked. Jim's reply stopped Warren cold. "You know why," Jim responded. "It is on account of the girl we are both interested in." Jim said that he believed that Carrie would never come back to Marion and that he had to get his affairs in order to entice her back.

"Here I *suffered*," Warren wrote to Carrie, "and wondered what to say, and be at least half honest." He told Jim that if Carrie came back to the States, she would come as readily to Marion as to Cleveland. Then he again cautioned that the move might threaten Jim's health, and that in any event, if he was doing it for Carrie, he should consult her. That said, Jim seemed mollified. He told Warren of a letter Carrie had written him and then showed him two letters from Isabelle, written while she was alone in Europe and her mother was with Harding in the United States, though she did not say a word about her mother's absence. "You can imagine what an interest I had in this letters," Harding wrote Carrie. "How marvelously discreet she is! I wonder if she knows," he mused. "She spoke of you as if you were there, without actually saying so, alluded to the bully good time you were having, never a hint about your travels."[32] Though five thousand miles away, he doffed his cap "in spirit" to Isabelle for her carefulness.[33]

On Monday, January 6, a letter arrived from Carrie, which she had penned on the steamer back to Europe and mailed on December 23. He was thrilled to get it—he had been starved for any word—but it contained matters that were at once "mystifying, satisfying, edifying, terrifying, and electrifying" to him.[34] She wrote in a way that held him enthralled. "It utterly engrossed me. It made me blue when you were blue, discouraged when you were discouraged, renewed my rejoicing when you rejoiced, made me ready when you were ready. I never was quite so utterly influenced."

Then he finally unburdened himself of the matter that had been disturbing his peace of mind. "One thing in your letter is revolving in my mind more dominant that all else," he wrote. He thought he understood what she meant in her letter when she wrote that "something has crept into my heart that neither you nor I can help and I can't tell you." He confessed at last that he suspected it related to her statement that she thrilled to another man. "I marvel at my composure over your question—'Am I disloyal to thrill with pleasure at the thought of the nearness of a certain man, etc.'"[35] The question had floored him. She could not love as he did and feel that way, he assured her. It was obvious to him that his love for her had not been enough. Worse, she seemed to be sending him conflicting messages. At one point in her letter, she wrote, "Be mine! And keep me yours, all yours forever." Then she wrote of things in her heart she could not tell him. He admitted his fatalistic sense about it all. "If this man that stirs your heart is near you, if he is near Berlin and there is propinquity, I wouldn't harbor real assurance *another day*. If distance intervenes, if it is the echo of an old love, I'll hope that chastity and high purpose and noble character will help to hold you mine."

It was all jumbled confusion. He blamed himself. "God!" he wrote. "What a retribution will be mine if I have awakened—and cannot hold!"

He was perplexed and lethargic. He closed his very long letter by simply saying: "And I do love you so. God knows I'm sorry that I can't fill your heart to the exclusion of your thrills over thinking of another, but I can't help it, and you can't so there is no use to grieve!"[36]

Nothing left to do but reiterate. *"I really do love you so."*

CHAPTER 16

"Mrs. H Is an Invalid"

The year 1913 was to be a time of darkness and murkiness for Warren Harding. Carrie was in Berlin, apparently enamored with another man. She would not return that summer. Instead, Jim Phillips would travel to Europe and tour with his wife and daughter. Florence Harding's health would fail, and her father, a giant though malevolent figure in Warren's life, would die in the fall. Warren's sister Mary would also pass away unexpectedly. Death and illness overtook Harding that year, leaving him writing regularly about his sense of isolation and depression. He was forty-seven years old, his party broken apart, with Democrats in the White House and in control of the governor's mansion in Ohio.

The weather seemed to be in sympathy with Harding's unhappy mood. In January he wrote that he had "never experienced such a gloomy run of weather" and that even the sea had been "cutting its wildest capers." He told Carrie he was grateful that "you and yours were not on the Atlantic during the last two weeks."[1] He developed a severe cold, which left him wheezing and sneezing, and his work at the newspaper was so intense that he had not played bridge with his friends for a couple of weeks, "which is pretty strong proof that I have been a recluse and sticking to my desk or the house."[2] Carrie's letters from an excursion to St. Petersburg only made him feel worse. A man from her Berlin crowd apparently was on the same trip with Carrie and Isabelle. Warren attributed her short letter to his presence. "Rather disappointed in length," he wrote of a letter from Russia, "but I was prepared to expect that, after you wrote me that Ginger would be there. So glad for your sake that he was, and I understand how rejoiced you were. And there was lots to see and enthuse over. I would have immensely enjoyed seeing it all with you, but since I can't, I am generous enough to be sincerely glad that you could enjoy and enthuse and see it all under such fortunate circumstances. You made me very much wish to attend the opera and the ballet."[3]

The man named Ginger was not Harding's only rival.[4] "They surely did miss you in Berlin," he wrote. "Willie [Allen, a woman friend and expatriate] is officially dead in love with you—and you deserve it—and I hate that George [Allen, Willie's husband] is on sufficiently friendly terms to send you love and kisses by mail."[5] He was left yearning for comfort from Carrie in the mail. On Saturday, January 18, he picked up his pen at four-thirty in the afternoon to write of his pleasure at bundling and addressing copies of the *Marion Star* to be sent to Isabelle and of his enclosing a hidden message of love with the package, using the code, "which you will readily translate." But even though he had received a letter from Carrie just that morning, he was "unconsciously looking for one in this afternoon's mail." Bereft when none arrived, he said that he found himself "insatiable in some ways."[6]

Though he assured her that he was bringing his emotions under control—"I love no less, just think more"—he continued to have disturbing dreams about her.[7] She seemed to be having simultaneous, reciprocal dreams. "Strange about you dreaming I told you a dream," he wrote her in March, "—for I was writing you of mine, just about the same time. Ought not, I know, but the spell was on, and I wrote it—defiantly." He described a dream in which they were in the midst of a frenzied sexual encounter. "I'll skip the details," he wrote, "except that Willie stood looking on, unabashed and unembarrassed." In this incipient age of Freud, Harding puzzled through the meaning of this dream. "I have been trying to test out my dreams on the latest theory of what dreams are—the unconscious expression of suppressed thoughts." He said he was "not yet ready to subscribe to the theory without considerable review" but was struck by the "coincidence in my writing you of a dream almost simultaneously with your dream of my telling you." His conclusion: "Dreams are strange, truly, some very delightful, some very harrowing—and we can't choose."[8]

Then, as if to put an exclamation point on his dark emotions, the weather in Ohio turned deadly. "The end of the week again," he wrote on March 29, "and such a week. Perhaps you have read of the flood. From Easter morning till Thursday night it rained, sometimes poured, and Ohio was never so visited with ruin."[9] It was the Flood of 1913, Ohio's greatest weather disaster. In Dayton, the Great Miami River rose and flooded fourteen square miles of the city, with swift currents ten feet deep running through the streets. The rainfall totals across the state averaged six to eleven inches in forty-eight hours, affecting Cleveland, where the Cuyahoga River washed away docks and rail yards, Toledo, where the Maumee River crested at ten feet above flood stage, and Cincinnati, where the Ohio River rose twenty-one feet in twenty-four hours. In Dayton alone, 123 people were killed, with another hundred drowning in Columbus. All told, almost 500 people died and over 40,000 homes were severely flooded or completely destroyed.[10]

Marion escaped the worst of it, but power and gas were cut off for days, and most communications with the outside world were disrupted. With little telephone service, no trains, and the telegraph wire dead ("we hadn't a dot or dash from Tuesday night to 10 o'clock today"), the *Star* had few sources for information about the disaster that was unfolding. "[A]nother week like it and I would be dead or insane, if I were in this business," Harding wrote to Carrie.

Jim Phillips jumped in with his usual impulse to civic responsibility and started raising funds for relief. Warren was noticing that Jim was becoming distant with him. Before the flood, Harding had called on him to discuss an increase in rates for advertising in the *Star,* and Jim became touchy—"and it makes me think he is 'offish' toward me," Harding wrote.[11] Yet at virtually the same time, he reported that Jim had asked the Hardings to join him on his trip to Europe that June. "I think it could be brought to pass," he wrote of Jim's invitation, "but it must not be." Warren did not doubt that "[m]any features [of the trip] would be enjoyable, but I couldn't endure the hardships, even if there was no rebellion other than that of my own breast to contend with. The time has passed when I might be near you and with you day after day and still deny the insistent calling of the heart, body and soul to possess you."[12]

The flood left a path of devastation across Ohio, good for newspaper circulation but "appalling" with respect to loss of life and property damage. Warren wrote that he even pitied "the thousands of poor animals which were its victims."[13] "Old man Noah never saw any thing worse," he wrote. "I shall hereafter believe the Bible story of the flood."

In the spring he bought books by the score from Brentano's in New York and read voraciously, keeping up with the latest bestsellers and continuing his interest in the love associations of the great leaders of history, such as Thornton Hall's *Love Affairs of the Courts of Europe.*[14] He sent Carrie almost as many books as he bought for himself.[15] Harding made few attempts to send private letters to Carrie in the summer of 1913, and those he sent were returned unopened. Jim did travel to meet with Carrie and Isabelle in June.

That summer Warren took on a ten-week-engagement with a Chautauqua speaker's circuit, agreeing to speak thirty to thirty-five consecutive days for fifty dollars per date plus traveling expenses.[16]

Warren's unmarried sister Mary, who was legally blind and a teacher at the Ohio State School for the Blind in Columbus, planned with him to find employment for their spinster younger sister Daisy, who was coming home from her extended visit to the Far East and Burma. Daisy returned via Europe and just missed hooking up with Carrie in Bellagio, Italy.[17] "Daisy tells me she missed you by an hour or two, and thought she saw you looking out the window of a passing car," Warren wrote to Carrie. With only a high school certificate, Daisy was going to face some difficulty finding a teaching job, but Mary wanted her to move in with her and apply for work in Columbus. "I think it would be so nice for us to have a little flat down here together, as it is, we have no home," Mary wrote to Warren.[18] Ever since their father had remarried a much younger woman, Warren's sisters no longer felt at home in Marion.[19] Moreover, Mary was poorly paid by comparison to her male counterparts, and as a consequence, she needed to board with someone just to make ends meet. She let her brother the politician know about it: "The idea of putting women out to board on a hundred dollars [a year] less than a man is preposterous. Every man teacher connected with our school gets three hundred to live on and the ladies two."

Harding attended several family reunions that summer. He and several of his siblings, including Deacon and Mary, joined in the Crawford-Harding reunion. Warren's grandmother on his father's side was a Crawford, which made him a blood relation of William Crawford, a Revolutionary War soldier and surveyor for George Washington. Crawford was tortured and burned at the stake at the battle of Olentangy in 1782. Harding wrote to Carrie that his Crawford relatives liked to hold their reunion near the site of the battle because "the sizzled Colonel Crawford was a kinsman."[20] In late August Warren spoke at a major family reunion of the Van Kirk family, from his mother's side, in Washington, Pennsylvania. Almost five hundred relatives attended, and his speech was so well received that he was elected, over his protest, president of the reunion association.[21]

Jim Phillips sent Warren postcards and letters from Europe, keeping him up to date with their travels. In a public letter to Carrie in the middle of August, Warren said that he had never known such a dull summer. Nor could he remember a hotter one. "I would think it because I am fat," he joked, "but thin people say the same."[22] He tweaked Carrie with a reference to how women in Marion were dealing with the heat. "The women seem to be meeting the situation coolly, by diaphanous, silhouette skirts and forgetting some of the things they used to wear. I hear that many a transparency attracts riveted gaze on the streets, but my eye-sight is poor and I never wear glasses on the streets, so I cannot speak from personal observation."[23]

But in the midst of his news and joking, he sounded a somber note. "Mrs. H has been in poor health since July 4, taking treatment every day at the san [referencing the Sawyer sanitarium, White Oaks]."[24] He mentioned nothing more, but the situation would grow dramatically worse, and by September, Florence Harding was critically ill.

Jim, Carrie, and Isabelle traveled across the continent that summer, visiting Italy, Switzerland, Sweden, and England. Jim wrote to Warren that he was leaving Europe on September 6 and that Carrie would post a letter confirming his departure.[25] The ship he traveled on was the behemoth of the Hamburg-American Line, a 52,000-gross-ton passenger liner just placed in commercial service in June. The *Imperator* (Harding wrote to Carrie that it was pronounced Im-per-*raw*-ter) was the world's largest liner for its first few months of service until its sister ship the *Vaterland* (later SS *Leviathan*) was launched.[26] Everything about the *Imperator* was of immense proportion. She had a three-stack design with funnels that towered almost seventy feet above the deck, an elaborate and flamboyant indoor pool called the Pompeian Bath with a spectator's gallery, a gymnasium, and a finely appointed Social Hall festooned with palms and a huge, ornate glass skylight overhead, all watched over by a white marble bust of spiked-helmeted Kaiser Wilhelm II. The ship had a gaudy gilt figurehead on her bow—a giant eagle with outstretched wings, clutching a globe in its talons, with motto emblazoned: "Mein Feld ist die Welt" [the World is my Field].

On Jim's return trip, a fire was reported on the *Imperator*'s deck. A copy editor at the *Marion Star* picked it up from the newswires and asked Warren, "Didn't Jim P. cross on that ship?" Warren was amazed that night to see a squib in the paper that Jim *and Carrie* were returning to Marion. "Well, a dozen or more personal inquiries followed the next day," Warren wrote Carrie of the incident, which highly annoyed him but he could not show it. "Even the Mrs. asked me about it."[27]

With Jim on his way home, Warren released a torrent of letters to Carrie. On September 15, he composed a twenty-six-page missive, then another twenty-three pager over the next four days, and a twelve-page letter two days later.[28] The letters written prior to Jim's arrival in Marion on September 20 are missing the first four pages, meaning Warren continued to send "open letters" in front of his private letters to Carrie, just in case.[29]

Things had gotten progressively worse in Marion. To divert himself from the sickness at home, Warren wrote several escapist letters. In a letter written on September 15, he wrote of what he called "memory festivals," recollections of times he had spent with Carrie. "Great solace is memory," he wrote to Carrie. "Great solace at times, awful tempter at others, sometimes distressing. Balancing the account at times, I treasure my love memories of you as priceless things." He described how on the day Jim had left for Europe at the beginning of the summer, he had asked Warren to help him move his packed steamer trunk from the second floor. Warren quickly realized that it was a mistake for him to be in that space, even with Jim there. He couldn't help but travel back in time to the erotic moments he and Carrie shared in her home:

> There I had almost a riot of recollections, and it all seemed so strange. While I waited on the porch there was love memory and love's keenness there. When I tarried in the library there seemed a thousand caresses like memory-kissed. I made excuse to go to the music room, with its memories of "[indecipherable]," dear and delicious, so good to have, where hunger could not feast in fullness. J— took me up stairs, to help on the trunk in the upper hall. Trooping came the memory of our sacred day, and the bridal breakfast that was served there, I made my way to your room, where memory deepened and blessed even more—memory of the first time I saw you garbed for your couch, in those glorious flowing tresses, and you first became mine not deliberately, but love plighted itself; and there were memories there, in such a short time, of fuller visions of your great beauty, memories of grander realization, of ecstasies and raptures, of fascinating fondling and kisses hurried and heavenly, memories of you giving yourself as only you can give—the surpassing experiences of my life. Memories of you telephoning while I distracted your thought by making you fondle, while I held your breast in my adoring hands. On the upper porch, too, I recalled the August night two years ago, you were so exquisite and loving. And these I might run on, reciting with pen how my thought reveled, and I rather rejoiced that the house was to be locked, and walls that knew so much could not speak, and would be alone for a time and unprofaned.[30]

When he was not diverting himself with his memories, he was brought back to the grim existence that was overtaking his household. Florence was in what he thought could be her final illness. His father-in-law was definitely in his last illness. "The old gentleman has been losing ground—and losing his mind, almost imperceptibly the latter—all summer," he wrote Carrie.[31] "The woman married to him [his second wife] is to be genuinely pitied. Never was a person as imprisoned, under such disagreeable conditions. His feebleness is no affair of mine, but you can guess it has unavoidably had an influence on my affairs."

But it was Florence's condition, not his father-in-law's, that was taking up most of his time. "Worse still, the Mrs. became ill after the motor drive east [earlier in the summer], and has been a pitiful figure ever since. She has been desperately ill twice, and on the 26th of August was ordered to bed for two months, with the warning that it was the only thing that would save her." He was providing support, day and night, taking his dinners alone at his dining room table at home while Florence languished in bed upstairs. "One night I thought the end was near," he wrote Carrie. The entire town joined him in what they thought was a deathwatch. "The town has the story that she is in great danger. All this has its influence in my daily walks. It is all very trying."

His quiet battles over the years with Florence may have created distance and bitterness between them, but watching her struggle moved him with feelings of sympathy and concern. "I tell you, dearie, no matter how deep one's resentment may be, one must be humane when brought face to face with a fight for life. I can't write more of it." Knowing how touchy Carrie was to any reference to Florence, he reiterated that he remained true to her. "It has been very trying, *very*, and I have tried to be faithful to manly duty without any way lessening my love and fidelity to you. I wonder if you understand. Surely you do."[32]

"Mrs. H is an invalid," he wrote a day later. "Dr. S—[Sawyer] has told she is likely to die any day."[33] Florence's father, Amos H. Kling, was showing signs of resilience, but Harding knew the look of death when he saw it. "A.H. is a little improved, walks about some, but is doomed and looks it."

He wrote of how bewildering Amos Kling's second wife, Carolyn, was to him. She was thirty-eight years younger than her eighty-year-old husband (and thus six years younger than Harding and eleven years younger than Florence), and Warren, who obviously had more time to study her closely during Amos's decline, could not figure her out. "I have no idea what she thinks, but I am about the farthest in the world from her thoughts. She has always been a puzzle to me. Has been courteous and polite, seemingly considerate but always miles aloof." He knew her to be interested in a local judge. "She lifts up whenever they meet," he wrote Carrie. "She is quite taken with Judge S— but she is a candidate for sympathy in her present enslavement. No one else in Marion has a harder cross to bear."

Sitting at home on "gloomy, cold, disagreeable" Sunday, September 21, listening to John Philip Sousa on his Victrola and "smoking his head off" with cigars, Warren wrote to Carrie that Jim had returned to Marion the day before. "J—arrived in M—yesterday," he wrote, "and honored me with an early call in the afternoon, staying close to one hour. He looks exceptionally well, and is adorned with a little chunky, grey mustache with reminds me of the gallants of Munich and Rome. He seemed devoted to it."[34] Warren listened with keen interest as Jim described Carrie's friends in Berlin. Jim had delivered Warren's "esteemed respects" to one of Carrie's German friends but Jim told Warren that the woman received the greeting with dissatisfaction, as too cold. "What should I have said?" he asked Carrie. "I seem very unsophisticated, but can learn."

This Sunday afternoon letter was interrupted by the arrival of Warren's bridge gang. "Am glad they are coming, I need the distraction." They played bridge until eleven that night, and the next morning, September 22—Carrie's birthday (she turned forty)— Warren continued his letter. "Good morning, my girl with a birthday today. I'd like to give you a kiss greeting. I'd hold you in my arms and weld my lips to yours and give you a great, deep, breathless, heart-stopping kiss for each and every year you have brightened this old world." He told her of another revealing dream he had of her the night before: "I dreamed that J— [meaning Jim] and I journeyed over the Atlantic to visit you, and we reached Pension Polchow [where Carrie resided in Berlin] before you had any word of my coming, and you started to greet me with great cordiality when you looked and saw I was barefooted, and became so mortified you wouldn't even speak to me. Not much joy in a dream like that, but I caught your vision, which was some compensation."

John Sousa's band played a concert in Marion on Carrie's birthday, and a thousand people showed up for the outdoor performance at the pavilion. It was "beastly chilly" for late September, and so Warren passed: "I couldn't have been tempted to venture out."[35] Jim turned up for another long visit on Tuesday, bringing a pipe he purchased for Warren in Europe. "I am very fond of a pipe," he wrote Carrie, "but they do not promote my nervous or physical well being." When Warren reminded Jim that it had been Carrie's birthday the day before, Jim said he remembered and had had a notion to send her a cable. "See," he wrote Carrie, "you are a lot thought of."

His mood turned "grouchy" when he received a cold little note that Carrie had written before she had received his flood of letters. He was sorry she felt abused, having received so few letters, but he knew by the time she received the letter he was writing, she would have had enough to soothe her hurt. But he was not pleased with something she wrote about his rival named Ginger. He sarcastically responded to her comment that Ginger was "ordered," as any good Prussian would be. "Of course, he is 'ordered,'" Warren fumed. "I have been 'ordered' myself. It is great to be 'ordered' at the opportune time. Since J—told me he said he saw more of him than any other man I have but one response— 'you are your own mistress and will do what you prefer, and what I don't like I can lump,' and that's all there is to it." After all, he wrote, "Germany and the United States are free countries, and you are especially situated to do exactly as you please. But nix on the 'ordered' business."

Ironically, just when he seemed to be in one of his most tetchy moods, he found within himself the wherewithal to write at his best about the nature of love, the meaning of nearness, or "propinquity" as he called it, and the age-old question of whether love was something permanent or merely illusory, a passing fancy:

There, I have replied to your note and answered every suggestion therein, save one, which I reserved for the last. You wonder about genuine love, and say it doesn't require propinquity to keep it aflame. Perhaps not, but you will agree some day that propinquity will work wonders. I am not sure whether you were questioning the genuineness of my love or not. Of course I may be mistaken about it myself, but if I am fooled, no man ever truly loved. I have studied it a lot and scrutinized myself. If it isn't love, it is an alarming case of permanent infatuation. When a man can think of no one else, worship nothing else and craves nothing else than the one woman he adores, though he hasn't seen her in nine or ten months, and she is four thousand miles away, and can't possibly be possessed, it seems more than infatuation. I often wish it were less, I am so obsessed, but a mature reflection convinces me that it is really big to know such a love, and then I am content. When a man loves with all his thoughts, loves as he walks, loves in his daily business, loves as he reads, loves at his work and loves at his play, when every song of his lips in some way, intimately or remotely, is associated with the one beloved, he is very much in love, and it must be the real thing. I grant you have reason to think I yield to the sex call. I do. I am ever wanting to kiss and fondle, to embrace and caress, to adore and possess. I can't help it. That is not spiritual, I grant, but very real. It may be only a symptom of the greater love, or it may be a factor in the greater love's awakening. I do not know. But this I do know, my greater admiration, adoration, and worship has been inseparable from this experience. And it all endures.[36]

In the meantime, October, with its expected and unexpected deaths, awaited Warren Harding in Marion, Ohio.

CHAPTER 17

"I Have Had My First Lark since You Went Abroad"

The weather in 1913 continued to be quirky. To anyone with the power of discernment, the climatologic oddities seemed as if a presage of the disaster forming in Europe. "We are floundering about in the grip of one of the greatest snow storms ever, certainly the greatest ever recorded in the fore part of the November," Harding wrote Carrie on November 11.[1] Drifts were five to eight feet deep. Many farmers were caught unprepared for the early and unexpected snow. Harding told of pigs in small hog houses that were buried beneath drifts and that it took days for them to be rescued.[2] On top of it all, he was sick. "I don't know how I got it, but I have a wheezing cold and feel bum accordingly."

He had been under enormous personal stress for months. After a summer of decline, Amos Kling succumbed to illness and old age, dying on October 20. He was cantankerous to the end, refusing to pay for a nurse until he finally took to his bed four days before he died. After years of friction between the two men, Warren felt little pity for the old man. Writing privately to Carrie, he compared his father-in-law to a brute and a cold-blooded snake. "No, I wasn't distressed over AHK's death," he wrote to Carrie.[3] "But circumstances forced me to see him often during the last week he lived, and death is a spectacle and unavoidably gloomy to me."

His compassion was reserved for Kling's widow, Carolyn, who had borne a terrible burden in his final illness and then was treated shabbily, according to

Warren, in the will. Florence's brother Cliff received "nearly everything," including the Florida home and his stepmother now had to get his permission to stay in it over the winter.[4]

The day before Amos Kling died, Mary Harding, Warren's sight-impaired sister, made a visit from Columbus, taking the train to come up and check on Florence and to have dinner with Warren. Florence was still struggling, and Mary spent several hours with her. "She has a form of enlarged heart, with a nervous breakdown," Warren wrote of Florence's condition to Carrie.[5] "Some days she is improved, some days in a sorry state. Both Sawyers have told she wouldn't recover, they have said so to me and then changed their mind three different times, but brother [George or Deacon] has always insisted she will get well." In fact, Warren's younger brother had a sample of Florence's urine examined at a laboratory in Columbus and wrote to Warren that the report "was favorable."[6] He recommended a wait-and-see attitude. "Just be patient with Florence," George counseled Warren, "and don't worry. Give her time. She will come out ok." He recommended internists in Columbus, Cleveland, and Cincinnati, but Florence trusted the Sawyers—especially the father Charles, who everyone called "Doc." Doc and his son Carl had seen her through rough patches in the past, and she believed in their unique homeopathic cures, which she felt kept her alive.

Harding had been circumspect in writing about Florence's health, but he was growing weary of Carrie's lack of sympathy. "There has been little of it written to you because I could not bring myself to write of it, and knowing your dislike, it seemed best not to bring up the subject," he wrote on November 13. "Perhaps you would be less positive if you were brought in contact with her struggling to live—any how I could not have held my head erect if duty were needlessly neglected."[7] He told her his life had become a daily routine of attending to the sick. "One can't plan much ahead with a member of the household sick and doctors coming twice a day," he wrote. It was not that he had to do daily nursing; others were hired to attend to those duties. But he did have to be on call and was the primary caregiver at night. "I do little nursing, and love reading aloud; some nights I read a short story in the Saturday Eve. Post or a magazine. All that seems to be required is my presence in the house, so that Frank and Bernice [caretakers and housekeepers] can get out, after being on the job all day."

The Friday after her visit with Florence and Warren in Marion, Mary had a seizure at her home. Deacon thought the problem was controllable and so did not notify Warren, who, unbeknownst to Deacon, was in Columbus for business a few days later. Anxious to get back home because of Florence's health, Warren did not drop in to see either Mary or Deacon, something he would normally have done. The following day, Tuesday, Mary had another attack, a stroke that killed her. When Warren was told, he was disconsolate and reproached himself for not taking the time to see her the day before. "Dear, good, noble, big-hearted sister Mary died last night," he wrote to his sister Carolyn in Burma. "A better, dearer soul never lived."[8] He found great pathos in a letter from Carolyn that crossed in the mails with his, "telling with enthusiasm what she and her husband were planning to do for Sister Mary," he wrote Carrie. "While this letter was crossing the seas to me, my own letter was sailing to Carrie [Carolyn also went by Carrie] telling her of Mary's sudden death. Imagine the feelings of Carrie when my sad letter arrives."[9]

Warren helped his father with the mournful task of preparing Mary's casket and floral arrangements for visitation in his father's house. He remarked to Carrie of the coincidence of her writing about a strange sensation she had about him on the day he was attending to his sister's funeral arrangements. In an early November letter before she knew of Mary's sudden passing, Carrie wrote to Warren of an inexplicable but distinct feeling she had that caused her to think of him. She didn't know what the feeling meant, but it was strong enough that she wrote asking what he was doing at an exact moment on October 30. He wrote back: "In another place you wonder what I was doing at 8:45 p.m. on October 30. I happen to remember, very distinctly. I was over at father's, assisting in arranging the casket which contained my sister, and helping to fix the many beautiful flowers and complete funeral arrangements for the next day." He reminded Carrie that she was last in that same house when death had taken his mother in 1910—so his thoughts in fact had turned to her. "I thought of you, too, because you had called the last time death visited that house."[10]

Mary's death was harder on Warren than he would admit. A few weeks later, he went to Columbus to attend to her estate. He found from her bank records that she had given away almost half of her paltry salary to people in need. "Think of her, on the verge of blindness, giving over half her salary away," he wrote Carrie. "She was such an unselfish soul."[11] When he returned to the train station to catch a ride back to Marion, he bumped into "a gang" of his friends. "I have had my first lark since you went abroad," he wrote to Carrie of what happened next, "and it was quite unpremeditated." His friends were in high spirits, likely politicians all, and the superintendent of the Big Four Railroad lent the men his private car, which was hooked up to the train going to Marion.[12] "Well, there was poker and heaps of [indecipherable], and I was in the psychological mood. Everybody hit things up, and after dinner in the car, in the Marion yards, we went to J—S— home and put a grand finish on a swift beginning. I landed home at 2 AM, in considerable disfavor, but incapable of being sorry."[13]

A dog began to appear at his door that fall, for no apparent reason, but the animal epitomized Warren's time of trouble. "I have a new loss to add to my woes," he wrote Carrie. "A neighbor two doors to the west (I don't even know their names) had a little crippled black and tan dog, who has been twice run over by automobiles, who was blind in one eye, deaf, and had a broken leg. Somehow, I don't know just how, he got to coming to our house for his supper, and every night at six, right on the dot, he was on the job." In his loneliness, Harding found the creature, wretched though he was, to be an attentive companion. He began to ask the little visitor into his house. "So I got to inviting him in, to get his gratuity from the table while I dined. He was so appreciative that I enjoyed his company." Then, just as suddenly as the dog had materialized, he stopped showing up. After several days, Harding became concerned. "He hadn't appeared for four days, so I stopped last night to make inquiry, and found he had died. Really, I am sorry, though he was only the semblance of a dog after all his misfortunes."[14]

Not all the news he shared with Carrie was downbeat. Marion had "never been so gay socially," he told Carrie. Parties abounded. A group called the Tally Wags held an all-night dancing gala, with music scheduled until six in the morning. "Looks like overdoing," he wrote of the all-nighter, "but I suppose I gaze with 48-year-old eyes."[15] An Elks carnival in Marion resulted in what he characterized as "the greatest gambling orgy ever pulled off in this town." According to Harding, even "Monte Carlo and Cripple Creek are put in the shade." His unsophisticated secretary found herself caught up in the betting frenzy. "My stenog, who is ordinarily a pious Baptist, is rejoicing today over winning $6.00 and a fancy scarf," he wrote Carrie. Warren suspected that the pulpits in Marion's churches would "thunder" on the upcoming Sunday over the outbreak of gambling.[16] He did not participate, but not because he had a constitutional opposition to gambling. "I have not attended, though taking a chance is not offensive to my disposition, but I have prepared not to be identified with this open violation."[17]

He wrote about his latest choice in books, which included a work of fiction just published by English historical novelist Maurice Hewlett called *Bendish: A Study in Prodigality*.[18] He sent Carrie his copy, saying he didn't mark the book, but directed her attention to a few pages that caught his interest, no doubt love passages. He shared some lighter things, such as a parlor story about a woman with a tight skirt: "Did I ever tell you the cute dialogue between the young smarty and the tight-skirted chicken?" he regaled her. "Mr. Smarty noted her skirt and said, 'Say kid, your skirt is mighty tight about the *bottom* isn't it?' 'Yeah,' chirped the chicken, 'and *about the ankles too.*' Perhaps I scratched it before. Writing so much it is difficult to remember."[19]

When Carrie asked, he denied he had had an affair with a woman identified only as "Mrs. F." Apparently she was a friend of Carrie's and Florence's. He admitted they once were very intimate and "traveled heaps together," but she fell out of favor with Florence over some dispute involving Florence's stepmother. Mrs. F. remained friendly with Harding until 1909 when the Hardings and Phillipses went abroad. "She thought I cared for you, hinted it more than once," he wrote, "and slammed you a couple of times, and I told her that if all her friends were as good and pure and high-minded as you the world could be measured by a new and exalted standard."[20] Despite all this, he was adamant: "*No, I was never in love with, or the lover of, Mrs. F.*"

His letters kept her up to date with the latest zany stories from life in small-town America.[21] The Sawyers, whose White Oaks sanitarium always provided a storehouse of tales, had to care for one particularly disturbed young man that year. "Poor Sawyer has his troubles," he wrote Carrie. "He has a bug-house patient, a fine looking young fellow, who is epileptic and gets off for brief spells only." One such bout made news in Marion. The young man asked permission to find some work to stay busy, so he was assigned to a local farmer named Hesker. "Suddenly the boy went wrong, kicked down Farmer Hesker and attacked him with the prongs of the pitch fork," Harding wrote. Remarkably, the farmer survived. "How Hesker escaped nobody knows, he did get a prong through the arm, and that crazy man did not know that he had even been disturbed."[22]

And still, with all the tumult, there was plenty of love in his letters. In September, just after Jim boarded the *Imperator*, Warren wrote that he was thankful she still wrote the code word *matrix* in one of her letters (meaning "I am utterly and gladly all yours—today and always"). "I can't tell you how glad I am," he wrote her. "I didn't believe it possible, I was prepared to be reconciled to what must be, though I should have suffered terribly, so you may know how rejoiced I am to read it, after all danger is past."[23] He even spoke of when they might meet next. But he recognized that she had made the sacrifice two years in a row, traveling to meet with him in New York.[24] Moreover, those two assignations had resulted in bad feelings. "You ask when we are to meet," he wrote. "I wish I could answer. Of course you couldn't come again for a tryst—they have ended so unhappily. I don't know just why, but they did. Any how, the denial and frustrations and long, tedious journey can't be worth the cost in effort. You will not say so, but I know."[25]

Sometimes still he could write himself into a wild mood of sexual fantasy, when he called himself a "barbarian," but those moments occurred less and less frequently. For example, on September 15, he wrote:

*Y*ou are the dearest goddess to love and worship that ever was or could be, and incomparable to gaze upon, *and matchless to fondle, and embrace amid kisses. I tell you truly, you are the* very darlingest to love in all the world. I am crazy about you. *And when my thought is fixed in fondness I grow wild,* simply wild. *You simply do not, cannot guess how I need you, and want you, and ache for love's employments, as you inspire them.*

This love burst went on for several more pages, in which he recalled affectionately their days in Richmond and in London at the "dear old Devonshire." The next morning, the spell broken, he wrote as if he were a recovering drunk: "*A new day,* and sober again, tho not regretting the intoxication of fond thoughts of you."[26]

A fundamental cooling of their relationship had taken place over the course of the year 1913, and by November he was admitting he had grown cautious, pulling back from her in self-defense. She needed the attention of men—"you could no longer be happy without the society of men than you could fly," he wrote. "So I did the only thing I could do, reconciled myself to that order of things, and resolved to love and accept such love as you would bestow, and let it go at that. I chucked my ideal, because it was impossible."[27]

And though he did not yet see it fully, there were signs that Florence finally was starting to turn a corner. "The sick were doing well for a week," he wrote Carrie on November 18, "then a back-set the first of this week so that progress is not perceptible." Florence, like her stepmother, was not treated well by her father in his will. Amos Kling's estate was estimated to be worth more than $800,000, a fortune in a small town like Marion. Florence received only $60,000, an unfair share, but nevertheless significant money for a couple who had no children and an established and profitable business.[28] She decided not to contest her father's will, though she did immediately draw up her own will to make sure that Marshall did not squander what she had to leave, "or neglect his children," as Harding wrote to Carrie.[29] In the process of finding out about Florence's estate planning, Warren discovered that if he did not have a will, his entire estate would go to her and, worse, to Marshall if Florence predeceased her son. The thought that his brothers and sisters would get nothing so troubled him that he had his own will made up after a sleepless night of worry.[30]

While Florence did not inherit what many thought she would (or did) after Amos Kling's death, Harding was not particularly disappointed. Money never meant much to him after he reached the point of feeling financially secure. "It is good to have means, I know," he explained to Carrie, "but money is only a convenience." He elaborated on his feelings about money, having just seen his father-in-law die with so much money left in his estate:

I saw the poor old man dying, when all his money could bring him neither solace nor comfort. He may have enjoyed accumulating it, but never had much joy expending it. I'd like to have enough to feel assured, but I am positive that I will never care a rap to be rich. More, I am very sure I never will be. I think J—[Jim] aspires to be rich. He has some big scheme in his head. It never struck me that your [wealthy] Uncle Frisk has an extra good time. Why didn't he spend more, instead of seeking more? I've always thought I'd like a lot for a little while to show some of the wealthy what I would do, but I suppose if I had it I'd want more, and do just as they do to acquire it. Funny old world isn't it, and the touch of Midas is the same everywhere.[31]

"I shall not aspire again," Harding wrote Carrie about his political ambitions as 1913 drew to a close. But he found in November that there was still "political buzzing" about him, and he admitted that all the attention "tickles one's vanity a bit."[32] As in the past, his assurance to Carrie that he was through with politics turned out to be a pledge he could not keep. An open race for one of Ohio's seats in the United States Senate would prove to be too powerful an attraction for him to resist. Florence's slow recovery and his required attention to her would also turn his concentration away from Carrie and direct him into the political fire again. These two developments—renewed political interest and Florence's resurgence—would combine to open a major gap in 1914 between the two lovers.

But in the end, it may have been Carrie's own letter in the first weeks of January 1913 that started the chain of events that led to Warren Harding's Senate race. Harding changed upon reading that she had "thrilled" to another man—a sentiment she expressed perhaps in a moment of unguarded candor, or just as likely to inspire jealousy. His feelings would harden over the course of a long, trying year and eventually would guide him not only to the U.S. Senate but ultimately to the White House.

A war would intervene between Harding's time in the Senate and the White House, providing him with his moment of destiny, but it would further strain the bonds of affection between Senator Warren G. Harding and Mrs. James E. Phillips, private citizen.

CHAPTER 18

"I Was Literally Seduced and Urged into the Step"

Despite all his opposition to direct democracy, Warren Harding would reach the U.S. Senate, ironically, as the first popularly elected senator in the history of Ohio. Since the country's beginning, senators had always been chosen by state legislatures, but the Seventeenth Amendment provided that senators would be chosen "by the people" of the state. Ratified in 1913, the election of a senator in Ohio would happen for the first time in 1914. As the year began, though, it was not at all clear that Warren Harding would run for the job.

In January, his immediate concern seemed to be Florence's recovery and the welfare of his unmarried sisters, who continued to feel the shock of their sister Mary's sudden death. He wrote to Carrie that he could not come to Europe because he was being watched by the whole community, which knew of Florence's invalidism.[1] His family members seemed convinced that Florence would pull through if she was given enough time and rest. His sister Charity wrote: "We all feel so sorry that Florence is confined to her room and has been so long. It must be dreadful for one so energetic and always 'on the go' like Florence used to be. Her father's death must have been hard to bear, in her weakened condition."[2]

From Texas, Ed Scobey extended a cheery invitation to Florence and Warren to come south for her convalescence in the San Antonio sun and heat. "I think the Duchess would improve rapidly if I could hold her hand every day," he wrote to Warren on January 19. "I don't think you can beat the San Antonio climate, as a rule, in the Springtime; we usually have sunshine every day."[3]

Harding decided to take Florence to Florida instead of Texas. When Carrie found out about this trip, she became furious. She wrote him a series of letters in March, which he responded to in early April after returning from the trip. "This is to acknowledge your two notes of the 28th and 30th of March, received here at home last Wednesday," he wrote Carrie on April 11, "also the letter presumably written two weeks earlier, but bearing no date."[4] His cool reply was in contrast to the heat from her letters. "After reading and rereading, *reflectively*, several times, I am sure there is no reply for me to make. It is all my fault, your decision is made, and I can neither argue nor appeal. Contradiction would be unseemly on my part, and the ocean is too wide to admit of argument across its wide expanse." He tried to mollify her by telling her that he had taken a small photo of her that he worshipped to Florida, "but I suppose that knowledge would not please you." He even said he thought of sending her a photo of himself showing the mustache he had grown on his Florida sojourn, but he had shaved it before sitting in front of a camera. "You would have been amused," he ventured.

She was anything but amused. Two months later, in June, he was still responding to letters in which she fulminated against his trip with Florence. "I did not go to Florida in anger, or to punish you or defy you," he wrote defensively on June 4.[5] "I went because it seemed the only thing to do. The doctor said it must be so, and I know that an entire community was watching." The letters make it clear that the root of her anger was the fact that he went to Florida with Florence rather than traveling to Europe to see her. "I wanted to come," he wrote, "but you won't have it so unless I come alone. When you reflect—reflect deliberately—you will agree that I could not leave an invalid wife and be about three weeks without leaving my address. It would have been the equivalent of burning all bridges and involving you, and there could be no backward step."[6]

It was on this Florida trip that Harry Daugherty supposedly convinced Harding to run for the Senate. Daugherty, a lawyer and political operative from Washington Court House, Ohio, had been active in the party, holding such titles as chairman of the Ohio Republican State Executive Committee. Like Harding, he was a party loyalist and Taft supporter.[7] He would become Harding's attorney general, a man around whom shady dealings seemed to coalesce. Daugherty's claim that he found Harding in Florida in the winter of 1914 sunning himself like a "turtle on a log" and that he, Daugherty, "pushed him into the water" of the senate race is mythical.[8] Daugherty appears to have played a small role in Harding's decision to enter the Senate race. Harding was a man who kept his own counsel, and his correspondence shows that when he did take advice, it was from his friends Ed Scobey or Malcolm Jennings. Daugherty was more of a rival at this time than a confidant.

When Harding returned from Florida, he was still reluctant to make any decision about the race. "You have been home a week," Malcolm Jennings wrote Harding on April 11, "and I haven't heard from you, and I am getting a little anxious. I am afraid you will shave before I see that mustache and that will be a calamity. The reporters have been running to me for information as to your political intentions and almost everybody I see has a question to ask."[9] Harding had to weigh several factors in making a decision on the Senate seat. There is no doubt he was concerned about the effect of a major campaign on Florence's health and her recovery, and he knew how Carrie would react if he ran. The man who held the Senate seat, Republican Theodore Elijah Burton, had decided that he was not popular enough to withstand a direct election and made it known he would not seek reelection. Harding's *Marion Star* agreed with Burton's self-assessment. "Burton is a scholarly, Christian man, and a great, big statesman," the *Star* editorialized in December 1913, "but he does not appeal to popular acclaim."[10] Similarly in April 1914, the *Star* proclaimed that Burton was "one of the least popular men in public life."[11] But among the leading challengers who emerged for Burton's seat was Joseph Foraker, Harding's old mentor who twice had been selected as a U.S. senator by the Ohio legislature (1897 and 1909). Harding was not interested in competing against a former friend.

Foraker, however, was far from palatable to most regular Republicans, and he was certainly not acceptable to Progressives. He had been whisked out of office in scandal.[12] He was from the old-school political boss mold, seen as a reactionary, and influential newspaper editors like Dan Hanna of the *Cleveland Leader* thought that his candidacy would spell disaster for Ohio Republicans. Foraker had been one of President Roosevelt's biggest opponents in the Senate, and he fought with McKinley and Marcus Hanna in Ohio. After the disaster of 1912, the watchword for Republicans was reconciliation. State leaders looked for a candidate who could act as a harmonizer among the factions, and Warren Harding seemed just such a man. When Senator Burton officially announced he would not run on April 7 and Foraker made known his entry into the field, Burton thought momentarily about reversing his decision, but eventually he and other state leaders pushed Harding to enter the race. Republicans were certain that Harding alone had the standing to stop Foraker from getting the nomination. (The only other declared candidate of any note was a congressman from Findlay, Ralph Cole, who stood little chance of defeating Foraker.) Harding waited until almost the filing deadline of May 30 to declare. He had hoped that Foraker would withdraw under pressure, but Foraker stood his ground. On Thursday, May 28, unhappy that Foraker was still in the contest, Warren Harding declared his candidacy.

A week later, on June 4, it was time for him to justify what he had done to Carrie. "I suppose you will think I never mean anything that I say," Harding began, "but I am likely to get into politics again." He clarified that he still needed to collect sufficient signatures for his petition to qualify for the August 11 primary, but if he accumulated them, he wrote, "I will enter the race for U.S. senator." He did not go into detail on his reasons, but he did fix some of the responsibility on her, saying he entered the race because of his increasing disappointment and despondency over their relationship:

> *The papers have been full of it. I assented at a very late hour, and there may be difficulty in getting 10,000 petitioners, but I think I will have them and some to spare. It will be settled by the 12th. The nominating primary elections are August 11. If one is nominated he still has the campaign for election in November. I am to contest against Foraker and Cole. Grandma Burton withdrew. You will be less surprised on this news than I was myself. I was literally seduced and urged into the step. I do not know that I can win, but I know I can try. I shall not be worse off if I lose, meanwhile I will be pretty thoroughly diverted from such disappointing and dispiriting thoughts as I have harbored for several months.*[13]

The disappointment he referred to was the deep freeze in their relationship. He continued to be wounded by what he thought were her wandering ways with other men. "It has always been so with handsome women," he wrote, "it has always been so since love was first invented. Men near by are infinitely preferable to a prosy lover from a thousand miles away who can only write the same old story over and over again."[14] The letters between them in 1914 had grown scanty. He told of his reason: "I said I did not know what to write. By that I mean that it seems useless to write the love and fondness which are in my heart, useless to write my hunger and thirst, because, looking backward for a whole year, I can not recall when you have favored me with a line of love."[15] For her part, she remained aggrieved that he refused to come to Europe to see her after she had made the sacrifice two years in a row. They had reached an impasse.

Even Jim Phillips seemed to realize that something had been going on between Carrie and Warren. "J—never tells me anything about you anymore, except as I half-drag it out of him."[16]

Carrie and Isabelle were coming home that summer. In April, he thought they were going to sail on the *Washington* ("a fine ship, I have always heard") on May 3 from Bremen, Germany. "Funny thing—this habit one gets into," he wrote. "I still keep tabs on the sailing and landings, though I no longer have any assurance of letters." He told her that she would be "cordially welcomed home, by J—, by your friends, and by none more sincerely than the writer. It will be good to see you." By June it was clear she had decided to stay part of the summer in Europe to visit England and Scotland.[17] He again wrote that he was happy she was coming home. "In truth I never wanted you to go, and never wholly got over that feeling. However, if it was best and happiest for you, I shall never complain, because I realize, *full well,* that I am the source of your unhappiness and discontent."[18]

Warren wrote to Scobey later in the month that he was receiving plenty of advice about how to run his campaign, but he thought it unseemly to attack fellow Republicans in a direct election contest. In response to Scobey's urging that he make numerous campaign speeches, he wrote: "I shall make such speeches as there is genuine occasion for making, but should like to know how in thunder you expect me to go out and make speeches telling the dear people to look me over and see what a wonderful candidate for senator I am, or how I can consistently go out and bat either Senator Foraker or Ralph Cole over the head and tell the dear people they will never do?"[19]

Others in the world saw political change in much more violent terms. Across the wide ocean in Sarajevo, the capital of Bosnia and Herzegovina, a group of young men made plans for the elimination of the heir to the throne of the Austro-Hungarian Empire, an archduke named Franz Ferdinand. They would execute those plans ten days after Harding wrote to Scobey. The result, a double murder, would tumble the world into a century of disaster greater than humankind may ever again witness. It was the eve of Armageddon.

CHAPTER 19

"Sophie! Sophie! Don't Die! Stay Alive for the Children!"

Gavrilo Princip could not believe his good fortune. The Graf & Stift open sports car had taken a wrong turn onto Franz Joseph Street near the Latin Bridge, right in front of Moritz Shiller's café, where Princip, a diminutive teenager, had stopped to have a sandwich. After some yelling from an officer in the car to the driver that he had gone the wrong way, the car stopped and was reversing when two shots rang out from a semiautomatic pistol Princip wielded with deadly accuracy. A woman in the open backseat holding a bouquet of flowers was hit by one of the bullets in the abdomen, and the other bullet tore into the neck of the mustachioed man in a pale blue tunic sitting next to her, severing his jugular. Both would be dead within the hour.[1]

Princip, the assassin, was not yet twenty. He and five or six other Serbian nationalists had been stationed along the motorcade route where the car carrying the heir to the throne of Austria-Hungary would pass from a military base he briefly inspected to the town hall. Some of the young men were armed with bombs and grenades, others with pistols. All were charged with the duty to kill Archduke Franz Ferdinand, who was in Sarajevo by invitation of the provincial governor to witness military maneuvers and inspect some governmental buildings. Franz Ferdinand and his wife, Sophie, the Duchess of Hohenberg, arrived by train in Sarajevo around ten o'clock on Sunday morning, June 28, 1914. As they made their way to an appointment at the town hall, the first two would-be assassins lost their nerve. The third,

Nedeljko Cabrinovic, hurled his bomb at the car carrying the royal occupants. Either the archduke deflected it or it bounced off the car's folded-back convertible cover and rolled under the vehicle immediately behind the archduke's automobile and exploded, seriously injuring passengers and some spectators. The car carrying the archduke and his spouse, after briefly stopping, sped away to the town hall. The car's speed thwarted further attempts by the remaining assassins, including young Gavrilo Princip.

Once at the town hall, Mayor Fehim Curcic began his prepared speech of welcome: "Our hearts are full of happiness over the most gracious visit with which Your Highness," he began. The archduke, clearly agitated, interrupted. "Herr Burgermeiseter, it is perfectly outrageous!" the heir to the throne blurted out. "We have come here on a visit and we have had a bomb thrown at us." After some awkward silence, Sophie whispered into the archduke's ear, and he said to the mayor, "Now, you may go on."[2] The crowd cheered. After the mayor concluded his remarks, the archduke read a prepared speech and added an extemporaneous final line:

> It gives me special pleasure to accept the assurances of your unshakable loyalty and affection for His Majesty, our Most Gracious Emperor and King. I thank you cordially for the resounding ovations with which the population received me and my wife, the more so since in them is an expression of pleasure over the failure of the assassination attempt.

The formalities over, the archduke and his wife toured the town hall, which took about a half an hour, and then the archduke insisted that he go to the hospital to visit the people injured in the bomb attack. A dispute about security ensued. It was decided that the army could not be called out to line the streets because the troops did not have their parade dress with them on maneuvers. The Sarajevo police force would have to do. General Potiorek, chief of the regional government, and Count Franz von Harrach, who would ride on the car's running board as added security, suggested that the caravan take a direct route, avoiding the city center. The driver, not informed of the plan, took a wrong turn on the street where Princip by happenstance had stopped to have a sandwich, believing his mission to assassinate the archduke had failed.[3]

After the shooting, the scene was pure chaos. "As the car quickly reversed," Count von Harrach would recall, "a thin stream of blood spurted from His Highness's mouth onto my right cheek. As I was pulling out my handkerchief to wipe the blood away from his mouth, the Duchess cried out to him, 'In Heaven's name, what has happened to you?' At that she slid off the seat and lay on the floor of the car, with her face between his knees."

Harrach had no idea that the duchess had been shot. He heard His Imperial Highness say to his wife: "Sophie! Sophie! Don't die! Stay alive for the children!"

When Harrach grabbed the archduke by his collar to hold his head up and asked him if he felt any pain, the archduke said softly, "It is nothing." He repeated the line several times and then lost consciousness. Then he made a hideous, violent choking sound and died before they reached the governor's residence.

Gavrilo Princip was amazed. He had gotten his chance after all.

CHAPTER 20

"I Am Busier than an Old Hen with a Brood Full of Chicks"

"**W**elcome home!" Harding wrote Carrie from his room in the Hotel Statler in Cleveland on Sunday morning, July 19, 1914. He had received a letter from London sometime earlier telling of her travel plans back from Europe, but he failed to get off his own letter in time to greet her as she disembarked in New York. He finally found a moment to write a note that he hoped would find her when she returned to Marion. "Sounds strange, doesn't it, to come from me?" he wrote about his inability to find time to write her. "But, truly, I am busier than an old hen with a brood full of chicks."

At his office in Marion, he was employing two to five typists just to keep up with his crushing campaign correspondence. "I am in politics, up to my ears, with all its cares, worries, anxieties and heartaches, with all its excitements and compensations," he wrote.[1] His window of opportunity to write her this Sunday morning closed at 11:30 as he needed to board a train to travel to the western part of Ohio to deliver "a Chautauqua spiel." He would be back to Marion for a speech on Thursday, then on the road again for a Friday night speech in Warren, Ohio, a talk in Youngstown on Saturday, and then to Lakewood and Doylestown on Sunday. He was so busy he did not know if he could see her before the next week.

"Don't know how this political game is coming out," he wrote in his welcome letter. "Looks good some days, others not so good. It is diverting, surely, and has taken me out of the rut into which I had gotten, so even if I lose I shall be little out except expended coin and energy—both being considerable but not enough to break me."[2]

His note was warm but lacked the fervor and eagerness of his earlier letters. "You won't like me much any more," he wrote. "I am getting old and fat. Look at the snap shot in today's [Cleveland] *Leader*. I enclose it for your amusement and disgust. The sad thing about it is I look like this picture." He did not venture a guess on how she would be treated by the citizens of Marion when she returned; nor was he sure what she would think about being home except that she would probably find it dull. He made no reference to the feverish activity in Europe that was leading to ultimatums and troop mobilizations. "I hope you find it pleasant," he wrote of Marion, "that all you wished will come true, and that the world looks rosy."

Most Americans in fact were oblivious to the details of the events that were leading to war in Europe.[3] President Wilson himself was more concerned with insurrection and fighting in Mexico and the health of his wife, Ellen, who was unwell and not recovering. She would die just as war was declared, leaving him distracted and grief-stricken. Wilson had sent his close advisor, Colonel Edwin House, to Berlin and London in May to try to broker an entente among Germany, England, and the United States. House, alarmed at what he found, reported of the state of crisis hanging in the air, a month *before* Franz Ferdinand's assassination:

> The situation is extraordinary. It is jingoism run stark mad. Unless some one acting for you can bring about a different understanding, there is some day to be an awful cataclysm. No one in Europe can do it. There is too much hatred, too many jealousies. Whenever England consents, France and Russia will close in on Germany and Austria. England does not want Germany wholly crushed, for she would then have to reckon alone with her ancient enemy, Russia; but if Germany insists upon an ever-increasing navy, then England will have no choice.[4]

Carrie was returning to Marion just in time for its summer Chautauqua week and Harding thought it would be a good time for her "to see your friends and start the renewal of acquaintances." He hoped his schedule would allow him to be in Marion the day Minnesota congressman J. Adam Bede, a popular stump speaker and humorist, would engage in a "Famous Debate" with Emil Seidel, the Socialist ex-mayor of Milwaukee. The topic for consideration: "Socialism in America."[5] Entertaining as the debate was likely to be, Harding knew it was doubtful he would have the time to witness it in person. "I have this game of my own," he wrote Carrie, "and must play it, win or lose until August 11. Then, if I should win, I must go on playing until November. If I lose in August I shall be so dead politically that the obsequies will have to be hurried." With less than a month to go, he worried that he had been double-crossed by some who had encouraged him to get into the race in the first place. "When I went in I felt pretty sure of winning the August contest, but there are liars in politics as well as in other lines. If I am politically dead, *I'll know it*—which is one advantage gained."[6]

In Carrie's communications from London advising of her return plans, she underlined certain words, signaling their coded meaning. This pleased him, especially the use of the word "matrix," which meant "I am utterly and gladly all yours—today and always." Yet there was still caution in his writing. "*I am glad* you are returning," he wrote. "I shall see you at the *first* opportunity, and hope it will not be far away. I love you *truly,* I admire and adore, but [I have] changed, I do confess. I *awoke* to the realization it was insane to expect you to be mine in the exclusion that I wildly dreamed, and that fine jealousy that you so hated is dead. It took away something—only its horrid self perhaps—well, you ought to like me better."[7]

Four days after Harding penned his note from the Hotel Statler, on the morning of July 23, the ambassador from Austria-Hungary delivered an ultimatum to the Serbian government in Belgrade, giving Serbia forty-eight hours to reply. The so-called July Ultimatum contained a list of grievances and demands: Serbia must stop its agitation, suppress publications that incited hatred of the Austro-Hungarian monarchy, dissolve certain revolutionary societies, and allow Austria-Hungary to take part in any judicial inquiry into the assassination. Serbia accepted most of the demands with the exception of the participation of Austria-Hungary in any internal judicial proceeding. When the Austro-Hungarian ambassador was handed the reply on July 25, he read it, saw it was not unconditional agreement, packed his bags, and left the country. Diplomatic relations were severed. Austria-Hungary declared war on Serbia on Tuesday, July 28. The next day, Austrian troops crossed the border and began shelling Belgrade.

Russia, Serbia's northern Slavic protector, mobilized on July 30. Germany came to the defense of Austria-Hungary, causing France to mobilize. During the week of Marion's Chautauqua and the "Great Debate" between Adam Bede and Emil Seidel, as Carrie Phillips renewed her acquaintances and Warren Harding campaigned for the Senate, the world organized for war.

CHAPTER 21

"You Are an Enemy Alien"

Attorney Abernathy was trying hard to get his client back on track. It was getting late on Saturday, December 22, 1917, and he now had to ask for the third time whether the baroness' husband, the German army officer, made it back to London just as the war was declared. The baroness responded that he did come back from Singapore on a ship that traveled through the Suez Canal and that he stopped in France, where he hired a car to take him north so he could be ferried across the English Channel. Once in England, he was placed in a concentration camp for alien enemies.[1]

After saying all this, the baroness began to wander again. "I can't remember," she puzzled, "when war was actually declared between England and Germany."

The federal magistrate interjected: "August 4, 1914."

She thanked the magistrate and continued her narrative. "I gave up my house at Kensington Gate," she testified, "I was in a terrible state of mind because I did not want to leave my children and go back to the estate [in Singapore]. My husband wanted me to leave the baby in London and go back to the estate. My husband wrote me a letter and he knew of the war as I could tell by the contents of his letter, or in fact I don't believe he knew right at that time because he stated to me that he was going to land at Marseilles on August 1st, and would come by land, instead of coming around by Southampton."

Then she stopped, as if recognizing that she was stumbling to answer the question. "Now Mr. Abernathy," she said, "I just want to ask you one question." This had to be torture for Abernathy. He could do nothing but let her continue. "I have absolutely nothing to hide," she declared, "and I would rather tell these gentlemen absolutely everything, do you want me to go on?"

What was Abernathy to say to such a question? "Yes," he replied.

That seemed to comfort her. She admitted that in fact she had cabled her husband on board his ship when war was declared to warn him against his plan to disembark in France. She feared as a German officer he would be arrested. She especially worried that the title papers to the rubber estate, which he had in his possession, would be seized if he were detained. She moved into a hotel in London, fretted, and for the next eleven days visited the offices of the Peninsular & Oriental Steam Navigation Company to inquire about the ship.

"In the meantime," she continued, "I learned the fact that as the wife of a German subject I was an alien and I had to report to police headquarters." She had been unaware of the requirement to register until she was so advised by Major-General Sir Alfred Turner. "Major-General Alfred Turner phoned me and said my child you realize that under the present law you are an alien enemy and he said you had better go to police headquarters and he said I will come around and give you a letter to the Police Captain," she testified. "And he did and I went around to police headquarters as did everyone also who was a German subject. They simply took my name and everything about me, which I have gave them and then they gave me a little slip." The slip allowed her to travel about in a five-mile area around her hotel.

Sir Alfred was no insignificant figure in London. He had had a long and successful career as an officer in the British Army, serving during the Gordon Expedition and the Mahdii campaigns in Egypt and Sudan in the 1880s, and he was police commissioner under Lord Spencer in Ireland in Kerry and Clare during what the British considered to be some of the darkest days of the so-called Parnellite agitation (named for the Irish Protestant leader Charles Stewart Parnell).[2] Sir Alfred was active in society and had been the subject of a caricature in *Vanity Fair* in 1910. He was a Knight Commander (KCB) and a member of the Order of the Bath, a British order of chivalry founded by King George I in 1725. The baroness described him at the hearing as "a friend of mine." Though not in the testimony, Sir Alfred likely knew the baroness through the Beresford nobility in her mother's line.

The baroness looked to Sir Alfred to see about her husband's release from the English internment camp. Arrangements were made, and he was given his release on the condition that he and the baroness would return to the United States and that he would not to take up arms against Great Britain in the war.

The baroness's third husband, now Captain Zollner, would turn out not to be a man of his word.

CHAPTER 22

"This Was Surely a Great Victory"

In the years leading up to the war, England worried about the kaiser and his country's increasing naval power. Germany fretted that Great Britain could blockade its ports in the event of a war. Russia made everyone nervous, but especially Germany and Austria-Hungary, which stood to lose the most if the Russian empire became aggressive about territory. France still bristled over the loss of Alsace and Lorraine during the Franco-Prussian war of 1870-71, when the German empire was born. Ever since Napoleon had menaced the entire continent, all the great powers sought partners to offset perceived threats from enemies and to balance power among the nations. The aim was to make war seem so costly that none would dare make the first preemptive strike. Great Britain, France, and Russia joined in the Triple Entente to prevent German expansion in Europe; Germany, Austria-Hungary, and Italy formed the Triple Alliance.

When Austria-Hungary invaded Serbia and Russia mobilized, all of the alliances clicked in, and general war was declared with dizzying speed. Germany demanded that Russia halt its mobilization. The threat of invasion by Slav hordes heightened war fever in Germany. Great Britain's desperate attempts to force mediation of the Austro-Hungarian conflict with Serbia failed. The German Schlieffen Plan called for a swift strike against France, taking out Russia's ally early so Germany could concentrate on defeating Russia before it could fully mobilize. To accomplish its lightning blow, Germany had to avoid a direct assault on France's fortifications along Germany's western border, and this would necessitate a broad sweep through neutral Belgium, Luxembourg, and the Netherlands on the way to Paris. When Russia refused to comply with the German ultimatum to demobilize, Germany declared war on Saturday, August 1. Similarly, when France refused a German ultimatum that it pledge neutrality in the coming German-Russian war, Germany declared war on France on August 3 and moved into Belgium on August 4. In response to Germany's breach of Belgium's neutrality, England joined the war. As Sir Edward Grey, Britain's Foreign Secretary, notably said: "The lamps are going out all over Europe. We shall not see them lit again in our lifetime."[1]

Two days later, on Thursday, August 6, Ellen Wilson died in the White House at 5 PM with her husband holding her hand. "Oh my God," Wilson sobbed to the White House physician, Dr. Cary Grayson, "what am I to do?"[2] A funeral service was performed in the East Room on Monday, August 10, then the body was taken by train to Rome, Georgia, for burial in Ellen Wilson's hometown on August 11. Torrential rain greeted the president and his family at Myrtle Hill Cemetery, and the normally steely Wilson gave way, crying uncontrollably at the gravesite.

On the same day, Warren Harding won the primary contest for the Republican nomination for senator. The election was closer than Harding had anticipated when he joined the contest. In a day of very light voter turnout, Harding garnered 88,540 votes to Foraker's 76,817. Cole ran stronger than expected, racking up 53,237 votes.[3] Harding's hard work and tireless barnstorming around the state had all been necessary. Republican Party leaders were relieved that Foraker's comeback was defeated. But Harding took no pleasure in defeating his mentor and wrote a conciliatory note to the old man. "While I am experiencing that elation that attends a victory in the contest for the nomination," he wrote to Foraker nine days after the primary, "I cannot resist writing you the one regret that is in my heart, that is—I had to acquire it in a contest against you. My admiration for you, ever growing for nearly 30 years, is no less today than when I enrolled for a contest in 1908 [Foraker's reelection effort], which I knew at the hour of enlistment would end in failure."[4] He asked Foraker to stay active in Republican politics, as a source of inspiration, and sought his help in securing the Senate seat for their party. "I do not believe I am consumed with ambition," Harding wrote, "indeed my most earnest hope is for Party rather than a personal victory in which we can equally rejoice. You can wonderfully help."

Harding's narrow victory left him taking nothing for granted. "I feel confident I will be elected," he wrote to Ed Scobey on August 22. "However, I mean to do as much speaking as it is possible for one man to do. I shall not commence until the latter part of September, because I think too early a start would cause the work to become stale."[5] Good fortune, though, shined on Warren Harding in the general election. His Democratic opponent was reformer Timothy Hogan, twice elected attorney general of Ohio (1910 and 1914). Hogan had an Achilles' heal—he was a practicing Roman Catholic, and Ohio was not ready to elect an Irish Catholic to the Senate.

Nevertheless, Harding's old campaign manager, Malcolm Jennings, worried that there was trouble on the horizon. He found a mixed message in the primary election results. Prohibition, not war, had been the dominant issue. "You were nominated by the sober second thought of the Republican electors," Jennings wrote, apparently not recognizing his pun. "Cole has the support of the Anti-Saloon League, and Foraker that of the liquor interests, which proves that neither side has your interests cordially at heart and the result may be a whip-saw as it was in 1910."[6] Harding wrote to Scobey that he agreed that prohibition, an issue that always provoked the spending of huge amounts of money, was potentially the most dangerous problem for him. "I think we are going to have a very vigorous campaign in Ohio and can not see a single cloud in the sky except which results from the everlasting wet and dry issue," he wrote Scobey. Harding, being Harding, would straddle the issue. He adopted a compromise position: Voters should decide the question in each state on a nonpartisan basis.

Jennings saw other threats. Foraker's supporters included "the colored voters," Jennings wrote, and they were bitter over his defeat. Foraker, a Civil War veteran, had a fairly remarkable record on race relations. He had severely criticized Theodore Roosevelt on his handling of the Brownsville affair (where black soldiers were accused of "shooting up" a Texas town in a race-charged rampage in August 1906). The president had ordered the blanket discharge of the entire African American regiment without formal charges being brought against any of them.[7] Foraker believed the men were innocent and began a long effort to vindicate them. One scholar has ventured that this rift was important in solidifying Roosevelt's support of Taft as his successor in 1908, a year that Foraker himself had presidential ambitions. "So angry with Foraker did Roosevelt become that he increased his support for Taft's presidential candidacy in 1908," presidential scholar Lewis Gould wrote. "The case became one of the key events in setting up the transfer of power from Roosevelt to Taft that had such significant consequences for the Republicans in 1912."[8]

The war in Europe did not even make Jennings's list of issues to address in the campaign. In fact, Harding saw the European conflict as an occasion for Americans to cut their dependence on European goods and products. In an editorial titled "Our Golden Opportunity," Harding's newspaper pointed out that the privations of war would advance American self-sufficiency. "We might have gone along for years," his editors wrote, "content to look to the Old World for this mineral, that drug, that dye or that manufacture had the war not cut us off, in whole or part, from their importation."[9]

Little is recorded of Carrie's reception in Marion, and it seems the two lovers continued to keep their distance. No letters exist after July 19 until a Christmas poem Harding sent her at the end of the year.

Underscoring the remoteness between them, Warren told Scobey that he and Florence were going to take a two-week motor tour with the Sawyers in the Adirondack Mountains starting August 26, the very thing—vacationing with his wife—that had been so incendiary to Carrie in the spring.[10] Harding needed the break. When he made it back to Marion after the vacation, he wrote Scobey that he found Lake Placid particularly relaxing and delightful. "My only regret," he wrote on September 12, "was that I could not spend two or three weeks there and have the joy of your company and that of Mrs. Scobey."[11]

In San Antonio, Scobey was pleased with the primary result. "From now on you will be busy," he wrote Warren, "but any time that you have an opportunity, drop me a line and give me a little encouragement." Scobey missed his old friend, all the more so with his wife Evaland vacationing "up north" to avoid the Texas heat. "While she was away I took dancing lessons," Scobey proudly reported to Warren. "Now I can walk them clear off the board and do some hesitating, and men of your age and my age can hesitate better than we used to."[12]

Scobey's only substantive advice for the campaign in this letter consisted of a recommendation that Harding change his old campaign photo. "By the way, why don't you get some cuts made of your last photograph," he chided him. "The one that you have been using for the last fifteen years would look a great deal better if you would have a serial number under them as you look more like a convict than a statesman. Better spend $3.50 and show the people what a good looking man you are."[13]

Harding responded to Scobey's "breezy and curious letter" with one of his own. "I shall make no comment on the doddling tendencies of your old age. If you expect to dance all the latest capers and continue your foxy attitude toward all the young women, I shall expect my acquaintance to be maintained with you from long distance. The Lord only knows how you backslid during Mrs. Scobey's vacation in the North."[14]

By this point at the end of September, Harding was feeling better about his prospects for election, writing Scobey that "the situation, politically, seems to me to be of a very encouraging nature." He understood that opposition to Hogan came from anti-Catholic chauvinism, but he did not exploit the issue.[15] He stayed on his game, never really getting away from the nagging doubt that still followed him from his loss in 1910. "One never has an election until after the votes are counted," he reminded Scobey as he started the big push of the campaign. "It is always difficult to know what may come up during the progress of a campaign or what trick may change several thousand votes." By the end of October, Harding through his deft political moves and winning oratorical gifts was generating his own electoral steam roller. His popularity was immense. Even the cautious Jennings began to believe that Harding would be elected by a big majority.[16]

The result was a stunning victory: Harding won by over 100,000 votes, the type of lopsided victory that propelled him overnight into serious talk as a presidential aspirant in 1916, especially given his powerful Ohio pedigree. The turnaround from 1910 was remarkable and had to have been exceedingly rewarding for Warren. "This was surely a great victory," Scobey wrote immediately after the election, "and no doubt so by you having such a large plurality after having met a Waterloo four years ago. This brings us back to Lincoln that you can't fool the people all the time."[17] Harding responded that the magnitude of his triumph did indeed wipe out "all the unpleasantness that dated from 1910."[18]

Scobey encouraged Harding to come to Texas, this time to celebrate his victory. Harding had over a year before he would actually sit as a senator. By the peculiarity of the congressional schedule set by the Constitution, those elected to Congress in November 1914 would not be sworn in until December 1915, when the new session of Congress would start. "I wired you to come to Texas to spend the winter," Scobey wrote. "I want to talk with you about further aspiration. The Republican party is very shy on big men. The probable candidates, at this writing, it seems are Whitmar, Herrick, Burton, Borah and Hadley. Do you think any of these men have it over you on ability or oratory, or any qualifications that go to make up a good President? Think it over. Come down and we will try and lay some plan."[19]

Harding had been flattered by the flood of mail that touched on the presidential possibility after the election, but he knew enough to treat such matters with caution. "I have read carefully all that you said about the presidency," he responded to Scobey, "and am perfectly free to say that my vanity has been more or less appealed to by numerous messages of this character from all parts of Ohio and nearly all parts of the United States."[20] Republicans, he said, seemed to remember favorably his nominating speech for Taft at the 1912 convention, and his cool in the face of the mob that tried to shout him down. "I suppose I have as much capacity as some of the men who have been able to have themselves mentioned for that position," he conceded, "but I really think that one can spoil everything by being too ambitious and I am pretty well persuaded that I can be wholly content in making good in the office to which I have been elected. There is too much anxiety and stress and strain and expense connected with a nation-wide campaign and the thought is so appalling to me of asking my friends to follow that lead in such a contest."

Harding told Scobey he was "absolutely obliged" to get away for a long vacation.[21] In addition to exhaustion from the campaign, he was besieged by Republican office-seekers. He also wanted to escape from the mounting requests from across the nation for speeches. A dream of visiting Hawaii had been in his mind for some time, so he decided to make plans and invited Scobey to join him. "I wrote Mrs. Scobey yesterday making a proposition that she and you join us in making a trip to Hawaii this winter. Duchess and I are very anxious to go and we are a bit reluctant to go alone. When we do go, we shall come by way of San Antonio and whether you go or not, we shall probably make a visit, at which time, you and I can thrash out all these political matters."[22]

Scobey declined but continued to press Harding to come to Texas. "The trouble in your going over there will be that you have to spend too much time going and coming—come here and get a rest," Scobey responded.[23] He promised the beautiful women of San Antonio would be on display to grace his visit. "Since you [were last here] I have run across several chickens that would even make a United States Senator take notice." Scobey also had a personal agenda for insisting that Harding spend time in Texas. The Timkens were scheduled to come to Texas on their way to a vacation home in California where they were going to spend the winter. Scobey wanted to try to mend fences between Harding and Timken.

The Progressive party that Timken supported in 1912 was in transition and decline. In his restlessness Theodore Roosevelt planned and went on an excursion to South America at the end of 1913 and did not return until May 1914. It was supposed to have been a speaking tour, but once in Rio Roosevelt was cajoled by the Brazilian government into charting the River of Doubt from its headwaters to its mouth.[24] The expedition proved to be a calamity for Roosevelt's health. He almost died from malaria, a high fever, open abscesses, and other injuries. When he finally emerged from the jungle in the spring of 1914, his health was broken—though he was not yet sixty. He stumped briefly in the 1914 campaign, but he was not the same. For the rest of his life, Roosevelt's health would wax and wane. Roosevelt told his supporters in 1914 that the country had grown tired of reform and reformers.

On Scobey's reference to Texas chickens, Harding feigned indignity. "[I] do not think it is becoming for a Texas steer to be writing a dignified senator-elect about the attractiveness of Texas chickens," he reprimanded his friend. "You really offend me. If you don't cut out this affinity business and your interest in chickens, you will come to a speedy and disgraceful end. I regret that you have been deteriorating very rapidly since you got beyond the sphere of my helpful influence."[25] Despite Scobey's renewed offer that he come to Texas, Harding wrote that he was going to Hawaii. Not even the war and the fear of a potential submarine attack could hold him back. "If we should be blown up in the Pacific, I am sure it would save all funeral expenses and leave our friends free to go into mourning without any personal inconvenience."

That Christmas Harding wrote a melancholy poem to Carrie, lamenting their separateness. When he told Carrie of his plans to go to Hawaii, she turned fiery—"imperious" was the word he used. She demanded that he *not* go. He bristled at the command. Then, as he prepared to leave Ohio for Texas in the second week of January, she handed him a note. He took it but did not look at it until on the train headed to Texas. By the time he read it, it was too late.

CHAPTER 23

"I Expected My Husband to Stay in America"

Captain Zollner, like the Baron Kurt Loeffelholz von Colberg before him, was brutal with Iona.

"A short time after you were back over here did he treat you cruelly?" Abernathy asked her in a leading question that should have provoked an objection.[1] But she was deep into her testimony, and the magistrate would likely have let it go.

"Yes sir," she responded with atypical brevity.

Abernathy's phrase "back over here" referred to the fact that the baroness and Zollner had come back to the United States in the fall of 1914. Major-General Sir Alfred Turner had pulled strings with the British War Department, resulting in Zollner's release from the English internment camp, and he and the baroness sailed for New York. "I expected my husband to stay in America and try to do something with the rubber estate, at least try to do something for me," she told the court.

Either Zollner never intended to keep his word or the lure of the battle in Europe was too great. He may have worried he would miss all the excitement of a quick German victory. Early on it looked as if the Germans were going to deliver the knock-out punch in France within weeks, just as it had been drawn up in the Schlieffen Plan. By mid-August 1914, they had pummeled and destroyed the twelve forts surrounding Liege in Belgium with two Krupp-manufactured 43-ton howitzers, known as Big Berthas (named for Gustav Krupp's wife), each of which could fire a 2,200-pound shell over nine miles. The Germans, though, made two big miscalculations: They underestimated the fight that the Belgians would put up when their sovereign territory was invaded, and they misjudged the outrage of the world, especially among the people of Great Britain, over Germany's violation of Belgium's neutrality. Aggressive wars, even when dressed in defensive necessity, are never tidy things. Once in France, the Germans would be met not just by French defenders but four British divisions of the British Expeditionary Force.

More, the invasion of Belgium was a public relations disaster for Germany in the United States, especially as reports began to trickle in of atrocities committed by invading German troops against the civilian population. For many Americans, the Germans became the aggressor and the cause of the war. Public opinion in many quarters turned against them, despite Wilson's call for Americans to remain neutral in thought and deed. Theodore Roosevelt, for example, heard from his daughter Ethel, who had gone to Europe with the Red Cross, of stories "about German soldiers cutting off the right hands of Belgium boys to prevent them from shooting back."[2] T.R. became pro-Ally.

The United States, however, was deeply divided over the war. The country had a substantial German American population: 20 million of German birth or descent out of a total U.S. population of 100 million.[3] Many of these citizens and immigrants held strong feelings of loyalty for their homeland. They believed the war had been caused by the Kingdom of Serbia and its Slavic ally, Russia. Broadly cast, they saw the war as a colossal struggle of the civilized world, represented by Germany, against the Slavic hordes. "Have faith in us!" ninety-three world-renowned and noted German leaders in science, art, music, and scholarship wrote in a broadside circulated in the United States early in the war. "Believe that we shall carry on this war to the end as a civilized nation, to whom the legacy of a Goethe, a Beethoven, and a Kant, is just as sacred as its own hearths and homes."[4]

This theme resonated with Carrie Phillips. She admired the German *Kultur* that she and Isabelle had immersed themselves in during the three years they were in Berlin. Her private notes, kept with the Harding letters, are filled with references to Germany's fight to "uphold humanity and civilization."[5] "All strong nations, like strong characters, call forth envy," she wrote in these notes. Her musings, often convoluted, nevertheless provide a striking picture of a woman fully indoctrinated into the German ethos of world power, or *Weltmacht*. "A Government with the power as has been demonstrated to the world in the past four years," she scribbled, "must needs take a whole world to fight it down or be drawn under its influence, if not its domination eventually."[6]

For many German Americans and pro-Germans like Carrie Phillips, Germany was merely defending itself and protecting Austria-Hungary in its right to root out and destroy terrorists and the terrorist-supporting Serbian regime. As events unfolded, German Americans would blame England for interfering with Germany's right to self-defense and for its "starvation" naval blockade. Pro-German journalists and international law scholars considered the blockade a blatant violation of international maritime law and *the* provocation for German submarine warfare.

In Ohio, Warren Harding recognized this divide in the populace. Central and western Ohio had major German populations, and Cincinnati was known to be a German town. Newspapers across Ohio were still published in German. A large percentage of these German Americans were conservative Republicans. Harding had to tread carefully when it came to pronouncements on the war and its causes.

In the United States, a propaganda war opened up directly on the heels of the shooting war in Europe, aimed at winning the allegiances of Americans. The Germans were the first to jump into the fray. Arthur Link, Wilson's leading biographer, described the German propaganda operation in its early days:

> Fully aware of the necessity of winning American friends, the Berlin Foreign Office established a propaganda agency in New York in August 1914. Known as the German Information Service, it was headed by former Colonial Minister, Doctor Bernhard Dernburg, who came to America at the outbreak of the war as the representative of the German Red Cross. Associated with Dernburg were Doctor Heinrich Albert, head of the German Purchasing Commission; Privy Councillor Anton Meyer Gerhard, formerly of the Colonial Office; Doctor Alexander Fuehr, who had recently come from the Imperial Embassy in Tokyo; and George Sylvester Viereck, a young German-American journalist who had already begun editing a weekly *The Fatherland.* These were the principal operators of the German propaganda machine, but there were others associated with it in various helpful capacities—such as the Ambassador in Washington, Count Johann von Bernstorff, Professor Hugo Munsterberg of Harvard University, and William Bayard Hale, one of the leading journalist of the day.[7]

George Sylvester Viereck, one of the most intriguing of these characters, was a hero to Carrie Phillips. She admired his writing and was a regular reader of his newspaper. As the war progressed, she often mailed the latest editions of *The Fatherland* to Harding, underscoring special passages for his attention. "Herewith I am returning the papers from Viereck's which you marked and mailed," Warren wrote to Carrie on Senate Chamber stationery in late March 1917. Another constituent apparently also sent the paper to Harding, but anonymously. "I am returning the papers which I already had," he wrote Carrie, "marked by some unknown sender, and am keeping your markings to discuss some future day in a calm retrospect."[8]

Viereck allegedly was the grandson of Kaiser Wilhelm I. His father, Louis, was the son of Edwina Viereck, a leading Berlin actress, who reportedly had an affair with the kaiser during which she became pregnant with Louis. Paternity was claimed by a relative in the Hohenzollern family, a common method of handling such royal indiscretions.[9] Louis became a radical Socialist, a friend of Karl Marx and Frederick Engels, and may have been involved in a plot to assassinate his father. Frederick Engels's cousin married Louis in 1881, and Engels was one of those in attendance at the wedding. George was born from this marriage in Munich in 1884. The family emigrated to New York City in 1896, where George attended City College.

In August 1914 Viereck was laboring diligently in New York City on his weekly newspaper and founded the Fatherland Foundation—an organization dedicated to making "German-Americans proud of the hyphen."[10] To many during the war, the term "hyphenated American" became code for citizens who were disloyal, untrustworthy, and even treacherous. As early as 1915, Viereck began to campaign for German Americans to become active and involved in American politics in general, and the 1916 presidential contest specifically. "We must assert ourselves in politics," he wrote in *The Fatherland.* "We must bring back to America a sense of that Americanism for the sake of which we or our fathers have deserted the old world." He argued that German Americans should oppose a pro-English president and a Congress that "takes orders from London." At the same time, he said he did not want a pro-German Congress. He focused much of his attack on Theodore Roosevelt, whom he said had betrayed the Progressive Party and was "playing into the hands of the Anglo-Saxon war mongers."[11]

But behind Viereck's legitimate political agitation lay more sinister plans, and money—lots of German money. Viereck and others in the upper echelon of the German propaganda machine (which included the highest diplomats in the German legation) recommended such things as the secret purchase of well-known American newspapers, like the New York *Sun* and the *Washington Post,* to be used as propaganda arms.[12] The Germans secretly paid journalists, such as Dr. William Baynard Hale of the Hearst papers, to write and publish pro-German stories. This same propaganda group sought to incite American labor to general strikes in munitions manufacturing plants and other critical industries. Bombings and sabotage of weapons-producing plants, particularly in New England, became commonplace as the war dragged on. German reservists stranded in the United States when the war broke out were issued false passports from an operation set up in a building on Bridge Street in New York, allowing them to return to the German armed forces via a neutral country or to pass through the British blockade. (The English regularly stopped ships and demanded identification of passengers.)[13]

The plotters even discussed the provocation of international disputes and incidents between the United States and Mexico and the United States and Japan to divert attention from Germany. The Germans courted the American Irish, who hated England, and American Jews, who despised Russia.

The vast spy, sabotage, and propaganda network was interconnected and well funded. After the United States entered the war, Viereck admitted that he had received large sums from the Imperial German Government.[14] In a libel proceeding in 1922 involving the mayor of Chicago and the Chicago *Tribune,* Viereck's former secretary testified that he received $140,000 from the German Information Service in just the first two years of the war. She explained that some of the money was used to produce pro-German pamphlets and books, but some was used as "silence" money for agents in the field.[15]

After obtaining a false passport, Captain Zollner snuck out of the country. If the baroness was to be believed, he threatened her life to keep her quiet. "He said if I don't kill you, I will have somebody who will, and I was eating my breakfast at the time, but I hate to say these things, he threw a dish in my face of fried eggs."

On cross-examination, she admitted that she continued to stay in contact with Zollner through cables and letters, sent through safe intermediaries in Europe, once he returned to Germany.

"This is the brute that put you in this trouble and left you in New York that you were sending cablegrams to?" the U. S. attorney inquired with heavy sarcasm.

"Yes, sir," she meekly replied.[16]

CHAPTER 24

"Why Didn't You Say What You Wrote?"

Warren and Florence Harding boarded a train in Marion on Tuesday, January 12, 1915, to make the long trip to Texas for a short visit with the Scobeys. Their itinerary called for them to travel from Texas to Southern California and San Diego to meet with the Timkens before turning north to San Francisco to stay a few days and then board a steamer for Hawaii, a U.S. territory. Old Doc Sawyer and his wife, Mandy, accompanied the Hardings, as much to provide medical attention for Florence as for companionship. As a newly elected senator, Harding could make the visit a semiofficial junket, meeting with territorial government officials and inspecting construction of the new naval base at Pearl Harbor.

Despite the prospect for a rejuvenating vacation, Harding was disheartened as he departed from Marion. "Left home woefully depressed and distressed in spirit," he wrote Carrie, "and can't quite recover."[1] He finally read the letter she gave him after their argument over the Hawaii trip and he was saddened when he realized the cause of her anger. "Our parting interview broke me all up—I had no idea you felt as you did. I did not read your letter until I was on my way—then I understood but it was too late," he wrote her. "I kept saying to myself—'Why didn't she tell me,' 'Why didn't she let me understand.' Surely it pays to be frank and honest and wholly sincere."[2]

The storm between them had been intense. "I never dreamed you felt as you did. Had you only said so I should have chucked the trip and never thought of any humiliation. Was never wholly tied up to go until just few days prior to leaving, but you had only said, in a rather imperious way, that I should not go, and I felt that you would despise me if I yielded. I realized that we could never get on in the world if our actions were to be determined in that way, so I decided I would do what seemed to me to be best."

Warren had believed Carrie's objection arose from spiteful motives toward Florence. Thinking her simply bullying for the wrong reasons, his back stiffened. "Love seldom commands, but love can appeal so that love is eager to comply," he wrote of why he reacted the way he did.[3]

It was a classic lover's misunderstanding—a wound packaged and expressed as anger, followed by misapprehension and an equally heated counterreaction. But this spat brought to the surface feelings that had gone underground during a year of estrangement, and the quarrel had a transforming effect as far as he was concerned. "I really love you better than all the world, and worship and adore you," he reflected. "And when I found you really distressed my heart was broken. I know you differently than I ever did before. I had never seen you in tears, except those of anger. Now I love you more than ever. You are more humanly normal, less imperious, and I have found a new side of you to love." To him, their leave-taking had been an "awakening incident," which he hoped would spark a "greater love and sweeter happiness" when he returned.

What was her hurt? In her letter she reminded him that they had once shared a vision of visiting Hawaii *together*. "It never dawned upon me about our dreams of Hawaii—dreams of *our* trip there—until I read your letter. I shall go now in an indifferent and uninterested mood."[4] Despite his protestation that he was not blaming her, he was still troubled about her "thrilling" to other men, and he found a way to turn the tables and recast the discussion. "Yes, I did dream of the journey with you," he granted, "and I can recall a time when I would have flung aside all to go with you. But *that* would have been a fatal error unless we can find our way to love's mutuality, unless I can satisfy you as you satisfy me."

In the letter he wrote her from the Palace Hotel in San Francisco, in the very same hotel where he would die when president, he explained why he needed to get so far away. "Really, as I tried to tell you, I didn't choose this trip to enjoy the trip, but chose it because I needed to get away—far enough away to escape engagements, and wanted a sea voyage to quiet my irritable nerves. I was on edge, all in, and stale and weary. I *had* to get away, but I had rather stayed at home and gone to a hospital than to have caused you the grief you suffered over my going, and had I known how you really felt, *I would never had gone.* I will not do so again."[5]

She questioned whether it was his intention to cut off the relationship permanently. He responded by pointing to an assignation they had sometime in the late fall, probably after the election. "How can you say it—especially after our heavenly tryst?" he wrote. "Did you observe a waning interest or less admiration? Surely not. I am wilder than ever to possess you and hold you all mine. True I went into politics for diversion and distraction at a time when you seemed lost to me (and evidently you were, in part at least) but all the while I was thinking I could hold your esteem by being worth while, and never a day passed but I felt that political success could afford us opportunity that we had never known before."[6]

But before anything could be changed, he told her that her relations with Florence had to be normalized. His letter makes clear that since Carrie's return from Europe, Florence had been openly hostile to any association with the Phillipses. Packaged in a defense of his return to political office, he wrote:

> *I was sure I could have you all the more in darling trysts and believed, as I do now, that we could do many things in mutual enjoyment if we could only restore friendly family relations. I have been working to this latter end, and oft discouraged, sometimes by you, oftener at home. I have preferred the reestablishment through tact, rather than force, because greater compensation is promised. I'll write you a promise now, and you can remind me of it in my own writing if I seem to forget it—to wit: If you will only help, the Mrs. must be friendly to you and allow our families to associate, so that I may enjoy my pride in you—else I will make things so intolerable that she will not remain with me. I am quite determined.[7]*

Lying below the surface of all this confusion were Harding's continuing feelings of both anger and inadequacy in his relationship with Carrie. His letters at this time begin to refer to a man named Robinson, who seems to have been a rival for Carrie's affection. There is little information to identify Robinson, though he does not appear to have been the same man that Harding referred to as "Ginger" in his letters to Carrie in Berlin. Later correspondence suggests he was a man whom she met in Europe, but it is unclear whether he was an American visiting Germany or a German. Clearly he did not live in Marion, since she communicated with him mostly by letter. Beyond that, there is not enough information to say for sure who he was or where he lived.[8]

Regardless, Warren finally made a clean breast. "I may as well tell the truth," he admitted deep into his letter. "I suffered unspeakable torment when I found you so interested in Robinson. And not torment of him alone. But

I'll not prolong my confession—for you hate jealousy."[9] He claimed he had remained faithful to her ("I am so glad to love you in sweet and satisfying exclusiveness"), but he no longer believed she returned that fidelity (since he knew Carrie was not in love with Jim, he never wrote of feelings of jealousy over him).

He saw further proof of her unfaithfulness in inflammatory comments she made just before he left Marion. "But you dreadfully alarmed me," he wrote. "You did the other night. My heart aches yet with the grief I feel when you spoke of what you might do." His reference was not to a suicidal threat, but a warning that she might become promiscuous with another man. "Your threat concerning yourself does not seem compatible with the high character you have seemed to possess," he wrote. "I hope you were speaking heedlessly in momentary desperation. Please, please, I beg of you, please remember my hope of a good and noble woman is riveted in you."[10] Here, as at other times in his writings, it did not seem to occur to him that his Victorian view of "the noble woman" seemed entirely absurd given their adulterous relationship. His profound fear was that his trip to Hawaii had provoked her to contact the man named Robinson. "I do hope you did not write Robinson in your desperation. I pray you will not write him or encourage him to write you. Can't I make one man's love enough? God! This had been my abiding anxiety."

"Won't you please destroy?" he wrote in postscript to his letter. "You are not always careful with letters, and if you destroy, you won't need to be careful."

The day after he wrote his letter from the Palace Hotel, he boarded the ship for Hawaii. He wrote to Scobey that the weather in San Francisco was "disagreeable" on the day they would sail, "but that does not much matter." Harding loved the ocean, even when it was stormy. His party arrived safely in Hawaii on February 3. They stayed for ten days, returning on February 13. Scobey wrote a letter to greet Warren on his homecoming to San Francisco, cracking that he had been watching the papers and that he had not noticed any ships going down in the Pacific, "so I suppose you have not been submarined or mined yet."[11]

Harding responded with a letter describing their stay in Hawaii:

> We were made the guests of the territorial government during our stay there and were obliged to lengthen our stay beyond the original plan in order to accept the many hospitalities which they provided us. We couldn't pay for anything, not even our laundry, and they provided us a new Packard automobile

and a driver for every hour of our stay on the islands. More than that, they arranged a Hulu [sic] dance for us on the last night of our stay there, which is showing some considerable courtesy, in view of the fact the Hulu dance is no longer tolerated by the statutes. It had a semblance of lawfulness on this particular occasion, because the governor of the islands and the mayor of Honolulu were present and participated in the hurrah. The dance would not have been pleasing to you, because the Hulu girls yielded sufficiently to the conventions to wear grass skirts. I trust it will not discourage you when I say that they wiggle a darn sight better than you do the fox trot in your giddiest mood.[12]

The party returned to the United States in time to witness the glittery opening of the Panama-Pacific International Exposition in San Francisco. They were present for the dedication of the Ohio building where Ralph Cole, Harding's opponent in the Senate primary, orated impressively to Harding's ear. "I never heard him to better advantage," he wrote Scobey. The exposition was a world's fair, and it not only celebrated the completion of the Panama Canal, but also demonstrated to the world that San Francisco had rebuilt and renewed itself after the devastating earthquake of 1906. Warren wrote Scobey that the exposition was superb, "far beyond my powers of description."

When he checked into the Palace Hotel, Warren found a letter waiting from Carrie, a response to his long explanatory letter written before he sailed for Hawaii. He was not sure what to make of it but felt compelled to write her immediately, with an open letter to be delivered to her home, containing code words underscored to deliver a secret message. He posted it the day he returned from Hawaii, on Friday, February 19. It read in full:

Feby 19
Dear Sis:

Just landed, and raced through mail. Hardly know how to construe your note, and there is no use guessing. On the way over the Pacific returning I had penned some reflections and observations, but I will not assume they would interest or pleasingly divert you, though they were penned in the afterglow of one's unavoidable infatuation with Honolulu and the islands. I was tremendously sorry the Phillipses were not along and thought a thousand times of the delight you would have experienced. They are superb, incomparable, the most fascinating in all the universe. One is in constant admiration and unending enthusiasm over the charm of that country, and interested every moment by the Orientals. I hope you have quite recovered from your disagreeable illness. I was ill a bit myself but I was only mal-de-mer when our ship was tossing for two days in a 90-mile gale. When one travels he must expect that.

Please preserve for me my calendar and holiday greetings. I was conscious of having left them, but it was not because of a lack of appreciation. I was happy to be remembered, and know you will let me have them when I return, a couple weeks hence. Thank you for the note. With constant *regards*

Yours
W.G.H.[13]

From San Francisco, his party traveled to Los Angeles and visited with Warren's sister Charity Remsberg and her family, and then returned to Marion in March. It had been an amazing journey, and though he wrote Scobey that by the time they were in Los Angeles they were "worn out and had to hike for home in order to secure a rest," Florence showed no signs of being exhausted. "Mrs. Harding stood the trip all the way through very finely and is better for having made it," Warren wrote.

On March 12, the *New York Times* ran an editorial, entitled "Favorite Sons," and declared that the "Republican campaign of 1916 is now on."[14] Citing what it considered a "fairly impressive list," the newspaper saw Harding as one of the major candidates, even though he had not spent a moment in the Senate. "Ohio has no less than four [possible candidates]," the paper reported, "Gov. Willis, ex-Senator Burton, ex-Ambassador Herrick, and Senator-elect Harding." Ex-president Taft and New York Court of Appeals Justice Charles Evans Hughes also were seen as "two figures of really dominating size." The mention of Harding in this company was testament to his rapid rise to national prominence.

His friend Scobey of course noted the recognition. "I see by the New York papers and Cincinnati Enquirer that they are discussing your advisability and availability as the nominee of the Republican party, do not overlook this," Scobey wrote Harding at the end of March. "Of course, you cannot push yourself, but one can have friends that can help. Better get the Timkens to throw in a little money and go into the field, as I am confident that you can carry Ohio against any comers, providing you do not get too late a start."[15]

Scobey even began to needle Harding's newly appointed secretary, young George B. Christian, Jr., the son of the Hardings' next-door neighbors in Marion. "I wrote Mr. Harding some time ago and told him that I believe that he had as good a chance for the Presidency as anyone," Scobey importuned Christian.[16] "I don't get any encouragement from him about the future as he claims that I am never satisfied." Scobey thought the time was right and that Harding needed to be pushed. "I have sized up all these candidates, and without being prejudiced I am confidant that he measures

up in ability with any of them with the exception of Root and I don't believe he will be a candidate."

Events in the world continued to intervene, setting things in motion in
a chain of causality that would eventually lead to Harding's elevation to the
highest office in the land. At the time, none of it clearly pointed to what
would happen, but every turn of history was leading him to his fate. On May
1, the British liner *Lusitania* departed from Pier 54 in New York's harbor. Almost 2,000 passengers were onboard, including over a hundred Americans.
The German Embassy warned that vessels like the *Lusitania* would be "liable
to destruction," and George Viereck went further in his newspaper, actually
predicting the ship was likely to be sunk.

The war was about to finally come home to Americans.

CHAPTER 25

"Apparently Considerable Panic"

The Wilson administration faced a conundrum when the war broke out. The U.S. economy had been mildly depressed since Wilson took office (a fact that was exploited by Republicans, including Warren Harding, in the 1914 elections). When war came, normal trade was disrupted, but orders for munitions poured in, especially from the western Allies, and these requisitions eventually would help lift the nation back into prosperity.[1] The complicating factor was that as soon as it entered the war, Great Britain began intercepting traffic to and from the Central Powers, either directly through German ports or countries through which imports and exports flowed, such as the Scandinavian countries and Denmark. Germany responded with its submarines.

Under international law, such as it was, a blockade in order to be legal had to be "effective," that is, maintained by a force sufficient to prevent access to the enemy coastline. If a blockade was not complete, it was a "paper blockade" and therefore illegal.

Just six years before the war was declared, Great Britain had invited the leading European naval powers, Japan, and the United States to London, under the auspices of the Hague Convention, to hash out a code of the rules of blockade during war. The result was the so-called Declaration of London of 1909. The signatory powers to the declaration, in preamble, stated that the document represented an agreement of that which was already established law. Though the document fairly clearly identified what was allowed and not allowed in a blockade, it was more breached than followed as soon as the war started.

The United States intended to assert its right as a neutral to trade with all belligerent nations. In August, just days after the formal declarations of war, Wilson's secretary of state William Jennings Bryan sent telegrams to the combatants seeking an agreement that the laws of naval warfare as set forth in the Declaration of London would be followed. Germany and Austria-Hungary, aware of Britain's superiority on the high seas, agreed immediately. Britain waffled, reserving its right to capture neutral ships when it suspected that offending cargo was aboard.

In a time of war, belligerent ships have always had the right to stop and inspect neutral merchant ships for "contraband." If contraband was discovered, the ship was supposed to be taken to an allied or neutral port where a prize court could adjudicate the seizure of the contraband. If the situation required the sinking of the ship rather than taking it as a prize (where there was danger to safety involved in the capture), the intercepting ship had to ensure the safety of the crew and all persons on board before sinking the merchant vessel.

However, if a merchant ship was armed, it became a warship and was subject to immediate sinking, without warning.

The definition of "contraband" was a subject of much debate during the conference that produced the Declaration of London. Absolute contraband included materiel and supplies intended for armed forces—arms of all kinds, munitions, limber boxes, military wagons, clothing and equipment of distinctly military character, and raw material used in war production. Conditional contraband included foodstuffs, forage and grain for animals, clothing and fabrics for clothing, boots, and shoes suitable for use in war, gold, silver, and other articles that could support armed forces. Some articles were put on a free list and not subject to capture: rubber, copper, raw cotton, wool, and other raw materials used in the textile industries. Absolute contraband could be confiscated if destined for the enemy, regardless of the port of delivery, whereas conditional contraband was not subject to capture if the ship's destination was a neutral port.

Food would become a weapon of war. In Germany and Austria-Hungary, hundreds of thousands of civilians died of starvation over the course of the war as a result of the British measures and later the full Allied blockade in which the United States joined. While not as dramatic or famous as the sinking of passenger ships with civilians aboard, the "starvation" blockade was just as lethal to noncombatants and a cause of many more civilian deaths than submarine warfare.[2]

By November 1914, in response to the indiscriminate laying of mines by the Germans, the British declared the whole North Sea a "military area" and placed its own mines, all but shutting down trade through this vast area. As a consequence, neutral vessels that wanted to approach Scandinavia, Holland, or Germany had to sail south of Ireland and through the English Channel, which made it easier for British ships to stop and search them. The stranglehold tightened as everyone began to realize the war was going to last for more than a few months.[3] Germans believed that Britain was engaged in unrestrained trade warfare, and they were upset, as were many German Americans, that the Wilson administration had barely protested the British maritime policy. In January 1915, some Americans from a St. Louis firm, likely with German government backing, set out to test the British blockade, sending foodstuffs aboard the American steamer *Wilhelmina* for delivery to an American agent in Hamburg to feed civilians. The British impounded the cargo.[4]

As Harding was spending his first days in Hawaii in early February 1915, Germany announced it would undertake a campaign of unrestricted submarine warfare, *Handelskrieg mit U-Booten.* Henceforth, the waters around Great Britain, except for a small designated route, would be a war zone. All enemy ships would be subject to destruction, and no guarantee could be made of the safety of neutral ships that sailed the waters.[5]

The German embassy in the United States was instructed to use the American press to warn U.S. citizens and vessels to stay clear of the war zone.

Wilson reacted to the German declaration of unrestricted submarine warfare by announcing that the United States would demand "strict accountability" of Germany if American lives or property were jeopardized by a submarine attack. To German Americans, this response was further evidence that the president had taken sides with the British, since Britain had never received a similar notice of "strict accountability."[6] When Wilson asked the British to drop their embargo of foodstuffs to Germany in return for an agreement by the Germans to forgo submarine warfare (the Germans had signaled that they would accept this bargain), the British declined. Britain increased its blockade in March, announcing that *all* vessels carrying cargo to or from Germany, whether direct or through neutral ports, would be subject to seizure.[7] In the United States, efforts by German Americans to stop the supply of munitions to the Allies met with resistance by the Wilson admin-istration and went nowhere in Congress.[8] The United States protested the in-creased blockade of Britain with a lukewarm note on March 30.

Everything was set up for a disaster. And it came in May.

On the morning of Saturday, May 1, 1915, New Yorkers awoke to a dis-quieting message from the Imperial German Government in the newspapers, outlined in black border, warning about the risks of transatlantic voyages:

NOTICE!

TRAVELLERS intending to embark on the Atlantic voyage are reminded that a state of war exists between Germany and her allies and Great Britain and her allies; that the zone of war includes the waters adjacent to the British Isles; that, in accordance with formal notice given by the Imperial German Government, vessels flying the flag of Great Britain, or and any of her allies, are liable to de-struction in those waters and that travelers sailing in the war zone on ships of Great Britain or her allies do so at their own risk.

Imperial German Embassy
Washington, D. C., April 22, 1915

In some newspapers the notice appeared directly next to advertisements placed by the British shipping line Cunard for the *Lusitania,* which was to sail that day. The best evidence is that most of the *Lusitania*'s passengers saw or heard about the German notice before the ship sailed.[9] One historian has summa-rized the evidence of the contraband that was aboard the ship: "The cargo list also discussed munitions: 4,200 cases of Remington rifle cartridges, packed 1,000 to a box; 1,250 cases of shrapnel shells and eighteen cases of fuses from the Bethlehem Steel Company; a large amount of aluminum and fifty cases of bronze powder. In monetary terms, over half the *Lusitania*'s cargo consisted of material being shipped for the Allies' war effort."[10]

According to later published reports, the German ambassador, Count Jo-hann Heinrich von Bernstorff, knew of the specific threat to the *Lusitania* be-fore he placed the notice in the newspapers. A coded message sent by wireless from Berlin to the German embassy, which was intercepted on April 22, 1915, was later deciphered: "Warn Lusitania passengers through press not voyage across Atlantic."[11]

The German submarine *U-20,* commanded by Walter Schwieger, was ac-tive during the first week of May in the waters around the southern tip of Ire-land, directly in the lanes of the great passenger liners from America. On May 5, *U-20* attacked a British schooner, the *Earl of Lathom,* after firing a warning shot and giving a verbal warning through a megaphone for the crew to abandon ship. The ship was sunk ten miles offshore, and the British Admiralty sent out warnings to all ships, including the *Lusitania,* that there was a submarine menace off the southern Irish coast.[12] The *Lusitania* nevertheless entered the war zone on May 7. The morning fog caused her captain, William "Bowler Bill" Turner, to order the ship to reduce speed, but by noon, the sun was out, the Irish coast was visible, and the ship resumed speed, but not full speed.

At 2:10 PM Captain Schwieger aboard *U-20* gave the order to fire.

The torpedo hit with a thud and exploded. A second explosion followed. The ship began to list to starboard and became uncontrollable. Captain Turner tried to steer her to shore and reduce speed to allow lifeboats to be lowered, but the ship's controls did not answer. Order gave way to panic. "Great confusion on board," Schwieger wrote from the vantage point of his periscope, "boats are cleared away and some are lowered into the water. Apparently considerable panic; several boats, fully laden, are hurriedly lowered, bow or stern first and are swamped at once."[13]

At 2:28 PM the *Lusitania* sank below the surface, eighteen minutes after the torpedo hit. Of the nearly 2,000 on board, 1,198, including almost 100 children, perished. Of the 139 American passengers, 128 died, including millionaire Alfred Vanderbilt.

Newspapers in the United States reported that the news of the sinking was greeted with "expressions of amazement and enthusiasm" in Germany. "Hundreds of telegrams of congratulations are being sent to Admiral von Tirpitz, the German Minister of Marine, on the sinking of the Lusitania, which is considered by the Germans to be an answer to the destruction off the Falkland Islands of the German squadron under the command of Admiral von Spee," reported the *New York Times* a couple of days later.[14]

In the United States, pro-German editors like George Viereck wrote that the disaster was predictable. Viereck noted that American passengers had been warned and that they sailed at their own risk: "If an American is foolish enough to entrust his life to an English ship, in spite of the explicit warning of the German Embassy, he has only himself to blame if he meets with a serious mishap." Viereck brazenly called on Secretary of State Bryan to be impeached for failing to warn Americans to stay out of the war zone set up by the Germans. "Some time ago," Viereck noted, "Mr. Bryan warned all Americans to keep away from the Mexican war zone. If Mr. Bryan were not utterly neglectful of his duties he would long ago have issued a warning both to merchantmen and to passengers embarking for Europe to keep away from the war zone described by the German Government around England."[15]

In Cleveland on May 8, another member of the German propaganda hierarchy, Bernhard Dernburg, a representative of the German Red Cross, made similar incendiary remarks. When he tried to explain himself the next day in New York he only made things worse. "It is a catastrophe of war," Dernburg argued. "The Cunard Line is responsible. The British Admiralty is equally, if not more, responsible, for permitting innocent American travelers to be used as shields on a ship that was nothing more or less than an auxiliary cruiser and contraband carrier."[16] Dernburg was instructed by the German ambassador to return to Germany.

The Wilson administration came under intense pressure to declare war on Germany. Woodrow Wilson was stunned and stymied. For three days he said nothing, took walks by himself, played golf, went on long automobile rides, and isolated himself in the White House, puzzling through his next step. Thoughtless reactivity had taken the world into an unintended war that was now out of control—Wilson knew he had to approach it differently. On Monday night, May 10, three days after the sinking, Wilson broke his silence in a speech delivered in Convention Hall in Philadelphia to four thousand new immigrants. He later said he spoke words from his heart, extemporaneously. "The example of America must be the example not merely of peace because it will not fight," he said, "but peace because peace is the healing and elevating influence of the world and strife is not. There is such a thing as a man being too proud to fight. There is such a thing as a nation being so right that it does not need to convince others by force that it is right."[17]

Theodore Roosevelt was livid. He wrote privately to a family member that Wilson was a coward and a weakling, "cordially supported by all the hyphenated Americans, by solid flubdub and [the] pacifist vote."[18]

Wilson finally met with his cabinet the day after his too-proud-to-fight comments and presented his ideas on a note to be delivered to Germany. Various opinions were expressed in the meeting. Wilson's draft note took the high road, appealing to the German government to disavow the attack, as a government that had always "stood forthrightly for justice and humanity in international relationships." He insisted that Germany make reparations and take immediate steps to prevent the recurrence of attacks on Americans, even those traveling as passengers on ships of a belligerent. Some in the cabinet believed that Americans should be warned against traveling on belligerent ships and further that a note be delivered to London protesting the blockade of neutral shipping and the stoppage of foodstuffs to Germany. Bryan thought that time, above all, was needed to allow heads to cool and for further investigation of the facts. He hoped that the administration would suggest submission of the matter to international arbitration or settle it in some other manner at some later date.

Wilson did not want to delay or dilute his message to Germany. Wilson's first note was delivered to Germany on Thursday, May 13. It specifically referred to the German warning in the New York newspapers and stated that it was ineffective to excuse the sinking.

The Germans responded on May 28, expressing regret over the loss of the lives of neutrals but making the government's case that the *Lusitania* was a belligerent ship, an armed auxiliary cruiser in the British Navy. The response contended that the *Lusitania* carried munitions and Canadian soldiers.

Yet while they bristled externally, the Germans, too, were split. The chancellor of the German empire, Theobald von Bethmann-Hollweg, worried that Germany could not withstand U.S. entry into the war and cautioned that submarine warfare against neutrals had to stop. The German Navy felt that to do so would effectively mean the abandonment of submarine warfare. For the time being, the kaiser agreed with his chancellor, and U-boat captains were instructed in June to spare neutral ships, including large passenger liners.[19]

Wilson responded with a second note, stating that the *Lusitania* was not armed, that exploding armaments had not caused or accelerated the sinking, that no Canadian troops had been on board, and that the cargo of the ship was lawful cargo under U.S. law. Secretary of State Bryan thought the note too militant and believed that more time was needed to conduct a complete investigation. He also continued to believe that a note had to be issued to Great Britain as well.

Recognizing that his influence within the administration was fading, Bryan decided to resign. Privately, Wilson was glad to see him go.

Toward the end of summer, the Germans assured the United States that submarines would not sink ocean liners without prior warning. This concession came shortly after another unprovoked U-boat sinking of a commercial liner carrying almost five hundred passengers, the *Arabic,* a British freighter from the White Star Line. The attack resulted in the deaths of forty passengers, including two Americans. This time, Wilson threatened to cut off diplomatic relations with Germany, a first step to a possible declaration of war. When the Germans backed down, Americans saw the president as a hero, keeping the country out of war through a series of diplomatic notes without the need to fire a shot.

The sinking of the *Lusitania* led to greater surveillance of Germans and their diplomats in the United States. There had been widespread suspicion for some time within the administration that the Germans were using their embassy to conduct and direct espionage efforts in the United States. Because of the ambassador's diplomatic immunity, though, American agents had been limited in their ability to spy on the major players. On May 14, a week after the sinking of the *Lusitania*, Woodrow Wilson signed an executive order authorizing the surveillance of German embassy personnel.[20]

Wilson's executive order led directly to the discovery of a massive German plot to commit sabotage in the United States. With relations between the United States and the German Empire already on tenterhooks after the *Lusitania*, the question was whether the discovery of the plot would push the two nations to the brink of war.

CHAPTER 26

"Bernstorff Used Dyes as War Club"

Frustrated by his country's bungling and missteps, and concerned about the potential catastrophic impact of unrestricted submarine warfare on relations between the United States and the German empire, Ambassador Johann Heinrich von Bernstorff, the top diplomat in the German embassy in the United States, searched for other ways to put pressure on the United States to stop the British blockade. He hoped to awaken Americans to the role Great Britain's blockade was playing in creating the dangerous situation on the high seas. Urbane, incisive, the son of the German ambassador to England, Von Bernstorff's English was perfect, and he was acutely attuned to the mood in Washington.

He came up with the idea of cutting off the export of a German product so critical to American industry that its absence would have a crippling effect. To identify such a product, he did not need to think long or hard: the answer was German dyes. Germans had revolutionized the manufacture and production of synthetic dyes used in the textile industry; they held a near worldwide monopoly on dyes. As a consequence, dyestuffs had become an indispensable import for the United States. Because of the British blockade, German experts estimated that the stock of dyes in America had dwindled to the point that a complete embargo on dye importation "would throw 4,000,000 American workmen out of employment."[1]

The reason: a shutdown of the textile industry would have a ripple effect across the American economy. Even American economists conceded that "the dye industry controls the fate of three billion dollars' worth a year of American goods which cannot be made without its products."

The German advancements in dyes arose out of the fact that in the Wilhemine Era the Germans had become the leading chemists in the world. Breakthroughs in understanding and applying organic chemistry helped to power much of the exponential growth of the German economy under Kaiser Wilhelm II. The dyestuffs industry created a virtual national laboratory for chemical experimentation and innovation. To generate the astonishing variety of colors that the Germans came up with, scientists and engineers had to distill coal tar in great quantities, extracting the crude to come up with distinct dyes. This process, repeated over and over, had an amazing spin-off effect. The process produced an immense volume of chemical by-products, a cornucopia of waste products that could be used for other purposes.

From the dye industry the Germans discovered how to mass-produce high explosives like trinitrotoluene (TNT), which originally was used as a yellow dye. They developed important pharmaceutical products, including a refinement known as Bayer Aspirin (Bayer started as a dye producer). The Germans cornered the market on the chemical phenol, buying up all surplus produced in the United States to help Bayer make aspirin in its American plant but also to prevent its export to Great Britain for use in making TNT.

The German dye industry had another by-product: its representatives in America became deeply involved in German espionage and spying. Dr. Hugo Schweitzer, for example, a German-born chemist and president of the American branch of Bayer, was widely believed to have been a German spy who was a secret service employee of the German government.[2]

One of the other giants in the dye industry was a company called Badische Anilin und Soda-Frabrik (BASF). Badische was represented in the United States by an America corporation known as the Badische Company of New York. The stock of Badische in New York ended up in the hands of the owners of a company that was one of the major importers of German dyes in the United States: Adolf Kuttroff and Carl Pickhardt.[3]

Carl Pickhardt was Baroness Iona Zollner's uncle and father of Adolf Pickhardt, the young man who would eventually become engaged to Isabelle Phillips.

The Pickhardts were in an industry that Wilson's future attorney general, Mitchell Palmer, would conclude "was saturated through and through with German influence."

It was a breeding ground for spies.

CHAPTER 27

"It Is My Intention to Work at My Job Instead of Haranguing Dinner Parties"

Frank Burke of the Secret Service did not understand German, so he got nothing from sitting across from George Sylvester Viereck and Dr. Heinrich Albert, Privy Counsellor for the German government in the United States, as the two men chatted on the New York City train on a hot day in late July 1915. Burke had been told to shadow these men as part of the government's step-up in the surveillance of German diplomats. Burke saw an opportunity after Viereck got off the train and Albert appeared to fall asleep reading a book. Albert was startled when the train came to his stop, and he jumped up to work his way through the crowd, accidentally leaving his briefcase behind. Burke snatched it before Albert could get back on the train in a panic.

Albert chased Burke through the New York streets once he saw that Burke had the briefcase. After losing Albert by jumping on a fast-moving trolley, Burke took the bag immediately to his boss, the head of the Secret Service, William J. Flynn. Flynn scanned the documents, which were mostly in German, and saw enough to immediately report to his boss, the secretary of the treasury, William McAdoo. McAdoo was on holiday with his family in North Haven, Maine, but Flynn and Burke visited him there the next day with the documents.[1]

William Gibbs McAdoo was born and raised in the South but made his fame and money as a financier in New York City, helping to build the railway tunnel between New York City and New Jersey. His first wife, with whom he had had seven children, died in 1912. McAdoo was at the time the vice chairman of the Democratic National Committee and a loyalist to Woodrow Wilson in his run for the presidency. McAdoo married Woodrow Wilson's daughter, Eleanor Randolph Wilson, in a ceremony at the White House in 1914. He offered to resign as secretary of the treasury, but Wilson insisted he stay on to work on the recently created Federal Reserve.

After inspecting the Albert documents and some quick translations, McAdoo saw that "while they did not furnish any basis for legal action . . . they showed plainly enough that illegitimate activities were going on; that our neutrality laws were being violated. I saw an opportunity to throw a reverberating scare into the whole swarm of propagandists—British and French and German—and I decided that this could be done most effectively through publication."[2] Wilson and Colonel House were next to see the papers. They agreed with the suggestion to publish translations through the *New York World,* but only on the condition that the *World* not disclose the source of the documents.[3]

No one told the Bureau of Investigation, the investigative arm of the Department of Justice, of the discovery of the Albert documents. The day after the story broke, the chief of the Bureau of Investigation, A. Bruce Bielaski, sent an agent to the *World* to demand an explanation of how the documents came into the hands of the paper.[4] It took some back-and-forth before the matter was straightened out.

Bielaski conducted his own inquiry. The fact that he reported his results to the secretary of state, Robert Lansing (Bryan's replacement), was interpreted by the media as a sign that German diplomats were involved.[5] Though the source of the Albert documents was concealed, Americans, already outraged over the *Lusitania,* read all about the German deception and about the money that was passing through Dr. Albert's hands—huge fortunes spent on propaganda, on sabotage, plans to buy up press bureaus, to pay off journalists, and to purchase real and dummy munitions plants.[6]

The captured documents also proved that the Germans had been financing and fomenting counterrevolution in Mexico.

German spy hysteria grew and spread everywhere.

George Viereck was singled out for public flaying. A disparaging photo of Viereck, head in hands, appeared on the front page of the *World* next to copies of his letters to Dr. Albert showing that *The Fatherland* was being financed and controlled by the German government.[7] Theodore Roosevelt lashed out at "Viereck the hyphenate," calling for him to return to Germany to fight for the kaiser, where he belonged.[8]

U. S. neutrality was slipping away.

The investigation of Carrie Phillips as a German spy would not take place until after the United States entered the war in 1917, so there is no evidence of whether she became involved in the spy network in 1915. Nor do Harding's letters in 1915 shed light. After the letters from the Palace Hotel in the first part of 1915, either he stopped writing until the end of the year, or Carrie destroyed any letters he did send. The letters do not resume until December, when Congress finally returned and Harding would sit for the first time as a senator. Thus, no writings record Carrie's reaction to the sinking of the *Lusitania* or the Albert scandal.

Whatever the case, the events of 1915 clearly did nothing to cool Carrie's ardor for Germany or the German cause.

On December 11, 1915, Warren wrote to Carrie from Washington. It was the Saturday after Harding's first week in the Senate, when he had been sworn in by Vice President Marshall. According to custom, new senators were subjected to some form of hazing, and Harding's was to preside over the Senate when one particularly long-winded senator was scheduled to speak. When the man finally finished his address (before an all-but-empty Senate chamber), Marshall took back the gavel from Harding and said, "You have served your sentence. Hereafter you will be considered a full-fledged senator."[9]

Warren had done very little since returning from Hawaii the previous spring, telling Scobey that he spent "most of my time cavorting around and making speeches, having covered about forty engagements in that time."[10] But he stopped making speeches when he saw that it was causing people to talk about him as a presidential aspirant. "[T]here are a few poorly balanced minds, which have me becoming a candidate, but most of them will soon go to the asylums or ought to," he wrote Scobey, "so there is no use in giving them consideration."

As summer gave way to fall, Florence grew ill again. Ed Scobey's wife similarly suffered from another attack of sickness and was hospitalized. "I am greatly distressed to hear about Mrs. Scobey's series of indispositions," Harding wrote in September.[11] "The last time I saw her she looked so good that I didn't suppose she would go anywhere, unless it was to a divorce court seeking the deserved freedom from a gay and festive husband, like you have proven yourself to be." He advised Scobey to tell her not to fret. "Tell her not to worry about gastritis. I have had enough of it to fill 16 hospitals and have learned from experience that the only cure for it is to forget it."

Florence's illness was more worrying. By the middle of October young George Christian wrote to Scobey, "Mrs. Harding is still carrying out the doctor's orders very religiously and remaining most of the time in bed. She has some good days and then again some discouraging ones, but a good rest and some attention to her troubles, I think, will bring about rapid improvement."[12]

After Thanksgiving, the Hardings packed up in Marion and Florence rallied. Before leaving, she buried her son's ashes in a cemetery in Marion, Marshall having died on the first day of 1915.[13] The Hardings had had no time to locate a permanent house in Washington, so they rented temporary quarters. "We are located here at 1612 21st Street, Northwest," Harding advised Scobey on December 13, "the home of Ex-Secretary Herbert who was a member of the Grover Cleveland Cabinet. We were able to secure the home with all its furnishings and its small force of servants and are fairly comfortably situated, and think we shall enjoy it here very much."[14] He joined the golf club at Chevy Chase (where Franklin Roosevelt was one of his golfing companions), and Florence prepared to begin the social life of a senator's wife. Around this time, they were invited by Nick and Alice Roosevelt Longworth for a dinner party and an evening of poker, at which they met millionaires Ned and Evalyn Walsh McLean.[15] Ned McLean was the son of the wealthy and influential John R. McLean, who owned and published the *Cincinnati Enquirer* and the *Washington Post*. Evalyn McLean was moneyed in her own right—her father had struck it rich in gold mines in Colorado. She was the owner of the fabled Hope Diamond and became a friend and confidant of Florence's, taking her under her wing when she called on her at her home and found her sick again a few weeks after the poker party.

Evalyn's descriptions of Florence at this time provide some indication of how her illnesses had taken a toll on her physically. While she found Harding "stunning," Florence seemed old, white-haired, and frumpy—her "haughty" look fit Harding's nickname of "Duchess," Evalyn thought. "By the calendar she was five years older than her husband, but ill-health and a tendency to worry over what might happen, plus her nagging temperament, had helped to wear her body."[16]

☙

"It is a week since I bade you goodbye," Harding wrote Carrie on December 11, "and the days have been so extremely full that it seems an age." In language that was deliberately vague, Warren wrote to Carrie about some serious fight he had had with Florence before they left Marion. "Before leaving home I tried my very best to do the thing you desired," he wrote her on December 11, "which I *too* desired as much as you, but without avail." Since this was an open letter, it is difficult to know what the problem was but he was clearly trying to make some arrangement that Carrie desired. "The matter brought on a very serious controversy and so upset the order of things that our departure was threatened with delay on account thereof."[17] He wrote that he guessed that Carrie was perfectly furious and full of "I told you so's," but he asked that she suspend judgment until he could see during the holiday recess.

Congress would recess for the holidays on December 18, he thought, and he would be back in Marion on the twentieth. "Surely I shall see you as early as I reach home," he wrote, "provided it is agreeable to you."[18]

Harding was stimulated by Washington and its hubbub. "I have dined with my family but once—rather an unusual experience for me," he wrote Carrie. He said that perhaps it was the newness of the congressional session, but he had been deluged with visitors. "If I am always to be so busy I shall soon have my nerves worn to a frazzle," he wrote. Then in code, he added: "It seems like anyone in the *universe* wants to see one here, and there is *constant* call to meet people."[19]

He shared titillating gossip with Carrie about Woodrow Wilson's public romance with Edith Bolling Galt, a young widow Wilson turned to after his wife Ellen died. "You must hear the late intimate gossip of this town relating to the big Chief and his affairs of the heart," Harding wrote. "I can not tell you of the truth they contain, but they are highly diverting. When we last discussed the affair we (you and I) made the correct guess. There *was* a triangular tangle."[20] Wilson married Edith Galt a little over a week after Harding wrote his letter to Carrie, on December 18, 1915. The relationship set all manner of stories swirling, including rumors that a Mrs. Peck, a former flame of Wilson's, was offering to sell love letters she had received from Wilson.[21] Wilson met Mary Allen Hulbert Peck in Bermuda on a vacation he took without his wife when he was president of Princeton and recovering from a small stroke that left him temporarily blind in his left eye. Reportedly Wilson wrote over two hundred letters to Mrs. Peck, which she kept. He also is alleged to have sent her $7,500 of his own money while president.[22] The letters have never surfaced.

Harding wrote Carrie that he had received a letter from Isabelle, "saying she was leaving for home this week." Carrie had enrolled Isabelle in Mrs.

Dow's School for Girls at Briarcliff Manor, New York, a private school fifty miles north of New York City on the Hudson River.[23] "You will be as glad as she is, I am sure. I shall be happy to see her myself."

He joked with Carrie that that night he was going to meet "her old beau," William Jennings Bryan, at the Ohio Society dinner. Bryan was making the rounds speaking against the Wilson administration and for peace. Harding too was scheduled to give an address. "I am to speak—my final engagement, with one exception, for many months. It is my intention to work at my job instead of haranguing dinner parties, etc."[24]

That day, ominous newspaper headlines announced that Captain Franz von Papen and Captain Karl Boy-Ed, the military and naval attachés to the German embassy in Washington, were being recalled by the kaiser in response to demands from the U.S. government.[25] Through a series of carefully arranged leaks, likely from the Wilson administration, the men had been linked with various plots and scandals: from provisioning German cruisers with munitions off the U.S. coast, to passport frauds, to supporting the deposed Mexican president. The U.S. government would not give specific reasons for the recall of the diplomats other than that their "continued presence in the country was undesirable." While complying with the U.S. demand, the Germans insisted that the United States "show its reasons for this unwarranted and vicious action."[26]

The newspapers also predicted that Dr. Heinrich Albert also would be asked to leave the country, though that did not occur until after the United States declared war against Germany in 1917.[27]

Yet the Wilson administration continued to court German Americans. Officials in the administration and high-ranking Democratic senators privately lobbied George Viereck and other Americans of German descent for support of Wilson in the upcoming election.[28] According to Viereck's testimony in a postwar libel suit, President Wilson sent two emissaries, Postmaster General Albert Sidney Burleson and Missouri Democratic senator William J. Stone, to secretly meet with him to assure him of the president's neutrality and that the administration was "by no means anti-German." Stone, then the chairman of the powerful Senate Foreign Relations Committee, pointed out that if he was defeated along with Wilson, the hawkish Massachusetts senator Henry Cabot Lodge would succeed him as chair of Foreign Relations. That event, Stone argued, would mean disaster for Germany, since "Lodge belonged more in the British House of Lords than in the United States Senate."

As the year 1915 surrendered to 1916, Harding wondered privately what had happened to his relationship with Carrie Phillips. On December 22, still in Washington, he wrote her.[29] "I had hoped for a line from you before today, so I might pen an Xmas note such as would fully reveal all that is in my heart." He said he longed to "renew Christmas activities of the happy years between 1905 and 1914," but he could not for he was unsure of where she stood. "I'd like to specify, but I dare not venture, because I do not know your attitude." She had been "emphatic," he thought, that she was not interested in restoring the old feelings, but still he hoped. "God! For a twenty-four hours of supreme content and solace of days that were."

He signed his note: "*Constant.*"

CHAPTER 28

"He Was an American from the Word Go"

Baroness Iona Pickhardt Zollner had two sons with her first husband, Charles Warren Shope. Shope's death from cancer in 1901 led her to Europe, and to her second husband, Baron Kurt Loeffelholz von Colberg, and eventually to her third husband, Lieutenant Zollner, who was promoted to a Captain in the Bavarian Army sometime after their marriage. She and Zollner had one child, a little girl they called Nonie. Iona's first son, Beresford Shope, became a cadet at the U.S. Naval Academy at Annapolis in the fall of 1915.

"My boy had always wanted to get in the American Army or the American Navy, and I suppose I kept up his patriotism," the baroness testified at her espionage hearing, "because he was an American from the word go. If anything is said in favor of any other country, he will always say: if it is American, it is better."[1]

There was the matter of getting him into West Point or Annapolis. Beresford had not done well in his entrance examinations. At the time, the baroness was living at 959 Madison Avenue in New York City, and her congressman told her that he had given out all his appointments. So she traveled to Washington to speak with congressmen who had vacancies in the hope of securing a slot for her son. She said she made several trips, staying a week at a time, but her efforts failed.[2] She then visited the Navy Department itself and was successful in obtaining Beresford's appointment.[3] She testified that a retired admiral helped her, but her second son, Bedford Sutton Shope, sixteen years old at the time of the espionage hearing, told the U.S. attorney in an out-of-court interview that he was with his mother when she met with the assistant secretary of the Navy, Franklin D. Roosevelt, and that she had used her Roosevelt family relation—her brother Ernest had married Maude Fortescue, Theodore Roosevelt's first cousin—to secure Beresford's appointment.

Franklin Roosevelt was distantly related to Theodore Roosevelt but Eleanor was Theodore's niece. (Eleanor's father, Elliot, was T.R.'s only brother, and T.R. gave away Eleanor when she and Franklin were married in 1905, as Elliot had died a decade earlier.)[4]

When the U.S. attorney tried to get Bedford to repeat in court the Franklin Roosevelt connection to his brother's appointment to the Naval Academy, Bedford tried to deny it but admitted under cross-examination that the Roosevelt connection was mentioned to Franklin when Beresford's appointment was discussed. Specifically, the baroness mentioned Edith Roosevelt, who had been married to John Roosevelt, one of Theodore's legitimate cousins through his uncle Robert Roosevelt. John was Maude Fortescue's half-brother.

> Q. You said something about one of the Roosevelts being related to you by marriage?
>
> A. Yes sir.
>
> Q. That was Mrs. Edith Roosevelt.
>
> A. Yes, sir.
>
> Q. What was her husband's name?
>
> A. John.
>
> Q. What did he do?
>
> A. I don't know, a lawyer I think—I think he is retired, he is very old, he is 62.
>
> Q. Your mother used the interest in the Roosevelt family to get the boy appointed to Annapolis, did she?
>
> A. I could not say.
>
> Q. It was told Franklin Roosevelt of this relationship?
>
> A. Never mentioned to him a connection at all; besides it [the family relationship] is far too distant.
>
> Q. You were present with her?
>
> A. Yes sir.
>
> Q. Did she tell him that she was related by marriage, or that the boy was, to Mrs. Edith Roosevelt?
>
> A. She spoke about Edith, but did not say how connected, because Edith might have been a friend, that is too far [a family relationship] to claim.
>
> Q. What did she say on the subject?
>
> A. She may have mentioned Edith's name.[5]

Once Beresford entered the Naval Academy, the baroness began to visit him in Annapolis, boarding at a house not far from the grounds of the academy. She kept track of his friends, their comings and goings, and their families.

One of the cadets at the Naval Academy was a young man from New Mexico named John W. Spalding. Spalding was not the best of students, or perhaps he was not particularly ambitious. He would eventually be "bilged" from the Naval Academy (thrown out due to poor academic performance), and the baroness would pull strings to assist him in procuring an officer's commission in the U.S. Army. Lieutenant Spalding was the young man found under her bed in Chattanooga in his union suit in December 1917.

CHAPTER 29

"So Robinson Came!"

As a freshman senator in the minority party, Harding was limited in his choice of committee assignments. He was selected for the Commerce Committee, the Coast Defense Committee, and the Claims Committee, which dealt with private bills and petitions and was one of the busiest but least important of committees. "I should assume it was the 'hazing' committee for all new members," he wrote Scobey of the Claims Committee. "My observation is that the new member gets rather a poor deal in his committee assignments, particularly when he belongs to the republican minority and the democrats of the solid South are in the saddle. I am not complaining, however, because I find I have plenty to do and will be exceedingly busy this session learning how to become a Senator, in fact as well as in name."[1]

Even though he was hunkering down and narrowing his focus, he still had the national convention that summer much in his mind. His maiden speech in the Senate, delivered on January 28, was on the Philippines, and it was filled with his gospel of Americanism. He opposed the Democratic proposal to grant the Philippines immediate independence; he did not think the Filipinos were ready yet for self-government, though they would be someday. Like McKinley, Harding favored the concept of benevolent American imperialism. He approved the annexation of the islands taken in the Spanish-American War so that the people of the Philippines would learn democracy under the protection of the United States. "We are the first nation on the face of the earth that ever unsheathed the sword on behalf of suffering humanity," he told the crowded Senate chamber.[2] The Senate got its first taste of Harding's oratorical skills. His name appeared immediately thereafter in the press as a candidate to deliver the keynote address for the Republicans at their Chicago convention.[3]

Florence Harding seemed to continue in her recovery during their first month in Washington, but she overextended herself and was sick again in the second week of January. Warren wrote to Scobey that they attended a dinner party on January 8 and afterward Florence "was seized with what seemed to be very serious attack of the Grippe." Harding reported that doctors had admonished Florence to "cut out practically all of the possible social activities of the season and spend a very quiet winter if she hopes to get on a dependable footing again."[4]

With Florence under doctor's care but stable, Harding made a quick trip to Marion to see Carrie on Saturday, January 22, 1916. Revelations during this visit left him stunned and bewildered. Robinson, his dreaded archrival, had been to Marion to see her.

He wrote that he had "chucked" several important engagements to make the trip to Marion. Once there, he wished he had never gone. "If you designed to punish me," he wrote Carrie on Monday morning back in Washington, "you have succeeded fully." He said he had "come with heart a hungering," but then he was "suddenly plunged to the depths of anxiety."[5]

During the visit, Carrie showed Warren a letter written by Robinson. In it, Robinson professed his love for Carrie, and the letter clearly revealed that he had come to Marion. "So Robinson came!" he wrote with great distress. "I feared for a year but would not surrender. I know *now* of my failure."

He was so shocked that on Monday morning back in his Senate office he still wrote with high emotion. "It is more than thirty-six hours since I saw you, and they have all been given to you, amid the perturbation I could not shake off." He was reminded of a poet who once wrote: "For one to appreciate the pangs of hell/He first must know of heaven well."

He was dejected, and in his typical fashion he withdrew. "I sought the impossible, and I am defeated. I'll not complain, I'll not annoy, I'll not further pour out my perturbation. The inferences are so obvious, the impressions so unavoidable that—well, I can't be blind, but I can strive to be dumb. Perhaps I deserve it. You think so, anyway."

His hurt was obvious. "Anyhow, I am resolved to try to stifle the aching of my heart by plunging into a struggle to fit my self for the duties I have ventured to assume," he wrote. "They are big—vastly greater than I ever dreamed. I am finally awakened to my utter incapacity and incompetence but I can struggle to be partially fitted, and will." He even admitted that he made sure to be in the Senate chamber when it opened each day after noon so that he could hear the chaplain's prayer. "I need it. God help us all. I rather like the chaplain. He does not give God a lot of advice, but humbly beseeches his guidance, even as I inwardly supplicate him now. Perhaps I do not deserve to be heard."

His letter reads like a valedictory to Carrie. "I shall not get home again in a long while," he now conceded. "I wish you the continued peace and tranquility of which you wrote. . . . I shall always wish you the greatest wealth of happiness, all the triumphs of your brilliant womanhood and your charming personality, no matter what my own disappointments are."[6]

It was at such down periods that his friend Scobey seemed to be the elixir. Around this time, the two men exchanged a series of notes, discussing politics and the various misfortunes and maladies of their spouses. Harding wrote that he intended to support his predecessor in the Senate, Theodore Burton, in the upcoming presidential race, even though he felt Burton's chances were slim given his "lack of popularity."[7] New Yorker Charles Evans Hughes seemed the odds-on favorite, but Harding was not convinced he was the answer. "I have not a bit of enthusiasm for Hughes myself," he admitted to Scobey. Both Harding and Scobey worried that T.R. would take an active role in the convention and that he might even be scheming to gain the nomination himself. "It is possible the Colonel wants to eliminate everybody else and then appear as the only best bid left to the Republicans," Harding wrote. "I doubt if he could be elected, if nominated. I doubt if I should vote for him; I certainly would be unable to go on the stump and do anything towards his election." The old wounds of 1912 were still there, something Harding would eventually rise above, but he wasn't ready yet to forgive or forget.

Carrie responded to Harding's desperate letter about Robinson saying that she was surprised by his reaction. "Your letter received with gratifying promptness," he wrote back on Sunday, January 30, from his Senate office. "I found yours on my desk when I arrived for my morning tasks."[8]

He struggled to find a way to respond. She clearly was playing him off Robinson. "This is my fourth attempt to reply," he wrote, "but I do not seem able to write such a reply as I am willing to post. It is useless to detail my disappointments and I esteem you far too highly to yield to fault-finding or bitterness." When she challenged him that she did not think he cared about Robinson, he begged to differ, pointing to his reaction to seeing the man's letter to her. "Well, if you can believe that to be my attitude after *the poor fool* I made of myself when I read his revealing letter, and after I begged you to ignore it, neither word nor action will ever count."

He quoted a line from her letter about whether she could believe either of the men contesting for her affections were sincere. According to Harding, Carrie wrote about Robinson: "If his disappointment be real, I'll know some time." About Warren she wrote: "If you care, I shall also know." Her point was that time would reveal the truth. Harding said he would accept the challenge. "I assent to the test of revealing weeks, months and years." But he was fatalistic: "I know when I have lost."

When Warren Harding faced depression or anxiety, he usually tried to lift himself out of it by immersing himself in work. He had plenty of it to keep himself busy as a new senator. His job, and the increasing demand for his services as a speaker, kept him "tremendously busy," causing him to stay up most nights to work, reading up on current issues or drafting speeches. "Honestly, never was my time so pressingly filled in all my life," he wrote Carrie in February 1916. "Night calls for so much reading on pending questions that I seldom get out."[9] But he welcomed the frantic pace. "I can dissipate a lot of depression amid the engrossment of toil. It is my one relief."[10]

His speaking engagements included a much-coveted request to speak at the Gridiron Club, an invitation-only social club for Washington journalists. Harding received the singular honor of being invited to speak at the same dinner with Woodrow Wilson and Vice President Marshall. "Was tipped today that I will be called on for speech at the Gridiron dinner Saturday night," he wrote to Carrie on the Tuesday before the dinner, "and I must find time to think of something fit to say. There are but four speakers, the president, the vice president, J. Skates and one other. Jerry will have to hump himself a bit, because it is the most exceptional dinner crowd in the republic."[11]

He knew how special this request was for him. "I have been wonderfully honored by the Gridiron crowd. There have been three dinners since my election—this is the fourth, and I have been invited to all of them and asked to speak the second time. My appreciation of the favor grows when I recall that there are scores of senators who have never been invited to attend and not a dozen in the present body have ever been asked to speak. You see, you can't buy a ticket, one has to be asked."[12] The crowd on the night of this particular dinner was indeed extraordinary: The president and vice president, the Speaker of the House, most secretaries in the Wilson cabinet, foreign ambassadors, Henry

Ford, and Finley Peter Dunne, the noted Chicago humorist and cartoonist, creator of Mr. Dooley.

Seeing how boastful he was in his letter, Warren guessed what Carrie would think as she read it: "Here I go—in a moment you will be saying how pleased I am with myself. I am proud of the distinction, but I ought not be telling it to confirm your already fixed notion about my self-esteem."

Carrie continued to bedevil him with the Robinson matter, this time sending to him in the mail two communications, a letter and a telegram, that she had received from Robinson. "I had your note and the enclosure of R—letter and telegram," Warren wrote her on February 17. He was not pleased, though Carrie claimed she sent them to show a cooling of her relationship with Robinson. He sent the letter back, along with some sarcasm. "I am returning the letter herewith," he wrote her. "It was thoughtful of you to forward them, but it was quite unnecessary. My impression concerning R—has not changed since you first wrote me in such enthusiasm about him, rather my impression has been confirmed, first by the letter that made his avowal and his later visit and welcome to Marion."[13] He decided he would no longer be a "pitiable ass" in writing her further about the distress Robinson caused him. "It has taken a long while for me to awake, not because I lacked discernment, but because I made myself believe what I wished, rather than accept that which I saw." He confessed that one of the main reasons he had followed through with his Hawaii trip was because he had seen a Robinson letter avowing his love for Carrie.[14] When Robinson did come to Marion, Warren had to believe it was at Carrie's invitation. "Can I believe that a gentleman would come without assurance?" he asked. "God help me—I can not."

Meanwhile Harding continued to build his national reputation. His speech on March 11 in Pittsburgh was featured in a national Republican magazine accompanied by a full-page portrait of him.[15] He slowly began to speak out against the Wilson administration, particularly regarding the Mexican situation and the economy. On Mexico, he continued to believe that, like the Philippines, nothing would be settled until the United States imposed its beneficial influence on the anarchy that was spreading in the country torn by civil war. On March 9, Pancho Villa seemed to confirm Harding's fear when he crossed the border and destroyed parts of Columbus, New Mexico, causing Wilson to send General John J. Pershing after the raiders into Mexico in hot pursuit. Harding believed a tougher stand earlier in the conflict would have avoided the continuing chaos across the border.

He also came to believe that President Wilson had "no dependable policy" when it came to the war in Europe. He thought a New York newspaper's rendition of the "Wilson Tango" captured best the administration's lack of defined policy: "One step forward, two steps backwards, hesitation, side-step." Despite the German assurance that no passenger liners would be sunk without warning, there was an occasional dramatic breach. In March, another unprovoked attack, this time of a French cross-Channel steamer, the *Sussex,* resulted in a Wilson administration ultimatum that if the Germans did not abandon their submarine warfare against passenger *and* freight-carrying vessels, the United States would sever diplomatic relations.[16] The kaiser relented and ordered that no unresisting merchant or passenger ships would be sunk without prior warning or at the least without making provision for the safety of passengers and crew.[17]

For the time being, Americans had reasons to believe that the United States could avoid war. Woodrow Wilson would base his upcoming campaign precisely on this hope. "He kept us out of war" would become his campaign slogan.

Harding began to have portentous feelings, physically and emotionally. On March 4 he wrote to Carrie, "I was feeling poorly, have been for two weeks, was frightfully depressed and feeling strange sensations and I was not sure that something might not happen to me and was strangely reconciled if there should."[18] Perhaps it was the stress of overwork. Perhaps it was their strained relationship. Carrie had been writing that "everything was spoiled."[19] Earlier that month, she had even demanded that he cease receiving visitors from Marion or Ohio in his home in Washington. If she was not welcome by Florence, no one should be. "No Marion friends, no Ohio friends can be invited to our home, until you can be welcomed here," he wrote her. His letters do not reveal whether he spoke about this directive with Florence; likely he did not.

His anxiety for his own health grew to the point that he decided one night to visit his Senate office to destroy some letters Carrie had sent him lest they be found by someone in the event he died or became disabled. "So I went to my office at night, the *second* time I have ever gone at night, and destroyed the accusing pages," he wrote to Carrie.[20]

At the beginning of April, the Republicans chose Harding to be the keynote speaker and the temporary (and therefore likely permanent) chairman of the national convention at Chicago. He had been chosen over Philander C. Knox of Pittsburgh, former attorney general for McKinley and

Roosevelt, secretary of state for Taft, and senator from Pennsylvania, and James Robert Mann, Chicago congressman and Minority Leader of the House.[21] The honor was proof of his growing status. He seemed acceptable to Progressives and regulars within the party, none of whom wanted a repeat of the split of 1912. Hawks like Roosevelt, for example, viewed Mann as weak on national defense because he had supported the McLemore resolution, which would have barred Americans from travel on armed belligerent vessels.[22]

True to Harding's predictions, Theodore Roosevelt was testing the waters to see about a run in 1916. On the day Harding was chosen as temporary chairman, T.R. spent an active day at his office in New York receiving delegations from around the nation. His office was a mob scene, reminding his supporters of "the old days." The *Times* characterized T.R. as "in fine fettle and enjoying the excitement that had been stirred up by his appearance as a candidate for the Republican nomination."[23]

T.R. withheld judgment on the Harding choice. "For publication, at any rate, the Colonel refused to comment on the political situation, and would not even say what he thought of the selection of Senator Warren G. Harding of Ohio as the Temporary Chairman of the Republican National Convention," the *Times* reported.[24]

Harding's letters to Carrie during this time show that she was spending more and more time in and around the city. She spent the first weeks of May traveling east to New York, to visit with Isabelle at Mrs. Dow's School for Girls and to spend time in the city. The question is whether she and Isabelle were visiting the Pickhardts. There had to be some contact between the families given that Isabelle would become engaged to Adolf Pickhardt by early 1918.

Another perhaps more significant question is raised by Harding's letters to Carrie just before the Republican convention of 1916. With the convention less than three weeks away, he wrote a terse letter to her about her criticism of him for his "mad pursuit of honors." This no doubt refers to his potential dark horse bid for the nomination at the convention. He then mysteriously wrote: "I ran over to Baltimore last Wednesday and learned something which persuaded me of the futility of such pursuit." To add to the inscrutability, he followed with these sentences: "On my return I did the thing which makes further mad pursuit impossible. I write it because you may be interested."[25]

"Henceforth," he wrote her, "I shall make no mad chase for honors, but I do mean to try to hold myself honorable. . . . I shall keep my engagement at Chicago June 7 [the date of his keynote address at the convention] because it would not be well to do otherwise. The soul is impaired, but there shall be mechanical compliance with the compact."[26]

But what was it he learned in Baltimore, and with whom did he meet?

CHAPTER 30

"The Strength of the Warrior and the Skill of the Engineer"

The weather should have been a sign, an omen. For three days since the arrival of delegates in Chicago, beginning Monday, June 5, 1916, it had poured down rain, soaking everyone. Everything about the atmosphere was sodden and inhospitable. "The hall was cold and damp, dripping raincoats and umbrellas soaked the floor, but the bedraggled delegates made the best of it," the *New York Times* reported.[1] Worse, the saga of 1912 seemed to be repeating itself. A candidate the regulars preferred, this time Supreme Court Justice Charles Evans Hughes, of New York, was opposed by Theodore Roosevelt and his supporters, and Roosevelt vowed, as he had done four years earlier, to stay in the race to the finish. According to the *New York Times:* "The most definite statement that can be made at this time is that the Colonel is in a very determined mind, and is listening to the reports of what his workers in Chicago are doing with a grim determination to fight on until all of the cards must be laid face up."[2]

When Warren Harding began his keynote address on Wednesday, June 7, there was no life in the delegates, and for one of the rare times in his public speaking career, he flopped. His delivery was flat. "Republicans Lack Fire" was the headline of the *New York Times* the next day.[3] "Somewhere between 12,000 and 14,000 graven images gathered together in the Coliseum at 11 o'clock this morning and viewed each other with cold, unwinking eyes and chilled steel faces for something like three hours, then dispersed." It was hardly the tumultuous scene Harding faced four years earlier when he placed William

Howard Taft's name in nomination. Then he could scarcely finish a sentence without a fight breaking out; this time they yawned.

He tried to work the audience up, but they sat stolidly. "Nothing could tease them into a flicker of emotion," the paper reported. "Those who did produce noise," the *Times* noted, "merely opened their faces patiently in response to Mr. Harding's vocal signal and made as short a noise as possible, unaccompanied by any expression on their faces to indicate joy, anger, sorrow or any other feeling. When they stopped making this noise, they did so without effort."[4]

Did his poor performance have to do with the revelation in Baltimore and subsequent action he undertook to make "further mad pursuit impossible"? To be sure there was real contrast between his effort at the convention and a speech he delivered in Chicago at the Hamilton Club in April, the day after he had been selected as the temporary chairman. In Chicago, his gave the performance of someone who was thinking seriously of a dark horse candidacy, and his audience felt his energy as a rising national star.[5] In a hall dedicated to Republican heroes, he pointed out that the past of his party was connected to the present. Republicans, he asserted, had always rescued the country from disastrous economic policies of the Democrats, and they would do so again. He even played the Ohio card, reminding his listeners of the giants in the Republican party who came from Ohio, especially the beloved McKinley. He preached America first. "That's Republican doctrine!"[6]

His speech brought the audience at the Hamilton Club to its feet. "As he closed," biographer Downes writes, "the applause was deafening; during the next few hours the congratulatory telegrams came pouring in. The party had found a spokesman in whom all Republicans might find confidence."[7]

George Christian wrote to Scobey in May that "dark horse" sentiment for a Harding nomination was growing in Washington and that even Harding's efforts to stop it had "no effect."[8] When the convention opened in June, Hughes had a strong position, Roosevelt had an outside shot, but the situation could have been managed and worked into a stalemate, with a compromise candidate emerging.[9]

Instead of a vigorous effort, though, Harding seemed to be going through the motions.

While there is no direct evidence of who he saw in Baltimore in May, there is one line in a letter he wrote to Carrie in August that references an "utterance you made in B—when your temper was defiant."[10] On the copy of the letter in her collection, she wrote out the word Baltimore where he had placed the letter "B." One can speculate that she was the one who threatened him in Baltimore, when her temper was defiant, in an effort to keep him from running for president. She had been furious when he ran for the Senate, so it follows she would want to stop any dark horse campaign.

The convention did select Charles Evans Hughes as its candidate. Though highly qualified, Hughes was not a dynamic candidate. Roosevelt derisively called him "the bearded iceberg."[11] A graduate of Brown University and Columbia Law School, Hughes had been a prosecutor of corruption in the utility and insurance industries and a reforming governor of New York, when President Taft appointed him associate justice of the U.S. Supreme Court. On the bench, Hughes ruled in favor of the rights of women and upheld labor laws. A party regular who had a record acceptable to Progressives, he stepped down from the Court after receiving the Republican presidential nomination.

On the stump, Hughes was cerebral, stiff, and unappealing. He had none of Roosevelt's charisma and little of Harding's charm and self-deprecating humor.

Despite his momentary appearance as a candidate, Theodore Roosevelt was a sick man in the summer of 1916, still battling and weakened from his physically devastating exploits on the River of Doubt. "Three days after Hughes was nominated," a biographer has written, "the ailing Theodore coughed so violently he tore a ligament in his side and spent the next several days in pain."[12] In addition to his physical maladies, he knew his bolt from the party in 1912 brought the country Woodrow Wilson, and it was his antagonism toward Wilson that led him not to challenge the result of the Republican convention. When the Progressive Party nominated him later in June, he refused to accept the nomination and endorsed Hughes. This was a major turning point for Harding. On June 28 he began a rapprochement with Roosevelt, writing: "I have just read with very great satisfaction your letter declining the third party nomination and pledging your support to the Republican nominee, Mr. Charles Evans Hughes," he wrote. "I believe you will have your reward in the high opinion of your fellow countrymen."[13]

Meanwhile, the Germans were engaged in a death match with the Allies in the trenches in Europe, with military leaders in Germany believing their country had tied their hands by voluntarily calling off unrestricted submarine warfare. To counter anti-German sentiment in the United States and to bring attention to the illegality of the British blockade, the Germans came up with a public relations stunt. Once again they focused on the dye industry, but this time they decided to tweak Ambassador von Bernstorff's idea. They decided to make the point not by withholding dyes but by bringing supplies to the United States in a daring maneuver that would capture the world's attention and the American imagination. They would deliver the dyes via the latest German engineering marvel: the submarine. *U-Deutschland,* a commercial sub without armaments, was commissioned and built as a merchant vessel to carry cargo by operating beneath the British blockade, avoiding destroyers and weaving through underwater mines and submarine nets. The submarine's destination: Baltimore.

U-Deutschland left Bremerhaven under the command of Captain Paul Konig on June 23, carrying bags of mail and a cargo of concentrated dyes and medical drugs worth in excess of $1 million. The oversized sub was able to carry more than 750 tons, about half the cargo of a small freighter. The only weapons aboard were five pistols for her officers.[14] The craft could plow through rough and stormy seas, submerging on only electric power to avoid enemy ships.[15]

The submarine appeared at 1:43 AM inside the Virginia Capes on Sunday, July 9, and was escorted by U.S. Navy ships up Chesapeake Bay, dropping anchor at 10:30 that night in the Baltimore harbor. The successful crossing aroused intense interest and excitement, and made the boat and its captain instant sensations.[16] Once it was clear the submarine was unarmed, the crew was warmly welcomed by Baltimore's citizens and generally celebrated in the United States. Baltimore had a large and active German American population. Since the vessel was without arms, the legal question was: would it be treated as a merchant ship and allowed to engage in trade or would it be deemed a belligerent vessel and impounded? After an inquiry, the government decided to treat the U-boat as a trader.[17]

There was powerful curiosity in the cargo the submarine brought with it and perhaps more about the merchants to whom the cargo would be consigned.[18] Captain Paul Konig released a prepared statement to the press about his ship's cargo, using the opportunity to lash out at the British blockade. "We have brought a most valuable cargo of dyestuffs to our American friends, dyestuffs which have been so much needed for months in America and which the ruler of the seas has not allowed the great American Republic to import. While England will not allow anybody the same right on the ocean because she rules the waves, we by means of the submarine, commenced to break this rule."[19] The captain declared that this was the start of regular international commerce by submarine. He promised that a sister merchant submarine, *U-Bremen,* would be next.

George Viereck wrote in *The Fatherland* that the "arrival of the supersubmarine is Germany's heroic reply to England's repudiation of the Treaty of London." He took the opportunity to propagandize about German superiority: "Not all the armadas of Great Britain can debar Germany from her place among the nations. What power can defeat a people who combine the vision of the dreamer with the strength of the warrior and the skill of the engineer?"[20]

Ambassador von Bernstorff, Dr. Heinrich Albert, and members of Deutsche Bank traveled to Baltimore to meet with Captain Konig, the local German consul, and the mayor of Baltimore. They had lunch at the Germania Club and inspected the submarine.[21] Even Vice President Marshall's wife visited and was given a tour.

Though the identities of the persons or companies who would purchase and take possession of the cargo of the submarine were protected, there were reports of the likely suspects. Of the German dye importers in the United States, it was believed that Bayer and Badische (the company affiliated with Kuttroff and Pickhardt) were the largest purchasers of the stockpile of dyestuffs.[22]

Captain Konig and his crew slipped away on August 2, avoiding the British and French ships that had amassed outside the three-mile limit off the U.S. coast, determined to capture or sink the submarine that had made them look foolish. The submarine returned to Germany loaded with rubber, tin, and 341 tons of nickel, a precious metal needed as an alloy to make armor stronger. As a neutral, the United States obviously could not restrain the sale of armaments to the Germans given the scale of such trade with the Allies.

U-Deutschland would make one more transatlantic voyage in November 1916, this time to New London, Connecticut, disgorging a reported $10 million in gems, securities, and medicinal products. After the *Bremen* was lost on her maiden voyage (she was believed to have hit a mine), and as relations with the United States soured, *U-Deutschland* was converted to *U-155*, a warship. The submarine would sink forty-two merchant ships in three battle tours.

At the very moment of triumph for the Germans, a stunning event in the New York harbor reminded Americans of the deadly seriousness of German espionage within the United States. While *U-Deutschland* was spending its final days in Baltimore, German agents in New York and New Jersey planned the most spectacular sabotage of the war on American soil. A little after midnight in the small hours of Sunday morning, July 30, guards at Black Tom Island—a promenade just opposite the Statute of Liberty on the New Jersey shore—noticed a series of small fires burning in and around railroad cars and on some barges tied up along its piers. The guards immediately grasped the gravity of the situation. The area was packed with an estimated 2 million pounds of ammunition and other high explosives, all ready to be shipped to the British, French, and Russians.[23]

A series of minor explosions began just as a guard called the Jersey City fire department. But before firefighters arrived, a terrific explosion blew the munitions center sky high. More explosions followed, sending shrapnel and bullets flying for miles around. The Statute of Liberty was peppered with hostile fire, suffering over $100,000 of damage, and windows were blown out in office buildings throughout lower Manhattan up to Times Square.[24] People in nearby homes and apartments were thrown from their beds, many believing there had been a major earthquake. The clock tower of the *Jersey Journal* newspaper was struck by flying metal, causing the clock to stop at precisely 2:12 AM.

Firemen arriving both by land and by boats fought through a rain of bullets. Newly arrived immigrants on Ellis Island found themselves under attack by exploding barges that drifted nearby. "As they dodged bullets," the *Times* wrote of the firemen, "they poured oceans of water into the blazing barges, meanwhile being compelled to keep a reasonable distance, because they didn't know how much unexploded powder might be on the barges."[25]

By Sunday morning, everything within close range of the Black Tom's piers was completely flattened. "Visitors landing at Immigration Station on Ellis Island yesterday afternoon might easily have imagined they were on the track of the great war and entering a town that had been besieged for several days," the *Times* reported.[26] Fortunately, the death toll was light, but property damage was estimated in excess of $20 million.

Warren Harding was one of the visitors who arrived the very next day in New York City. He had come to New York to deliver the official notification of the nomination of the Republican convention to Charles Evans Hughes (a tradition known as "Notification Day") in a ceremony scheduled to take place that night at Carnegie Hall. Harding told Scobey he expected Florence to be with him on the trip, now that she was completely recovered from her winter illness.[27] Once again Harding had been asked to assume a place of prominence among the Republicans. The *Times* noted: "The only two speeches made will be one by United States Senator Harding of Ohio, Chairman of the Notification Committee, and the speech of acceptance by Mr. Hughes, which the entire country has been waiting for."[28]

Harding would have read in the *New York Times* that day not only of Black Tom but of the growing list of unexplained explosions in munitions and chemical plants all across the United States and Canada.[29] The initial reaction to the

Black Tom explosion was that it was an "accident." The owners of the piers and warehouses were charged with criminal violations of laws that prohibited the overnight storage of explosives near a population center like Jersey City, but with an election coming up even A. Bruce Bielaski of the Bureau of Investigation was reluctant to offend German Americans by mentioning the likelihood of sabotage. "All I can say at this time," he told anxious reporters of the investigation initiated by the Department of Justice, "is that we have received a preliminary report from one of our agent in New York. . . . Our investigator there seems to think that the explosion was an accident."[30]

Witnesses in postwar hearings before a commission set up to investigate Black Tom and other explosions pointed to a German safe house at 123 West Fiftieth Street in New York City as the center of German espionage in the area[31] Diplomats and sea captains visited regularly, and according to the witnesses, the Black Tom explosion was carefully planned there.

Charles Evans Hughes left his summer residence in Bridgehampton, Long Island, early Monday, traveling by train to Republican headquarters in New York City for all-day meetings.[32] Hughes's speech at Carnegie Hall was too long, especially given the heat of that night (it was one of the year's hottest days, causing three deaths and heat prostration across the city).[33] Harding kept his remarks mercifully short. "The convention uttered the principles of a confident, determined, reunited, and enthusiastic Republican Party, which turns to you in highest respect and trust as a nominee best typifying the party's purposes and people's desires," he told Hughes in front of the standing-room-only audience, including T.R. who sat in a box with his wife, their son, Ted, and Ted's wife, Eleanor.[34] Most of Hughes's speech criticized the Wilson administration's vacillating policies in Mexico. Hughes knew that Roosevelt's jingoism and harsh anti-German statements were harmful to the Republican chances in the fall, and he stayed away from comments that would alienate German Americans and many who wanted to stay out of the war.

The fear of alienating German Americans would give way to open hostility once the United States entered the war, and everything German would be seen in a different light. Whereas the arrival of *U-Deutschland* was generally acclaimed in America in the summer of 1916, when it came time to probe the activities of the Phillipses in 1918, the investigators and members of the American Protective League would find sinister significance in the facts that (1) Isabelle Phillips seemed to be engaged to a Pickhardt; and (2) the Pickhardts were known to have made one of the major purchases, possibly half, of the dyestuffs brought over by *U-Deutschland*.[35]

CHAPTER 31

"I Learned to Love with You"

"You ask me what the feeling is on the political situation," Warren Harding wrote to Ed Scobey on Tuesday, August 15. "I think the feeling is good, particularly regarding the far western states and the eastern states. I do not think that Indiana looks as promising as many Republicans would wish, but generally the Republicans are quite confident of winning the campaign."[1]

Harding had reason to feel some optimism, despite his personal beliefs that Hughes was not a very magnetic candidate and that his campaign manager, William R. Wilcox, was "not a very strong man to direct the campaign."[2] Wilson had won four years earlier only because the Republicans had split into two factions, and at least nominally that problem had been patched up. The East looked solidly Republican and the West seemed to be leaning that way. The Midwest, with all its German Americans, was up for grabs. The question was whether Wilson would correctly gauge American opinion as being largely noninterventionist. The president gradually brought out his peace theme, tentatively at first, and then it became *the* issue of campaign. A vote for Hughes was a vote for war. Theodore Roosevelt's militaristic shadow would follow and ultimately haunt the Hughes campaign. "If Hughes is defeated," Ambassador von Bernstorff cabled Berlin, "he can thank Roosevelt. The average American is and remains pacifist."[3]

Harding's optimism about politics was not shared in his private life. Carrie continued to disappoint him. The day before he wrote Scobey, he had started a letter to her, telling her of how saddened he was ("the worst in my life") that she had not come East to meet with him. They had met briefly, somewhere, on Monday, August 7, and he was desperate to see her again. "I wanted you. Somehow I expected it, though, frankly, I had no good reason for doing so. Especially when the weather changed I felt sure you would come, and wished it more than ever. I kept myself in reach of the 'phone Thursday, Friday and Saturday, thinking and wishing and half-believing there would be a call from Cleveland. I had everything planned, and I *prayed* you would come."[4]

He had gone to his Senate office on Sunday morning, August 13, in the hope that he would find a note from her. "I went to the office at 10 A. M. feeling sure there would be a note, and was determined to call you up if I should find none." There was indeed a note waiting for him, but not what he had wished for. After reading it, he knew her coming was "all out of the possibilities." He was dejected and wrote that, given her feelings, it was better that they not meet. He did not want to react immediately, saying he would need some time to think "deliberately" before responding fully to her letter.

Jim Phillips had written him twice from New York, and Harding did not know what to make of it. "Pray do not mention, but it has made me wonder," he wrote of Jim's letters. "Am answering, anyhow, so he will know I am here. Remember, you must not mention this, but it struck me as strange."

He told her that he intended to be back in New York the following week on August 23. "That is the anniversary of August 23, 1905," he wrote, "and I had dreamed of celebrating it at Le Marquis. It would have been so fitting, if all were well. It would take the whole twenty-four hours to say all I wish and demonstrate the undying and unchanging quality of the love I avowed eleven years ago." Then he stopped himself. "Enough now—I have written more than I intended. I shall write at greater length and will post when I feel I have said it as I wish you to understand it."[5]

But he clearly was obsessing over her. Despite his pledge to allow time and space before responding to her, he could not let a day pass before he was again writing her. On Tuesday, August 15, after three failed attempts (he tore "to small bits" his first three efforts at writing), he began a letter that he would complete over the following four days, in between "scores of interruptions," eventually filling up forty highly emotional pages.

At week's end he composed a cover letter with the forty-page missive and sent both, hoping they would reach her in time for their August 23 anniversary date.[6] "The following pages have been scratched at various hours on different days," he wrote in the cover letter. "Some lines will not please you, they may annoy or anger, but you asked me to be frank. I have been. If you grow offended and decide not to finish, please destroy, and assure me of that fact."[7]

He started his long letter with the premise that he had lost her, he knew it. "My chief request, my big sorrow is that your love has flown," he wrote. "You write it, you say so, you enact it, therefore I must believe." And he could trace when it all began to unravel:

> *L*ooking back now, with my vision cleared a bit, I can recall the turn of the tide when you were in Europe. I think I once possessed the intuition which could manifest it. But I blindly hoped on, nevertheless. The R—[Robinson] correspondence and my recollections of what you had written me from Europe concerning him ought to have warned me, *and did warn me momentarily, and put more bitterness in my cup*—in our cup—*than* any one thing *that ever happened. Finally, I argued that you need never have told me, and I was* fairly cured *when* he *came. A sane man could have construed that coming, but I loved enough to be* mad, *and* half-blind *and know a* fool's self-satisfaction *and* consuming egotism. *I* might have seen *but would not.*

He wondered if all her disclosures about Robinson were simply her way of testing him. Then again he had begun to question if things she said—and those she left unsaid—were her ways of trying to deliberately destroy their relationship.[8] When they last met on August 7, as they embraced, she said something that left him unhinged. "You said, a week ago Monday, *not in anger, but deliberately, even between kisses,* that 'the *only reason you hadn't given yourself to any one was that you had not met an agreeable person for such bestowal.*'"[9]

"God!" he exclaimed. "I thought my ears would burst with that smarting blow."

That was it—the statement that set him afire. "I'll not recite the varied and horrifying trains of thought that frank statement started," he continued. "I wished that God might strike me dead, not alone to spare my grief, but to punish me for my part in making a reckless woman of one so good and pure as I believe you to have been when I came into your life!"[10]

He admitted that he had known temptation and that in spite of it he had remained exclusive to her. "I know the 'agreeable' person always appears," he wrote. "I know in pique or anger or disappointment there comes some one who momentarily seems agreeable, though he may be loathed later on. I know something of the inclinations of desperate moments, and having heard you say *that*—I wonder, and ponder and wonder anew, and am a lover adrift in an awful storm, praying for calm and groping to find it. No wonder I became a barbaric madman, and frightened you. I was mad—insane. I am not sure I am fully recovered, either."[11]

This was the reason he was so upset that she did not come East. He could not get over this revealing statement. "Thinking *more soberly* now," he wrote, "I am convinced *we ought never meet* since you feel that way. The halo is darkened. The priceless spirit, the ineffable exclusiveness and anointing sweetness and purity *in thought* at least is gone. How can I worship now?"

And he had worshipped, he said. She was the one, the "*soul* and *inspiration* and *compensation* of *the best years of my life.* Mind you, I am confessing my madness." But he could not help it—she was his great love:

> *It made* me live *and* know an added *joy in living. It made me* do, *to be more worth while to you. Perhaps you think, indeed you have said, that I have loved to be* gratified. Pray never believe that. *A mere passion could be gratified as readily as you command praise and admiration. I know whereof I speak. I have walked where most men meet temptation. But I know no passion* except for you, because I love you. *Impassioned love for you is an expression of the soul of reverent love, and the joy of it has been the miracle that* only real love *knows*. It has been enough for me, *that is—I have wished no other, though I could delight in a hundred times* more of it with you, *but it has* not satisfied you—*not half. Believe me, I am* not *ugly,* nor fault-finding. *You can't help it,* no handsome woman can. *You require the admiration and association of men. You prefer the tribute before the world to the secret worship.* I don't blame you. *It is your nature.* I wish I could offer the open tribute. *I might not wholly win you, but I'd like to be in the game, if circumstance permitted me to give my attentions and reverences and admirations as a man ordinarily may show the best of his heart. I'd win you or* make a miserably hard task for any one else *to do it.*[12]

Her complaint, he repeated, was that she could "be put aside and taken up again at will."[13] Not with him, he protested. "I never sought to put aside, but have always sought to take up and crush you to my heart and hold you there."

Then he came to what he understood to be the main question she wanted answered, in truth and frankness. It was simple: what did he intend to do?[14]

He said he knew he had been loyal—"a lover's loyalty"—so that could not be what she meant. His answer, therefore, was equally simple: "I mean to go on loving you, not because I choose to, because I would be happier if I did not. *But I'll go on loving you*—worshipping sometimes—*wanting you always—craving you often*—because I can't help it. It has never been otherwise."[15]

He said he lamented his coming into her life—for her sake. But he felt no regret for himself, though he too had suffered much. "But I know a rapture demands its compensating pain," he wrote, "and I'll willingly suffer all that I owe, for the rapture I have known." It had been eleven years since he had first declared his love for her. "Recalling the great revealment of eleven years ago, I am going to write now, deliberately, reflectively, honestly, I love a hundred times more now than then. I learned to love *with you.* I know something of the immeasurable feelings, the inexpressible soul. I admire more, I adore more, I worship more, I hunger more, I thirst more. Strange words to be writing the woman who declares she does not love, and proclaims one love as good as another. Yet I write it, because it is so."[16]

As he wrote, he dodged appointments and turned away visitors, but he was a man possessed, determined to get it all out, once and for all. "You see," he wrote on Saturday morning, August 19, "I got to write less than five lines yesterday though I started at 11 a.m. It was a busy day for me. I offended a number of people by being unable to see them—one from so far away as Oklahoma. There are days of slavery in the public service more exacting than any known in private life."[17]

On Saturday, he wrote out thirteen dense pages, completing what seemed "like a hard letter to conclude."[18] He was determined to get her the letter by August 23, the anniversary of his declaration of love.

He addressed in detail her continuing complaint about him staying in his marriage. While she thought it was a matter of choice for him, he felt otherwise. His situation was different from hers with Jim. "You forget health conditions," he wrote of Florence's recurring illnesses. "You pooh pooh them, but I dare not write what I am professionally told, not alone by one whose judgment you doubt [likely referring to Dr. Sawyer], but by others—including those here [in Washington]." If he left Florence, two things could happen: She could again fall sick, and the community would never forgive him for abandoning her; or, if well, she would seek revenge against Carrie in ways he thought would be catastrophic.

He asked her to really think of the consequences of a break with Florence. "You say no break would come," he wrote. "There is your error. It has been near more than once, and I have sought seemliness for your sake—and my sake—and *all our sakes.* Because, *just as sure as fate,* once a break comes, an insanely jealous woman who believes you robbed her of a husband's love—though you received rather than robbed, would seek vengeance against you. Once the fire started we would be consumed. Once aroused you would have a real demon to deal with on your side and I shudder to contemplate all the possible results." Nor was he thinking of his Senate seat. "I could simply forfeit that without inconsolable grief," he insisted. "But all I have, all I could rely on to do for you and yours, is of a kind that open scandal would ruin, and we should face an awful situation. I *must* think of these things—I owe that same consideration to you, and you ought to think of them." He reminded Carrie that she herself had commented on what she thought was a tendency toward insanity in Florence's family. "If you have correctly pointed out a family danger of insanity, recall the added danger in dealing with one such. Surely you have not counted the possible cost of unheeding action."[19]

He said he continued to hope to restore relations between Carrie and Florence. "You haven't helped," he chided her. "You have said some things and they have been repeated. You are not tactful. This is not a criticism. I merely record a contributing factor to the difficulty I encounter. You say you speak as you think. But it is not always wise. It would be better not to do it."[20]

Misunderstanding built on misunderstanding.

He concluded this letter by asking her to destroy it. "Such a letter is a peril," he cautioned. "I know and ought not send it. I endanger you, and no sane man ever pens such a missive. But no sane man ever loves as I do." Referring to a time when she gave him a package of all the letters he had written to her, and his later return of that package to her, he wrote: "I realize that you have a package which would be sufficient to hang me, figuratively, to justify my being shot literally, and involve and ruin us all. But I do not regret or fear. I always felt I was writing to my Lady of Quality, who could be sane when sanity is needed, and when I returned a package to you I added new proof to my trust in your caution and wisdom. But do please destroy for your own sake. It is risk enough to trust the mails in sending."[21]

Having unburdened himself with his long letter, he returned to the political campaign. He was dispatched to Maine in the first two weeks of September to speak on behalf of Republicans as part of the party's strategy to make a good showing in the state's early elections. The statewide elections in Maine were held in September (because of weather and an early harvest season) and its results were seen as a bellwether for the national elections. "As Maine goes, so goes the nation," was the slogan. More often than not, the country seemed to follow the Maine trend. As a consequence, every four years the major parties expended considerable effort in trying to win in Maine.

The Republicans took Maine that September. Scobey wrote to Harding congratulating him for his role in the victory. "Now since you have been on the stump and helped carry Maine," he wrote, "kindly advise what you think of the outlook in general. About all the news we get down here is democratic 'inspired' stuff, and they try to make us all believe Hughes' campaign is a failure."[22]

In the White House, Woodrow Wilson, too, wondered what it all meant. Certainly the Maine results were disturbing. Wilson's concentration on winning caused him to put off a secret German request that he actively mediate an end to the war. This was a missed opportunity, but Wilson had to ensure his political survival before he could think about saving the world.

CHAPTER 32

"No, This Makes Me Too Promiscuous"

T he week after Harding was in New York on the anniversary date of August 23, a seemingly obscure article appeared on the fourth page of the *New York Times,* announcing the promotion of Paul von Hindenburg to chief of the General Staff of the German Army.[1] Hindenburg, the old field marshal, was the hero of pivotal battles against the Russian armies on the Eastern Front. His ascension to power was a sign that reactionaries were making headway with the kaiser. Hindenburg's predecessor, Erich von Falkenhayn, fell from favor when his campaign to "bleed the French white" at Verdun failed.

Making matters worse, Romania entered the war against Germany on August 27.[2] Romania had been ruled by kings of the House of Hohenzollern since 1866, so its entry into the war against Germany was personally devastating to Wilhelm and worrisome to the German high command. By contrast, the Allies saw Romania's entry on their side as clear evidence that "the fortunes of the Teutonic powers are ebbing."[3]

"The opinion of those best informed here," a *New York Times* correspondent wrote from London on August 30, "is that the true measure of the effect which Rumania's entry into the war has had upon the German higher councils is shown by the removal of General von Falkenhayn and appointment of von Hindenburg as Chief of Staff." Hindenburg brought with him Major General Erich Ludendorff, his partner in the Russian campaigns and an outspoken foe of von Falkenhayn. The selection of Hindenburg was seen as a positive development by those within the German military who had been advocating for the resumption of unrestricted submarine warfare. Germany's chancellor, Theobald von Bethmann-Hollweg, did not share this view. He was a moderate on the subject, and he opposed the resumption of all-out submarine warfare.[4]

Behind-the-scenes attempts by the Germans to arouse Wilson to intervene before the hawks took over came to naught. So unsure was Wilson of his reelection that he wrote out a note to his secretary of state, Robert Lansing, to be delivered on election day, advising that if Hughes was elected, Lansing should resign, and Wilson would appoint Hughes as secretary of state. Then Wilson and Vice President Marshall would resign immediately. Under the Constitution's order of succession and the law in effect at that time, the secretary of state would become president of the United States. Thus Hughes would not need to wait another four months (until March 4, 1917) to take office.[5] Wilson thought the serious and fluid state of affairs in the world made this unprecedented step necessary. "Such a situation would be fraught with the gravest dangers," Wilson wrote of his potential defeat in his wax-sealed letter. "The direction of the foreign policy of the government would in effect have been taken out of my hands and yet its new definition would be impossible until March."[6]

Warren Harding traveled that fall in support of Hughes, finding his way to Wyoming and Montana to make speeches for the Republican nominee.[7] In an undated fragment of a letter to Carrie from the Plains Hotel in Cheyenne, he wrote: "We are a mile and a quarter above sea level here," he wrote her, "and I feel it. It was nearly so high as Butte, Pocatello, and Ogden. Makes it difficult to sleep—it stimulates."[8] The campaign seemed to lack inspiration for Harding. "In spite of the interesting places, the trip is tiresome, exceedingly so," he wrote. "But there is *constant* work and *constant* thought," he signaled her in their code.

The election turned out to be one of the closest in American history. On election night, November 7, Charles Evans Hughes went to bed firmly believing that he had won the presidency. He carried most of the major states in the East in landslides, and the Midwestern states, except for Ohio, were trending his way. In the middle of the night, though, the results in Western states began to shift toward Wilson. By the next morning, the election was still too close to call, though several major newspapers named Hughes the winner. The important states in doubt were New Mexico and California. It took several more days for the results to become known, but Wilson won California by less than 4,000 votes. Hughes did not officially concede until November 22. "It was a little moth-eaten when it got here," Wilson said of Hughes's concession note, "but quite legible."[9]

Ohio stood out in the Midwest as a Democratic stronghold. Wilson carried the state by almost 90,000 votes, and Democrat James Middleton Cox was returned to the governor's office, defeating his Republican opponent Governor Willis by 6,600 votes.[10] Harding attributed the Ohio result to "the farmer republican, who voted for Wilson just as the farmers did in Kansas, and we had the radical laboring forces throughout the state which gave their support to Wilson because of his advocacy of the eight hour day."[11] Harding was willing to give Wilson his due. He believed that Wilson would no longer be eligible to run (not yet by constitutional proscription but following to a longtime tradition that a president would serve only two terms), "he will be a better president." Moreover, seeing the groundswell for the eight-hour day, Harding officially switched his position. "It may shock you to know," he wrote Scobey, "but I mean to translate the vote of the country into an actual eight hour day. The people have voted strongly for such a thing and I propose to be an active participant in bringing it about."[12]

He sarcastically commented on the consequences of his own change of mind, writing Scobey: "I suppose as soon as the eight hour day is established, the agitators who make their living through agitation, will immediately get busy on a six hour day. If the reformation goes far enough, nobody will have to work at all. Then we can let God do it."[13]

Harding did not despair of future Republican success in Ohio. He saw the election result as peculiar to circumstances and rectifiable. "We are not in a bad way in Ohio," he wrote Scobey in early December, "though we have been most thoroughly licked." He pointed a finger specifically at Roosevelt, knowing his militarism and anti-German stance cost votes in Ohio, for the majority of Ohio German Americans were Republicans. "Most of the Progressives came back to the party, but the farmers and radical laborites voted strongly against us and Col. Roosevelt succeeded in driving away the German vote which we had expected to save the situation."

He did not want to engage in post elections what-ifs or recriminations against Hughes. "It is of very little value to discuss the weakness of Mr. Hughes as a candidate," he wrote Scobey. "The impression is very general here as well as in Ohio that he would have fared much better had he gone to his summer residence after the speech of notification and acceptance and remained there and retained the halo about his head which came on his exceptional nomination."

❧

Around this time, Carrie consulted a lawyer in Columbus for some reason. A three-page follow-up letter written by the lawyer, dated Saturday, November 18, was kept among Carrie's collection of Harding letters. The lawyer's letter was written with such care that little is expressly stated: the lawyer is not identified, the parties involved in the dispute are not identified by name, and the actual dispute is not stated. It was as if the lawyer worried the letter might reach hostile hands.[14]

Yet there are some clues about why she conferred with the attorney. First, Carrie kept the letter with the Harding letters, which leads one to infer that it was about their relationship. Second, the attorney's letter refers to "four people interested most": Carrie and her "consort" and an unidentified woman and her "consort." The unidentified woman is identified as a wealthy woman and her husband as someone who has a "very public life." The lawyer does mention Isabelle, sending his "warmest regards for both you and my love to dear Isabelle, who surely is so charming that no one would wish to do anything that would injure her youthful felicity." This statement suggests that the lawyer knew Carrie and Isabelle before the consultation, that Isabelle participated in the interview with the lawyer, or perhaps both.

The "subject matter or the bone of contention," according to the attorney's letter, was "of such a delicate nature, and from its very nature, it is in a field by itself, so that the ordinary standards of weighing the different interests of the four involved is entirely different from that of weighing property rights or settling ordinary disputes." But, though it is not expressed, some accusation against Carrie was of such an "infamous charge" that it amounted to criminal libel, "punishable in the penitentiary, as everyone knows." The unidentified woman who made the accusation had an "informer," whom she refused to identify or produce. It also appears that the offensive statements were made more than a year earlier, since the lawyer advised that a civil action on the charge could no longer be brought in court because more than a year had passed since the words were uttered. Carrie's only recourse was to the criminal courts. "To establish criminal libel," the attorney wrote, "it means evidence that is convincing beyond a reasonable doubt, and it would be simply your word against her word, and she would have to be defended by her husband, his friends, and all her wealth."

Pulling this evidence together, it seems likely that Carrie was offended by some charge or gossip made public by Florence Harding in Marion. It is not clear whether Florence's "informer" told her of the adultery or that Carrie was a German operative, or something else altogether. But given that the interested parties are two couples, one could guess that adultery was the charge.

What is clear is that Carrie forced a showdown. The lawyer wrote: "[I] have come to the present tentative conclusion, at least, that you not only were given abundance of ground to be offended and that you were justified in calling the interested parties promptly and then and there forcing the issue, which was perhaps the result of womanly intuition, rather than of long reflection as men should have done." According to Carrie's version, as repeated by the lawyer, "[t]here was no countermove the other party could make except to play the act of the burglar when caught under the bed, claiming he did not know where he was and had no evil intent, etc."

Carrie told the lawyer that the accusing woman was shamed and challenged by Carrie's presentation of the facts. "Up to that point, the other party was thoroughly cowed and humiliated and your line of conduct was commendable and showed wisdom and tact and I cannot understand how she has ever been able to counteract or make a return play to the searching review you gave the whole matter promptly and speedily before the people most interested." Carrie's "searching review" was, again according to her, "approved by the other two, whom you called in."

The lawyer, after several days of careful thought and bringing his "very best judgment and experience in human controversies," concluded that her best course was to do nothing further. Taking official action would make the matter more public than it was, and "publicity in a matter of this nature is worse than the disease." More, Carrie's confrontation seems to have intimidated her accuser and stopped further whispering. "As it now stands, you have three against one, and she is suffering the agonies of the damned by reason thereof. No doubt, she is being treated by her husband with proper indignation, but the minute the public enters into it by outside people, his very public life compels him to make a semblance of loyalty and that commits him, at least, publicly to her side of the case and against yours, whatever he may say privately."

The attorney visit is not mentioned in any of Harding's letters, so it seems apparent that Carrie weighed her options and took the lawyer's advice.

On November 29 Carrie mailed a letter to Warren in Washington, which he found on his Senate desk the day after Thanksgiving. Once again she was in New York. They had seen each other sometime before she wrote, when she came to Washington, and they apparently were intimate. "Am so glad you had a happy day in W—," he wrote her on the morning of December 1. "You rejoiced me and I dwell in bliss, though I was fearfully disappointed in myself. You never disappoint at the alter [*sic*] of love. Nothing destroys your matchless fascination. You are beyond compare."[15]

He reported to her that he and Florence had moved into a new home on Wyoming Avenue in Washington and that he spent an "inordinately dull Thanksgiving" in his new "topsy-turvy house" and had gone to a hotel for Thanksgiving dinner.[16] He enjoyed reconnecting with his fellow senators, though some had not been reelected. "It is amusing," he wrote, "to greet the fellows on their return—some coming with the glow of victory, some in the depths of disappointment. There are some individual defeats which are deeply felt."[17]

"I could almost swear I saw you and Isabelle in the moving pictures of the Army-Navy game—though it may have been my ready imagination," he added.[18] He did not seem surprised that the two women would have been at the football game. Perhaps he knew at this point of the relationship between Isabelle and the naval officer Adolf Pickhardt.

Harding's December 1 letter to Carrie seemed to represent a renewal of sorts of their association. But he insisted she must be honest with him about other relationships in order for them to start over on a "firm foundation." He went on at length about an Italian man named Roscano, whom Carrie and Isabelle had met in their travels in Europe. Harding recalled Isabelle innocently mentioning in the presence of her father and Harding that Roscano had "spent evenings in the Phillips' room" and that he had offered Isabelle and Carrie the use of his villa in Italy.[19] He even remembered talk of Roscano giving Carrie unmounted jewels. And all of it made him wonder anew if he had made Carrie a wanton. He dredged up a time after she returned from Europe when they were kissing and she suddenly "broke away and exclaimed, 'No, this makes me too promiscuous!'"[20]

So he wanted the "absolute, frank truth," he wrote her. "I'd rather correct misunderstandings and tear out and cast aside the blunders," he wrote, "than try to build in doubt. I dislike to write these things, but you said: it is better to have it out, and be frank and be understood so I am writing from the depths of my heart."

After it all, he still believed that their "day of fruition must come." He still looked to a future time when they could be together. "It requires vast patience to thwart the fates in a world which worships convention, even though the worship is an outward form and belies the inner conscience."[21]

For the moment, Carrie seemed to be back in a courting mode. She hinted in her note that she wanted to come to Washington on her way back from New York "for a brief meeting."

"I'd love it," Warren wrote. "But I'm ashamed to make you do the traveling and experience all the boredom for so little pleasure as I can afford. I write truly. I have thought of my selfishness until I am ashamed. I'd like once to introduce you to a season of love as a lover ought to bestow it."[22]

He wished her a "dandy time" in New York. "You do so enjoy the N. Y. whirl—and I am glad, because I rejoice to see you so happy."[23]

CHAPTER 33

"Today We Raise the Question of Peace"

The clock was ticking. Two armed merchantmen, the *Marina* and the *Arabia*, were sunk by U-boats without prior warning at the end of October and the beginning of November just as the election season in the United States was winding up. Wilson did not want to elevate these isolated events to the next level of diplomatic challenge, especially since both vessels were armed. Now that he had been reelected, incidents like these prompted him to renew his efforts to try to negotiate an end to the war. His biggest problem was that the Imperial Chancellor of Germany, Theobald von Bethmann-Hollweg, was almost out of time. The German military command increased pressure on the kaiser to reopen full submarine warfare. The British did not help matters when they instituted a policy of arming as many merchant ships as they could and thereafter declaring it was their policy to destroy all German submarines on sight.[1] The French also ordered their merchant ships to take aggressive action against German submarines. The German high command argued with the kaiser that these moves made it mandatory that Germany respond with all-out submarine warfare.

Bethmann-Hollweg hoped to give Wilson his opportunity, sending conciliatory notes on the *Marina* and *Arabia* and privately encouraging the president to take the initiative on peace negotiations.[2] But the matter was urgent, the chancellor warned. If much more time passed, all sides would need to make preparations for spring offensives, and then the military would gain the upper hand. On December 2 the kaiser, at Bethmann-Hollweg's suggestion, ordered submarine commanders to avoid any further incidents like the *Marina* and the *Arabia* while peace options were being explored.[3] As Ambassador von Bernstorff told Colonel House in a late November meeting, "peace was on the floor waiting to be picked up."[4]

Wilson worked on a peace note but faced opposition within his administration. Secretary of State Lansing worried that a U.S. peace proposal might be accepted by the Central Powers and rejected by the Allies, leaving the United States in a predicament. If the Germans found Wilson's peace ideas acceptable, would the United States really turn its back on the Allies and support the Germans? It was unthinkable to Lansing, who believed the war had become one about democracy against autocracy. At all costs, the United States needed to support England and France, not only because they were the country's main trading partners and debtors but also because it was in the national interests of the United States to have democracies dominate the postwar world. Democracy, Lansing thought, was the only sure guarantee of a lasting peace. Colonel House had similar thoughts. The extended internal debate, along with attention that had to be paid to nagging domestic issues, caused Wilson to delay in completing his peace note.[5]

The postponement was costly; the Germans beat the United States to the punch. On December 12 Chancellor Bethmann-Hollweg appeared before the German Reichstag, its parliament, to announce, to thunderous applause, that Germany was prepared to end the war. The country had fought the war for defensive purposes only, he said, and though his nation had proven its invincibility through the test of arms, it had no interest in annihilating its enemies. As he spoke, Germany was in fact experiencing some military successes: It had halted the Somme offensive and defeated Romania. Bethmann-Hollweg had convinced the kaiser that this moment of strength was the best time for Germany to risk a peace overture. If the effort was rebuffed, Germany could argue it had no choice but to start up all-out submarine warfare, and in that event the United States might be persuaded to stay out of the war. Bethmann-Hollweg also had run out of patience with the U.S. president and was not convinced that he would ever launch a peace initiative. Chief of Staff Hindenburg and General Ludendorff hotly opposed Bethmann-Hollweg and insisted that if his peace proposal failed, they must be given carte blanche to begin unrestricted submarine warfare immediately. Kaiser Wilhelm agreed to give the chancellor's idea a chance, but he agreed with his top military men that if the peace initiative failed, ruthless submarine warfare needed to commence without further delay.

"Today," Bethmann-Hollweg told the Reichstag, "we raise the question of peace, which is a question of humanity."[6]

Over the next few weeks, the Allies—Russia, England, and France—all would reject the German offer of a settlement. They smelled a double deal, believing it was a strategy to set up the return of unrestricted submarine warfare. Many of these Allied leaders also felt that they had to defeat Germany militarily before discussing peace terms.

In response, Wilson frantically finished his own peace note, hoping to issue it before anti-peace sentiment hardened in the capitals of Europe. He had it sent by wire to the American diplomatic embassies in Europe on December 20. The president made it clear that the note was not connected to the German initiative, though the timing obviously made it seem as if it were. Wilson's diplomatic overture requested that the belligerents on all sides state the terms under which they would stop fighting and work toward peace. Unfortunately, Wilson made the singular blunder of equating the war aims of the Allies with those of the Central Powers. "[The President] takes the liberty," the note read, "of calling attention to the fact that the objects, which the statesmen of the belligerents on both sides have in mind in this war, are virtually the same, as stated in the general terms to their own people and the world." This statement caused the Allies, especially England, to explode in protest.

It also stirred up a severe reaction in some hawkish circles within the United States. Theodore Roosevelt, breaking his self-imposed silence from the day before the election, issued a statement, lashing out against Wilson and calling the note "profoundly immoral" in likening the war objectives of all the belligerents. He even charged that the administration had leaked information about the note to investors who profited in the stock market from foreknowledge.[7] The rhetoric was so bitter that even the normally Theodore-friendly *New York Times* called it "Mr. Roosevelt at his worst."[8]

Wilson's own secretary of state worked against the note's success. Robert Lansing, without discussing the matter with Wilson, caused a furor the day after the note became public by issuing his own statement. His statement read that the United States was "drawing nearer the verge of war ourselves, and therefore we are entitled to know exactly what each belligerent seeks, in order that we may regulate our conduct in the future." His spin that the United States was on "the verge of war" caused a panic on Wall Street.[9] In the circumstances, it could only mean war against Germany, something Lansing believed should happen.

Wilson summoned Lansing to the White House and insisted that he immediately publish a correction.[10] "I learned from several quarters that a wrong impression was made by the statement which I made this morning," Lansing wrote the same day, "and I wish to correct that impression."[11] He said he did not mean to suggest that "the Government was considering any change in its policy of neutrality" and that it was "needless to say that I am unreservedly in support" of the president's call to the belligerents to state their terms of peace.

Wilson's most important biographer Arthur Link has suggested that Lansing in fact did aim to sabotage the president's peace efforts. As further proof, he points to the fact that Lansing privately met with the ambassadors of France and Britain over the next few days to assure them that Wilson's preferences lay with the democracies and that the United States would "deal only with a reformed and democratized Reich."[12] Link concluded from the evidence "that the Secretary of State was maneuvering to promote American intervention on the Allied side."[13]

Harding's only substantive public statement at this time was that he had hoped that "the first serious peace suggestions would contain a proposal for disarmament."[14] History would all but forget that as president Harding oversaw the first successful worldwide disarmament conference, the so-called Washington Naval Conference. He was nothing if not consistent in his public pronouncements. He did tell some Ohio reporters that he would avoid mediation by the United States at this point. "The fellow who tries too soon to bring about peace between combatants often gets swatted himself," he remarked.[15]

At this moment, Theodore Roosevelt reached out to Harding and asked that they meet in New York. Whether Roosevelt was smoothing feathers looking toward the 1920 election or simply taking Harding's measure as a rising power in the Republican Party, Harding was impressed with his private meeting. "I went over at his request," he wrote Scobey, "and was very glad to have the meeting, and found it a very satisfactory one." He was surprised how much he liked the Colonel. "He made a rather more favorable impression on me than I have ever had heretofore, but I cannot say as to what impression I left with him. My best guess is that the Colonel is looking forward to a candidacy in 1920, and felt that it might not be unwise to be on friendly terms with me. . . . The most enjoyable part of the interview was the revelation of his thorough understanding of the republican members of the Senate," he wrote. "He had the Progressives down to an ant's heel, called one of them an S.O.B. and suggested that another was impossible."[16]

The year 1916 ended with Harding still in demand as a speaker. "I do not know whether my case is different from other members of the Senate," he wrote to Scobey, "but I do know that invitations for speeches average one or two every day, and if one should bring himself to accept these invitations he could have no time for his official business or his attendance at the Senate."[17]

"Such is human nature when one is hopelessly in love," Harding wrote to Carrie on January 11, 1917, of his continuing obsession with her.[18] "Perhaps I should invoke the scriptural reminders for my comfort—those whom he loves he chastens—etc. But it is a fact, I live for a letter every day—am disappointed if none comes, and rejoice when even a tiny note arrives, though it contains only a bit of criticism or reproach." He had written her a New Year's letter filled with "reverie" and in "grateful recollection" of New Year's past, but he destroyed it because it became stale before he felt free to post it. "I hesitated to mail because I had written without restraint," he wrote, "and ought not do it, when there is a single doubt about prompt and safe delivery."[19] She had written him twice in the first days of 1917, apparently keeping close tabs on him.

He reported that he was keeping his promise to refrain from having visitors or entertaining at his Washington home. Although he was "a little embarrassed and may seem the queer one" as a result, he maintained he was acting "exactly as agreed." He was not complaining. He found this "new order" freeing, allowing him to spend more time out in Washington social life or going to the theater. "I am broadening," he told her, "I am seeing more, and experiencing real diversion." He said he had become "such a recluse that I was frazzled and a real black number."

Her letters were less about love and more about the war and the recent peace initiatives. "You penned me a line about war and peace," he acknowledged. "I am wearied of the talk," he wrote. "There is so much lying and scheming and plotting and conniving here that one doesn't know whom to believe, hardly among his friends. War seems to rend the sincerity of the world." He did not want her to think he was taking an anti-German position by these remarks. "I am not referring to one side or the other. One has to study every utterance, diplomatic or otherwise, because the content is so much hidden. I may not succeed, but I *try* to be fair. The recent diplomacy of the chief executive is suspected on both sides here. I couldn't vote to approve, because I did not know all he knew and I mean to enjoy the full confidences of those I join in sponsorship."[20]

He told her that, at the moment, he was "catching the very devil *by mail* for my attitude on prohibition in the district." The Senate voted on January 9 on the so-called Sheppard Act, making the District of Columbia totally dry. It was the beginning of a wave of laws that would culminate in the Eighteenth Amendment to the Constitution. Wets tried to derail the act by proposing that the matter be put to a vote of the residents of the district. Harding voted for this proposal, consistent with his pledge when he ran for the Senate to submit the question of prohibition to a vote of the people and follow what they wanted. It was an odd stance for one who believed so strongly in representative government, but it allowed him to delicately sidestep an issue that was so explosive with voters. The amendment to the Sheppard Act did not pass, Wilson refused to veto the law, and the district went dry.

"I hope you do not wholly disapprove," he privately wrote to Carrie. "I voted as I said I would when asking for my election and have kept the faith. More, it was ridiculous to vote this cosmopolitan capital dry, where the enforcement is beyond the possibility of expectation. Might as well try to stop trysting at the Willard 'alley' or the Raleigh roof, or liaisons in Baltimore." He knew to expect the "hot fire of criticism" when it came to any vote on a prohibition law, but the storm he faced made him yearn for the day he could retire to a farm, a recurring dream of his.[21]

He said he would trade that farm for a moment of solace with her. "The truth is, I am everlastingly and incurably and abidingly in love with you— involuntarily and unceasingly. I was right—this is the big love, the one that comes and abides, no matter how disappointing or disagreeable it persists in being to you."[22] They had met recently, sometime before the new year— likely the meeting she requested in the December correspondence. It appears he went to New York to see her. "I am thinking of the incomparable fascination and the glory of you as I felt it in a hurried and stolen experience in our last meeting," he wrote. "I came for that, and for that alone, if the truth be written, and felt compensated, though its meagerness was like one tiny ray of light when the *universe* was struggling to be aflame." He underlined universe to transform it into its coded meaning ("all—there are no words, like Montreal").

"All my wishes seem thus meagerly assured, but hope isn't dead and love can be held eternal."

Days before Harding penned this melancholy letter to Carrie, on January 8-9, the military leaders of Germany met with the kaiser for the final showdown on recommencing ruthless submarine warfare. Bethmann-Hollweg came from Berlin but could no longer delay the inevitable. The Allies had rejected his peace offer—the British with terms so onerous that they were guaranteed to be unacceptable—and Wilson's vague note seemed pointless. The Germans thought the Allies were already planning spring offensives, and the kaiser finally relented, ordering unrestricted submarine warfare to begin on February 1. The German military believed that if the submarines could work without restraint, they could bring England to its knees in fewer than six months, cutting off war supplies and food. They knew full well that it meant war with the United States, but they gambled that the great sleeping giant would be unable to mobilize and field forces in time to make a difference. The order signed by the kaiser called for the sinking of all enemy merchantmen without warning.[23]

The Germans were right about the United States being ill prepared to enter the contest with any speed, but they were wrong in concluding that, once in the war, America would not employ all measures to provision England, despite the submarine threat. Moreover, they had overestimated how much damage their submarine fleet could cause to the armada that would sail against it; and they underestimated the effectiveness of antisubmarine measures developed since the start of the war.

President Wilson continued his frenzied backstage negotiations to stop the war. He was still reluctant in his heart to engage America in war, startling Colonel House when he told him that he believed Americans were not willing to go to war even if some Americans were killed on ships heading for Europe.[24] Wilson decided to go beyond his peace note and address the Senate to outline his own thoughts on the terms under which the war could be brought to a conclusion and what the United States would want in return for joining in a league of nations to enforce any future peace.[25]

Thus, on Monday, January 22, at noon, Vice President Marshall rose in the Senate and read a message from President Wilson asking permission to address the body that afternoon. An hour later, Wilson appeared and delivered his "peace without victory" speech. Making his argument for a new world organization to enforce peace, Wilson said, "The question upon which the whole peace and policy of the world depends is this: Is the present war a struggle for a just and secure peace, or only for a new balance of power? If it be only a struggle for a new balance of power, who will guarantee, who can guarantee, the stable equilibrium of the new arrangement? Only a tranquil Europe can be a stable Europe. There must be, not a balance of power, but a community of power; not organized rivalries, but an organized common peace." If both sides meant what they had said—that it was not their intention to crush the other side—then there had to be a peace without victors.[26]

"Victory would mean peace forced upon the loser, a victor's terms imposed upon the vanquished," he argued—prescient words indeed. "It would be accepted in humiliation, under duress, at an intolerable sacrifice, and would leave a sting, a resentment, a bitter memory upon which a peace would rest, not permanently but upon quicksand. Only a peace between equals can last." He was proposing a Monroe Doctrine for the whole world. No nation would extend its influence over any other nation or people. Each nation would be free to find its own way, to determine its own government.

But it was too late. The submarines had been stocked with supplies and food, given their new instructions for all-out attack, and they were already sailing from their bases to points where they would lay in wait, incommunicado.[27]

Scobey was glad to hear of Harding's private meeting with Roosevelt and wondered what might have occurred had the two men been closer before the last convention. "I am sorry this could not have been brought about a year or two ago, and if he had been friendly to you, you might have been the nominee at Chicago, and if you had been, you would have been elected. The women of the West [women had the vote in some western states even prior to the Nineteenth Amendment] would surely have been for you on account of your manly form and scholarly face. Women don't like whiskers [referring to the bearded Hughes]."[28]

Warren seemed to be physically absorbing the momentous events he was witnessing. He had been out of sorts since the start of the year, and his younger brother George's sudden and serious illness put additional weight on his shoulders. George, or Deacon, suffered some attack of "inflammatory rheumatism and heart trouble," according to newspaper accounts, and there was real alarm that his condition might be hopeless.[29] "May be obliged to come any day on account of brother's illness at Columbus," he wrote to Carrie on January 20. "He is the best man I ever knew. More, I am blue myself. Hope doesn't brighten where I most wish it might."

His conclusion: "I am in the depths and will await some ascent."[30]

CHAPTER 34

"I Know You
Are in Rebellion"

At four in the afternoon on Wednesday, January 31, the German ambassador, Johann von Bernstorff, arrived at the State Department to meet with Secretary of State Robert Lansing. Bernstorff's usually sunny disposition was gone. His manner grave, he handed Lansing two notes announcing that unrestricted submarine warfare would begin the next day, February 1. A messenger had been dispatched to New York earlier in the morning to deliver a letter to Colonel House containing Germany's terms for peace. Lansing saw tears in his adversary's eyes as the ambassador solemnly told him, in his perfect English accent, how deeply he regretted this renewal of submarine warfare. Then the ambassador shook Lansing's hand and said good-bye.[1]

Lansing met with the president that night at the White House and recommended an immediate break with Germany. Wilson was shocked by the news, which had come to him earlier in the day from an Associated Press report. He spoke of an idea he had had recently. He thought that the war in Europe now threatened "white civilization" and its domination over the world, and he was coming to believe that the United States had to stay above the fight in order to rebuild a broken Europe after the combatants had exhausted themselves. Lansing wrote: "He said that as this idea had grown upon him he had come to the feeling that he was willing to go to any lengths rather than to have the nation actually in the conflict."[2]

Wilson anguished over what to do. Should he break diplomatic relations immediately or wait for some incident on the high seas to force his hand? Colonel House came to Washington from New York and met most of the day, February 1, with the president. On Friday morning, February 2, Wilson golfed with his wife in Virginia, returned to the White House that afternoon, and met with his cabinet for several hours. The question arose of whether diplomatic relations should be terminated. "He [President Wilson] immediately followed this question with a somewhat startling statement," Secretary of Agriculture David Houston wrote. "He would say frankly that, if he felt that, in order to keep the white race or part of it strong to meet the yellow race—Japan, for instance, in alliance with Russia, dominating China—it was wise to do nothing, he would do nothing, and would submit to anything and any imputation of weakness or cowardice. This was a novel and unexpected angle."[3]

Wilson went to the Senate Office Building that evening and met with a large group of senators, coming, he said, "seeking light." Harding was not among the group. After this conference, the president decided to break diplomatic relations with Germany immediately. The next day, Saturday, February 3, Wilson appeared before a joint session of Congress to announce that all diplomatic relations between the United States and the German Empire were severed. The German ambassador would be given his passport and told to return to Germany, and the American ambassador in Berlin was being called home. Wilson told Congress he still hoped for peace.[4]

On Sunday, February 4, Harding wrote two long letters to Carrie. The first was a public letter, meant for "family consumption." The second was "for you alone, because I love you so much, so genuinely, and so longingly that I must utter it."[5]

He said that the week leading up to the break in diplomatic relations with Germany had been "the hardest week since I have been in Washington." He had had no time at all to write her. The news about his brother Deacon was first on his mind. "On Monday, 29th, I had such distressing news from brother that I was in the depths all day. The reports on Tuesday were better and have grown better daily since. Yesterday the doctor in charge gave a favorable prognosis and I have felt so much better because I do love and revere my brother. I wish I were half so good and worthy."[6]

Compounding his crazy schedule that week, delegates from the National Chamber of Commerce descended on Washington from Tuesday to Saturday. Harding not only met the scores of delegates from Ohio but continued to build his national network of friends, and he was kept busy all week, going to lunches, dinners, and the theater. "Most of them were important people," he wrote Carrie, "many of them had shown me courtesies, and it was good to see them—I was glad—but it took all my time and nearly wore me out. This will explain why I have not written, though I very much wished to and was in the mood."[7]

In his public letter, for Jim's benefit, he wrote that he had been called the week before to Columbus because of George's illness and that he had come through Marion late on Friday, January 26, but had no time to check in with the Phillipses before he returned to Washington. This was a ruse. In fact, he traveled to Pittsburgh on Saturday the twenty-seventh and met with Carrie that night, then went to Columbus to see his brother, returning to Washington from there.

"If I needed it," he wrote Carrie in the private letter, "I was fully *reconsecrated* at Pittsburgh. I was so blessed. I have felt differently ever since. I have pondered it much, and reflected in great deliberation, and I am sure of myself when I say I had rather have your full, loyal and devoted love than any thing else and all else in the world. It is the greatest thing in my life."[8] After their meeting, he wrote that he "journeyed to Col. in such a heaven of happiness. It was not the *most* but the *best* ever. I have dwelt in rejoicing ever since—was so helped, and want you all my very own forever and always."[9]

On international events, Harding's public letter was a warning of sorts to her. "I suppose you are not a little perturbed over the diplomatic break with Germany," he wrote. "Really, I do not see any other course which reasonably might have been adopted. Ruthlessness on the seas to neutral commerce does not harmonize with the advocacy of freedom of the seas on which I thought Germany and the United States might agree. I fear it means war, and pray that it does not." He pointed out that even most of the pro-German members of Congress approved of the break. "I know you are in rebellion, but I think I might say to you that only two men in all the Congress oppose the action thus far taken—though there are many pro-German sympathizers in Congress as earnest as you."

He said he did not expect to modify her "sympathies" and that he hoped armed conflict could be avoided, but if war came, she must put her country first. "I do know there is genuine regret over the possibility of a conflict with the Central Powers," he wrote of the general sentiment in Congress.

"If it does come," he cautioned her, "you will be American first of all." Even if she protested that she could never take such a position, he knew what was in her heart, he wrote. "In spite of your reverence and sympathy and love for Germany (much of which is justified), you are after all an American and ever must be, and you will wish that the anxieties—and great trials, perhaps, will exalt the American soul and spirit." He concluded this public letter paraphrasing from the famous toast given by an early American naval officer, Stephen Decatur. "It is a difficult time for a public servant, it is trying for individuals, but there can be but one answer in the end. 'My Country—May it ever be right! But right or wrong, MY COUNTRY!'"

When the Senate voted a few days later on a resolution introduced by Senator William J. Stone of Missouri supporting the president's break with Germany, Harding was one of seventy-eight senators who voted to endorse Wilson's actions. Five senators opposed.[10]

The day after voting for the Stone resolution, Harding wrote another extended letter to Carrie, this time on Senate Chamber stationery. "This is your reception day," he wrote to her on February 8. Carrie and Isabelle had planned a tea and a dinner in Marion, perhaps a sort of coming-out party for Isabelle. "Just now filed a telegram to I—," Harding wrote, "so you would know I was thinking of you and wishing you well, tho' too far away to send my cards."[11]

"I have your appeal on the international situation," he wrote Carrie of a note she sent on the war issues, "which I was glad to read and found worth while." She had also enclosed a personal card, expressing a message of love. He prized the card, he wrote. Though he wrote that her comments "on the war and over international relations" were not unwelcome, he did not want to engage in a debate with her. He knew the enormity of the situation he faced as a U.S. senator, and he recognized that no one person was capable of discerning the right course. "Much of what you write I very cordially agree with," he conceded. "Some things I do not. Perhaps you are as biased in your reading as you think I am. But I do not exactly say that. I am trying to read both sides, because my duty requires it. On the whole it is a very serious matter with me, because I must vote and be recorded, and help to vote for a hundred millions [the U. S. population] and must answer directly to five millions [Ohio voters]." He could not help but "feel the responsibility, the gravity and am not insensible to my incapacity," he wrote in his typical humility. "But I do not contend with you. It is not wholly because I can not make reply, because on many disputed points I could reply to my own satisfaction. But I can not bring myself into controversy with you. When we are not agreed I prefer to recognize that differences of opinion do exist and am content not to urge my own."[12]

The weight of the times continued to cause great anxiety, bringing him close to nervous exhaustion. "These are trying days here," he wrote, "not alone because of the strain of foreign relations, but the general and insistent pressure of many important things. I feel like a workman with a great load which he is never permitted to put aside, and my nerves are showing the strain. I do so much wish to see you. I need you. You always help so much. *You are the supreme compensation.*"[13]

He then wrote an illuminating and touching piece about his brother's near-death experience, his relief that he was recovering, and the perspective it brought him on the relative importance of his life when compared to his only male sibling, the father of four children:

You must not wear yourself out. You must save your nerves. So must I. Brother's illness was wholly due to overwork and weakened resistance, and he had a desperately narrow escape. He is better, and I am so relieved. It has taken a great load off my mind. I know his merits, his usefulness, and had that family of four children in mind. He must live for them. Of course I'd have been a real brother as best I could, but I couldn't take his place. Oh! It is so good that he is getting better. I could go and it would little matter. Perhaps you would care—of course you would—but generally and specifically it would not much matter, and even you would be better off. And there would be instances of actual rejoicing. But let that all pass, it is not important and less diverting.[14]

With the break in diplomatic relations, the debate in the Wilson administration turned to the idea of "armed neutrality." As a result of the renewal of submarine warfare, the question became whether the United States should allow its merchant ships to be armed with guns to defend against attack. More, could the government install and man defensive armaments on merchant vessels? The economic threat was great. Exports had begun to pile up on American docks, as shipping companies and their crews were unwilling to risk sailing without some protection against hostile fire. It was not an easy question for Wilson; he knew that any increase in violence made it all the more likely the country would be drawn into war. He also was well aware that many Americans, especially in the West, were still for peace at any price.

Over the next few weeks, Harding grew more and more drained and stressed. He wrote Carrie on Saturday, February 10: "I am out of gear myself—don't know just why except that my nerves are getting frazzled. It takes me far into the afternoon each day before I am able to get up steam."[15] A day later on Sunday the eleventh he wrote her twice, once at noon and then started a second letter that evening. He considered these to be St. Valentine's Day messages, meant to be delivered to her by the fourteenth. But he clearly was fighting off some sort of major depression or illness. "How you could comfort me right now. And I do so need it. I am so wistful and need the solace that only you can give. One ought never write except cheerfully, and I'll try not to be too blue, but I am in a doleful rut and need a blessing. I am not sick, but I am not well. Can't define it exactly, except to say 'out of form.' Surely I am no good, and it is a fight to keep from being more blue than indigo."[16]

It was her physical presence he needed so badly. "This is not a man long-ing for passion," he protested, "it isn't really at all. I just want you—your pres-ence, your eyes, your voice, your spirit, and *you, you, you!* I know I should be lifted up into quite another existence."[17] In his most direct reference to the fact that their relationship began with a courtship and did not become inti-mate for three years, he wrote, "It is a very wonderful thing for a beautiful, and fascinating woman to be still more beautiful and still more fascinating after twelve years of love's worshipping and more than eight years of intimate revelation."[18]

That night he began his second letter. This one, as it survives, has pages that are missing or partially clipped. Harding refers to a lunch he had with Sir Gilbert Parker. Parker was a Canadian novelist and member of Parliament who became the head of British propaganda in the United States when the war started.[19] Recognizing that this meeting might irritate Carrie, Warren made sure to comment that he and Sir Gilbert spoke only of characters in his nov-els and that he never raised "a word about the war."

He suspended his writing on Sunday night and the next morning ar-rived at his Senate office and opened a letter from her that caught him off guard. She sent a stinging reproof. Likely upset over his support of the break in relations with Germany, she raised the very topic she knew would drive him crazy. "This a.m. I had your letter (in two parts) which you finished writing on Saturday," he wrote her on Monday, February 12. "I can't exactly tell you its effect on me."[20] He was shocked by its tone and content. She not only filled up her letter with criticism of the American government and him, but she again raised the specter of finding another lover.

His response was acidic, so uncharacteristic for him. "I can find no faults in your criticism of the American government," he wrote, in mocking deri-sion. "It is weak. Our system is wrong, manifestly. There is no national spirit—else you would not write as you do." He tartly remarked on her love of Germany and tied it to her expressions in the past of her desire for a Ger-man lover. "Whatever else betides, I hope to hear your later verdict after your ardent love for Germany has made you the wife of a German patriot in the Fatherland. Recalling some of the observations you penned to me during your early days in Berlin, I have a faith that all inconsistencies will be reconciled. Since you wish such a consummation I am bound to be sufficiently a gentle-man to wish you the realization of your dearest wish."[21]

Just that morning, on his way to the office, he had stopped at a book-store to order "a little package of books as a Valentine remembrance" and purchased a "box of Martha Washington candies to be sent to Isabelle," all to be delivered on the fourteenth. His blissful mood was shattered, though, when he read her letter. "I am at a loss," he replied, "to understand why you arraign me as you do in your last. Surely nothing has been done, nothing has developed, nothing has been undone to justify it. I must assume that it is the abiding hostility—the unchanging dissatisfaction which is ever in your heart. And when you are finished indicting me, you renew the declaration that you would willingly and unhesitatingly give yourself to another. If this was written to distress me, the object is *well* achieved."[22]

He was besieged that week with telegrams and mail and visitors, "all telling me what to do." He was determined to take in all points of view, knowing the stakes, even those that were "disturbing my patience and adding to my concern."[23] He wrote Carrie at week's end that it was not her pro-German invectives that had so troubled him about her last letter but her repetition that she would give herself to another. "You choose to reiterate and emphasize the thing which always perturbs me. You see, I know how punctilious you are about warnings, and you repeatedly tell how you will give yourself to another, how you are justified in so doing, how I have forfeited my claim, how I have said by my acts that I do not want you, and so on."[24] He said he had been plunged "into an inferno of doubt and suffering."

Without recognizing it, he was doing the very thing he warned against the week before when he wrote of his brother: working himself to nervous exhaustion. "My nerves are worn to a frazzle," he wrote her on Friday the sixteenth. "I sometimes fear they are going to break. The strain of public problems, never more grave, and the anxiety of personal matters continue to make a trying burden. However, enough of the doleful. I'll thrash it out with myself and reap as is my lot."[25]

Though he said he would eschew any debate on the war, he found himself back in the discussion when he tried to answer her suggestion that the question of war be put to the people directly, through a national referendum. "A brilliant woman of your unusual intelligence," he wrote her on Senate Chamber stationery, "knows that I am sworn to support the constitution and you could not have a referendum on war without changing the constitution, and that organizing effort could hardly be accomplished short of two years, if hurried."

"I do not know now whether I shall vote for war," he informed her. But he knew he was charged with making that decision, and he intended to do what his conscience told him, regardless of how it affected him personally. "I may not be called upon to so vote. When I do vote for it I shall do so with such conviction that I shall enlist to fight as I vote." He then stated the first iteration of a theme that he would repeat in speeches on the war: that it was a test of popular government, another fire through which the republic must pass to prove itself worthy of being called one nation:

> *Perhaps the assertion of American rights will lead, as you suggest, to our ultimate subjugation. Very well, if the Kaiser can conquer the world, I'll swear my allegiance to him. He will deserve it. Meanwhile we may test popular government of a polyglot people. We are testing it now, without war. I wonder if it will stand the strain. Sometimes my fears rise far above my confidence. We are not one people. I am not alluding to German Americans alone. Scandinavians, Italians, English, Scotch, Russians, all lack the sense of America against the world. I know. I see it right here in Congress. It is very trying to find myself torn by conflicting emotions. I do love my country. I do love you. I should prefer to please you, to win your approval above that of everybody in the world. I have tried to see your point of view. I agree to much of your contention. You are an able advocate. I am prejudiced toward what you wish, because I love you and want you. But I must also think, and I must act, and I must answer for my acts. It is very trying. It is wearing me out. I still hope for peace. God knows, I mean to be right. I can only do my best, and will. And I'll love you every hour while I seek to meet the obligation and oath I have assumed.[26]*

The next day, his body gave way. He came down with "the Grippe," as he called it, an influenza that sent him to his bed for the next five days. "I have been having the Grippe since Saturday," he wrote to Malcolm Jennings on Wednesday, February 21, "and this is the first day at the office. The Duchess is complaining of being seized in the same manner, so you see we are not entirely without our reasonable amount of trouble."[27] The time away put him "hopelessly behind" in his correspondence, he wrote Carrie. "On my letters I need hours and hours. Full a hundred or more are on my desk requiring my personal attention. A senatorial answer will not do."[28]

In the Senate, the battle lines were forming for what would be called "the bitterest parliamentary wrangle in the history of the country."[29] Since the term of the Sixty-fourth Congress would expire at noon on March 4, Wilson sought congressional sanction for his proposal to arm merchant ships and pre-approval of "such authority which I may need at any moment to exercise."[30] The pacifists did not want to arm the ships, fearing it could only lead to war. The nationalists and interventionists, such as Senator Lodge, wanted ships armed but were uneasy about giving the president vague and seemingly wide-ranging powers to exercise as he might in the nine months before the next Congress would assemble in December.[31] They wanted Wilson to call a special session of the new Congress to meet immediately after the expiration of the old one.[32] Wilson would go only so far as to call the Senate alone for an extraordinary session to approve treaties and the like, beginning March 5 at noon.[33] Yet war could be declared only by the action of both houses of Congress, so the question still remained: Should the president be given broad war-like powers while Congress was out of session?[34]

Wilson went before a joint session of Congress on Monday, February 26, to ask for assurances that it would support him in his request for armed neutrality. "No doubt I already possess that authority without special warrant of law, by plain implication of my constitutional duties and powers," he contended, "but I prefer in the present circumstances not to act upon general implication. I wish to feel that the authority and the power of the Congress are behind me in whatever it may become necessary for me to do. We are jointly the servants of the people and must act, together and in their spirit, so far as we can divine and interpret it."[35]

Wilson told Congress he did not propose war, or steps leading to it. "I merely request," he said, "that you will accord me by your own vote and definite bestowal the means and the authority to safeguard in practice the right of a great people, who are at peace and who are desirous of exercising none but the rights of peace, to follow the pursuit of peace in quietness and goodwill—rights recognized time out of mind by all the civilized nations of the world."[36]

Congress had no way to know it at the time, but Wilson knew when he approached Congress that a secret message had been intercepted from the German government to the Mexican government that would propel the United States to war. Before he could disclose it, the administration had to first authenticate the document. What the document proposed was so preposterous on its face that Wilson wanted to make sure it was not a hoax.

The document originated from the German foreign service office and was authored by a man named Arthur Zimmermann.

CHAPTER 35

"We Shall Make War Together and Together Make Peace"

On Thursday morning, March 1, 1917, the *New York Times* printed the following text:

[Supplied by the Associated Press as an authentic copy of the German Foreign Minister's note to the German Minister in Mexico]

On the 1st of February we intend to begin submarine warfare unrestricted. In spite of this, it is our intention to endeavor to keep neutral the United States of America.

If this attempt is not successful, we propose an alliance on the following basis with Mexico: That we shall make war together and together make peace. We shall give general financial support, and it is understood that Mexico is to reconquer the lost territory in New Mexico, Texas, and Arizona. The details are left to you for settlement.

You are instructed to inform the President of Mexico of the above in the greatest confidence as soon as it is certain that there will be an outbreak of war with the United States, and suggest that the President of Mexico, on his own initiative, should communicate with Japan suggesting adherence at once to this plan. At the same time, offer to mediate between Germany and Japan.

Please call to the attention of the President of Mexico that the employment of ruthless submarine warfare now promises to compel England to make peace in a few months.

ZIMMERMANN[1]

CHAPTER 36

"A Little Group of Willful Men, Representing No Opinion but Their Own"

As the president addressed the Congress on Monday, February 26, word spread in the chamber that the night before, in stormy waters 150 miles off the coast of Ireland, the Germans had torpedoed the Cunard liner *Laconia*, with the loss of American lives. By quirk, two of the Americans killed included a Mrs. Hoy and her daughter, whom Mrs. Wilson knew personally.[1] "The Laconia constitutes the overt act which the President has indicated would be a first step toward compelling a more vigorous policy in dealing with Germany," the *New York Times* reported the next day.[2]

Yet even this outrage seemed to have no real impact on the senators who wanted peace above all else. Wilson said he would take no action on the *Laconia* matter until Congress acted on his request for broad powers to protect American ships and lives. The leader of the antiwar group in the Senate was Robert La Follette, a Republican from Wisconsin. La Follette and several other senators seemed determined to filibuster the armed neutrality bill until the congressional session expired. Republican senators had already started a filibuster to prevent the passage of critical appropriations bills, as a means of forcing the president to call for an extra session of Congress. Knowing of the continuing recalcitrance of the peace senators, Wilson, after conferring with his secretary of state, authorized the release of the Zimmermann note to a representative of the Associated Press on Wednesday evening, February 28, for publication on the morning of March 1.[3]

The note had arrived at the State Department on Saturday night, February 24. The sender was the American ambassador in London, Walter Page, who had been handed the text of the ciphered telegram by Arthur Balfour that afternoon. Zimmermann's note originally had been sent in code on January 19, through multiple channels, including, incredibly enough, a secure line provided as a courtesy to the German embassy in Washington by the State Department.[4] The German message was originally supposed to be carried on the third trip of *U-Deutschland,* which was scheduled to travel back to Baltimore, where it could be delivered to the German ambassador in person. But the submarine was delayed, so the note was sent by wire, through neutral Sweden and directly to von Bernstorff on the State Department wire.

Amazingly, Zimmermann took all the suspense out of whether the telegram was a fake by admitting to sending it. On March 3, newspapers reported Zimmerman's acknowledgement of the telegram and his attempt to justify it.

Events in the Senate raced along. La Follette and those in sympathy with him still persisted in their efforts to kill the armed merchant vessel bill. "The Senate," the *New York Times* would report, "through the stubborn opposition of eleven pacifists, failed to reach a vote."[5] La Follette and his colleagues filibustered for the entire evening of March 3-4. In the middle of the night, sixty-eight senators signed a manifesto stating their desire to vote with Wilson, authorizing the president to arm American merchant vessels. "Under the rules of the Senate allowing unlimited debate," the manifesto read, "it now appears to be impossible to obtain a vote prior to noon March 4, 1917, when the session of Congress expires." The senators wanted their statement in the record "to establish the fact that the Senate favors the legislation, and would pass it if a vote could be obtained." Signatures were gathered through 1 AM and the manifesto was entered into the record sometime around 3 AM.[6] Warren Harding was one of the signatories.

As the debates and manifestos swirled around him at his desk in the Senate, Warren wrote a letter to Carrie on Senate Chamber stationery. "A line to acknowledge yours received today," he started his note on "Eve of March 3." "I was glad to have it. I ought not need to repeat that I am always glad to have your letters, personal or otherwise. I have read them all. I have endeavored to read all the clippings, pamphlets and books, but in the last few weeks could not find time for the books. I was in bed five days and got almost hopelessly behind."[7]

He wrote to her that these were "busy and strenuous days as well as anxious ones." But his tone had changed; he seemed more sure of his stance. He had listened to the debates, shifted through the evidence and the positions, and was affected by the sinking of the *Laconia* and the revelation of the Zimmermann note. He even had spoken favorably about Theodore Roosevelt recently, for which Roosevelt penned a thank-you letter on March 2.[8] "I wish to thank you for your recent references to me," T.R. wrote. "Incidentally, I am certain that what you said is exactly true! We have invited war by our feeble, timid, shuffling course!"[9]

Harding explained his position to Carrie. He finally had reached a moment of clarity and he wanted her to understand:

> *Perhaps I have an awkward conception of my duties. Very likely I take myself too seriously and scatter over too much and concentrate on too little. One thing sure I have a real job, which I perform very poorly, but not near so than many who are in the same position. I have been listening these days pretty carefully to the debates, holding an open mind, anxious to learn. As the hours pass my convictions are deepening. I believe I am right on my public position. I believe it so much that I am willing to rest my fortunes, and I have the self-consciousness which holds me serene. It is distressing to disappoint one's friends, and worse to disappoint those we love. I wanted to answer your appeals—to meet them. You have impressed me more than all others who take your point of view. Hundreds have written me on behalf of Germany, but none so ably, so clearly and so forcefully as you. You have awakened my admiration to new heights. You are a wonderful woman, one in a million. I wish I could agree for another reason—because I love you. We like to respond to the expectations of those we love. I am pained that I have not been able. On a public question of such vast importance I can't run counter to my solemn belief. But I do tell you I am sorry.[10]*

The letter gives only the slightest glimpse of the drama in the Senate that night. "I am not pretending to write a [complete] letter," he wrote her of his short five-page effort. "I am stealing the time and there is strain and anxiety and excitement all about." He said he was canceling all his plans for the immediate future, including a trip planned to the Philippines in April (he was on the Senate committee overseeing the Philippines). "I wouldn't go now for a fortune," he wrote, reflecting the increased concern over submarine warfare, even in the Pacific. "A perfectly good editor might be sent to the bottom of the sea," he wrote. "That wouldn't be the worst way to go, but I do not mean to invite such a fate."[11]

The next morning, Sunday, at about 8 AM, La Follette entered the Senate Chamber, fresh from a short nap, hoping to make a major address on the war, but the Democrats would not allow it. The presiding senator refused to recognize him and allowed others to speak. La Follette went into a rage. "I do not care what point of order the Senator makes," he shouted. He then stormed down the aisle to the well of the Senate, as other senators moved to interrupt. "I will continue on the floor," La Follette roared, "until I complete my statement, unless somebody carries me off the floor, and I would like to see the man do it!" But the Democrats had planned their response; they had outmaneuvered him.[12]

At 10:45 Woodrow Wilson showed up at the Capitol with a detachment of Secret Service men in tow, along with his wife, physician, secretary, and some members of his cabinet. He went to the President's Office, which is across a fourteen-foot-hall from the Senate Chamber, and he began signing legislation and attending to other work.[13]

His purpose for coming was to be sworn into office by the Chief Justice Edward D. White in a private ceremony, because it was a Sunday. The press, though, loved the drama of counterpoint. A *Times* reporter wrote:

> *He came in with Mrs. Wilson, Colonel House, Secretary Tumulty, and some members of the White House staff, threw off his overcoat and began work at once. As he did so, La Follette, on the other side of the wall that stood fourteen feet away, threw himself into his chair with a growl as the immovable [Democratic Senator] Hitchcock declined for the tenth time to let him have the floor, and shouted, leaning over to the stenographers: "I have the right to be heard. Get that down." Hitchcock, outwardly unruffled, went on at the same slow pace of speech to deliver the address which had for its one object the throttling of La Follette's great oration, for which the Wisconsin man had been preparing for weeks; La Follette sat watching him, with a red face and furious eyes.[14]*

Because the Chief Justice and the president were deep in friendly talks ("close confabulation," the papers termed it), the actual ceremony of oath-taking did not take place until 12:04, just as the tempestuous Sixty-fourth Congress was gaveled out of existence. "This was the real inauguration," the papers wrote, "for it matters not how many times the President may repeat the oath-taking now, and whether in public or private. He is going to repeat it tomorrow in public that the people may not be disappointed, and that the old form may be observed. His second term began at noon today, and there never was an inauguration like it."[15]

Later that day Wilson issued a statement to the American people, blasting the senators who had killed all legislative efforts in the last two weeks of Congress. "The termination of the last session of the Sixty-fourth Congress by constitutional limitation disclosed a situation unparalleled in the history of the country, perhaps unparalleled in the history of any modern Government," the statement began. Wilson was showing the bitter temper that would so ill-serve him after the Paris Peace Conference when he would again do battle with the Senate. He particularly was astonished that a small number of senators could hold the government hostage to their own views. "A little group of willful men, representing no opinion but their own, have rendered the great Government of the United States helpless and contemptible," Wilson's statement read. He felt there was only one remedy: Change the Senate rules.[16]

The Senate did change its rules. On March 8, the Senate passed a resolution changing its unlimited debate rule, which had prevailed for nearly 110 years.[17] Limited cloture thus came to the Senate. Two-thirds of the Senate could vote now to bring a measure to vote, allowing senators not more than one hour to express themselves thereafter.[18] Wilson's chief objection to calling an extra session of the entire Congress was therefore eliminated. He now knew an attempt to filibuster in the Senate would have some limits.

As a consequence, on Friday, March 9, the president announced that he intended to arm American merchant ships based on his own constitutional powers. At the same time he finally called for an extra session of *both houses* of Congress to meet April 16, without stating the exact purpose. Everyone believed it was for the purpose of acting on a declaration of war.[19]

All the tension and strain had its effect on Harding's desire to see Carrie. He wrote her that he had received a letter from her husband on March 3 and, from it, he understood that the Phillipses were coming East. "If it were any other time I would urge you to come alone," he wrote her. "But we have been so busy, the city is so full and so many from Ohio, and I have felt so miserably that I have felt it would be unwise and very disappointing to you. Maybe the way will soon clear and you can visit Baltimore."[20]

For the moment, all was quiet with Carrie, but a speech in Cincinnati would dredge back up all the bad feelings, again.

CHAPTER 37

"My Countrymen, the Republic Is on Trial"

"It has been exceedingly strenuous work here during the month of February," Harding wrote to Ed Scobey on March 12, 1917. "For a long time we had a continuous inpouring from the pacifists who were mainly pro-German, and then after the La Follette filibuster we began to hear from the other side." Harding recognized that whatever position he took, he was likely to upset someone and risk his seat in the Senate. "I have a pretty strong conviction that a man in public life these days is very likely to wreck his political career, no matter what course he may pursue," he wrote Scobey. "However, I am perfectly content to follow what seems to me to be the American course and allow the political future to assert itself in whatever manner it may."[1]

Malcolm Jennings saw an opportunity for Harding to come home to Ohio and lead in this confused, conflicted, and highly charged political environment. "For a number of weeks," Jennings wrote from Columbus on March 13, "I have heard, from people here and from all parts of the state, the sentiment expressed, 'I wish Harding would make a great big speech, along patriotic lines, appealing for unity of purpose and for the expression of that loyalty which is inherent in ninety-nine out of a hundred of our citizenship . . .'"[2] He suggested that Harding chose as his venue for such a speech the most pro-German city in the state: Cincinnati. The Business Men's Club had issued an invitation for Harding to speak there on March

31 and Jennings encouraged Harding to accept for several reasons: "It is known as a German city, but is disposed to resent any aspersions of its loyalty; you will be assured of a big audience naturally friendly to you and of sympathetic treatment by the newspapers." The Zimmermann note, in Jennings's mind, had had a particularly decisive effect on those who had been unreservedly pro-German prior to its revelation. "The disclosures as to the official activity of Germany in this country during all the months of the war, the revealing of their willingness to wage war upon us in company with the bloody bandit minded Mexicans, the heathen Chinese, the Japs or any other race or tribe or tong which could be induced to turn guns upon us, has aroused intense feeling against the Bully of Europe," he wrote.

Harding replied on March 19 that he had taken Jennings's advice and accepted the Cincinnati engagement.[3]

Woodrow Wilson, meanwhile, struggled with his decision to call the nation to war. He fretted in private meetings about how war would change American democracy. Events in Russia and three more submarine attacks against American ships, though, seemed to end the debate in his mind. The removal of the czar opened the ability for him to argue that the war would serve a transformational purpose. No longer would the war be seen as a meaningless commercial fight among alliance-laden, old-world powers: Its purpose would be to rid the world of autocrats and dictators. The war would become a crusade to promote and protect democracy, because the democratic form of government was the only stable type that could assure the lasting peace of the world.

Before the Romanovs fell, the inconvenient fact was that despotic Russia was one of the Allies, making it hard to maintain the position that the war was about freedom and the elimination of tyrants and despots. On March 15, though, this obstacle was removed. After a long series of internal political struggles and domestic strife caused by the privations of war, simple food and labor strikes in Petrograd led to the downfall of the Russian czar. It began with an army mutiny. "The people's cry for food reached the hearts of the soldiers," the *Times* reported on March 16, "and one by one the regiments rebelled, until finally those troops which had for a time stood loyal to the Government gathered up their arms and marched into the ranks of the revolutionists."[4] Czar Nicholas II, stopped short of the city on his way back from the front, abdicated and a new provisional government was formed with Prince Lvoff, a leading liberal and nobleman, as its premier.[5] For a time, Russia would struggle with democracy.

Wilson greeted this dazzling news with joy. The fall of Nicholas was seen as a herald to a similar change in Germany. In fact, the German chancellor, Bethmann-Hollweg, appeared before the German Reichstag on March 15 and delivered an extemporaneous speech in reaction to the news in Russia, pledging reforms and the democratization of Prussian political institutions after the war. "Woe to the statesman who cannot read the signs of the times," he warned.[6]

On March 22, the United States became the first nation to formally recognize the new Russian government.[7]

Secretary of State Robert Lansing told Wilson that it was the right "psychological moment" to declare war on Germany, sensing that the impetus of the Russian Revolution and the stirrings of the anti-Prussian spirit in Germany might "even cause revolution in Germany."[8]

Wilson met with his cabinet on Tuesday, March 20, and asked each member whether he should call Congress to a special session earlier than April 16 for purposes of declaring war. Over the weekend, the nation had learned that three American ships, the *City of Memphis, Illinois,* and *Vigilancia,* had been destroyed by German submarines, with loss of life.[9] Many believed Germany was acting as if a state of war already existed between it and the United States. The cabinet, even Josephus Daniels, the peace-loving secretary of the navy, advised war.[10]

The next day, March 21, Wilson called Congress to extra session on April 2, "to receive a communication concerning grave matters of national policy."[11] The war would become a war to make the world safe for democracy.

As Warren Harding prepared his remarks for his Cincinnati address, he wrote a public and a private letter to Carrie Phillips. On Friday, March 23, he wrote a two-page public letter to her on Senate stationery.[12] He returned George Viereck's newspapers, which she had sent him, along with some letters from Carrie's friend from Berlin, Willie Allen. "I am extremely well, best ever," he wrote. "It would be a crime to be better. Haven't been so well in years. One or two people have sized me up when I was quite tired and thought I looked jaded, and somebody reported such an impression in Columbus, but it is all wrong. I am fully well."[13]

In his private letter, written two days later, on Sunday, March 25, he clearly was working out in his mind what he would say in Cincinnati. "You have written freely and forcefully in behalf of Germany, and I have read, fairly open-minded, and always respectfully because it was you who wrote," he started, referring to a recent letter she sent him. "You think I am too ignorant. Perhaps you are right, but I could have countered many an argument. I refrained, out of deliberate reflection. It was not agreeable to my taste to pursue an argument with you." What troubled him was not that the world was intervening, or even who was right or wrong in the contest. He was disturbed more about the lack of American identity, the seeming loss of the American soul. Pointing to a marriage and family that had broken up over fighting about the war, he wondered what it all meant, for his country, and for his relationship with Carrie. "Where are we drifting—where is the world drifting—if war is to rend happy homes and make a breech between lovers?"

He assured her he had no particular prejudice against Germany, nor was he acting in rashness or out of a spirit for revenge. "I have not been hasty or hysterical," he wrote. "I have pondered the situation with soberness and solemnity, ever mindful of the great responsibility. How unthinking and unfair you are when you accuse me of playing politics! I represent a state with hundreds of thousands of German Republicans. Nobody knows better than I do that I seal my political fate by displeasing them. I know it makes me a one-term official to oppose their desires, but I prefer to perform a duty in good conscience even though I know it means the end of my public service."[14]

He was influenced, he admitted, by recent events and by his revulsion for the senators who had formed the "willful little group" whom Wilson had excoriated. "Politics have impelled Stone, La Follette, Norris, Gronna," Harding asserted. "I know whereof I write. You quote Stone and pay him glowing tribute. You would not if you knew him. After eighteen months of pretty intimate observation I rejoice that I am not classed with Stone, La Follette and Norris. You would be of the same mind if you only knew. You would not trust or respect one of them. Surely justice and righteousness and honor would not plant themselves exclusively in such a minority."[15]

His neutrality had been tested, and it finally ended when the Zimmermann note was exposed. "I may be wrong—I have never claimed any degree of perfection, but when I knew of the German plotting and conspiring, and observe the murderous course of the Kaiser," he wrote her, "I can have no other choice. If the Kaiser can dictate to the world, I'll be his vassal, too, but not without an effort to sustain the honor of self-respect of the land which has given me opportunity and such reward as I have merited."

He wrote to her, again, that he was keeping their secret compact—no entertainment at his home, no dinner parties except stag affairs, and he had not returned to Ohio with Florence. He advised that he was coming out to Ohio later that week, to attend to state party matters in Columbus, and he would be staying at the Neil House while there on Thursday. He expected to spend Friday in Marion and then travel to Cincinnati to give his speech on Saturday night.

On Wednesday morning, though, as he was leaving Washington, he had to scratch out a rushed note to Carrie warning that Florence would be traveling with him.[16] "There is a need to see Dr. Stephan, there is business with the dress-maker at Col., there are matters to look after in M—," he explained. "These reasons are evidently genuine and I can not forbid. One can not deny his wife going to her home. I have tried to dissuade."

He thought Carrie would be so displeased that she would not care to see him, and he apologized, but thought it better to forewarn her. "You have heretofore said that half my offense was in not telling you."

"My countrymen, the republic is on trial," Warren Harding started his speech in front of a packed house of businessmen in Cincinnati on Saturday night, March 31. "Popular government is brought to the supreme test."[17] Harding stood at a speaker's table that was adorned with a small statute of Abraham Lincoln, with the words "With malice towards none" inscribed at its base. His fellow speaker that night was Governor James M. Cox, the man against whom he would run for president of the United States three years later. But on this night, as the *Marion Star* reported, there was "no party, no race, but just plain Americanism."[18] The ostensible purpose for the dinner was to honor men of the Ohio National Guard, who were returning from service on the U.S. border with Mexico.

In the speech, Harding's premise was that the United States faced as great a trial as it had during the Civil War. The country needed to demonstrate that it worthy of being called one nation. The United States and its people had to show they could withstand the divisions created by the European conflict and that the very liberty that allowed its leaders unlimited debate would not be misused in ways that prevented the nation from acting. "It makes seemingly a contradiction," Harding said, "but at the very moment when revolution has given birth to a new republic, cradled in the very throne of Russian autocracy, we are approaching the test of our nationality amid the reign of boasted American freedom. We are soon to demonstrate whether we constitute a mere pathetic figure in the strife of human progress, where abuse of liberty has paralyzed nationality; whether we are merely a collection of peoples inhabiting a certain area of the world, boasting freedom but without a national soul; or whether we are a republic strong in our nationality, imbued with pride and purpose, honest in intent, lofty in spirit and confident in a noble destiny, ready to sacrifice and suffer for the sublime fulfillment."

But had the fires of the great American melting pot gone out? At the least, were those flames "deadened"? His mail, he asserted, showed deep division in America; it revealed "magnified proof of a polyglot character." The sentiments in the letters he was receiving from across the state and the country gave witness to a lack of solidarity and an "incohesion that dulls the soul of nationality." He was not hopeless about the situation, but he felt the need to "cry out to my country for reconsecration. We must save the temple of the Republic. Let us have a soul in our national life. Let us light the way of these United States with the spirit of the founders and the spirit of the saviors, and make and hold it a Republic of one people."

To Ohioans who still knew Civil War veterans and who had lived through an almost unbroken string of Ohio-born or bred presidents who helped stitch back together the broken Union, the words "the spirit of the saviors" held a power a modern hearer might miss. The founders, including the early presidents, were mainly Virginians; but since the Civil War, Ohio could boast of giving birth to the men who would *save* the country: from the tatters after the Civil War, through the dangers of Reconstruction, and into the modern era as a nascent world power.

He spoke to the pain the war would cause those of German heritage. His purpose was to empathize and soothe hard feelings. He could have been speaking directly to Carrie. "I can understand the sorrow that will weigh in the heart of many an American of German birth or extraction, to find his adopted land and the Fatherland plunged in the arbitrament of arms.[19] I wish I might spare him the conflict between sympathy and duty. I know nothing more beautiful in all the world's passion for country than German love for the Fatherland."

Then he came to a point of distinction in his thinking. "I venture to remark, in passing, that human progress does not depend so much on the form of government as it does on the human agencies which administer it."

He blamed not the German people, nor the German form of government, but the particular leaders. This was an important distinction for German Americans. "Russian autocracy, weakly headed, halted its people in bondage and corruption, while a German monarchy wrought a people's progress in forty years for which history has no parallel."

In some ways, Harding's analytical framework was more subtle than that being developed by Wilson and Secretary of State Lansing. To Harding it was not the case that all autocracies were war producers and all democracies guarded peace. Harding was influenced not only by Carrie Phillips but his own travels, on multiple occasions to the German Empire. And, as importantly, he called on his reading of history. Napoleon, he reminded his listeners, "wrought his early slaughter in the name of the First French Republic." Caesar likewise fought in the name of the Roman Republic before Augustus assumed benevolent power after Caesar's assassination. A similar tragedy was playing out in Germany, one that Harding could see would have consequences for generations to come. "The human agents failed, and the German people, though the empire is saved and its borders are unchanged, will stagger under the load that a century will not wholly relieve, and all Europe, bereaved, maimed and burdened, will stagger with them."

In the end, while the Allies may have not "always adhered to the letter of international law" in their blockade, the lawless sacrifice of human life by Germans, Harding said, was never defensible or acceptable. "There was not and can not be any justification of the utter contempt for neutral rights and horrifying disregard of the rights of humanity."

Two days after Harding's address in Cincinnati, Woodrow Wilson left the White House on the rainy night of April 2, with a heavy escort, to take the short ride up Pennsylvania Avenue to the Capitol, to address the newly formed Sixty-fifth Congress. The night was full of drama. Pacifists had come to the District of Columbia in droves, and they threatened to disrupt proceedings, even assaulting Senator Henry Cabot Lodge as he entered the Capitol Building. Rain fell softly and the dome of the Capitol was lit up against a dark sky. Members of the Supreme Court arrived, sans robes, and took up seats directly in front of the speaker's platform. The diplomatic corps was there in full evening dress. Both houses of Congress assembled. As Wilson entered, the entire chamber rose and cheered. "It was two minutes before he could begin his address," the *Times* wrote.[20]

Wilson read most of his address, leaning slightly on the green baize–covered desk and looking up only occasionally. He laid out the efforts of the United States to avoid war with Germany. Close attention in the hall "deepened into a breathless silence, so painfully intense that it seemed almost audible," as he drew close to his call for war. One line, partway through, caused the greatest sensation: "There is one choice we cannot make, we are incapable of making," he read, "we will not choose the path of submission." These words brought an emotional response, led by the chief justice of the Supreme Court. "Chief Justice White," the newspaper reported, "with an expression of joy and thankfulness on his face, dropped the big soft hat he had been holding, raised his hands high in the air, and brought them together with a heartfelt bang; and the House, Senate and galleries followed him with a roar like a storm. It was a cheer so deep and so intense and so much from the heart that it sounded like a shouted prayer."

Wilson then made his full-scale attack on German autocracy. Setting forth U.S. motives and objects in entering the war, he said that the essential purpose was to "vindicate the principles of peace and justice in the life of the world as against selfish and autocratic power, and to set up among the really free and self-governed peoples of the world such a concert of purpose and of action as will henceforth insure the observance of those principles."

"The world must be made safe for democracy," Wilson declared in what would become the most memorable line of his presidency.

In an indirect bid to foment revolution in Germany, Wilson spoke to the German people directly and in a code they would understand. "We have no quarrel with the German people. We have no feeling toward them but one of sympathy and friendship. It was not upon their impulse that their Government acted in entering the war." His concluding remarks echoed Martin Luther's best-known phrase "Here I stand. I can do no other. God help me. Amen." Wilson's version: "God helping her, she can do no other." With this, the chamber again reacted with a strong and ringing ovation. Almost alone, Robert La Follette stood motionless, arms folded tight against his chest, "chewing gum with a sardonic smile," but the rest of the senators stood and cheered, waving American flags they had brought for the occasion.

Two days later, the Senate took up the debate on the war resolution. It went on all day, taking over thirteen hours. Warren Harding was one of the last to speak, nearly at eleven at night, just before the vote was taken. He summarized and repeated portions of his Cincinnati address but added a specific disclaimer that he was *not* voting for war to make the world safe for democracy. After saying he would be brief, he said to the presiding officer of the Senate:

> I want especially to say, Mr. President, that I am not voting for war in the name of democracy. I want to emphasize that fact for a moment, because much has been said upon that subject on the floor. It is my deliberate judgment that it is none of our business what type of government any nation on this earth may choose to have; and one can not be entirely just unless he makes the admission in this trying hour that the German people evidently are pretty well satisfied with their Government, because I could not ask a better thing for this popular Government of the United States of America than the same loyal devotion on the part of every American that the German gives his Government.[21]

He was voting for war, in the end, to support "the maintenance of *just American rights,* which are the first essential to the preservation of the soul of the Republic."

His speech was delivered so late that it barely received notice in the press the next day. In fact, the *New York Times* completely botched his message. "Senator Harding said . . . that he was voting for the resolution in the name of world democracy, because he believed it was the right of any nation to have any form of government its people desired."[22] Harding was not pleased. "The trouble with my speech in Congress," he wrote Scobey, "seems to have been that it was delivered about eleven o'clock at night, which was too late for any attention in the morning papers and too far in advance to draw any notable attention from the evening papers the next day."[23]

War meant war hysteria. After the disclosure of the Zimmermann note at the end of February, Americans saw German spies everywhere. "ALIENS A PROBLEM HERE" was a banner of the *New York Times* on March 20, the day Wilson's cabinet met to discuss a declaration of war.[24] American ambassador James W. Gerard, who had recently returned from Germany, spoke of the need for greater awareness and action to deal with enemy aliens and spies within the United States once war was declared. Speaking to the Chamber of Commerce in New York, Gerard said that if war were declared, "this country faced the question of interning alien enemies or leaving them free to blow up bridges and do other damage."

Other headlines grimly warned of such things as, "RED CROSS BANDAGES POISONED BY SPIES."[25] In Philadelphia, the head of the Red Cross cautioned women making bandages to "clean house" and review lists of volunteers in order to "make sure of the loyalty of every one." He claimed that it was recently discovered in New Jersey that bandages made for American soldiers had been "soaked in poisonous chemicals and then dried." In addition, some of the bandages allegedly had been filled with ground glass, "so that when they were used on open wounds they would cut and cause suppurating sores."

Some Americans felt moved to enlist in the fight against internal foes. Right after the Germans began unrestricted submarine warfare, a Chicago businessman, Albert M. Briggs, vice president of Outdoor Advertising, Incorporated, decided to offer a dozen automobiles to the understaffed Chicago office of the Bureau of Investigation. He expanded the idea after meeting in Washington with the chief of the Bureau of Investigation, A. Bruce Bielaski. A national organization was proposed and after Bielaski consulted with the attorney general, he wired his Chicago office to encourage Briggs to create his volunteer organization.[26]

Plans immediately began to take shape. The volunteer organization would aid the Bureau of Investigation and would bill itself as an "auxiliary of the Department of Justice." Its leaders and members would be the foremost businessmen of their towns, "citizens of good moral character."[27] The organization would have a police-like structure. A reliable man at the top of industry would be identified as the "chief" for the city; the chief would in turn work with "lieutenants," preferably executives in different companies or industries in town; and these select few would enlist "officers" to carry out the legwork and the everyday spying for the group. The chiefs and lieutenants were issued badges, to identify themselves, one to the other, and to local police and Bureau of Investigation agents.[28]

The organization would be named a few weeks later, just as the United States entered the war. It would become known as the American Protective League.

CHAPTER 38

"First Met Him at a Hop"

John William Spalding had been a midshipman at the Naval Academy at Annapolis since December 1913, but two years and eight months after entering the academy, he failed in his examinations and was thrown out in February 1917, just as the Germans reinstituted unrestricted submarine warfare.[1] He wandered about for a few weeks, taking short trips to Baltimore and Washington, where he witnessed the public inauguration of President Wilson on March 5.

And then he returned to Annapolis, moving in with the baroness and her teenage son, Bedford, in a boardinghouse. Bedford and the baroness had been living there, on and off, since the previous September, when her elder son, Beresford, reentered the academy after flunking out following his first try in 1915.[2] Beresford Shope had introduced Spalding to his family. "First met him at a hop," younger brother Bedford testified in his mother's espionage hearing of his acquaintance with Spalding, "before the Army and Navy game, casual acquaintance then and when he came back from the [Wilson] Inauguration he happened to be staying at the same boarding house where my Mother and I stayed and we became close friends."[3]

This was the same Army-Navy game that Harding wrote about in one of his letters to Carrie. He could have sworn, he wrote, that he saw Carrie and Isabelle at the game in a newsreel.[4]

The baroness claimed the reason Spalding was found in her bedroom was because of her heart condition. She recounted the earliest time Spalding came to the rescue when she fell ill. "I get terribly weak and my heart seems to give out," she said in describing one of her spells in Annapolis, "and I just called and called." Spalding responded from another room in the boardinghouse, she said, "and he got my boy and they came in and stayed with me."[5] Thereafter, it became the habit of the young men to take turns sitting up with her when she had an attack.

On May 14, 1917, a month after the United States declared that a state of war existed with Germany, the baroness and the young men moved out of the boardinghouse and leased a home just outside the gates of the Naval Academy. She testified that she intended to take in borders, family and friends of the midshipmen who would come to visit over the weekends. She tried to avoid being too conspicuous. "So I had these different ladies and their daughters for week-ends," she testified, "and during June Week, which lasted I think about four days, I had the mothers of several midshipmen and girls of several midshipmen staying with me but I never went to any of the hops or anything because I believed that under the circumstances it would be better for me to simply stay at home, so I did."[6]

There was a reason the baroness wanted to keep a low profile. Her presence just outside the gates of one of the major military institutions in the United States caught the attention of military secret service and the superintendent of the academy, Captain Edward W. Eberle.[7] Though she had been born in the United States, she was the former wife of a German baron and was currently married to a German army officer who had skipped parole and returned to Europe on a falsified passport to rejoin his army unit.

Her situation was precisely what the administration wanted to guard against when President Wilson issued a proclamation regarding enemy aliens within the United States after war was declared.[8] Enemy aliens were subject to instant arrest or removal from the country. Under regulations issued by Wilson, enemy aliens were prohibited from possessing firearms or weapons, signaling devices, such as wireless apparatus, or cipher codes. They were not permitted to print or publish any attack or threat against the government or Congress of the United States. And specifically, enemy aliens were prohibited from approaching or being found within one-half mile "of any Federal or State fort, camp, arsenal, aircraft station, Government or naval vessel, navy yard, factory, or workshop for the manufacture of munitions of war or any products for the use of the army or navy."[9]

Though technically not an enemy alien since the proclamation did not apply directly to females who were married to enemy aliens (that change would be made in 1918), the baroness received a visit from a Captain Fowler of the Navy Secret Service shortly after she moved into the house outside the Academy's gates. He told her that she had been watched for months and that her mail had been opened and read. Her son Beresford was told by his superiors that in order to avoid any embarrassment he should tell his mother to leave Annapolis. The baroness consulted her New York lawyer, who told her that the Navy's actions were "perfectly absurd." She claimed at the hearing that she was given a letter of introduction by her attorney to Attorney General Thomas Watt Gregory. She went to Washington, where she met not with Gregory but with Navy officials, who supposedly told her that they had investigated her and could find nothing against her. "I had a clean bill," she testified.[10] She said she was told the enemy alien laws were actually meant to protect her.

She returned to Annapolis, but within a month she would leave, taking Spalding with her.[11] His next destination would be Fort Leavenworth and a brief Army career.[12]

CHAPTER 39

"You Suddenly Threatened Me with Exposure to the Germans"

Once the United States entered the war, the question became whether it could get its forces to the front in Europe in time to make a difference. As Theodore Roosevelt put it: "It would be an evil thing, a lasting calamity to this country, if the war ended and found us merely preparing an army in safety at home without having sent a man to the firing line, merely having paid some billions of dollars to other people so that with the bodies of their sons and brothers they might keep us in safety."[1]

Many high up in the War Department believed that sending untrained, green American troops would be disastrous, if not a burden to the Allied troops already engaged. Yet France in particular was desperate to see additional forces as soon as possible. Although most Americans were unaware of the fact, France was on the verge of economic collapse. England, too, was in precarious shape. No one knew if Russia, under its new government, would continue to fight or make a separate peace with the Central Powers. The Germans wondered how quickly American troops could be trained and when they might begin to appear in the field in substantial numbers. If they could mount an offensive that would shatter French and British lines before the Americans arrived, perhaps they could force the Allies to respond positively to the German call for an armistice and join in a true peace conference.

As a consequence, the Germans needed eyes and ears in the United States to keep them apprised of the pace of American mobilization.

The Wilson administration agreed with the Army and refused to send troops abroad until they had been adequately trained. The president planned to increase the transfer of munitions to the Allies, to provide them with additional funding and loans, and to coordinate U.S. naval forces with the British and French navies for joint operations against German submarines, but he did not want to send American troops overseas until a million men could be trained and readied, with adequate provisions made to keep them supplied in the field.[2] The British had learned a bitter lesson early in the war, the Americans believed, when they sent many of their best-trained soldiers to France for an offensive at Mons, only to find that significant numbers were lost with no appreciable gain in the field. The Wilson administration did not want to repeat that mistake. They felt that it was better to keep the most experienced soldiers home to intensively instruct and prepare the new recruits and conscripts.

Before any action could be taken, though, Congress had to pass a bill calling for an immediate nationwide draft.

Roosevelt thought the Wilson plan a calamity. Believing that the Allies needed an immediate shot in the arm, he felt that a smaller expeditionary force should be sent abroad as soon as possible, and that *he* should lead the force. T.R. tried to meet with Wilson on April 3, the day after the president's call to Congress for a war resolution, but Wilson was too busy to see him. A week later, on April 10, T.R. sat down with Wilson for forty-five minutes. Following the meeting, Roosevelt stood on the steps of the White House facing the press with Wilson's secretary, Joseph Tumulty, there to act as censor in the event the Colonel went too far. "I came here desiring to see the President personally and reiterate what I had said about his [war] message and to lay before him in detail and explain just what I desire to have his direction to do, in the case of the division," Roosevelt told reporters, "and why it was my earnest hope and belief that it would be well that he should authorize me to raise such a division to be sent as part of any expeditionary force to France at the earliest moment."[3]

For a brief moment, there was genuine hope among leaders in both major political parties that a true war coalition was going to form around a Wilson-Roosevelt rapprochement.[4] But that optimism would be short-lived.

First, there would be a fight in Congress. Warren Harding stepped forward to guide the effort in the Senate for Roosevelt to be put in charge of a division. In this, his first major effort to lead in the Senate, Harding would show his innate political skills and his personal appeal, which would serve him so well in the 1920 campaign for president. Moreover, the effort would be entirely consistent with his long-term goal of restoring party harmony and promoting healing in a party still rent from the breach of 1912.

Harding proposed an amendment to the Army bill that would allow Roosevelt to raise four infantry divisions for service in France. In his lengthy speech on Saturday, April 28, Harding continued his theme that the only proper purpose of America's entry in the war was to rebuild the American soul. With references that mirrored his private debate with Carrie, he spoke of the disunity that had to end now that the United States was in the war. "Our own land has its hundreds of thousands impelled by love or hate, and see only the European issue, without a concern for the fate of our own Republic, now inseparable from the peace terms to which Europe must come," he told his fellow senators. "Germany must be brought to terms, or the world becomes her dominion." He charged that the "great awakening" had not yet come in America; the pity was that it would never come "except in the echoes of national disaster and the convulsive sobs of an American tragedy."[5]

He did not expect the Roosevelt division to detract from the universal obligation of conscription. Roosevelt's men would come from the ranks of men too old to be drafted or who might otherwise be exempt, but their immediate presence in France "would put new life into every allied trench and a new glow in every allied campfire on every battle front in Europe."[6] Though a similar measure in the House was defeated, Harding's amendment was passed by the Senate, with nineteen Democrats voting with the Republicans.[7] The final law contained a compromise version of the Harding amendment, which left it to the discretion of the president to send troops under Roosevelt.

Typical of this period of his life, Roosevelt said things that hurt his own cause. At times he seemed actively to sabotage his own interest. On the same day that Harding was carefully orchestrating his appeal to the Senate on Roosevelt's behalf, T.R. spoke out critically against the Wilson administration in meetings in Chicago, trying to make his case for an immediate entry of troops into the fighting. "During the last two years and a half of peace we have been foolish enough not to prepare for war. Now that we are at war, let us avoid the further folly of failure to prepare for the great tasks of peace, the tasks with which we will have to deal now while at war, and which will be of overwhelming importance as soon as the war is over."[8]

He sounded more like a man running for office than a loyal warrior willing to follow unquestioningly the orders of his commander in chief.

Not surprisingly, Wilson politely but firmly declined T.R.'s offer a few weeks later. On May 18, Major Douglas MacArthur of the General Staff distributed the official announcement to newspapermen at the War Department that an expeditionary force, under the command of Major General John J. Pershing, would proceed to France "as soon as practicable." Simultaneously, Secretary of War Newton Baker gave the press a statement that President Wilson would not "avail himself" of the services offered by former President Roosevelt. In a classic Wilsonian sting, the statement said the president had no doubt that politically a Roosevelt appointment would be to "very fine effect," but that "the business now at hand is undramatic, practical and of scientific directness and precision" and that the president did not regard "Colonel Roosevelt as a military expert."

And as to specifics of how quickly Pershing's force would be ready, the Wilson administration explained that this information was a military secret. The statement MacArthur issued about Pershing's expeditionary force "requested that no details or speculations with regard to the mobilization of this command, dates of departure, composition, or other items, be carried by the press, other than the official bulletins given out by the War Department relating thereto."[9]

Roosevelt's loss was Harding's gain. Harding received great personal praise and national recognition for his skillful handling of the Roosevelt matter in Congress and for his leadership. As importantly, he advanced his growing relationship with Roosevelt and ingratiated himself with T.R.'s good friend and most important ally and advocate in the Senate, Senator Henry Cabot Lodge. "My dear Theodore," Lodge wrote to Roosevelt on April 30.[10] "It was, as you may suppose, a very great pleasure to me, and the deepest kind of personal satisfaction, to have the 'Roosevelt Amendment' pass the Senate by a noble majority of 25. Harding, who presented it, managed it with great skill and tact. He made a speech in the morning and I followed him. When the time came for the vote Harding made a second speech, for five minutes, and [Hiram] Johnson [of California] made a very able speech in the same length of time; then we swept it in." Lodge suggested that it would gratify Harding if Roosevelt wrote him a note of thanks. T.R. did, and Harding responded saying that Roosevelt's son and daughter had both called him to express gratitude for his adroit work on behalf of their father.[11]

Harding's pal Ed Scobey wrote that his wife energetically supported Harding's campaign to get Roosevelt into the fighting as soon as possible. "Mrs. S. says she is like you, she wants T.R. to go to the front; the farther in front the better it will suit her," he joked. Harding, for once, did not join in Scobey's humor. He was developing a watchful appreciation of his old foe and showing typical Harding grace.[12] "You can say all you please about him," he wrote in response, "he has a personality which cannot be put aside and he has the qualities of Americanism which have very largely restored him in the

affections of the people." Still, Harding reassured Scobey, caution would prevail when it came to T.R. Harding would not be swept away by Roosevelt's
charm. "He and I are getting to be quite Buddy," he wrote Scobey, "but I do
not think you need to have any apprehension of a seduction. I mean to maintain my virtue at all hazards."[13]

During the first week of May, Harding returned to Ohio to take up the re-
organization of the broken state Republican Party.[14] On May 2, he and former Governor Myron Herrick arrived together in Columbus to meet with
party leaders. The regulars were being led by Harry Daugherty, the Progressives by Walter Brown. Harding named four Progressives to a restructuring
committee out of nine members, and his bow to them "raised some considerable howl from the regulars," he wrote Scobey, but he believed that he could
rebuild a united party only by opening the doors to his past adversaries.[15]
Without fully seeing it, he was beginning to build the very base that would
ensure his landslide victory in 1920, starting in his own state.

Sometime around the time of this trip to Ohio, Harding wrote a highly
defensive, twenty-three-page letter to Carrie Phillips.[16] She had written him
a vinegary letter after his speech in Cincinnati and the declaration of war,
calling him an "abhorrent" hypocrite. "I may be a hypocrite in your eyes—I
know you think it—but I am not a hypocrite in any tribute I have uttered to
German progress or any expression of sympathy I have spoken to Americans
of German origin over the involvement of their adopted country in war," he
wrote. "I have never said I wish Germany to triumph, because that would
not be true. But that is another matter. I am only concerned with your repeated quotation and your charge of public hypocrisy."[17]

Her accusation of insincerity related to something she contended he said
to her in private—that it would be a good thing for the United States to have
a fight with Germany. He denied making such a statement to her, or in his
speech. "You quote the silly lie about my having said 'a little scrap might be
a good thing,'" he wrote. "Can you think me so dumb headed as to say a
thing like that to a pacifist delegation, even if I thought it? In my address I
refuted that statement in Cincinnati." In fact, he did correct the record in his
Cincinnati speech. The statement "a scrap would not be a bad thing for the
country" had been falsely attributed to him by a speaker at a Cincinnati peace
rally who had mangled, perhaps deliberately, Harding's public pronouncements about the war. He deplored the war, he told the Cincinnati audience,
but felt that, if it came, it would make America stronger, more unified. "I

would not seek war for even so desirable an end as that," he said then, "but if it comes and our American people are thereby reconsecrated and are made one people, with undivided allegiance and distinctly and exclusive American ideals, there will be some fit compensation for the artful cost, and the republic will endure."[18] He never said war would be a good thing. "If you read the speech," he chastened Carrie, "you know *what I said* which has been twisted into that silly misrepresentation. Ordinarily I would think you the last to insist on repeating a badly tortured statement, but you have done so in your letter, so I write the denial directly to you."[19]

The entire tone of her letter and the charge of hypocrisy was nothing new, he wrote. She had thought it "for a long while." The most recent allegations caused him to dredge up a time in Baltimore, when, during an intimate encounter, she suddenly threatened to expose him to the Germans. "My mind reverts momentarily to the shock I received at Baltimore, when out of the very halo of blissful existence, when sweet and holy reflection made an air of paradise, you suddenly threatened me with exposure to the Germans, as though I had professed to ask some favor of them when I was unfit for even their toleration," he wrote. "A bolt of lightning from a clear sky could not have given greater shock. I was innocent of the cause, and later I was distressed and disillusioned, because I came to understand where I stood in your estimate and preferences."

Harding had an exact memory of the Baltimore encounter (though he did not clearly place it in time in the letter), and reminded Carrie of how it played out. "I had been calling on you. You insisted on war talk, which I always preferred to avoid. I respected your sympathies, and always preferred the concord of love to contention and argument. Your feelings outran your love for me, and you grew bitter and unheeding, and said I was 'pitiably ignorant' and 'unfit for my responsibilities' and other harsh and irritating things." The onslaught caused him to finally explode and he said disparaging things about Germany, likely that he harbored strong hatred for the country. "Under the sting of such utterances from you, under the lash of your unrestrained speech, when you treated me with unendurable contempt, I, too, momentarily lost control of my tongue and made some such reply as you have repeatedly quoted. I do not contend that it was wholly justifiable, but you offended and stirred my temper, and I said a thing I did not mean and had no sane reason to say. I was too irritated to be sane." What he said was "an embittered retort to your lashing," he contended, "rather than a revelation of any hate in my heart."

Carrie's histrionics from that past tête-à-tête echoed in her most recent letter. She assailed the war declaration and his part in bringing it about. He responded: "You say we have blundered and that I 'have helped betray my country.' It does not lessen my ordinarily high regard for your opinion to reply that I voted in the best conscience and the highest sense of duty which I am capable of feeling. I am not infallible! Alas! So few of us are." Her attack went beyond a political argument; she assaulted him personally, and he responded with angry sarcasm. "Worse, I am 'ignorant' and a 'hypocrite' in your sight," he wrote. "But I still insist that I did my best in a full realization that I must answer to those who commissioned me. A vote is an unalterable record—*no dodging, no escape.* I shall be held to account. If it is a blunder, if it is a betrayal, I shall have to pay. If I am condemned in the final judgment of this witnessing generation, I wish you the certain joy of witnessing my punishment."[20]

A permanent break between the two seemed at hand. "There is doubtless your impelling conscience in writing me that you can no longer be mine," he despaired. Her declaration did not surprise him. "For a long time," he wrote, "I have been the pained witness to resentment driving all love from your heart. Perhaps you do not hate me (not yet) but I could not be blind to the swift-growing change." He narrated the events that had led over time to this point of ultimate estrangement: He had offended her when he took Florence to Florida in the winter of 1914 to recuperate from her serious, life-threatening illness. In her resentment, Carrie said the breach widened while she was still in Europe. Then, after winning the Senate seat, he went to Honolulu in 1915, "the unforgivable offense." Though she said she had pardoned him, he no longer believed it ever had been true. "You have never forgotten for a day, or forgiven for one full hour in which I have had a part in your thoughts."[21]

He again proclaimed he had been exclusive and loyal to her all these years, but brought up two "conscience-burdened nights" when he had apparently confessed some sort of wandering to her:

I am sure there will never be another affair. It is unthinkable. I had resolved in that, long ago. I came to that conclusion at Decatur, when I spoke with a load in my heart never borne by another speaker, save one who spoke once at home after an anguished night in Cleveland. I had rather die than live either of these conscience-burdened nights again. You write that probably my utterances [on the war] have won the approval of another. Oh, no. You need not believe that. There is no other. It would not ordinarily be surprising if there were, for you have not written a word of commendation or approval in years. It is quite human, especially for an egotist (I am so conceited and self-satisfied, you have told me) to crave a bit of approval, and I wished it from you above everybody else in the world, but I wished in vain. Instead I have heard or read only severe criticism and condemnation, sometimes attended by pity for my ignorance. In spite of such extenuation for seeking sympathy and encouragement elsewhere, there has been no seeking and none has been offered. I have only communed with my inner-consciousness and have tried to be worthy —though you will have difficulty in believing me capable of even that.[22]

Carrie's response to this letter can be found in some notes she made on Hotel Statler stationery, apparently drafted while she was in Cleveland, where she seemed to spend a great deal of time in these years.[23] These notes are the only remaining record of what she thought during this period of time and address several of Harding's points from his long letter. They also appear to be jottings she later used to compose a letter she sent to him from Cleveland on May 23.[24]

For example, she wrote out that he did say to her that a scrap with Germany would be a good thing. "The 'silly lie' denied made in Cinci speech—you said it to me," she wrote. "I didn't know it was said by you till then. I only speak of the things you said to me." She also contested directly calling him a hypocrite. Her logic: she hated hypocrisy, she knew what he thought of Germans, and she had read his Cincinnati speech. That is all she said. He was the one applying the label of hypocrite to himself. Of Baltimore and the threat of exposure to the Germans, she wrote: "I made a perfectly sane and sound statement on the subject of Germany's victories. You flew into a tantrum and made the ugly remark when I told you that under the circumstances you should never ask anything of Germans or I should have to tell them what you thought of them—*perfectly fair*." She was referring, she wrote, to German voters in Ohio. "You surely wouldn't think of asking favors of them now? They put you where you are—perhaps it isn't counted a favor?"[25]

She claimed that she was the one who tried to avoid war talk and that he was the one who always brought it up. "*You did it yourself,*" she scribbled, and underlined for emphasis. "*I know* for I tried in particular not to [talk of war] till I had a right to when it came to our country entering. I tried to do all I could. I might have saved my time and put it to better use but I'm not sorry. If every one had done as much to save [the country from war], in proportion, I think it would not have been."[26]

She asserted that he had it all wrong about her sympathies now that the United States had entered the war. Her sympathies were "*for America,* not *Germany,* as you've supposed." During this time, she could have pointed to the seemingly patriotic role that the Uhler-Phillips department store was playing in Marion. In April and May, Uhler-Phillips ran advertisements in the

Marion Star supporting the American Red Cross. Saturday, May 12, was declared "Red Cross Sales" day, with portions of the proceeds from all purchases going to the Marion County Red Cross. The store's ad read: "Everybody, quite naturally, wants to assist America's great 'Red Cross' movement—a notable humanitarian project whose sole object is to relieve suffering and keep alive the gentle spirit of civilization—in the midst of a world shaken and stunned by the black thunderbolts of war."[27] The *Marion Star* reported that Uhler-Phillips's fundraising activity "was a success and netted a nice sum for the Red Cross society."[28]

Despite this public show, Carrie continued to privately mock America's entry into the war under what she considered the ruse of safeguarding democratic principles, or even Harding's limited purpose of protecting just American rights. Referring to Harding's meeting the English propagandist Sir Gilbert Parker, she wrote:

> *Sir Gilbert Parker—not worth mentioning—any way all snobbery and when the real ones came they couldn't stoop to associate with any one so down in governmental affairs as the upper and lower houses? What is it we're fighting for "democratic principles"? Yes, that's it, and* liberty!—*and* humanity. *We had a negro equality man* under democracy *lynched yesterday—great* pretexts *there, of ours! Or if we say "just American rights" that only holds good with* English enemies, *not England herself, or France? No, just* England's enemies, *the Germans! I remember I was glad to read he, Sir Gilbert, has the "good taste" never to mention war. No, no offence if he were here on a political mission—to some—the country has been well over run with them but not until we publicly announced we "were in" (good expression) did we acknowledge them.*[29]

Her mention of the killing of a "a negro equality man" likely was a reference to a lynching in Tennessee that was widely reported in the press on May 22. In that incident, a black farmer named Ell Persons was burned to death in a steel cage set up in the countryside outside Memphis. Ell Persons supposedly had confessed, after being severely beaten, to the decapitation murder of a young white girl. The description of the vigilante execution in the newspapers nationwide was hideous, yet the papers reported it as almost a matter of routine. "The burning of the negro was delayed for several hours pending arrival from Mississippi of a crowd of citizens who had sent word ahead that they desired to witness the ceremony," the article in the *Marion Star* read. "The city of Memphis was agog with excitement. Many business houses failed to open their doors and the newspapers closed their editions early so that employees could go to the scene of the lynching."[30] According to accounts, the condemned man's white captors "leaped about the fire and howled like madmen," while a shouting crowd, estimated at 10,000, looked on as the flames engulfed the terrorized farmer.[31]

As all this bile and bitterness played out between Warren and Carrie, a young woman originally from Marion wrote a letter to "Hon. Warren G. Harding" in Washington asking for his help in finding a job. A high school graduate, she had completed a stenographic program in New York City that spring and wanted a secretarial position in the world of business. Her father had been a well-liked physician in Marion, known to Warren Harding, but had died unexpectedly a few years earlier, leaving a widow and family of five children, including the young woman.[32]

The young woman's name was Nan Britton.[33]

CHAPTER 40

"I Guess My
Spirit Is Broken"

Nan Britton's book, *The President's Daughter,* was published in 1927 and became a national sensation. The book and the authenticity of its many claims, including that Harding fathered Britton's child, Elizabeth Ann, have been the subject of intense debate over the last three quarters of a century. In the book, Britton asserts that her relationship with Warren Harding began after they exchanged a series of letters in May 1917. Her first letter, asking for help in getting a job, she claims was sent on May 7. According to her account, Harding responded that same week, writing that he remembered her and her family. Although he had no position available in his office, he promised to recommend her to the war or navy department if she could provide a note of recommendation from an employer. He told her that there was a good possibility he would be in New York in the next week and would be happy to meet with her in person.

She alleged that she wrote a second letter at on Friday, May 11, thanking him for his reply and encouraging an in-person meeting when he came to New York. Her letter, if believed, was fairly forward for a young woman three years out of high school who was writing to a man who was her father's age and a U.S. senator. "I am hoping that you will be in New York next week and that I can talk with you; I am inclined to believe that an hour's talk would be much more satisfactory," she says she wrote. "There is so much I want to tell you; and I am sure that I could give you a better idea of my ability—or rather the extent of my ability, for it is limited—and you could judge for yourself as to the sort of position I could competently fill."[1]

To her surprise, she received a second letter from Harding, this one on May 15, written in longhand on stationery with the words "Senate Chamber" embossed in its top corner. Although she kept none of his alleged letters, she states that Harding wrote that he intended to be in New York in the next ten days and that it would "be a pleasure to look you up."[2] If her version is to be believed, Harding showed up in New York shortly thereafter (her book gives no date), telephoned her at the secretarial school she was attending, and made an appointment to meet her in the lobby of the Manhattan Hotel at Madison Avenue and Forty-second Street.

They met at the Manhattan at ten-thirty in the morning, had an initial drawn-out conference in a reception room, and then he invited her upstairs, according to her story, to the bridal suite, where, immediately and after closing the door, they began to kiss—though she contended they left the bed "undisturbed." That same afternoon, after a luncheon at the Manhattan, he purportedly took her all over New York via taxi, streetcar, and on foot, to meet with various people for extended interviews at three different locations, culminating in multiple conferences at the offices of the United States Steel Corporation in the Empire Building, with, among others, the company's chairman of the board and its comptroller. She wrote that she and Harding then returned to the hotel for a second stint of kissing. She alleged that throughout the day he told her that he "loved her more than the world" and that he wanted to make her "his bride."[3]

By any measure this was an astonishing day, at the least requiring remarkable energy and stamina. Britton also wrote as if there were nothing far-fetched about him confessing his undying love for her on the first day of their meeting outside of a few brief greetings on the street in Marion. This from the man who spent three years courting Carrie Phillips before their relationship turned physically intimate.

Britton asserts that Harding returned to New York and met with her again before she left in early June to visit her sister in Chicago, prior to starting her new job at U.S. Steel.[4]

Harding's letter at the end of May to Carrie Phillips does show that he went to New York for a day, on May 24, but he told her that he had been quite sick during the past ten days and was having trouble recovering. His office had received a note from Carrie on Thursday, May 24, in which she advised him that she could leave Cleveland, presumably to meet him somewhere East. "Your note of Wednesday now saying you could leave C— [Cleveland] evidently came to the office Thursday while I was in New York," he wrote Carrie on May 28.

"If I had only known in time we could have met in N.Y. on Friday, for I might as well have gone on Friday as Thursday. It happened to be dull work in W— [Washington] and I could have had leisure any day, except that I have been physically and nervously miserable. I can not shake off this cold and cough which put me in bed a couple of days, ten days or more ago, and I feel like a mere remnant of years ago. I do not understand why I can not throw it off."[5]

Harding did return to New York three days later, but only for a few hours late on Sunday night, May 27, when he made a futile search for Carrie. "It is not written to complain," he wrote Carrie on May 28 from the Copley Plaza Hotel in Boston, "but I must tell you that you gave me an anxious three hours last night and you may believe I thought of you every minute of all that time." He looked for her in the train stations and the lobbies of the Biltmore and Manhattan before boarding a midnight train to Boston, tired and disappointed.[6]

If his writing was truthful, he believed she was going to meet with him, either in New York or Boston, and that they had gotten their signals crossed. He had hoped that she could have met him in Boston so they could travel together back to Ohio, where he was scheduled to give a Memorial Day speech to a massive crowd in Columbus on May 30. "We would have time to thresh out everything," he wrote of the prospect of a long train ride together back to Ohio.

Another letter written about this time suggests he did in fact return to New York before going to Ohio. "You will recall very distinctly of my trip to New York, Boston, and New Hampshire, and my return to New York and then coming to Ohio," he wrote to Carrie.[7] The trip sequence appears to conform with Nan Britton's story. But his time was severely limited. He wrote to Carrie from Boston on Monday morning, May 28, after taking the midnight train from New York. He conducted whatever business he had in Boston, apparently stopped in New Hampshire and New York, and then appeared in Columbus on Wednesday morning, May 30, to deliver his oration. His stops in New Hampshire and New York had to be only in passing.

The fact that Nan Britton seems to have a correct chronology of his travels either shows the truth of her account or raises the question: Did she base her book on dates and locations she got from Warren's letters to Carrie Phillips? Were copies of some of the letters in circulation in Marion after he died? Did Isabelle Phillips share the letters, or copies, with Britton, her contemporary from Marion? Britton wrote in *The President's Daughter* that she and her sister knew Isabelle; in fact they were direct backyard neighbors. (Britton gave Carrie and Isabelle pseudonyms in her book—referring to Carrie as "Mrs. Henry Arnold" and Isabelle as her daughter "Angela.")[8] Britton wrote that Isabelle was aware of her teenage crush on Harding and teased her about it. "Angela Arnold, knowing of my adoration for Mr. Harding, one time stopped my sister Elizabeth on the street and told her to 'tell Nan' that her hero had been up to call upon them and had sat the bottom out of one of my mother's favorite chairs! The truth of it was that it was probably a frail chair and Mr. Harding's weight had broken it."[9]

Strained as Britton's story seems, it is not out of the question that she started some sort of a relationship with Warren Harding in May of 1917, though perhaps not exactly the one she described in her book. The timing does correspond with a period of high discord between Warren and Carrie as evidenced by the bitter writings just after war was declared.

The war clearly had taken a toll on the relationship between Warren and Carrie and his letters in May and June show that he felt helpless to change things. "I am not embittered, *I am sorry,*" he wrote to her after she failed to show up in New York. "I shall go on in my own way, reveling in memory, loving the love which filled and sweetened my life. I don't want the memory to be spoiled." His apparent acceptance of a break between them left him feeling a sense of loss—not at all the upbeat, peripatetic, and healthy man who moved so briskly through the pages of Nan Britton's book.

Harding's address in Columbus, Ohio, on Memorial Day was an affair ablaze with patriotism. "Preceded by a parade, in which 10,000 men took part, Columbus celebrated its Memorial day with a big mass meeting, in which Senator Warren G. Harding was the orator," the *Marion Star* reported. "The day's exercises were very impressive, the presence of military organizations soon to be called into federal service furnishing the reminder of the nearness of actual participation in the great war."[10]

Harding repeated his now-consistent war message before the gathering: the war was to protect American rights, not to change another country's government. "It is none of our business what type of government any nation on the face of the earth may have so long as that nation pays its respects to international law," he told the enormous crowd.[11]

After his speech, he said some things that got him into trouble. Speaking without prepared remarks to a group of women, he attacked the Liberty Loan campaign that had just been launched by Secretary of the Treasury William McAdoo, calling it "hysterical and unseemly."[12] He said he thought the United States was perfectly capable of raising funds for the war without such a campaign. These remarks found their way into a

Columbus newspaper and the following week he was severely condemned by Democratic senators on the Senate floor. They charged that in making these remarks he was pandering to the German American voters in Ohio.[13]

Harding did not deny his statements—in fact, he repeated them for the record in the Senate—but he retorted that he had made them in the context of being made aware of administration policy from executive sessions of the Senate that he was not at liberty to disclose. He said that if the facts from those secret sessions could be made public, "it would prove a sensation to the hundred million of Americans, who are on the anxious seat today." He declared that much of the "sentiment uttered concerning our part in this war is balderdash." He was "wearied," he fumed, of all the talk of dethroning the Hohenzollerns and Hapsburgs.

Though he clung doggedly to his defense, he was chastened by the experience. For a time, he became a whipping boy for the administration. Secretary McAdoo said of Harding's statements: "Such remarks are purely political and should not be dignified at such a time in our history with a reply."[14]

In his isolation, Harding wrote Malcolm Jennings that he assumed his friend did not approve of "the course I recently took in the Senate in defending myself against democratic attack."[15] Though he did not regret what he said, he recognized his error. But he insisted that if a democracy was going to conduct a war, it could not appear to be so free and open as to seem hysterical and disorganized. "I have no hesitation in saying, after sober reflection, that I am glad I said the things which I did. The real solemn truth is that we have said so much about democracy in this country that we are on the verge of a chaotic democracy and are developing conditions which seriously cast a doubt upon our ability to defend ourselves."

He continued to think that America's lack of preparedness left it vulnerable and that its focus had to be internal first before setting out to transform the world. "I do not think we are yet ready for the reformation of the world and we ought not to be encouraged in a pitiable endeavor to instigate revolt against governmental authority at a time when we are soon to see governmental authority in this country put to a more than serious test."

Though they were back in a period of estrangement, Warren and Carrie still maintained a regular correspondence. She sent him two letters, on May 27 and 31. She even called him by telephone, and then apologized in her letter for interrupting him and for the mix-up over their plans to meet in New York.[16] But the fact she did not come East sent a clear message to him. "In one sense

I was rejoiced to read that you were safe at home," he wrote. "In another sense I was distressed, because the explanation revealed that you had rebelled against keeping the engagement which had afforded me great happiness while the anticipation lasted."

Her civility did not mean she was willing to drop all discussion of the war, but he wrote back, "I will not discuss." Tellingly, he wrote in the past tense when describing his loyalty to her. "I gave you the best and most faithful and most infatuated love a man can ever bestow. I was loyal and gladly all yours in spite of the failure I made of it, and I can't put it aside as you are able to do. So I just love on, wishing and hoping, and regretting grievances."[17]

His next letter, three weeks later at the end of June, confirms that he believed, or perhaps wanted, their relationship to be over. On Saturday, June 30, he wrote that he had been in Indiana and Chicago the week before and stopped in Ohio for part of a day on this trip, but he "did not find much enjoyment therein." He obviously did not see her. "I used to look forward with happy anticipation to all journeys to Ohio, but that has all changed now."[18]

The reference to Indiana and Chicago provides another direct hit with Nan Britton's story. In *The President's Daughter,* Britton wrote that while on vacation with her sister Elizabeth in Chicago in June of 1917, she received a forty-page love letter from Harding, which caused her to tell her sister of the budding relationship. A week later, she alleges that she received another letter from Harding, telling her that he had been asked to speak in Indianapolis and inviting her to meet him there.[19] She claims she took a train and met him in the Indianapolis train station. "I was curiously enough, quite free from nervousness as I walked through the iron gate where he stood waiting," Nan wrote, "and wondered why *he* seemed so nervous."[20] They registered in a hotel in Indianapolis, and then she accompanied him to Connersville, Indiana, where he spoke, checking into yet another hotel, though she asserts there were no "climatic intimacies" during these visits. That night after his speech, she says, they took the midnight train back to Chicago. "The remembrance of that trip from Connersville to Chicago is very beautiful although it, too, was free from complete embraces."

His description of the Indiana/Chicago trip in his correspondence to Carrie could be seen as confirmatory of Britton's account. Complaining of the intense heat and work in Washington, he wrote Carrie that he had to escape the capital just to catch his breath. "One has to break away to get a fair breathing spell," he wrote her on June 30. "I was away last week—Indiana and Chicago, and felt a strange freedom which I would gladly have prolonged."[21]

There is little doubt that he considered their intimate relationship over. He even ventured that he thought their compact—that he not entertain at his home in Washington or otherwise socialize with Florence—was at an end. "When you wrote me the end had come for you, and notified me you would do what I would not do, that I couldn't have you any more, that you were no longer mine (with inferences to be made accordingly), I supposed nothing mattered much." He assured her that if Florence's presence in Marion was an irritation to her, they would avoid coming home in the future. "There may be a day of necessity now and then, but no continued presence, no residence, no constant annoyance to you! I am willing to sacrifice for your comfort."[22]

He did strike a note of concern about what Carrie might do now that the relationship was over. "I am ready to do anything except to wreak things in a way to engulf us all, and all directly associated with us. . . . I am yours to command—except to explode a bomb to destroy us all."[23]

During the month of June, General John Pershing finally reached Europe. "The arrival in England of Major General Pershing, who is to command the first American army in France, is coincident with the successful completion of the first registration for the selective draft by which large bodies of troops for the reinforcement of that army are to be obtained," the *Times* reported on June 9.[24] The country was now on a full war footing. Young men were required to register for the draft; camps were being built to handle the enormous influx of would-be soldiers. The Wilson administration undertook a series of measure to protect information about the comings and goings of the country's armed forces.

Since the United States entered the war, reports had been circulating that the Germans knew in advance of the sailings of military ships. In late May, for example, newspapers printed a story that a fleet of American destroyers under the command of Rear Admiral William Snowden Sims encountered mines "strewn at the harbor mouth of the port to which they sailed," because German spies in the United States had provided the German navy with information about the schedule and route of the ships.

The response of the Wilson administration was the Espionage Act. The act made it a crime, punishable by death or imprisonment for thirty years, in a time of war and with the intention to communicate the same to the enemy, to collect, record, publish, or communicate any information with respect to the movement, numbers, description, condition, or disposition of any of the armed forces, ships, aircraft, or war materials of the United States.

As originally drafted, the espionage bill contained expansive press censorship provisions, focusing mainly on the publication of troop movements.

Wilson contended that he required comprehensive censorship powers over the press to protect the public safety. In early voting, newspaperman Harding was one of the senators who opposed any press censorship in the bill.[25]

When Malcolm Jennings responded to Harding's letter about his dustup in the Senate over the Liberty Loans, he admitted that he thought Harding had handled himself poorly. Begging his old friend's indulgence, he responded to Warren's letter with a long one of his own, explaining where Harding had been right and where he had been wrong. Harding was right, he wrote, to remind the people that the war was a struggle of self-defense for the United States, not one for promoting some "abstract altruism" like world democracy. "So many of our people forget that our own government itself is a representative republic and not a pure democracy, and I think, to the extent you expressed this view, you were performing a much needed public service."[26]

But Harding was wrong to seem disloyal to the president during a time of war. "I may be wrong," Jennings wrote, "but I believe that martyrdom only awaits the conscientious patriot who dares to criticize the leader of a nation at war and I also realize that there must be criticism if there is to be good service." He recommended that Harding take every opportunity to state his instant readiness "to give the President, in this crisis, everything for which he asked but, at the same time, I would ask the President, on his part, to forget partisanship and call the strongest men of the nation to his council tables." A war, such as the world had never seen before, required autocratic power, Jennings maintained. "Congress is too big in numbers, too little in quality, too full of ambition, too illy-informed, too talkative, to make or conduct a war."

Jennings was urging dictatorship, but in his view, this would force Wilson to rely, more and more, on "men of capacity who can do things and that will mean, more and more, Republicans."

The opportunity for Harding to take up his old friend's advice would present itself soon enough in the person of a *New York Times* reporter named Richard Barry. Warren Harding was about to show his patriotism and devotion to his nation in its unalloyed state. He would rise above all the partisanship—his country needed a strongman. Civilization itself was at stake.

CHAPTER 41

"Secrets of the Hohenzollerns"

Carrie Phillips was in a white-hot fury. She had picked up the *Marion Star* on a Saturday at the end of June 1917 and found a new series titled "The Secrets of the Hohenzollerns."[1] The article was the first in a serialization of a novel written by William Le Queux, a British mystery writer and author of popular espionage thrillers and invasion fantasies. Le Queux purported to be writing what had been revealed to him by a Count Ernst Von Heltzendorff, who claimed to be the personal adjutant to Kaiser Wilhelm's oldest son, Crown Prince William. The count, whose services for the crown prince ended some years earlier, was an insider gossiping about the "gross scandals and wily intrigues" of the kaiser's family and his private circle during the years leading up to the outbreak of the Great War. "I feel, in my retirement, no compunction in exposing all I know concerning the secrets of the Kaiser and his profligate son," the count supposedly wrote to Le Queux from his exile in France, according to a letter published with the series in the *Star*.

Carrie was enraged at the series, especially the manner in which it was portrayed as nonfiction by the *Star*. "For one who knows," she wrote in scathing notes she kept with the Harding letters, "she hadn't read it twenty lines till the lie was given in the article. One who is not truthful in little things can scarcely be believed in the greater ones."[2]

She was in an unhappy and very dark mood as she wrote and the Le Queux series only served to further irritate her, causing her to remark on the superiority of the German nation and its leadership when compared to the vile English and their scandalous press filled with pulp-fiction writers. "But these things themselves will never hurt Deutschland," she wrote of the matters written in the series. "Deutschland is no different than any other nation in the world, save in the superlative degree of her efficiency. The Kaiser, the Crownprinz—no different than other men privately."

Then she wrote in a sinister way of what a similar exposé might reveal of the hidden life of the owner and editor of the *Marion Star* himself. What if he were betrayed by someone intimate to him? "Supposing," she posited, "taking the life, the life one lives only before his God, the life [of a] man [that] is not supposed to be revealed, *were revealed*—as in the case of the Crownprinz, [and] it is told by his friends, even his *most loving* friend and not by a bitter enemy who had been a trusted and loving friend and servant of almost great rank and birth (no doubt)?" She had material she could reveal, she mused, matters that would be scandalous for the owner of the *Star* but hardly of note to the emperor of Germany and members of his royal family. Her notes, though cryptic, were explosive in content, especially with regard to Florence Harding:

> *I ought to explain perhaps. Well, to begin with the editor before he became editor and to the present. If things known only to him and his God were revealed over the term of years mentioned by his most loving friend and given the* best possible *face, shouldn't you think it would make quite as good reading, for the class such stuff appeals to, as this of the Hohenzollerns* [as told] *by Heltzendorff? Of course we must take into consideration the differences in station, profession and prominence, etc., of the parties in question, giving all the* deference in the world *to their experiences. Now then take the* [editor], *he married a divorcee, or he could not have had her by law. Now, early in the life of this same person she was common property (by word of mouth of one of the participants, so he hinted). Anyway we* know *that she had a child in a few months (short) after her marriage to* one of them [likely Marshall], *not my informant. A bastard baby helped to be made legal, at best, given the name of the (guilty)? one. Now after this marriage before the divorce had been secured this person becomes pregnant by still another at least we* know *of one time and there were others. He married her. Now we are not mentioning others, women who had held a near and dear part in the life of this man spoken of, the editor and owner of the above mentioned paper who prints the inner most thoughts and actions of the Ruler and near Ruler of Germany with whose nation we are "in a state of war."*[3]

Was she suggesting that Florence Kling DeWolfe was pregnant when Warren Harding married her? The notes are too murky to draw definitive conclusions. And if so, what happened to this pregnancy? Again, the notes are unclear: "Of course there were no children born and, I think, in one of the same articles which no doubt will now follow in the 'jerkwater' press [illegible], I saw where the Kaiser had been so ruthless as to murder a man, that is, he said there was only one thing he could do with honor so he committed suicide. At least the man took his own life. The child or children above in question were not given a chance. They were murdered. Awful word isn't it."[4]

Warren's letter to Carrie on June 30 gives no specific hint that she wrote to him anything as inflammatory as is contained in her private notes, but he nevertheless was circumspect in his response to whatever she wrote. He politely acknowledged the arrival of a book and newspaper clippings she sent him. "I have read the latter [the clippings] and hope to have the book digested by the time Monday comes. These are busy times here, and it is so hot except at night, out of doors, that one does not get much accomplished." This is the letter in which he told her that, to escape the heat, he had traveled to Indiana and Chicago and had experienced "a strange freedom" that he happily would have prolonged. If the clippings were from the Le Queux series in the *Star,* or if the book was the one that Le Queux wrote about the secrets of the Hohenzollerns, Warren did not refer to them as such. Nor did he apologize for the series appearing in the *Marion Star.* But this was the letter in which he wrote: "I am yours to command except to explode a bomb to destroy us all."[5]

Carrie drafted an answer to this June 30 letter, one of the few copies of a complete letter that she kept with Harding's letters. It is not clear whether she sent an exact duplicate of this draft to him, but he responded on July 11 to one that at least was similar. Carrie's draft provides a window into her thinking at the time, and, as with her notes, she turned the searchlight on him.

She started the draft at nine-thirty on Saturday night, July 7, saying she was alone, as if she were somewhere other than at home, perhaps in a hotel in Cleveland or New York. "I haven't the slightest desire to write something tonight, but owing to the fact that there could be a misunderstanding I feel I ought. I have the time to and can always be alone here."[6] She noted that in his last letters he expressed a belief that their relationship seemed to be over and that the end had been *her* idea. She may have sensed that he was calling her bluff, or perhaps she was picking up on his attention to Nan Britton, if in fact an affair had begun. Whatever the case, she undertook in this draft to set the record straight: Her actions were in response to things he had done, not because it was her preference to end their relationship.

She then addressed his statement that she seemed "perturbed" over the apparent breach of their compact that he have no social visitors in his Washington home. (He had written that he had not even been in Washington during the time she was concerned about.) Yes, she wrote, she was upset, but not over visitors. "If they came before, what could I expect now?" she asked. She had learned, she said, to expect nothing from him since January 1914—referring to the time when he took Florence to Florida to recover from her lengthy illness.

She turned to his comment that he was hers to command except to explode a bomb to destroy them all. "I should not be required to 'command' you to do that," she wrote mockingly. "I could do that myself without the least bit of help from you."

Instead, she would simply replay for him all the major commitments he had broken over the years—promises that he would leave Florence, that they would make a dramatic escape out West, create a new life and possibly welcome their own children:

> *I remember of your telling me many times that all I had to do was "say the word" and you would divorce her (she isn't yours really for her husband was living when you went through the wedding ceremony), that I should "pretend to visit friends in the West" and you would meet me and we would "leave all behind and start anew." We would travel until a hoped for time came, and then stop till we were able once again to journey on—beautiful dream. Yes, but that was some time ago. This was renewed once again after a defeat in 1910—[but] relentless political aspirations bring [from him questions like], "What do you want to do, leave me?" [or statements like] "All I hear is reproach and condemnation." Remember we have reached the goal now, before we had failed. Love is all, nothing counts but love. "I love you more and better than everything else in the world." All you need is to command. "Your word is law." The simplest favor was denied. All promises were broken and I was "imperious," "demanding," "lacking in all courtesy," and "trying to wreck you," when I believed in you and asked you only to keep your word to me that I might not lose my faith in you.[7]*

The string of disappointments, she wrote, were finally too much for her. "How long do you think a self-respecting woman could endure the things I have?" she fumed. "I could not make you love me. You loved me or you did not." In her view, *he* was responsible for their rupture—his actions, not his words, showed her the truth. "You made the decision. Why aren't you satisfied? You have all you have ever craved, little has ever been denied you that *you* have cared for."[8]

Helping to fuel much of this anger was a deepening fissure between Florence and Carrie. The two women were apparently at each other's throats.

Carrie wrote that gossip had provoked her into writing a warning letter directly to Florence in Washington. She sent a copy to Warren, so he would know that the letter had issued. "Nice, you no doubt have the letter I wrote—the copy was not precisely the same but nearly so," she wrote. "I'll have no gossip if I can help it. If I find I have in spite of my protest I'll feel compelled to start something quite worth while to counter it. I can." She wrote that she had been protective of their relationship in part to guard Florence from embarrassment. "I have been asked point blank, a question by a person here and I *lied* outright about it to shield a person who wouldn't turn a hand to please me and is under all sorts of obligations to me. Strange isn't it! Yes, the letter will let you know. I sent it so that you would know what I had written and that I had."[9]

Carrie was not sure, given the extent of hostility that had surfaced between the two women, whether Florence would even read her letter, but she suspected her inquisitiveness would get the better of her. "She may not mention having received it," she wrote. "I think she is far too curious not to read."

The warning letter may have been the result of an incident like the one that was recounted in a newspaper article about Florence several years later, after Warren had won the presidency. On February 20, 1921, a few weeks before the inauguration, the *New York Herald* carried a long, glowing profile of Florence, written by her lifelong friend Jane Dixon. As evidence of Florence's remarkable character—and confirmation that she was "100 per cent American"—Dixon told of a very public event where Florence called out Carrie for her unpatriotic, pro-German comments. Dixon did not use Carrie's name, but the description of the woman reprimanded was clearly her, recognizable to anyone who lived in Marion during this time. Though the story may have been invented, the article detailed that sometime after America entered the war, the whole town, including the Hardings, turned out to "cheer and 'tear' their farewell" to a group of Marion boys who were on their way to Europe. "At the crux of the excitement," Dixon related, "a local matron who had spent some time in Berlin educating her daughter and who had managed to be bitten by the dog of Kaiserism, made some slighting remark anent the send-off." Dixon wrote that Florence overheard the remark and turned on the offending woman. "In a manner all the crowd might heed she publicly rebuked the foolish matron, leaving her to nurse her spleen against Uncle Sam in solitude, a move the entire town has since followed."[10]

Warren's response to Carrie's early July letter was perfunctory. "Your endeavor of clippings and copy of letter [to Florence] *all* received," he wrote on July 11. "The copy of the letter revealed a very dignified character and I hope the result is helpful."[11] It appears that he was not going to get involved this time in a direct dispute between the women if he could help it.

In the same letter, he advised that he was going to Chicago on "an important business trip" and that he would be at the Congress Hotel until Friday night, July 13. He held out an olive branch: "I could come to Marion on the return, but have no wish to come there unless I could see you, and you wish it so."[12]

She did not see him. She failed to get his note in time, she wrote to him. She explained that she was at the resort and amusement park in Sandusky, Ohio, known as Cedar Point. "It was unimportant anyway," he wrote on Sunday, July 22.[13] "Of course I would have returned from Chicago via Marion if you had been home and had expressed a desire for me to come, and not hearing I cut out Ohio and went directly to New York for a day, and then came home." Nan Britton wrote in her book that by July, she was back in New York boarding on West 136th Street and working at U.S. Steel, and that Harding came to see her in the middle of the month.[14] She describes him as arriving from Washington not Chicago, but that aside, this appears to be another direct hit in her book. "I like the diversion which New York affords to all who come," Warren described the trip to Carrie, almost as if he were baiting her. "It is a good place to get out of the rut."[15]

He and Florence finally did discuss the letter that Carrie sent to Florence. They had a sharp exchange. "I read the *copy* of the letter you sent to the house," he wrote to Carrie in a July 22 letter. "That is I read the *copy* you sent to me. In due time I inquired about the original and an answer thereto, got into a very ugly and disagreeable row and dropped the matter." Carrie apparently wanted him to press for a response, perhaps an apology. He refused. "I will not humiliate myself to ask again," he protested. "I thought you wrote in commendable dignity, I have no criticism, except that had I known you meant to write I should have asked to suggest the best time and some things to say which might have helped. But it is quite all right. You have gained something even though it goes unanswered. Perhaps it has been answered— I don't know."[16]

In Germany, the Imperial Chancellor von Bethmann-Hollweg, who once called treaties with Belgium "scraps of paper," was forced to resign over the weekend that Harding spent in New York. There had been a revolt brewing in the Reichstag by the Social Democrats, Progressives, and Center parties, all of whom favored a proposal for a moderate peace. They drafted a document to reflect their views known as the Reichstag Peace Resolution. The resolution, passed on July 20, reminded the world of the kaiser's proclamation at the beginning of the war that Germany had no intention of conquering any land and that it fought the war strictly for defensive purposes.[17] "The Reichstag labors for peace and mutual understandings and lasting reconciliation among the nations," the resolution read. "Forced acquisitions of territory and political, economic, and financial violations are incompatible with such a peace."[18]

There were rumors that the kaiser himself was about to resign. But even with the peace resolution and the government shake-up, the Germans intended to fight on, as long as enemy governments refused to agree on a peace without conquest or domination. "The German nation united is unconquerable," the defiant Reichstag members reaffirmed.[19]

In Russia, under its fragile new democracy, Prince Lvoff was replaced as premier by Alexander Kerensky, who had been minister of war.[20] But Russia was exhausted after three years of war, and mutinies, sparked by extremist agitators, were breaking out among military units at the front.[21] Eventually the coalition government—the vaunted democracy championed by the Wilson administration—would collapse and Vladimir Lenin and his Bolsheviks would gain power. Russia would be out of the war before the end of the year, allowing Germany to concentrate its efforts on the Western Front. Wilson's war to make the world safe for democracy was about to meet its greatest foe in revolutionary Russia, the country that he pointed to as the promising model.

The world war would continue.

In Marion, the *Star* carried a news story about how German spies were keeping close watch on vessels leaving ports. According to a report, an American barkentine captain who had been a prisoner aboard the German U-boat that had sunk his ship arrived back in the United States and described how the U-boat commander knew of the sailings of other American ships from German spies. "GERMAN SPIES EVER WATCHFUL" was the headline in the *Star* on July 23.[22]

In Washington, Warren Harding remarked, almost in passing, in his July 22 letter to Carrie that another reason he had gone to New York straight from Chicago was because he understood the Phillipses were entertaining a special visitor during that time in Marion. "I also knew," he wrote, "that you were having company—Lieut. P. I hope it was a happy week for Isabelle and a pleasant one for all of you."[23]

"Lieut. P." was no doubt Lieutenant Adolf von Scheven Pickhardt, USN.

CHAPTER 42

"The Chickens Had
Scraps from the Table"

"Mrs. Zollner, tell us, did you become very attached to Mr. Spalding?" Mr. Abernathy inquired of the baroness. She was still on direct examination in her probable cause hearing, taking her attorney's questions.

"I did," she responded.

"And did he become very much attached to you?" he followed.

"He did."[1]

Her claim was that the former midshipman had fallen in love with her, even though she was old enough to be his mother. But the facts were that she had kept him with her teenage son Bedford in the house just outside the gates of the Naval Academy and made sure that he studied for and took the entrance exam for Army officer training. Documents found on her person when she was arrested in Chattanooga also seemed to show that Spalding was acting with her in concert to provide intelligence to the Germans.[2]

Bedford stayed in Annapolis until July 6 when he returned to New York. There the baroness's young daughter, Nonie, was being attended to by trusted caretakers and hired servants. The baroness and Spalding continued to live at the house outside the Naval Academy until early August.[3] By then the academy had closed and the midshipmen were on their summer cruise.[4] The baroness asked to be released from her long-term lease of the house, purportedly because she had a physical breakdown, "a nervous collapse," at the end of July—conveniently occurring precisely when the midshipmen took their leave. The doctor ordered her to go away, she said, so she took Spalding to Atlantic City, where they spent the balance of August at a hotel on the ocean.[5] Bedford said he was not surprised that his mother had the breakdown. She had been prone to heart trouble all her life, "more so in this country because we had no permanent home."[6]

On or about August 22, they received the good news that Spalding had passed his entrance exam and would be expected in Kansas at Fort Leaven-worth in September.[7] The baroness admitted on cross-examination that she was "very anxious" to get Spalding into the Army. "No doubt about it," she agreed with the U.S. attorney who pressed her.[8]

During the first week of September, Spalding allegedly wrote out a strange statement, a copy of which was found among the baroness's posses-sions in a hotel safe when she was arrested.[9] It was explained at the hearing as simply a form of affidavit that the baroness could use, if necessary, to support her breaking of the house lease in Annapolis, though its bizarreness makes it seem more like a coded message, perhaps about conditions at the Naval Acad-emy, reflecting such things as ship strength, or company or brigade readiness:

September 3, 1917
To Whom It May Concern.

I hereby state that when Baroness Ione Zollner took over the Terry House, from Mrs. Howard, May 1, 1917, she found it in a filthy condition, even the linens and unwashed dishes were found hidden away in boxes. The Baroness was com-pelled to employ several (4) cleaning women for 3 days to make the house hab-itable. These women used disinfectants to take the vile smell from the kitchen.

Probably this smell and filth were augmented by cats who were not house broken and whom Mrs. Howard expected the Baroness to keep. She did feed them on the back porch, but they soon left. I judge because their tastes were not cultivated to the superior food she gave them. Likewise, I believe the chickens were overfed.

The chickens had scraps from the table where eight people ate three times a day. Also the chickens had corn, which cost $3.50 twice a day. Of course after the Baroness left on August 3 she was not responsible for the chickens for Mrs. Howard said she would look after them.

Mrs. Howard left, as she claimed, 14 sheets, that is to say she said that she had a pair of sheets for each bed (7 beds). Personally I never saw but 4 sheets of hers. I left 13 sheets then about 7 more and the Baroness had eight sheets marked and 6 new sheets. I have now, after Mrs. Howard searched the house and laun-dry, 5 sheets.

Mrs. Howard left the Baroness no towels.

> *As to the condition of this house when the Baroness entered, she has other witnesses.*
>
> *When she left she paid Mrs. Clara Coons a week's wages to clean the house. Clara says she did clean it. She has witnesses for this.*
>
> *I entered the house three weeks ago after it had been occupied by a family of four who did not own a broom with which to sweep and at that time the house was reasonably clean and much cleaner than I ever saw it when Mrs. Howard was living in it.*
>
> Lt. J. W. Spalding, U. S. A.

The baroness paid for the holiday at Atlantic City, then she and Spalding traveled to Washington, where they stayed for a couple of weeks at the Congress Hall Hotel, near the Capitol, a place frequented by congressmen.[10] She paid the bill for this stay, then she advanced Spalding's expenses to travel to Fort Leavenworth in the third week of September.[11] Spalding again wrote out an affidavit, found among the baroness's effects in the hotel safe, praising her for her willingness to pick up his transportation costs when the U.S. government had refused to help: "This is the second time in my knowledge that this lady whom the ignorant claim is a German spy has helped officers of the U.S. Government."[12]

Spalding would be in training for eleven weeks before being sent to Fort Oglethorpe, just outside Chattanooga. The baroness would arrive soon after his assignment to Chattanooga, and she would take an immediate tour of the cantonment, chatting up the officers and the enlisted men.

CHAPTER 43

"Need of Dictator Urged by Harding"

"What the United States needs and what it must have if it is to win the war is a supreme dictator with sole control of and sole responsibility for every phase of war activity, and this today means practically every phase of Government." Thus began an astounding article from an interview of Senator Warren G. Harding conducted by Richard Barry of the *New York Times,* which splashed in the newspaper's Sunday magazine on August 12, 1917, complete with a quarter-page drawing of Harding.[1] Even in an etching he projected a solemn and forbidding look. "Need of Dictator Urged by Harding," was the title of the piece.

Harding met with Barry on the veranda of the Capitol, just outside the Senate floor, to let his views be known. All summer the Senate had been bogged down with wrangling over prohibition, price fixing, food, feed and fuel control, the aviation bill, and increased spending and taxation.[2] Harding was growing frustrated with the pace of mobilization and Congress's seeming inability to adopt immediate war measures. Though he feared creeping socialism more than most in Congress, he had adopted Malcolm Jennings's position that the times required extraordinary action and emergency measures. He wrote to Jennings on July 6 that he would vote for the food control bill—which he did on July 21—but not without significant reservations: "I will vote for the food bill and fuel control, [and] will thank God if industrial paralysis does not follow, and will also ask him to forgive my of-ficial sins."[3] A few weeks later, he again bemoaned the Wilson administra-tion's war for democracy. "While we are making the world safe for democracy," he told the Senate on July 19 during the food control bill de-bate, "we are going through the processes of revolution, and they are very likely to give the world a socialized democracy."[4]

Harding spoke to Barry within earshot of orations on the Senate floor about the food control bill. Some of the very same senators who had opposed war now stood against the food bill, but were joined by some very conserva-tive senators for very different fiscal responsibility reasons. Harding had learned from the debacle over Liberty Bonds that dissent was dangerous in time of war, so he stood clear of the debate, knowing it would lead to a charge of pro-German pandering. "Over the whole Senate lay the castigations of John Sharp Williams of Mississippi accusing every obstructionist of potential, if not actual pro-Germanism," Barry wrote.[5]

Never again would Harding be seen as an obstructionist. "At lunch the Senator from Ohio had remarked, casually, that the United States was drift-ing toward a dictatorship," Barry wrote. "Later he was asked to amplify and, if possible, to justify this idea. He was quick to add that he meant it in no of-fensive sense, but that at the same time he was profoundly sure of the desir-ability of a dictatorship and had no desire to postpone the day of its arrival."[6]

Disclaiming any status as professional historian or constitutional lawyer, Harding nevertheless held forth on his view of American history and the Con-stitution, both of which he said supported his position that a temporary dic-tator was both necessary and consistent with the American form of government. He saw George Washington's approval of Alexander Hamilton's strong executive as confirmation that the founders intended to leave every av-enue open for "casting to one man in a crisis all power." Likewise, Abraham Lincoln accumulated power during the Civil War to the point that, toward war's end, "Congress as well as the Cabinet had all but abdicated in favor of one man who had proved himself a safe dictator for the destinies of the nation."

"The same thing must occur in this war," Harding concluded, "and the sooner it comes the better for all of us. We will never be actually in the war, never be a menace to Germany in a modern military sense, until it does come." He was not concerned that the dictator would be a Democ-rat. Wilson was elected president, so he was the one to be given the power. "I must say he is not my choice, but the people of the country have cho-sen him, and he is the only one to whom we can turn. Why quibble with events which are already accomplished." Nor did it bother him that the United States would become like Germany, the very kind of autocratic power it sought to defeat. "Our advantage over the Germans is that we would put on autocracy as a garment only for the period of the war, whereas they wear autocracy as the flesh that clings to their bones," Harding explained. "Once the war is over, we would discard autocracy, just as we did after the Revolution and the rebellion."[7]

Around the time he was giving his interview to Richard Barry, Harding made a quick political trip out to Cleveland, then stopped in Marion, and may have again diverted to New York to see Nan Britton, if her story is true, before returning to Washington to propose a major amendment to a resolution on prohibition.

In his letter to Carrie Phillips on July 22, he advised that he would be in Cleveland on Saturday, July 28, and that he might come to Marion the day before or the day after.

On July 28, a Saturday, he was in Cleveland to give a speech to thousands of Republicans at Luna Park, a giant amusement park on the east side of Cleveland. The event was the annual picnic of the League of Republican Clubs from around the state. An article in the Cleveland newspaper reported that the organizing committee had distributed 125,000 tickets for the function, "and the majority of the holders kept the turnstiles clicking at a merry rate in the early hours of the afternoon."[8] Harding met with dozens of party leaders in the morning and delivered his speech to the party faithful in the afternoon. While this was a party function, Harding reminded his listeners that the country needed to be united during a war. "This is not a war of political parties, nor the tragic screen for the display of political partisanship," Harding told the audience. "Partisan lines have been utterly dissolved in writing American conscience and American determination into all war enactments. It matters little whether one is Democrat, Republican, Socialist or Independent, until there are first guaranteed the rights, privileges and safety of triumphant American citizenship. First of all he must be an American for America, a patriotic citizen with an American soul."

Carrie must have responded to his letter of July 22 saying she would see him, for he traveled to Marion from Cleveland, either that night or the next morning. His letters confirm that he saw her, though his description of their meeting seems polite and distant, almost formal. "The recent hospitality extended to me was appreciated and most agreeable," he wrote on August 4.[9] "It was good to see you." The *Marion Star* for Monday, July 30, confirmed that Harding stopped in Marion on Sunday.[10]

On Tuesday, July 31, Harding was back in Washington, giving an address on the floor of the Senate on his amendment to the so-called Sheppard resolution, which was legislation to send the proposed constitutional amendment for nationwide prohibition to the states for ratification.[11] Harding's amendment to the legislation provided that the proposed constitutional amendment would expire if not ratified by the states within ten years. Though his initial proposal of ten years was defeated, Harding's amendment was passed when he reduced it to a six-year proposal.[12] A time limit was critical to Harding's support for the prohibition amendment, as it was to other senators, because it made it more likely that the amendment would not pass but still left the issue in the hands of the people. He did not want the prospect of nationwide prohibition hanging over the nation for some indefinite period—it needed to be passed within some reasonable time or not. The Harding amendment passed, as did the Sheppard resolution on Wednesday, August 1.[13]

Nan Britton places Warren Harding in New York on Monday, July 30, between the time he was in Marion, on Sunday, July 29, and the time he proposed his amendment to the Sheppard resolution on the Senate floor on the morning of Tuesday, July 31. The date, Monday, July 30, is not insignificant to Britton's story: It is the day she claims she lost her virginity and "became Mr. Harding's bride."[14] Years later, when she was defending her book in a libel court proceeding she initiated in Toledo, she made much of this particular day. She even introduced a hotel register, supposedly from the records of the Hotel Imperial in New York, which allegedly contained Harding's handwriting. Britton pointed to a handwritten entry on the register, "G. H. Harvey & wife" from Cleveland, as proof of their visit.[15]

Her description of the day, as with so many of her accounts in her book, was filled with details that lend credence, at least on the surface, to her story. Harding came to New York the morning of July 30. She wore a pink linen dress, "which was rather short and enhanced the little-girl look which was often my despair."[16] They went to a hotel on "Broadway in the thirties." The day was exceedingly warm, and the bellboy who took them to the room threw open the window, but they were up high enough not to be bothered by the traffic noise below. "I became Mr. Harding's bride—as he called it—on that day," she wrote.[17] They were startled by an unexpected phone call and then a knock at the door. Two men, apparently from a vice squad, came in and threatened to arrest them. Harding was dejected and told Britton to tell the truth about her age—she was twenty. At the last minute, one of the men noticed Harding's name in gold lettering on the inside of his hat and recognized him as a U.S. senator. The men then decided to let them go, and a relieved

Harding handed one of them a twenty-dollar bill in gratitude. "Gee, Nan," Britton recalled Harding saying to her, "I thought I wouldn't get out of that under $1000!"[18] The spooked couple went to Churchill's for dinner, and he returned to Washington on the midnight train.

But did this encounter, so pivotal to Britton's story, really take place?

Though it would have been an enormous logistical challenge for Harding to get from Marion, Ohio, on Sunday, July 29, to New York City on Monday and then to the Capitol on Tuesday, it may have been possible, given the regularity of night trains and his propensity for taking midnight trains. Yet he would have had to cover vast distances in three days. In light of the intense public interest and scrutiny that the prohibition measure was receiving across the country, let alone in a media-savvy city like New York, would Harding really have been so reckless as to have an assignation in a New York hotel, knowing that he was going to sponsor a high-profile amendment to the Sheppard resolution the next day? Further, would he dine in a popular restaurant in New York with an unknown young woman on the day when the prohibition debate was at its climax in the Senate? Would he risk his reputation and career, when surely he knew that his whereabouts would be watched and noted?

These questions alone cast serious doubt on Britton's story.

But the most significant problem with her chronology is the fact that the *New York Times* reported that Harding was polled by two of his fellow senators in Washington on Monday, July 30. The article is unusually clear that Harding was in the Capitol on that Monday. "A poll of the Senate today [dateline Washington, July 30] by Senators Sheppard of Texas and Curtis of Kansas indicated that the Sheppard resolution for a Constitutional amendment on nation-wide prohibition would be adopted 66 to 27," the article read.[19] Harding was listed among the sixty-six likely to vote for the resolution. The newspaper characterized the poll as a "fairly accurate gauge" because it "was taken of eighty-nine Senators who were at the Capitol," and, more, the canvass by the two senators was conducted "outside the Senate Chamber, while debate on the resolution went on." Four senators included in the poll even though they were absent from the Senate were listed specifically in the article: Tilman, Fall, Gallinger, and Goff. If Harding had not been present, it would have been a simple thing to mention him as absent. One must conclude that Harding was in the Capitol responding to the Sheppard and Curtis poll on Monday, July 30, not in New York having sex and dinner with Nan Britton.

The most reliable evidence, therefore, suggests that he returned to Washington directly from Marion to attend to urgent business in the Senate. This pokes a serious hole in the Britton story.

On Saturday, August 4, Harding wrote to Carrie thanking her for her recent hospitality in Marion, sending her newspaper clippings, and complimenting her on a note she sent him about the *Plain Dealer* article written of his speech at Luna Park. "You would make an invaluable editorial writer," he enthused, "except for your preconceived prejudices."[20] He noted that she would probably be occupied with the Chautauqua week in Marion, but now he himself had little interest in this event, which he used to enjoy so much every summer. "I have heard so much speech-making and wind-jamming that my Chautauqua taste has subsided. Perhaps it is the poor quality I encounter," he added in a shot at some of his fellow senators.[21]

The summer of 1917 had been consistently hot. "Heavens!" he exclaimed. "But I had a hot ride from Marion eastward," he wrote of his trip back to Washington. "We have almost roasted this week, ruining temper, disposition and appetite, and making sleep almost impossible. I am ready to vote a medal to the inventor of the electric fan. He is a real benefactor."[22]

Nan Britton claimed that during August Harding came again to New York and visited with her and that he sent her a gift on August 11—a wristwatch—for her twenty-first birthday. She also said he unleashed a torrent of love letters, one being sixty pages in length, and that she received a special delivery letter from him almost every Sunday.[23]

None of these alleged letters have survived.

As August dragged on, Carrie and Isabelle packed up their things and headed for an extended vacation on the East Coast, without Jim. They made their way to the Andencraig Inn, a hotel on Main Street in a sleepy town on Long Island Sound called Port Jefferson.

That summer, thousands of construction workers just a dozen miles south of Port Jefferson worked to create a major cantonment for New York City area draftees. The camp was located just outside a town named Yaphank, which was in the middle of Long Island. Yaphank was conveniently situated on the Long Island Railroad, allowing easy access to and from New York City.[24]

Though Carrie and Isabelle likely did not know it, their activities and movements were being watched and monitored. The American Protective League in Marion had decided she and Isabelle were dangerous and they started keeping tabs on their whereabouts.[25]

CHAPTER 44

"No Women Are Insensible
to the Courtly Attentions
of Army or Navy Men"

*T*he young men drafted over the summer were finally being called to camps. Nearly 687,000 men were scheduled to report in the first weeks of September to cantonments around the country established by the Wilson administration. "By the original plan of the War College Division of the General Staff," the *Times* reported in early September, "the country was divided into sixteen divisional training areas, with special reference to density of population in different parts of the United States, so that each of the sixteen camps would have about the same number of men of the right age to draw upon."[1] The camp just south of Port Jefferson, New York, would come to be named Camp Upton in honor of a Civil War general, Emery Upton, who long advocated that the United States should have a permanent army.[2]

Like all the cantonments, Camp Upton was huge. Built to house up to 40,000 men, the government constructed over 1,500 buildings, with a railroad terminal, barracks, wash houses, mess halls, officers' quarters, headquarters, stables, and sanitary and sewer lines.[3] The camp opened on August 25, with recruits scheduled to arrive in phases beginning in September.[4] Camp Upton would acquire some lasting theatrical fame because Irving Berlin, a Russian-born, twenty-nine-year-old draftee from the Lower East Side, spent time in the camp and wrote a musical called *Yip, Yip*

Yaphank (its most remembered song was "Oh! How I Hate to Get Up in the Morning").

Those reading the newspaper accounts of the making of America's great national army would have been sobered by official projections of the numbers of men who were likely to be lost in the war. Major General Tasker H. Bliss, Chief of Staff, told the press that "it is estimated at the War Department that the wastage of men by death, wounds, and all other causes will be 60 per cent a year," the *Times* reported as the draft camps opened. "So keeping a continuing force of a million men on the battle line through one year means 600,000 replacement troops trained in reserve. Should there be two years of war for America's armies, still other reserves would be needed to fill the ranks of the replacement troops themselves."[5]

In light of these bleak predictions, one wonders about former college president Woodrow Wilson's published letter expressing his envy of the men being sent to the trenches in Europe. "Please say to the men on Sept. 4," he wrote to the man organizing the New York draft parade, "how entirely my heart is with them and how my thoughts will follow them across the sea, with confidence and also with genuine envy, for I should like to be with them on the fields and in the trenches where the real and final battle for the independence of the United States is to be fought, alongside the other peoples of the world, struggling, like ourselves, to make an end of those which have threatened the integrity of their territory, the lives of their people, and the very character and independence of their Governments."[6]

Warren Harding wrote to Carrie from Washington in care of the Andencraig Inn in the town just north of Camp Upton on Saturday, August 25, the day the cantonment officially opened. She and Isabelle had already been at Port Jefferson for some time: Carrie had knitted some socks for Warren, which he acknowledged in his note. Harding's letter makes it seem as though this was the first time Carrie had visited Port Jefferson as a vacation spot. "Thanks for your note, and many, many thanks for the very beautiful sox," he wrote. "You are extravagantly generous and thoughtful, but it is sweet to be remembered, and I am very happy about them. I am glad, too, that things have turned out well, and the place is attractive and a pleasant time is in sight."[7]

During a stop in Washington along the way, Carrie did see Harding and asked of him some favor that he could not honor. "Was really sorry I could not be more helpful," he wrote. "Yes, every thing was all right here, except that I could not see enough of you." Since her visit had been around the time of their erstwhile anniversary date of August 23, he was moved to write of his love for her, even though he thought she no longer returned it. "But I do not forget the reason for remembering," he responded to her complaint that he had forgotten the date. "And I can do more than you, I can write, as I said then, 'I love you and want you.' And God knows I do—both love and want you. There were two separate moments when you were here when I realized it as never before. *God!* To have had you, and possess you, and been blessed, and compensated and transported to bliss restored! I wished all that and more. But you wouldn't write a word of love! Well, I don't want you to if you don't feel it."[8]

They apparently discussed the idea of him coming for a visit to Port Jefferson. He told her that he could not because the War Revenue Bill, which was in endless debate in the Senate, had "made little progress." But he did invite her to come to Washington if she had an idle day or two. He told her that "Jerry" had been interested in her visiting, "though too concerned to fully express," he teased. "He had largely lost interest in any part of present day activities, but he could be wonderfully inspired by you. I think you ought to do it." He cautioned her not to wire him but said it would be all right if she called him any day at the Capitol at noon.[9]

A week later he wrote to her again. She was still in Port Jefferson, with no apparent plans to leave. She wrote two notes to him during the week, one dealing with a newspaper profile that discussed his potential presidential prospects and another that suggested to him that she might be relenting and that they might recommence their intimate relationship. "I can't get away from a grateful clinging to your suggesting that I *might* have the craved happinesses which were momentarily glimpsed when you were here," he wrote to her on Friday, August 31, using Senate Chamber stationery. "Well, I wish them. I hunger and thirst for them, and when there is encouragement I dream fondly of them. I could drift to anticipation, *glad* anticipation now. My heart, my head, and whole being calls."[10]

A clipping from a Philadelphia newspaper that he sent her discussed him as a potential presidential candidate in 1920, probably as a result of publicity surrounding the *New York Times* magazine piece on his suggestion of a dictatorship. The report must have provoked her, so he tried to soothe. "And I should have asked you to disregard the unjustifiable reference to larger ambitions," he wrote her about the Philadelphia article, "because I do not harbor them. I know how you feel, and how you would quickly defeat me if I assumed to aspire, so I have long since put all that utterly and finally aside. We may now forget that phase for all time."[11]

"I can't come out for the weekend," he wrote in response to another invitation from Carrie. He was still weighed down with work and duties in

Washington, as debate on the Revenue Bill droned on. "If you were only half cordial and some time recalled the joy of loving and being loved, I would suggest your coming here when you can," he wrote. "Frankly you are so distant and aloof (in your letters) that I am embarrassed to suggest any meeting which puts the excess of travel on you. It is literally true, I am reluctant to ask and powerless to urge."[12]

He commented multiple times on the presence of military men in the area where she and Isabelle were staying and his understanding that they were fraternizing with the men. "I am honestly glad you are having a good time," he wrote. "I rather suspect you are doing the things you like. No women are insensible to the courtly attentions of army or navy men, and I know you have ample and admiring attention because you are one in ten thousand and men delight to show you deference and admiration. I'd rejoice to bestow myself, though I could not do it so gracefully as many you encounter."[13]

His letter to Carrie the day after the War Revenue Bill passed found her still at Port Jefferson, though she and Isabelle had moved to the Belle Terre Club. This time his jealousy was more evident, as it was apparent that Carrie and Isabelle were socializing with the enlisted men more than he wanted. In a short, testy letter, he wrote:

Sept 11
My Dear Sis:

I owe you an acknowledgement of your note, which was received and read and reread to make sure of its import. My deliberate conclusion is that I am constantly an irritation or a disappointment or both, probably the latter. Either one is intolerable and both together become insufferable. So I forbear intruding. More, I can see you are having a fine time, the things you like and that you deserve. I can readily understand how much attention you and Isabelle receive, and I know how much each or both of you merit it, in appearances, charm, intellectuality and all the attractions of womanhood. I hope you can arrange to stay so long as the conditions and associations are agreeable.

Sincerely
Gov.[14]

Carrie and Isabelle already had spent over eighteen days at Port Jefferson, using Harding's August 25 letter as the starting point. Based on the report of an investigation that started that month, it appears that the Carrie's trip actually started in the second full week of August. On Monday, August 13, the chief of the Marion branch of the American Protective League (APL), Asa C.

Queen, sent a telegram to Charles De Woody of the Bureau of Investigation in Cleveland, Ohio, advising him that Carrie Phillips would be arriving that afternoon on the Cleveland 355 Big Four train. "Investigate whereabouts," he cryptically wired, without further explanation.[15]

Queen was thirty-one years old when he sent this telegram. In business, he was associated with the Old Merkel Implement Co. in Marion and later would become a cashier at the Marion Savings Bank and one of its largest shareholders. His final career was as an owner of the Schaffner-Queen firm of funeral directors. He was an active Mason and would be elected to receive the thirty-third degree in Masonry, the highest degree in the Masonic Lodge—a distinction he shared with Warren G. Harding and only four other Marionites at the time.[16] Somehow this young man became the chief of the Marion branch of the APL. And something Carrie Phillips was doing in August 1917 caused him to send up a flare.

Charles De Woody of the Bureau of Investigation handed off the Queen telegram to an associate in the Cleveland office, Charles Jenkins. Jenkins attempted to investigate but was confused about exactly what Queen wanted him to do. "As the telegram contained no description or other information relative to Mrs. Phillips I tried to get Mr. Queen on the telephone, failing which I talked to Mr. F. Campbell, the postmaster at Marion, Ohio." Frank Thomas Campbell was a farmer who was an active supporter of the Democratic Party and a state Democratic central committeeman from the Eighth District—hence his appointment as postmaster when the Wilson administration came into power in 1913.[17] Campbell was either an officer in the APL or a regular collaborator, since he seemed to have had some idea of why Jenkins called him, but not precisely what Mr. Queen had in mind. "Mr. Campbell informed me that Mrs. Phillips had visited Germany about three years ago and since her return has been very pro-German," Jenkins wrote in his report. "Her husband keeps a store in Marion. Mr. Campbell was unable to furnish any information that would warrant keeping Mrs. Phillips under surveillance. He gave me a description of Mrs. Phillips."[18]

Jenkins went out and met the train "but saw no one answering the description of Mrs. Phillips among the passengers."[19]

Records of this investigation do not reflect any further activity until the beginning of 1918, but a letter written by Harding to Jim Phillips in the spring of 1918 confirms that Carrie and Isabelle were placed under surveillance during their time at Port Jefferson. Their trip to Washington was likewise observed. "Now about Washington," he wrote to Jim in a bit of a panic on May 1, 1918. "I must not, cannot say it to Carrie, and I had rather she did not know I am saying it to you, because she could misconstrue it, but she and Isabelle ought not to come to Washington now. Nor ought they go to New York. I had some inquiry made about things said, and the Washington trip last year led to suspicion about [her] acting as an informer (ridiculous, of course!) and the suspicion was confirmed by the long stay at the naval base at Port Jefferson."[20]

A few days after he wrote his bad-tempered and self-pitying note of September 11, he received a note from Carrie that left him in a better mood. She was by this time in New York City and had sent along a note from her American expatriate friend from her Berlin days, Willie Allen, who was now living in Washington. Carrie sent the note along because she wanted him to see that Mrs. Allen referred to him as "your wonderful Gov." Carrie wrote that she hoped to come to Washington to look up Mrs. Allen at some point. He responded that he was delighted at the prospect of her visit and would help with accommodations. His tone was brighter, calmer than his last note. "I am so glad that you and I[sabelle] had such a bully time at P. J. [Port Jefferson]," he wrote to her on Friday, September 14. "I know full well you enjoyed it, and how you fully deserved all the many attentions shown you."[21]

Thus, by September 14, Carrie and Isabelle had left Port Jefferson and were in New York City, staying at the Manhattan Hotel. They would remain there at least through the end of September and possibly into October after a brief visit to Washington in the first week of October. Two letters from Harding, dated September 17 and September 27, are addressed to Carrie at the Manhattan Hotel.[22] She did visit Washington around October 3 and stayed at the Raleigh Hotel, but a note Harding left for her in the hotel lobby states he missed her and would try again in the morning.[23]

Nan Britton's writing about her supposed relationship with Harding during this time becomes very vague. After providing a number of exact dates and events, her book about the fall of 1917 is filled with side stories, about her move to another boardinghouse and an attempt to get her mother a job in Cleveland, allegedly with a helpful note from Harding to the superintendent of public schools.[24] Perhaps this gap in details can be explained by the slowdown and then lack of Harding's letters to Carrie in the final months of 1917. There are no letters in the collection between October 3 and December 22.

No matter how disheartening things seemed in 1917, Harding continued to court Carrie, telling her he was still open to a renewal of their relationship, despite the months of disagreements. "Give my abiding love to Mrs. Pouterson," he wrote to her in New York on September 14 using her old code name, "and tell her that when she comes I hope to see her and wish for a reunion."[25]

He returned to form in his signature too: "Yours, *Constant.*"

CHAPTER 45

"Isabelle, You Are a Sudden Child"

"I note your comments on the Russian situation," Harding wrote to Ed Scobey on September 13, 1917. "Russia has all gone to pot."[1]

In the first days of September, the Germans won the battle for the Baltic coastal city of Riga, which was the right anchor of the Russian defensive line. The loss represented the beginning of the end for Russia militarily and made it likely that Russia would enter into a separate peace treaty with Germany. The victory was a lift for the Germans and made it all the more imperative that they deliver a decisive blow to the Allies before the Americans could enter the field in numbers that would tip the scales.[2]

Harding saw the weakness in Russia as further proof that encouraging revolution for the sake of promoting world democracy was dangerous. "Democracy has made a miserable failure of it there," he continued with Scobey, "because the people are not educated to self government and the new order following the revolution was inaugurated under the control of the socialist element." He had talked with Elihu Root, the former secretary of state and Nobel Peace Prize winner, who had recently toured Russia, and reported that Root felt that Russia would recover, but Harding was skeptical. "Manifestly," he correctly predicted, "Russia is out of the war so far as any material help is to be given to the Allies."[3]

Those in the United States who still hoped for a peaceful solution to the war before American troops were engaged continued to speak out, but political discourse and debate was becoming less and less acceptable to Americans and the Wilson administration. Robert La Follette was about to discover the cost of dissent. In August, he offered a resolution in the Senate demanding that the United States define its war purposes, that the Allies state the terms under which they would accept peace, and that America's allies disavow any claim to territorial acquisition or indemnity as part of a peace settlement.[4] La Follette's resolution was countered by Senator William H. King of Utah, a Wilson supporter, who demanded that the war continue until Germany had "acknowledged and expiated its crimes."

On September 20, before the Non-Partisan League at its convention in St. Paul, Minnesota, La Follette gave a speech supporting his peace resolution, but then in answer to questions from the audience, he made some fatal blunders. He said that while America suffered violations of neutrality at the hands of the Germans, these infractions did not justify the cost of America's entry into a full-scale war with Germany. "I was not in favor of beginning this war," he is reported to have said. "We had no grievances," a stenographer took down—a line later disputed by La Follette. He continued: "The German Government interfered with our rights to travel on the high seas—as passengers on munitions ships—of Great Britain. On these grievances, which were insignificant, considering the rights and consequences involved, we went to war."[5]

In answering another question, he also seemed to defend the sinking of the *Lusitania*. "A passenger on a foreign ship carrying munitions is technically in foreign territory," he shouted over a very restless and growingly agitated crowd. "The citizen who enters such a ship takes his life in his own hands. I believe that the American munitions makers encouraged Americans to ride on such ships to give them a semblance of protection."

"You're yellow!" someone from the crowd hollered.

Across the country, a howl went up to have La Follette thrown out of the Senate, and there were even demands for his arrest. The Minnesota Public Safety Commission adopted a resolution seeking expulsion of La Follette, which was offered by Minnesota senator Frank B. Kellogg on September 29.[6] La Follette was hanged in effigy in Wisconsin, and state legislatures demanded his ouster from the Senate. The Toledo Executive Club sent Governor Cox of Ohio a resolution suggesting that La Follette be deported and sent behind enemy lines to join the Germans.[7] In the Senate, La Follette was given three hours on Saturday, October 6, to respond to the charges of disloyalty and sedition. His oration is considered one of the most important in American history on the right of free expression in a time of war. "Neither the clamor of the mob nor the voice of power will ever turn me by the breadth of a hair from the course I mark out for myself, guided by such knowledge as I can obtain and controlled and directed by a solemn conviction of right and duty," he read from his prepared remarks, avoiding his usual bombast. As La Follette spoke, Woodrow Wilson sat across the hall in his President's Office in the Capitol signing legislation, likely taking a moment to wander over from time to time to listen in.[8]

Senator Joseph Taylor Robinson of Arkansas delivered an impassioned and highly personal denunciation of La Follette after he spoke. In the process, Robinson condemned anyone caught spying for Germany. "If I had my way about it," he growled, "every spy proven to be such would be executed, and every German hireling in the United States would be placed in jail."[9]

Thereafter, La Follette's attempts to clear his name were persistently blocked by parliamentary moves in the Senate.[10] He became the focus of intense public scorn as a traitor to his country, and his reputation never recovered.

The same war hysteria that created conditions for the formation of the huge American Protective League (APL) led to the roundup of 1,200 men, mostly miners, suspected of collaborating with the International Workers of the World (IWW) by vigilante groups in Bisbee, Arizona. The captured citizens were stuffed into boxcars and deported to New Mexico, where they were left in the desert on July 10, without food or water.[11] The Army had to intervene to save the stranded men.[12]

Increasingly the APL began to crack down on labor organizers, especially the IWW, under the guise of protecting vital American industries in wartime. The chief of the Bureau of Investigation, A. Bruce Bielaski, alerted his agents to pay special attention to the IWW because he said the labor organization was "taking advantage of the needs of the country occasioned by war to advance its own interests utterly without regard for the welfare of the people as a whole."[13] Authorities began to allege that the IWW was linked to German plots and German money.[14] Frank Little, a member of the IWW's executive board and one of the leaders of the labor troubles in Arizona was taken from a boardinghouse in Butte, Montana, by masked men on August 1 and hanged from a railroad trestle on the outskirts of town.[15] When his body was cut down, a card was found pinned to his underclothing reading: "Others Take Notice. First and Last Warning." In a speech he gave just before his murder, Little had referred to U.S. troops as "Uncle Sam's scabs in uniform." Across the nation, APL operatives and Bureau of Investigation agents arrested thousands of IWW workers.

The war unleashed passions not only over labor but also over race. Blacks migrating north to fill positions in war industries came under attack. On July 2, the most violent race riot since the Civil War broke out in East St. Louis, with nine whites and thirty-nine blacks killed. Wilson said nothing, which led a New York newspaper to carry a cartoon, reminiscent of Carrie's biting comments: "Mr. President, Why Not Make America Safe For Democracy?"[16]

Warren Harding stayed out of the La Follette mess. "Congress is quitting today," he wrote Scobey on Saturday, October 6, the day La Follette delivered his defense on the Senate floor. "I cannot tell you how glad I am that such is the case. We are about all worn out and it is vitally necessary to get away and recuperate and get back to normal again."[17] It had been one of the most amazing and active sessions of any Congress. "There has never been a Congressional session in history that approaches the record of the extraordinary session of the Sixty-fifth," the *Times* editorialized. "Not merely has it made preparation for war on a huge scale, but it has far surpassed the records made by parliamentary bodies of other democracies on their entrance into the war." As evidence of this Congress's productivity, the paper pointed to the declaration of war, the passage of the Selective Draft Act, the Espionage Bill, the Food Control bill, the Revenue Bill, and the construction of the merchant marine, not to mention the passage of the prohibition resolution.[18]

Harding was ready for a long break. "I am leaving early next week for a week or ten days at Senator Weeks' mountain home in New Hampshire," he wrote Scobey. "A half dozen or more are going up there to breathe the mountain air and live in the freedom of the wilderness and try to get their nerves in order if they can do so while playing golf and poker." He expected to return to Ohio from there but did not relish the prospect of being called on to speak on prohibition or municipal electoral issues, and he wanted to avoid "everybody who is wanting to get into the army or wanting out of it." He was seriously considering another trip to Hawaii instead, knowing Congress would not reconvene until December. "This trip would appeal to me very strongly were it not for the fact that there are two or three German raiders loose on the Pacific and I should rather be a live senator than a dead hero. However, I do not know that the danger is sufficiently great to hinder the trip."[19]

The fact that he would even consider another trip to Hawaii—knowing the turmoil his last trip there caused with Carrie—speaks to the state of his relationship with Carrie. His letters in late September confirm a return to frostiness between them, after a slight thaw, which he registered in his letter of September 14.

But more significant in these letters than the evidence that the relationship was reverting to iciness may be a line Harding wrote that would appear to bear out what Marion's postmaster would later report to the Bureau of Investigation—that Carrie and Isabelle were entertained by the Pickhardts in New York City in the fall of 1917. "Hope you had a merry time Saturday," Harding wrote to Carrie in New York. "Am interested to know you are converting Mr. P—. You can do it. Nearly every thing you wish will come your way. Sorry I cannot translate your foreign expressions. I must assume you are half-exclaiming to yourself."[20] The letter, dated September 17, seems to relate to a dinner or other social engagement at the Pickhardts on Saturday, September 15. One reading of the letter is that Carrie was attempting to win over Adolf Pickhardt's father to the idea of his son's engagement to Isabelle, a matter that may not have been viewed favorably by a family of social standing in New York City like the Pickhardts. Whatever the case, the dinner or party would have taken place just days after Carrie and Isabelle left Port Jefferson following their lengthy stay there—suggesting perhaps a debriefing concerning conditions at Camp Upton. The Marion postmaster's report that places Carrie and Isabelle at the Pickhardts in October of 1917 either is a misdating of this dinner or party or shows that Carrie and Isabelle were entertained multiple times by the Pickhardts in New York that fall, activity that would be consistent with an incipient engagement.

Carrie kept little in writing that deals directly with this alleged engagement. Among her papers is an envelope attached to her own rambling pro-German notes that has written on it, "Lieutenant Adolf von Scheven."[21] It is a unique name. Adolf Pickhardt's middle name was von Scheven, taken from his mother's maiden name.[22] A draft letter in Carrie's handwriting, also discovered with the materials she kept with the Harding letters, discusses the relationship between Isabelle and a young man named Adolf. In the undated draft, Carrie informs a friend that an announcement would be forthcoming regarding Isabelle's engagement to Adolf:

> I agreed right then and there and went with her to the Cable Office to send to A—. I do think it quite hurried but they both wish it very much I am sure. I write to tell you all this for I know you will want to know all at the earliest possible moment. I remember you saying so sweetly, Isabelle is a lovely girl, we have all lost our hearts to her. ~~I wished to say and could have said just as lovely thing about the son but refrained. I have told him only that I had not the slightest objection to him.~~ I was glad, or course, she is a darling girl. I know

Adolf slightly but feel I know him well, really. We are very fond of him, both Mr. Phillips and myself. If it is their wish to be married in the near future, we shall agree. Adolf thinks, I believe, that the reason I have never given them any encouragement is because I do not want to give Isabelle up & selfishness. He told Isa he did not blame me but he wanted her too.

Bless their hearts—that is real trouble for them! I wish they never had to have any more serious than this to face, in all their lives. No, that was not the reason. I must tell him that. I feared interfering in any way whatsoever. I have only been as certain as it is possible to be in the past few weeks. Even then I waited. It is well with me if they wish it, they are both adorable. I love Adolf.

I wish I could talk with you. I feel this falls far short of the sort of letter I wished to write but I must let you hear at once for, two weeks from the time this reaches you it is to be announced.

I think Adolf will cable you. If you will, mail a list of those whom you wish to receive communication. Upon receipt of this we will mail out about the fifth. My answer to Isabelle when she told me what she wished to do was—"Isabelle, you are a sudden child." I think you will agree, too. She seemed to think not, for she very much wished to [be married] before Adolf left the states a year ago, she said. I should like very much to have you come out if you feel you can. Any of you or all. Isabelle too would like Dorothy. I think she is writing her this evening. Some friends of hers from Cleveland, Tiffin and Columbus are to be asked. These days are difficult ones for every undertaking, all we can do is our best and hope.[23]

The report of Frank Campbell written in February 1918 confirms that it was his belief from intercepting mail that Adolf Pickhardt was "the betroth of Isabelle Phillips." Campbell had in his files several tracings of Lieutenant Pickhardt's handwriting from "envelopes of the numerous letters received by Miss Phillips." The censor stamp on one of the exemplars shows that Pickhardt was on the USS *New York,* an armored cruiser, in foreign service when he wrote to Isabelle on January 4, 1918.[24]

Congress adjourned on October 6, and Harding went on his vacation with the other senators to the mountain home of Massachusetts senator John Wingate Weeks where he ate too much, smoked too much, and played plenty of golf and poker. He decided against the Hawaii trip, "not because of the German raiders, but because the senators enrolled for the trip do not appeal to me as traveling companions," he wrote Scobey.[25] In contrast to these objectionable senators, Harding admired the practical, competent, and hardworking Weeks and came away from his extended vacation with him even more charmed. "You are right about Weeks," he wrote to Scobey. "I have seen him at close range for a week, and esteem him more than ever. He would make a great President."

Theodore Roosevelt, though, was still the man to beat in 1920. "But I think T.R. more probable," he wrote Scobey. "You have to hand it to T.R. He is a real American." In fact, Roosevelt had begun to pick up Harding's theme that the war was not about making the world safe for democracy. In a speech given in Johnstown, Pennsylvania, the day after the La Follette remarks in St. Paul, T.R. mimicked Harding's mantra. "We did not go to war to make democracy safe," he told a group from the Red Cross, "and we did go to war because we had a special grievance," he said in reaction to La Follette's alleged statement that America had no grievance with Germany. "We went to war because after two years, during which, with utter contempt of our protests, she had habitually and continually murdered our noncombatant men, women, and children on the high seas, Germany formally announced that she intended to pursue this course more ruthlessly and vigorously than ever."[26] He called La Follette a "shadow Hun," and recommended that the government should deport him. "I would like to send him as a gift to the Kaiser."

In his letter to Scobey, Harding downplayed his own prospects as a presidential candidate. "People who think of me are as foolish as you are, which is sure foolish. But I never fool myself. I am neither fit nor capable, though it would be worth while to give you a party at the White House. That is the only one lure."

Instead of the Hawaii trip, Warren decided to take a leisurely automobile trip back to Ohio with Florence, stopping along the way at Corning, New York, to pick up glassware for their Washington house. Then he and Florence quickly left Marion to travel to San Antonio to "loaf" with the Scobeys. He wanted to avoid any more speechmaking, though he continued to be one of the most sought-after speakers in the nation. "There are about five hundred calls for speeches just now," he wrote, "but I haven't the punch in me, so I am dodging and declining. I am hoping to develop some restored pep in the next six weeks."[27]

He told Scobey that he looked forward to spending his fifty-second birthday—November 2—in Texas. "[Y]ou can surprise me with a highball while I ponder the tendency of men to become good as age comes on," he projected. "You know how it is yourself."[28]

After more than a week stay with the Scobeys ("Mrs. Harding and I are agreed that we never had a more delightful time in our lives"), the Hardings traveled to Chicago for some shopping and then returned to Marion, where Warren took on the editorial responsibilities for the newspaper for ten days to allow his editor, George Van Fleet, to take a short vacation. "I found the work most delightful indeed," he wrote Scobey once he was back in Washington on December 6, "except I was incessantly disturbed by calls for speechmaking which could not be ignored."[29]

In Petrograd, Lenin and his Bolsheviks turned out the Kerensky government and assumed control over a few days in early November. The *New York Times* knew so little about Lenin that they misspelled his name "Lenine," and many thought the Bolshevik revolt would be short-lived.[30] The Russian democracy had not even lasted nine months, and for the second time in a year, Russia was shaken by revolution. A peace accord with Germany, punitive to the Russians in the extreme, was negotiated and signed in March 1918 at Brest-Litovsk. Russia indeed had "all gone to pot," as Harding said.

The war was about to turn deadly serious for America and its troops. Ships transporting U.S. servicemen were gearing up to sail in great numbers across the Atlantic for destinations in France and England.

Harding continued to be concerned about the slowness of America's preparations for war. He specifically took on the Shipping Board, demanding an inquiry, which he would lead, into the reasons for all the delays in shipbuilding. The U. S. Shipping Board was established to build and operate merchant ships to support U. S. war efforts. "I do not care to introduce this resolution of investigation and be subjected to the intimation that it is a partisan interference or suggestion; but I tell you, Senators, the winning of the war depends upon our strength on the sea," Harding told the Senate on December 18. "We must have a merchant marine if we are to hope to succeed, and I think it is a crime that the money placed in the hands of the Shipping Board should have been so ill handled that there should have been an entanglement of red tape and inefficiency of a character to delay the great American shipbuilding program."[31] Public hearings in front of the Commerce Committee of the Senate began.

By year-end, Harding was fully engaged in the shipping investigation and feeling soured by what he was finding. "I will not undertake to write to you some of the revelations which we have had before the executive sessions of the Commerce Committee relating to the labor situation in the shipbuilding world," he wrote to Malcolm Jennings on December 31. "It has much inclined to drive me into a pessimistic state, which you will admit is not my normal disposition."[32]

One thing he did know for certain: "No one who notes things carefully can escape the observation that we are in the midst of profound changes and

I find myself wondering every night what the end is going to be," he wrote. "Many a moment I am convinced that we are doomed to the rule of something similar to the Bolsheviki on the one hand or a very strong military autocracy on the other."

Though his Christmas felicitations to Carrie were friendly—he sent smokes for Jim, sweets for Isabelle, and books for her—it was clear that they were completely distanced from one another. "It doesn't seem much like Christmas here, where one has no intimate friends and no merriment like the good old days," he wrote on December 22 from Washington, where he was buried in the shipping investigation. "I had dreamed of coming to M— for the holidays, but unwittingly loaded myself up with important work which will require me to be industrious whether I prefer it or not."[33] He no longer signed his letters "Constant." He was formal but cordial. "And I do hope there is a Merry Christmas at the Phillips' home. I am sure there will be, and I only wish I might step in to breathe the cheery atmosphere."

Had he known of events taking place that very day in Tennessee, he might have been less cheery about the prospects of a merry Christmas in the Phillips household. No doubt the family was closely following events as they unfolded in Chattanooga, where Lieutenant Adolf Pickhardt's first cousin, Baroness Iona Zollner, had been arrested and charged with espionage.

CHAPTER 46

"I'm Talking to the Wife of a German Officer, Now Ain't I?"

When told by the U. S. marshals after she was arrested for espionage that they had retrieved documents from the hotel safe, including her purse, the baroness almost collapsed. She needed whiskey to steady herself.[1]

One of the documents in her purse was a receipt from the Congress Hall Hotel in Washington, showing that she finished her two-week stay there sometime around September 24 or 27.[2] She had maintained a room in the hotel for a number of weeks after seeing Lieutenant Spalding off to Fort Leavenworth. (He testified that he left for Fort Leavenworth in the first days of September and arrived there on September 9.)[3] Then she said she returned to Annapolis, where the midshipmen were back in residence. Forced to leave when the superintendent of the Naval Academy again complained about her lurking nearby, she was banished to New York City in October, around the time when Frank Campbell reported that Carrie and Isabelle attended a social event at the Pickhardt residence in which a woman of German nobility was also present.[4]

During November, Spalding sent multiple telegrams to the baroness in New York from Fort Leavenworth. He signed them all by what appeared to be a code name, "Preacher," though the baroness testified it was simply a nickname he acquired during his time at the academy.[5] He kept her advised of when he would be transferred to Fort Oglethorpe.[6] He finished his training at Fort Leavenworth on November 22 and was in Tennessee about November 26. Though he said he would be with his company on the rifle range until December 10 or 18, and therefore could not see her, she pressed him, and he eventually relented. "Don't carry out threat of letter," he telegrammed her on December 1, the Saturday after Thanksgiving, "I will do as asked. Hotels bum. Best is Patten."[7] She arrived in Chattanooga four days later, on Wednesday, December 5. At the espionage hearing, the baroness's son Bedford swore that his mother was stopping in Chattanooga on her way to Florida.[8] But on cross-examination, the baroness was forced to admit she was not on her way to Florida and that she had lied about it when she was arrested.[9]

She left her sixteen-year-old son, Bedford, back in New York, even though he was to have an operation, along with her six-year-old daughter, Nonie, who was the product of her marriage to Zollner.[10]

On the train from New York, Iona traveled with and obtained contact information from a Mrs. Beutner, a resident of Knoxville. Beutner's husband, Victor, was registered as an alien enemy and because of his suspicious activity he had been under intense surveillance by the Bureau of Investigation as a German spy.[11] An article in the Chattanooga newspaper stated that Victor Beutner was interviewed an hour or two before the baroness's arrest by U.S. Marshal Thompson; Beutner was in Chattanooga the night she was arrested. Mrs. Beutner was interrogated after the baroness was in custody by both Thompson and U.S. Attorney Kennerly. She was questioned about why the baroness had secured her address, but, according to newspaper accounts, she refused to cooperate—"she was impenetrable."[12]

Eleven days after the baroness's arrest, during her espionage hearing, Victor Beutner dropped dead of an apparent heart attack, supposedly caused by an unexplained fire at his house. "Advices from Knoxville were to the effect that Beutner's heart attack was due to excitement when his house caught fire," the Chattanooga paper reported.[13]

When the baroness arrived in Chattanooga late on December 5, around midnight, she checked into the hotel suggested by Spalding, the Patten Hotel.[14] Spalding met her at the train station and registered her at the hotel under the name "Baroness Iona Zollner, New York," telling Mr. Parker, the clerk at the hotel, that she was his sister.[15] Spalding also took a separate room for himself.[16] He later testified that he wanted her to come to Chattanooga because he "liked her company and liked to be seen with her."[17]

The next morning, the baroness rode in a small bus to Fort Oglethorpe to make her first inspection tour of the cantonment. "I motored out to Fort

Oglethorpe today," she wrote Bedford on the evening of December 6, "3/4 of an hour ride in a 'jitney' over the most awful road." The camp was in the backwoods. "I bumped and banged and swayed from side to side like one of those silver balls on the top of a fancy fountain—you have seen them and know what I mean." She described the camp, located on the site of the major Civil War battle known as Chickamauga. "Well on top of a plateau on the old battleground, hundreds of crude and the most primitive houses have been erected. Good gracious darling you have no idea of the awful primitiveness— tiny iron beds, mattresses like iron—and just wooden benches—absolutely no comfort—worse than any hovel or shanty."

She stayed at the camp the entire afternoon and went everywhere, taking careful note of its condition. "I stayed all afternoon," she wrote Bedford, "and met all of Preacher's friends—saw everything!" She struck up conversations with men in the officers' club, and she was watched after when Spalding had to participate in some training exercises. "When Preacher had work, one of his friends stayed with me," she explained to Bedford. In the letter, she underlined certain words once, twice, three, or four times, as if part of a code.

She instructed her son on what to say if anyone inquired as to her whereabouts. "If anybody calls—you know I am here to get that affidavit from Preacher! I am in Washington and here."[18] She admitted at her hearing that she had not come to retrieve a legal document from Lieutenant Spalding.[19]

According to the testimony of one of Spalding's fellow officers, Lieutenant W. B. Oliver, the baroness came out to inspect the cantonment twice.[20] Oliver also said that every officer in the camp had been carefully told that there were strict military orders not to disclose the troop movement to anyone.[21] Nonetheless, the baroness had in her purse a secret code given to her by Lieutenant Spalding, which he was to use when his division, the Sixth Infantry, was ready to ship out. On an envelope from the Congress Hall Hotel, Spalding had written out what would be referred to in the espionage hearing as "the code." If he wrote to her the words "Everyone well," that meant that his unit would be leaving soon for Europe via New York City. If he wrote "Everybody well," it would alert her that his unit would sail for Europe via Norfolk. And if he wrote "All Well," this would mean they were leaving for Europe but he did not know from which port. If he could see her before he left, he would write "Lovingly."[22]

Early on the morning of Thursday, December 13, a week after the baroness made her first inspection tour of Fort Oglethorpe, the hotel detective at the Patten Hotel, Thomas Stiff, knocked on her door at one or two in the morning. Spalding was found in the room hiding under the bed in his "union suit." They were arrested and arraigned in Police Court and charged with vagrancy. She pled guilty and paid a fine.[23] Spalding forfeited his bail; he returned to the Fort in the middle of the night.

That morning, Friday, December 14, the baroness moved out of the Patten Hotel and registered in another hotel in Chattanooga, the Park Hotel, this time using her middle name, "W. Sutton." She had consulted with a Chattanooga attorney, Carl Abernathy, whose office was across the street from the Park Hotel. He told her to stay in town to attempt to control any adverse press.[24] The newspaper did in fact carry a story of the arrest that afternoon, though both the baroness and the lawyer tried to convince the editor not to run anything.[25]

When Spalding returned to camp after his arrest he told his friends that he had been out late seeing the baroness off at the train station. Later in the day he asked two friends, Lieutenants Sullivan and Carter, to accompany him to town for dinner at the Park Hotel with the baroness—thus admitting to them that, in fact, she had not left town.[26] After dinner, the baroness and Spalding retired to the hotel's writing room and then walked across the street to Mr. Abernathy's office. Lieutenants Sullivan and Carter went out to the theater. In the attorney's office, the baroness, Spalding, Abernathy, and another lawyer named Clark exchanged lighthearted banter. Mr. Clark's jokes and stories were so entertaining, the baroness testified, that she "nearly had hysterics."[27]

When Spalding took the baroness back to the Park Hotel, they passed two men sitting in the lobby who were waiting for them. U.S. Marshal John R. Thompson and Deputy Marshal T. F. McMahon watched the couple enter the hotel. Spalding strolled with the baroness to the hotel elevator and bade her good night. Thompson and McMahon shadowed Spalding as he left the hotel, then Thompson put his hand on the lieutenant's shoulder just as he was to cross the street and asked his name. Spalding spun around and was confrontational.[28]

Thompson and McMahon went back into the Park Hotel, took the elevator to the baroness's floor, and knocked on her door. After identifying themselves as U.S. marshals, they said they wanted to speak with her. She said she would not submit to an interview without her lawyer being present and was allowed to call Mr. Abernathy, who came right over. While the two federal marshals waited in the hotel parlor for Mr. Abernathy, Spalding returned with his two friends, Lieutenants Sullivan and Carter, and the four men nearly came to fisticuffs. McMahon told them that "if they came for a rough house we would accommodate them."[29] Sullivan and Carter backed off when they learned Thompson and McMahon were federal marshals, and they left, taking Spalding with them.

Abernathy and the baroness joined the marshals in the hotel lobby. McMahon jumped right into the investigation, shaking his finger in the baroness's face and saying, "Ain't you a German spy? I am talking to the wife of a German officer, now ain't I? Now ain't I?"[30]

The baroness lied about being married to a German officer, then lied about being divorced from him. (She had started divorce proceedings in Maryland in November to gain control over her assets, in particular the rubber plantation in Singapore, but the divorce was not finalized.) And she lied about being on a trip to Florida. After she lied about whether she was receiving mail at the Patten Hotel, Thompson confronted her with a letter he had confiscated from the hotel earlier that day—a letter from Bedford, sent from their home in New York City. The contents of the letter were so strange that McMahon felt sure it had to be some kind of code.[31]

Thompson placed the baroness under arrest, though he allowed her to stay in the hotel that night and to go across the street to Abernathy's office for further consultation. When the marshals realized she had taken Bedford's letter when she and Abernathy went to his office, they crossed the street and demanded its return. After some denials, she produced the letter from her purse, allowing the marshals to see that she had other letters in her purse. They demanded that she turn over these documents, which she did: they included Spalding's telegrams from Fort Leavenworth and some of Bedford's telegrams. Then the marshals returned to the hotel and searched the baroness's room.

The next morning the hotel clerk told the investigators that the baroness had deposited items in the hotel safe when she had checked in. These were turned over to the federal officers and included Spalding's code about when ships would sail for Europe. Later that day, when the baroness was advised that the marshals had recovered her things from the hotel safe, she almost collapsed.[32] "Mr. Abernathy came to me and said she looked like she was in a very critical condition," Thompson remembered, "and wanted to know if I could arrange to get her a little whiskey."[33]

The baroness was formally taken into custody at the city jail. She claimed her treatment in the jail was akin to torture. She said McMahon threatened her that if she did not tell all she would be imprisoned the rest of her life and Spalding would "be shot on Sunday morning." She grew ill and frail, lost weight.[34]

The Bureau of Investigation gathered evidence in several cities for the government's case. Agents in New York searched the baroness's home on Madison Avenue and obtained letters and telegrams she had sent to her son from Chattanooga. Another agent interviewed a sister-in-law of the baroness in Boston. Chief Bielaski telegraphed from Washington advising that the baroness had been investigated by Naval Intelligence for her activities out-side the Naval Academy and in fact had been given "a clean bill of health."[35]

The most breathtaking evidence introduced at the hearing came from one of the baroness's own family members—her brother Adrian C. Pickhardt. The sister-in-law in Boston who was interviewed by the Bureau of Investiga-tion agent was married to, but separated from, Adrian. When a telegram re-port of Mrs. Adrian C. Pickhardt's interview with Agent Schmidt from the Boston office of the Bureau of Investigation was read into the record during the hearing, there were audible gasps from the audience.

Boston, Mass. Dec. 20, 1917
[Bureau of Investigation Agent Edward] Finlay,
James Bldg.
Chatta. Tenn.

Mrs. Adrian C. Pickhardt reports her husband's sister, Baroness W. Sutton Zoll-ner born Brooklyn, N. Y., about eighteen seventy two married Charles Sckoppe who died leaving two boys, boys probably now attending Annapolis College. She then went to Germany married Baron Koberg [sic] who she later divorced. Later married Capt. Zollner of Austrian Army. She resided in Germany about twenty years. About nineteen fourteen Baroness and Capt. Zollner entered port New York storage claiming American citizenship. Later Zollner stole Doctor's passport in New York on which returned to Germany. Mr. Pickhardt stated to wife he knew his sister was in employ German Government this country and while working Ayer cantonment he furnished information military importance to Baroness for which he expected receive money. Mrs. Pickhardt now separated from husband. Will furnish any information her possession. Copy this telegram sent Department.

Schmidt[36]

The cantonment at Ayer, Massachusetts, was Camp Devens.[37] Established to house draftees from Maine, New Hampshire, Vermont, Massachusetts, Rhode Island, and Connecticut, at its height it held about 50,000 men. If Mrs. Pick-hardt's story was true, Adrian Pickhardt, at his sister's urging, spied on Fort Devens for the Germans while working there, and he expected payment for information that he relayed to her. During the hearing, the baroness attacked her brother "Addie," calling him a spendthrift, a drunkard, and a gambler who had wasted his life on dogs and horses.[38]

The hearing took place over two days, beginning on the Saturday before Christmas, December 22. The atmosphere was electric. Just days earlier, the evangelist Billy Sunday, known as the "base-ball evangelist" because his gesticulations while speaking were so wild, was physically attacked in Chattanooga and then in Atlanta by pro-Germans who took exception to his anti-German statements. In Atlanta on December 20, Sunday said he "didn't believe God would be on the side of a dirty bunch that would stand aside and see a Turk outrage a woman." A crazed pro-German charged the stage. The *New York Times* reported that Sunday "fought a fast and furious fight with a German sympathizer on the platform. . . .While the exchange of blows was about even, Billy had decidedly the better of the argument before the crowd near the platform separated the contestants."[39]

After listening to all the evidence against the baroness, U.S. Commissioner Samuel J. McAllester decided that there was probable cause for holding her for trial under Section 2 of the Espionage Act. In ruling, he said that the defense had explained all questionable evidence except "the code found in the baroness's possession, and the affidavit concerning the Howard house in Annapolis, which mentions strange things concerning the physical condition of the place, cats, chickens and bed linens."[40] Abernathy asked for bail, but McAllester denied it, and the baroness was taken back to jail.

News of her arrest and imprisonment would eventually make its way into a Sunday magazine feature in February 1918 in the *Cleveland Plain Dealer,* entitled "The Love Tricks of a Woman Spy."[41] That article would push into higher gear the ongoing investigation of Carrie and Isabelle Phillips, as it added another piece to the puzzle. Marion Postmaster Frank Campbell recognized the name Pickhardt, since he had been monitoring mail from Lieutenant Pickhardt to Isabelle Phillips for some months. The dots were connecting.

The heat was about to be turned up on Carrie, Isabelle, and even Jim Phillips—and also Senator Warren G. Harding.

As the New Year of 1918 began, Warren Harding still could not forget the bliss he had known with Carrie Phillips six years earlier in Montreal, when he was simply a newspaper editor and she traveled all the way back from Europe to see him. On New Year's Day, he wrote out his first long, loving letter to Carrie since the United States had gone to the war.

CHAPTER 47

"It Thrills Me, Merely to Live It Over in Recollection

Jan 1/1918
My Dear Sis:

The first line of the New Year shall be to you, because you are first in my thoughts. When the year came in I was thinking of a wonderful bit of the New Year's greetings I experienced a half dozen years ago in Montreal, when I heard the bells of that city mingled with the transcending song of a heavenly duet, where the song was of rapture unutterable. I wish I could convey it to you as I am thinking of it—the grandest ushering in and the most entrancing and exalting greeting that mortal beings ever experienced. I thrill in the recollection. It was not deliberate, but fate and fortune timed the music to glorify the occasion and exalt the celebrants. I would have given anything in the world to have rejoiced again in that sublimity, precisely according to the surpassing experience of that never-to-be-forgotten acclaim of the New Year. Heaven has nothing more heavenly and earth has no bliss or raptures to surpass it. Perhaps I fail to even half convey, but it was so supreme, so beyond words, so perfect, so excruciatingly sweet and transporting, that no other impression of gladdest existence can ever compare. I am reveling in the memory of it now. It thrills me, merely to live it over in recollection. No overwhelming enchantment ever compared to it in my life. The duet was attuned to the infinite—some higher realm at least, and souls sang in the loftiness of it, and the old year died in the fires of flaming hearts, and the light of the New Year shone with consuming ecstasy. Oh, me! To live it again! To start a New Year thus, and revel in the remembrance, if the reenactment were not possible. Only a heavenly goddess, lovable and loving beyond compare, could strike the divine chord in which they sang that New Year's morn, and set a new exaction in the heights of perfection. And I was there, enthralled! It is so good to have the infatuating memory. I'm a slave to memory now. I know it is a sad confession. Those who live in memories are said to no longer achieve, that their faces are turned backwards, but I am a slave to it because of the riches of recollection amid the desert paths of realization. I have come to know myself in deliberate contemplation and studious reflection. I did give the one all-consuming, all-engulfing, all-worshipping, all-exclusive love. There is the surpassing and all-consecrated one love. I gave it to you. It is yours now. I am not insensible to the frank notice you have given me that you are no longer all mine. I have no right to expect it. But I'll always believe that you changed amid pique or resentment rather than on answer to your heart's "desire". "Egotist!" I hear you exclaim. Probably so, surely so in your estimate, but I am writing myself revealingly. I judge your heart by my own though I long since realized (no egotist now!) that I was not enough to reign exclusively and be the very all to you. No man is to a handsome woman. Every story of all time confirms. I realize it all now. *I had to surrender ideals and stifle a very natural, barbaric jealousy to come to understanding, but I finally came to see and understand. Nevertheless I recall reading "love is not love which alters when it alteration finds" and I do love, and love now in spite of "alteration found," of which you gave full notice. I may grieve, but I love, because I can't help it. And I admire and adore, and hunger and thirst, and crave and desire, because you are the grandest and darlingest and best to love in all the world. Listen to my deliberate and abiding conviction—you are the surpassing and incomparable one. This is my judgment in joy or grief, in exaltation or disappointment. I think you the best and darlingest in all the world, the most splendid, the most inspiring, the sweetest and most charming, the most brilliant and most refined, the most fascinating and most compensating, not rivaling a goddess, but a very goddess yourself. Please note, I am not writing in passionate intoxication. I am not raving in delusions. For I have none now. I am saying deliberately, reflectively, the estimate I think and feel, and bear with me in all my thoughts, so many, many of which are of you, all the day and most of night.*[1]

CHAPTER 48

"Let Me Lecture You a Bit"

Two days after writing to Carrie, on January 3, Harding wrote a letter to Ed and Evaland Scobey: "I find myself owing letters to both members of the family, and being in a mood to square the account I mean to cancel two debts in one stroke."[1] Despite the gloomy times and bad news on the war front, his spirits were up. He was fighting what he believed was the good fight against the incompetence of the Wilson administration in the conduct of the war, and he worried about the spread of Bolshevism in the United States, but he still found a moment to be lighthearted about the rationing and conservation all around him.

He had just lost his best stenographer, Mrs. Jones, who had decided to marry, and another assistant, who had enlisted in the Army. He was going to have trouble finding good replacements for both of them, he wrote. Washington was so overcrowded from the war boom that it was difficult for anyone to secure a decent place to live on the modest salaries paid by the government. Worse, the town was freezing from a coal shortage brought on by the war. He wondered if the Scobeys had heard the little rhyme that captured all the grief, poking fun at rationing guidelines issued by Wilson's Food administrator, Herbert Hoover:

My Tuesdays are meatless
My Wednesdays are wheatless
I am getting more eatless each day
My house—it is heatless
My bed—sheetless

They've gone to the Y.M.C.A.
My coffee is sweetless
The bar room is treatless
Each day I grow poorer and wiser
My stockings are feetless
My trousers are seatless
Be gosh! How I hate the damn Kaiser!

He was becoming more and more of an open critic of the administration, as he learned details of the bureaucratic ineptitude, abuses, and critical delays— the starts and stops—from the Shipping Board investigation. He was re-thinking his call to make Wilson the dictator of the war effort. "An incompetent administration in the greatest crisis of the world is making me a pessimist," he wrote Scobey. "The investigations (absolutely necessary to change the trends and shake things up) are rather disheartening. I believe we shall win, but we waited too long to start getting ready, and have been going on low gear when we ought to be in high speed, with a fearless and capable driver." He also foresaw that the rising tide of communism and socialism would infect the United States, regardless of the war's outcome. "Meanwhile, the Bolsheviki are getting stronger in America every day, and after the Kaiser is cared for, we can prepare to combat the Maximalists, the Bolsheviki and Radical Socialists in our own midst," he warned. "Busy times ahead."[2]

Despite the fact that the United States had been in a declared war with Germany since April of 1917, by January 1918, only about 100,000 men had been sent to England or France, and they had been mostly in training. The alarm that Harding had sounded in December about the lack of America's readiness was provoking other Senate investigations.[3] Secretary of War Baker, appearing before a restive Senate Military Affairs Committee on January 28, gave assurances that the War Department would have "500,000 men in France in early 1918 and could land 1,500,000 men in France by the end of this year, fully equipped, if shipping facilities were available."[4] Harding had been right: having enough ships to transport the troops was "the crux of the problem."[5] There was talk in Congress of the creation of a war cabinet and a new position of director of munitions to relieve the administrative burden on Baker.

In hearings a little over a week later, Baker said, among other things, that the War Department would not depend entirely on American ships to transport its troops; it expected assistance from the Allies.[6] At the same time, he warned that the United States had come into possession of information that the Germans were planning a powerful submarine offensive against U.S. transport ships. The submarines had been recalled, it had been reported, and were being refitted and resupplied to gear up for attacks against ships transporting American soldiers to Europe.[7] As Baker spoke to the Senate committee, officials in Ireland and England learned that the British steamship *Tuscania,* carrying over 2,000 American soldiers and in a heavy convoy with other ships, had been torpedoed and sunk off the coast of Ireland. It was the first ship carrying American troops to be lost.[8] Two hundred American soldiers died, the most killed in one day since the Civil War.

In the days following the shock of the first major loss of American soldiers, angry officials in Washington told the press that there was "deep seated opinion among high officials here that the successful attack on the Tuscania was due to advance information from this country on her sailing and destination."[9] America's allies blamed the United States: "It is said that the allies feel America is failing to guard troop movements and military secrets closely and is needlessly gambling with the loss of thousands of lives," the *Cleveland Plain Dealer* reported out of its Washington bureau on February 9. Attorney General Gregory was singled out for criticism. The Department of Justice was seen as being weak on German spies. "Either the mesh has been too big or the net has not been drawn in, for considering the known activity of German spies, the number of captures has been amazingly small." Calls for the death penalty for spies increased. "I believe that the prompt execution of a few would accomplish more than filling every prison in the country with them," one citizen wrote in a letter to the editor of the *New York Times.*[10]

The next day, Sunday, February 10, the *Plain Dealer* ran its Sunday magazine feature, "Love Tricks of a Woman Spy," with a quarter-page rendering of Baroness Iona Zollner, "arrested in the presence of an American army officer, and interned after the discovery of a secret code book and letters." The story "revealed how this sinister fascination of femininity is used to lure secrets from the foe and advance the cause of the country in whose behalf the woman spy is plying her skill."[11]

Three days later, on Wednesday, February 13, Frank Campbell picked up his phone in Marion and made an urgent call to the Post Office Inspector in Cincinnati. Jim and Isabelle Phillips were on a train bound for Cincinnati, but he believed their ultimate destination was Chattanooga. He supposed they were taking papers of some sort to the incarcerated baroness. Jim and Isabelle were scheduled to arrive at four-thirty that afternoon on the Erie Train No. 3, he told the Postal Inspector. The message got bollixed up by the time it reached Bureau of Investigation Special Agent Calvin Weakley of the Cincinnati Bureau of Investigation office. Weakley told fellow agent John Menefee that the woman with Jim Phillips was Baroness Zollner herself, posing as Phillips's daughter. Despite the confusion, Menefee secured the use of an "A. P. L. machine" (a car loaned by a member of the Cincinnati American Protective League) and went to the Cincinnati, Hamilton, and Dayton train depot.

When Jim and Isabelle got off the train, Menefee shadowed them to another train station, the Eight Street Station of the Queen & Crescent Railroad.[12] While they were attending to their bags, the cab driver told Menefee that Jim had said they were going to catch a train to Lexington. Jim and Isabelle found out they had been misinformed of the departure time of the train to Lexington—it was not leaving until 8 PM. Jim and Isabelle got back into the cab and were driven to the Sinton Hotel in downtown Cincinnati. Jim registered under his name; Isabelle did not register as a guest. Menefee obtained the registration information from the hotel clerk and also learned that Jim had said the woman with him was his daughter and that she wanted to use the room to freshen up but she would not be staying overnight.

Menefee realized that the stakeout was going to be more complicated than he originally thought so he called Agent in Charge Weakley and requested assistance. Agent Leonard Stern was the first to show up. While Jim and Isabelle ate dinner in the hotel dining room, Menefee, Stern, and the hotel manager went up to Jim's room and rifled through their luggage. They admired Isabelle's expensive suitcase and handbag and noted that she had a complete set of ivory toilet articles, but otherwise found no incriminating evidence. They did look through Isabelle's diary; that day she wrote that she was arranging her clothes in order to visit "Marie" in Lexington, Kentucky.

The agents discussed what to do next. Menefee instructed Stern to go to the train station where Isabelle was supposed to catch the eight o'clock train to Lexington and call him at home if Isabelle got on the train as expected. Once assured she was on the train, Menefee would call an Agent Thompson in Lexington to meet the train and follow the woman.

Agent W. H. Valentine arrived to support Stern. Two additional agents also showed up: Albert D. Cash and Claude Light.[13] Valentine reported that after Jim and his "supposed daughter" finished dinner, they went to their room for a short while. They came back down to the lobby, left the hotel, and got into a cab. Valentine and Stern tracked them in Mr. Isaac Rowe's borrowed APL vehicle. At the train station, Jim and Isabelle both entered the Pullman car and got Isabelle situated. Just before Jim left the car, the agents observed him giving Isabelle "some papers of legal size and a ten dollar bill." As soon as Jim disembarked, a "very good looking man" sat down next to Isabelle and engaged her in conversation. When Jim saw what was happening through the train window, he grew agitated and motioned Isabelle to come back to the end of the coach, where he remonstrated with her. She went back to her seat and Jim got off the train. Stern called Menefee to say the woman was on the train, and Menefee called Thompson in Lexington to meet the train.

Meanwhile, Jim began negotiations with a cab driver to take him back to the Sinton Hotel. Agent Valentine overheard Jim arguing about the proposed fare—Jim "resented the charge of $1.50 asked by the cab driver." Valentine saw his opening. He said to the cab driver that since he needed a cab to go home and the hotel was on the way, why not allow the two men to split the fare? The cab driver agreed, and a pleased Jim got into the cab with Agent Valentine, having no idea he was an agent for the Bureau of Investigation. The two men held a long conversation on the ride back to the hotel. According to Agent Valentine's filed report, Jim made strikingly pro-German comments:

> Phillips' remarks were very pro-German, stating that Wilson had bit off a bigger bite than he could chew and that the German army was superior to ours and that the men we were sending over there were nothing more or less than cannon fodder. He interrogated this agent very closely as to the sentiment existing in Cincinnati and what proportion the German populace bore to the populace of Cincinnati. This agent responded that the population of Cincinnati was composed of about seventy-five per-cent German. This seemed to please him very much and he continued his interrogation along the lines of what cantonments, the amount of men that we had in the cantonments and the amount of men that we had sent across. He laid particular stress upon the sinking of the "Tuscania" stating that it was it was a remarkable piece of work and showed the ability of the Germans when a submarine could escape the heavy convoy that accompanied the "Tuscania." He also added "I wonder if the authorities ever made a thorough investigation to ascertain whether or not the fate of the 'Tuscania' might have been an internal explosion."

Jim exited the cab at the hotel, and Valentine pretended to go home. He traveled just a short distance before he left the cab and met with Agent Stern, who had been in a cab trailing them. The agents decided to wait thirty or forty minutes and then to return to the hotel to try to engage Jim in further conversation. They agreed that Agent Valentine would go in first and try to reconnect with Phillips. Stern would then stroll in and be introduced as Valentine's friend.

The plan worked. Valentine found Jim in the hotel lobby, struck up a conversation, and then Stern entered and was introduced. The agents then took Jim to the hotel bar and continued to have "a running conversation" until almost 11 PM. Again, Valentine reported the conversation:

Phillips does not speak German himself but he is very familiar with Germany and claims to be a friend of the Kaiser. His supposed daughter was educated in Germany, having left there sometime in 1914. During the course of Phillips' remarks he referred to a small memorandum book, where, apparently, he had the different cities under the proper index as he turned to Cincinnati very promptly and asked these agents if we knew a Mr. Hellenschmidt, who is connected with the German Volksblatt [newspaper] of Cincinnati. He claimed that he had accompanied Mr. Hellenschmidt on a trip through Germany. He also mentioned a man by the name of Newen, who is supposed to be an Attorney in Cincinnati. The remarks of Phillips were in all respects quite pro-German and he seemed to take delight in describing the conditions of Germany and the thrift and ability of the German people coupled with their wonderful military establishment.

Jim also bragged before going to bed that once while his wife and daughter were in Germany and the kaiser was reviewing troops, Isabelle, in the crowd, innocently waved at the kaiser, and he saluted back. He told the men that his wife spoke German very fluently and then said good night.[14]

In Lexington, Agent Thompson met Isabelle's train and watched her. He reported that "shortly after she alighted from the train she joined some man and in company with this man, went to a house which is of questionable character and in fact is known to be conducted as an assignation house." Thompson waited outside for some time, but Isabelle and the man did not emerge, so he ended his surveillance.[15] He subsequently revised his report to correct his error in reporting that Isabelle went with a man to an assignation house. He and two APL men had gotten confused and followed the wrong woman. They afterward figured out that Isabelle was visiting Mrs. Norman F. Hertzer, "Marie," her cousin. Isabelle had been a bridesmaid in Marie's wedding to Norman Hertzer in Cleveland in June 1917.[16]

The next morning, Thursday, February 14, Agent Light called at the Hotel Sinton and discovered that Jim had just left for an eight o'clock train. Light jumped on a streetcar and went to the depot, where he boarded the train and located Jim in the dining car. Light remained on the train until it pulled out with Jim on board. Jim Phillips was headed back to Marion.[17]

Based on a letter Warren Harding wrote to Carrie, it is likely that as Jim was returning to Marion, Warren was just leaving. On Sunday, February 19, Harding wrote to Carrie from Washington, apologizing for his speedy exit but he had not written since his departure because he became violently ill after he left her. "I have been wishing to scratch you a line since my hasty leaving of Marion, but I was poisoned or knocked out by some train food and have felt perfectly miserable since," he wrote. "Friday and Saturday I ached so terribly I could hardly restrain from crying out. Am a bit better today. Am eating little and drinking gallons of water, trying to rid my system of the poison. Maybe it's the grippe. It was good I left as I did."[18]

He knew that he was being watched in Marion. "I am sure there were people at the station to see if I got away," he wrote. "Hope they were satisfied. One has not only to be reasonably good but must be sure to maintain the appearances. This is a great old world."[19]

It appears that he and Carrie had become intimate again. "Let me say that I was immeasurably helped by our brief interviews. I was inestimably comforted. Please know this. *I was rejoiced.* You are so wonderful," he enthused. "There is no other like you."

But he did not rouse himself from his sickbed simply to write her a note of thanks or to express his love; he wrote to warn her. Someone in Washington had told him that "a prominent woman" in his hometown was trying to dissuade young men from signing up for the armed forces. From the description, Harding recognized that the woman was Carrie. He was concerned and cautioned her to watch her tongue:

Having said all this in utter and very deliberate sincerity, let me lecture you a bit. It is quite all right for you to express yourself freely on war matters to me. This does not say you are right, but there is no harm in free expression to me. I can understand. But do, please, I beg you, be prudent in talking to others. If things go as you have foreseen, in the serene aftermath you can have your consolation. Remember your country is in war, and things are not normal, and toleration is not universal, and justice is not always discriminating. You know I am only for your good. If you are right, your triumph will be complete, if you are wrong you will have no words to eat, and meanwhile you will be secure from misrepresentation. I am moved to write this from an echo of things said of you, not by any unfriendly tongue, but by some who do not understand. When I tell you I heard here, from one who did not know I knew you, of a prominent woman in my town discouraging young men from entering the service (other things made clear who was meant). I trembled lest some embarrassment might attend. It is improper in any nation in the world to do that when war prevails. Of course I knew you did not go so far as that, but the story shocked me because it revealed the possibilities of rumors. Please, I beg, be very prudent. Let's get through these trying days without needless irritation or embarrassment. You have the intellect, the soul, and personality, please command the poises befitting your superiority.[20]

Having given his warning, he wrote that he looked forward to their next visit. She again was going to Cleveland for a couple of days or more—he didn't seem to find this troubling. He told her that he was thinking he might be in

Philadelphia on Saturday, February 23, "and it might be convenient to look up the Poutersons there." He in fact was scheduled to inspect the shipbuilding works at Hog Island in Philadelphia on Monday, February 25, with members of the Senate Commerce Committee, so he likely was thinking of going to Philadelphia for the weekend, if she could break away. The rendezvous did not take place.

When he did visit the gigantic works run by American International Shipbuilding with four other senators on February 25—they all had 30-cent lunches with the workers—he was impressed with the massive undertaking. It was the largest shipyard in the world with fifty slipways. Harding claimed with some self-aggrandizement that the improvements and progress he saw were the result of the "furor which has been stirred up" in Congress. He proclaimed that he did not think any member of the committee felt there had been "any graft or profiteering."[21]

While "echoes" of things that Carrie had said may have been repeated to him by someone in Washington, Harding likely had no idea that questions regarding the loyalty of Carrie, Isabelle, and Jim Phillips were about reach to the highest levels of the Wilson administration. The day after Harding wrote his warning letter to Carrie, Agent in Charge Calvin Weakley in Cincinnati asked Frank Campbell to provide more background on the Phillipses and his statements about them being connected to Baroness Zollner. Campbell responded with a long letter on February 20, which somehow found its way into the hands of Democratic congressman John Alexander Key, from Marion, Ohio. Key gave Campbell's letter to Wilson's attorney general, Thomas Watt Gregory. That Saturday, when Harding said he might be in Philadelphia, Attorney General Gregory dictated a memo to the chief of the Bureau of Investigation, A. Bruce Bielaski:

February 23, 1918
Mr. Bielaski,

This was given to me by Congressman Key of Ohio. While it does not seem to be particularly definite I think some attention had best be given to it and these people carefully investigated and also postmaster Campbell at Marion, Ohio, interviewed to see if any more definite data can be secured. See that it is given attention.

T. W. G.[22]

On the next Thursday, February 28, Bielaski wrote to his agent Weakley, advising him that Campbell's letter had made it to the attorney general. He ordered Weakley to have an agent conduct interviews in Marion, including one of Campbell himself. He further advised that Baroness Zollner had been released on bond with the understanding that she would not go near any military or naval base during the period of the war. In fact, the baroness's attorney, C. C. Abernathy, had applied in the middle of January to the federal judge, Edward T. Sanford of the U.S. District Court in Knoxville, for a bail hearing, which was granted and held on January 16. Judge Sanford unexpectedly granted bail and released the baroness under an agreement that she would stay in her home in New York, refrain from communicating with American military personnel and anyone in Austria or Germany, and report in to District Attorney Kennerly twice a week regarding her whereabouts.[23] No trial date was set.

Edward T. Sanford was a Republican, a graduate of Harvard, and a fervent and passionate supporter of Theodore Roosevelt. In 1907, President Roosevelt had plucked Sanford out of obscurity in Tennessee, appointing him assistant attorney general of the United States and nominating him a year later him as a district judge for the U.S. District Court, Eastern District of Tennessee. Given his history, it is fair to surmise that Sanford wanted to see T.R. nominated for president in 1920. Whether this had anything to do with the sudden and inexplicable release of the baroness is unclear. Was he told by the baroness's attorney of the marriage of the baroness's younger brother to Theodore Roosevelt's first cousin and that this messy information might come out in a full-blown trial, embarrassing T. R., who had made it his business to be the foremost anti-German in the country?

Might there also be some significance that Warren Harding nominated Sanford to the U.S. Supreme Court in 1923?[24] Sanford served on the Supreme Court with Chief Justice William Howard Taft for seven years until his death in 1930.

Bielaski, whose Democratic boss Thomas Watt Gregory was under intense public scrutiny for failing to aggressively pursue German spies, likewise was strangely lukewarm, if not hostile, about prosecuting the baroness. Just after she was arrested, before the evidence had even been gathered, Bielaski sent a telegram to his special agent in Chattanooga confirming that Naval Intelligence had given the baroness a "clean bill of health" and curtly added: "Unless evidence specific violation of law [she] should be immediately released."[25] And later at the end of February when writing to Special Agent in Charge Weakley of the need to follow up on the attorney general's request to continue the investigation into the Phillipses, Bielaski editorialized further on the baroness's seeming innocence: "With reference to the Baroness Zollner mentioned therein [meaning Frank Campbell's report], you are advised that there was practically no information against this woman indicating that she was a German spy, and she was released on bond with the understanding that she would not go near any Military or Naval base during the period of the war."[26]

Was it significant that Bielaski had been appointed chief of the Bureau of Investigation by a Republican, William Howard Taft? His attitude toward the baroness is hard to explain.

Bielaski's follow-up on Spalding was likewise lame. Over a month after the espionage hearing and after the baroness had been released on bail, Bielaski had agents interview Spalding's family members in New Mexico, specifically to see if Spalding had given them the same code about ship movements that he had given the baroness. The request was silly; the code had been published in all the newspapers covering the hearing, accounts Spalding's family members surely would have read. Not surprisingly, Spalding's family told agents that they too had been given the exact same code, yet they could not produce an original in Spalding's handwriting. ("I was unable to secure the original as they were unable to locate it," the agent wrote.)[27] Nevertheless, Bielaski let the Spalding matter drop.

Frank Campbell, however, had no doubt that the Phillipses were German spies. In his February 20 letter, he lined up the evidence:

1. The Phillipses were loud and vocal proponents of Germany in the war and investigators in Marion had collected affidavits to verify their pro-German statements. Though Jim Phillips was "the tool of his wife," he too was believed to be a German sympathizer, "a condition thought brought about solely through the influences of the wife and daughter."

2. Carrie and Isabelle had spent years in Germany prior to the outbreak of the war.

3. Campbell had intercepted frequent mail from Adolf Pickhardt to Isabelle Phillips, and they apparently were engaged.

4. Carrie and Isabelle spent considerable time outside Marion, paying extended visits to New York and Washington, where they spent "fabulous sums," well beyond the means of Jim Phillips's $5,000-a-year salary.

5. Carrie and Isabelle were entertained at the Pickhardt residence in New York and were believed to have attended a social event when Baroness Zollner was also present.

6. The baroness was related to Adolf Pickhardt, and she had been arrested in Chattanooga in a hotel room with a young Army officer along with "papers of sufficient damaging character to cause her to be held as a German spy."[28]

Campbell did not even mention—perhaps he did not know of—Carrie and Isabelle's long stay outside Camp Upton earlier that fall and how it mimicked the same sort of activity that caused the baroness to be arrested in Chattanooga in the first place. Nor had he seen the statement from the baroness's sister-in-law that her husband, Adrian Pickhardt, believed his sister was a secret agent being paid by the German government, and that he, too, had spied, at her request, on a major national cantonment.

It is hard to tell whether Harding knew any of this as it was transpiring in late February. On March 3, he spoke at a large patriotic gathering of the Maryland Branch of the Council of Defense in Baltimore and made his most jingoistic comments of the war. "Among us are miserable spies," he told his audience. Germany, he asserted, had dealt harshly with spies discovered in its country, and so should the United States. "In justice to these 100,000,000 American people, there is but one place for the man with the bomb or torch. That place is against a wall. We must be for America first."[29]

On the same day, the *New York Times* announced that Theodore Roosevelt had recovered sufficiently from an almost fatal recurrence of the jungle fever and infection that he brought home with him from his journey up Brazil's River of Doubt that he might be released from the hospital.[30] In fact, he was a very sick man who would be dead within a year.

Also on the same day in Europe, the Russians signed the Treaty of Brest-Litovsk with the Germans, giving up a third of Russia's population, half its industry, and most of its coal mines. The Bolsheviks, in a fight for their very existence, were desperate for peace at any cost—the treaty was a complete capitulation.[31] Lenin relocated the capital from St. Petersburg to Moscow and hunkered down for a nasty civil war. The Germans accelerated the movement of its troops to the Western Front for the spring offensive, designed to be the knock-out blow that would force the Allies to the peace table.

The Allies, including now the United States, knew the big campaign was coming. As early as February 11, Secretary of War Baker issued a statement saying that the "long-heralded and widely advertised German drive on the western battlefront may soon materialize."[32]

On March 21, the Germans launched the first of what would be five major offensives, this one against the British Fifth and Third armies. The Americans were about to get into the fight in big numbers, and it would be bloody.

In Cincinnati, Agent Leonard Stern made his preparations to visit Marion to talk to some people about the pro-German activities of Jim, Carrie, and Isabelle Phillips. He probably had no idea that he would get an earful about a sitting U.S. Senator.

CHAPTER 49

"War Is Hell"

Bureau of Investigation Agent Leonard Stern took the afternoon train on the Erie Railroad on Friday, March 8, from Cincinnati to Marion and arrived in town a little past 3:30 PM. He immediately reported in to Postmaster Frank Campbell and set up meetings for the following day to interview five men.

The next morning, Saturday, March 9, Stern spoke with Campbell; Asa Queen, chief of the Marion Branch of the American Protective League (APL); Ralph Lewis, a grocer who would marry Warren Harding's sister Abigail ("Daisy") after Harding had died; a Mr. Owens; and a Mr. Wysall, the fuel administrator for Marion County. The men all confirmed the same story: They believed Carrie and Isabelle Phillips were German agents.

They also told him something Stern did not expect to hear: that Senator Warren G. Harding was having an almost public affair with Carrie Phillips.

Stern corroborated most of what Frank Campbell had written in his February 20 letter along with details. Jim Phillips had been a member of the Uhler-Phillips firm that ran a large department store, but he had sold his stock and was now merely employed at the store, making a salary of $5,000 per year. Carrie and Isabelle were "extravagant" in their expenditures and lifestyles, spending more than Jim could possibly earn. "In fact, it is commonly reported that Phillips' wife and daughter have practically drained him from every cent he ever had and that Mr. Phillips is now considerably worried over financial matters." Jim himself was not seen as suspicious except that he was pro-German in his remarks, "which is accounted for by the influence of his wife and daughter."

Stern concluded that Isabelle was engaged to Adolf Pickhardt, who was stationed on the USS *New York*—though the engagement was "rumored and not confirmed." They all had read the *Cleveland Plain Dealer* article on Baroness Zollner and believed Adolf was the son of millionaire Wilhelm Pickhardt, thus making him the baroness's brother. "The Phillips ladies are known to be extensively entertained in New York by the Pickhardts," Stern recorded. He was shown and read two or three letters from Adolf Pickhardt to Isabelle, but he found nothing overtly disloyal in them. The letters were "of an endearing nature and such letters as a young man may write to any young lady." He recorded that the letters were "heated for tracings and held up to the light," but no secret messages could be seen.

"The gentlemen interviewed by this agent regarding the Phillips are firm in their belief that Mrs. Phillips would do anything to help the German cause." She spent nine-tenths of her time away from Marion, Stern was told. Much of that time, his informants believed, was spent with Senator Harding.

"It seems that about four years ago Mrs. Phillips and Mr. Harding, who is now United States Senator Harding from Ohio, were found in a compromising position in a hotel near Marion, Ohio, and from that time until the present time it is common gossip in Marion that Mrs. Phillips is practically furnished with funds by Senator Harding," Stern reported. "In fact, it seems to be open and notoriously known, as it is stated by different citizens of Marion, that whenever Mr. Phillips leaves town that Senator Harding is always in Marion. Mrs. Senator Harding is said to be an invalid."

The men who spoke with Stern suggested that Harding did not know of Carrie's ties to the Germans and was unaware that Carrie was using him for information. "These men state that Mrs. Phillips, under the guise of wishing to gain information regarding the whereabouts of her prospective son-in-law [Adolf Pickhardt], secures information from Senator Harding, who secures the same from the Navy Department in Washington and gives this information to Mrs. Phillips; that she then in some unknown manner relays this information to friends of the German Empire and they firmly believe and state that Mrs. Phillips should be closely watched while in Washington and other eastern cities."

Stern reported that much of what he heard sounded like small-town gossip. The only substantiation came from the fact that the two women traveled extensively and had been entertained by the Pickhardts. He wanted to interview the Phillipses, but they were out of town.[1]

It appears Stern was given a copy of a letter that Asa Queen had written to his superiors in the Washington headquarters of the APL. Queen had written on February 14, in response to an inquiry letter received a month earlier from the national head of the APL, Charles D. Frey. Queen's letter shows that the APL had asked its operatives in Marion to open an investigation into the activities of the Phillipses in the middle of January, a month before the *Plain Dealer* identified the baroness as the daughter of Wilhelm Pickhardt. Queen wrote that his group had begun an active inquiry well before January—obviously dating back to at least the August 1917 telegram he had sent to Cleveland advising that Carrie was on her way to there. Queen's letter contains much of the same information found in Frank Campbell's letter—indeed, since it predated it, it was likely the source for Campbell's letter. There are some additional tidbits in Queen's letter not found in Campbell's letter, such as a connection between the Pickhardts and the submarine *U-Deutschland*. Queen accurately reported an understanding that the Pickhardt firm was one of the major purchasers of the dyestuffs brought to Baltimore in the daring voyage of the merchant submarine. And his letter hints of the Harding relationship with Carrie, where Campbell's letter was silent on this account. Of Carrie, Queen wrote: "She has direct, intimate connection with public officers, viz. senators and men in the service, and seems to have advice of public affairs before it reaches the Press."

Queen was unambiguous in his conclusion. "Since then we have concentrated considerable effort towards securing evidence against these parties. The Captain of the Merchants Division in our organization was detailed on the case and we are now convinced that these parties are German spies and that they are receiving money from the German Government."

Queen's letter was circulated within the Bureau of Investigation. On March 18, the agent in charge of the Cleveland office, Bliss Morton, transmitted the letter to Charles De Woody, now stationed in New York. Bliss said he would keep an eye on Carrie in Cleveland. "It is suggested that the parties with whom Mrs. Phillips connects in New York and Newport be investigated," Morton wrote.[2]

This information, so potentially explosive for Warren Harding, would sit for well over a month on the desk of Chief Bielaski of the Bureau of Investigation. Perhaps he wasn't sure how to handle it; or perhaps he wanted to think over the advantage it might bring him. Whatever the case, it was not until April 29 that Bielaski finally responded to the February 23 request of the attorney general of the United States to "give attention" to the Phillips case.

❧

Someone tipped off Warren Harding. Maybe someone in Marion told him of the agent who came to town asking questions. By mid-April, though, he knew enough to consult with Jim Phillips and then he sent very carefully worded notes to Carrie. When her response seemed to be somewhere between hostile and blasé, Harding turned to Jim again and implored him to intervene to prevent a full-scale disaster.

The first letters Harding sent to Carrie have not survived but are referenced in a letter he wrote to Jim on April 22. "Several days ago I wrote to Carrie along the lines you suggested relating to the bond campaign and got a reply which in substance said you ran your own affairs. I rather felt my appeal very futile." He tried writing again, he wrote, "very seriously and earnestly, warning of her impending dangers." Clearly, Carrie was at risk of being arrested, and just as clearly, it had nothing to do with the bond campaign. "She is under the eye of government agents, and it is highly urgent that she exercises great prudence and caution." Harding then wrote as if to a censor who might intercept and read his letter—making his denials of any wrongdoing on Carrie's part. "I know, of course, that she is not deserving of surveillance, but feeling grows intenser, and prejudices are more pronounced as the casualty list grows, and I could beg of her to be prudent and above the impassioned prejudice of passing days."

He apologized for burdening Jim but felt the stakes were too high to remain silent. He knew Jim was no more likely to influence Carrie than he was, but somehow she had to recognize the gravity of what was happening. "I can't appeal very effectively," Warren conceded. "I wonder if you can command. Frankly I doubt it. Perhaps you can appeal. It takes more than tact. But it is really serious." She had to understand she was actively under suspicion and surveillance. "She forgets we are in war—hellish war—and she forgets how Germany treats those who are against the government. It is time to think. If she is loyal and prudent, the cloud will pass. She must be. If she isn't, there is certain humiliation and distress and annoyance and embarrassment in store." Jim had to intervene and "save her from herself."[3]

During this time, Harding kept up appearances. A week before writing to Jim, on April 13, he was one of the principal speakers at a luncheon given by the influential National Security League. The lunch was given in honor of Senator Harding and Senator Robert Owen of Oklahoma at the Hotel Astor in New York City. Harding reported on the progress on the shipbuilding program and again took some credit for righting what had been a chaotic situation. The German submarines would soon be unable to sink enough ships to overcome the number coming on line, he reported to his audience. Compared to the reluctant warrior he had been a year earlier, Harding now seemed to have both feet in, stridently calling for Germany to be brought to terms. "Originally we of the Republic went into the war in defense of American national rights," he said, "but now we find ourselves becoming part in a warfare for the preservation of civilization, and if this great Republic did not do its full part it would not be fit to live in. And so the committal is unalterable." On this day, no patriot could out-patriot him. "We can go further," he said of Lloyd George's declaration that England would never surrender as long as she had a ship at sea. "There is and can be no surrender for us so long as honor is worth while and there is energy and resource to make war in the cause to which we are committed." America would rise above any difficulty. "If we have builded well thus far, we are only begun in demonstration of capacity." The very American soul, he rhetorically concluded, was aflame and committed to victory.[4]

On Monday, April 29, Harding was on the Senate floor arguing against his earlier position that America needed a dictator to run the war. Since the previous summer, he had seen too much of the bungling and ineptitude of the Wilson administration and was recoiling from so much centralization of power in the federal government. Senator Lee Slater Overman of North Carolina, a Wilson proponent, had introduced a bill at the behest of the administration to give Wilson vast powers to prosecute the war. Harding was one of only thirteen senators to vote against the measure. He said if there was a lack of coordination among the executive bureaus and agencies, the president alone was responsible. He pointed out that subordinates in various government bureaus from whom Congress sought information were already insulting the Senate. "They speak contemptuously of Congress," he said. "An Assistant Secretary had the effrontery to say the other day that the Administration could get along very well in the conduct of the war if it were not for the interference of 'numbskulls on Capitol Hill.'" In his complete about-face, Harding now said that he was not willing to let Congress surrender its oversight functions, "so as to create a smoke-screen for the President for retreat from our established form of Government to dictatorship."[5]

Whether a coincidence or not, that same day A. Bruce Bielaski wrote out a memo to Attorney General Gregory advising him about the results of the investigation into the Phillips family, including the sensational news that Harding was having an affair with Carrie. "I have the honor to inform you that on February 23, 1918, you sent me a note handed you by Congressman Key, of Ohio, regarding J. E. Phillips, his wife, and daughter, of Marion, Ohio," Bielaski wrote. "The last two were said to be pronounced German sympathizers and Mr. Phillips was said to be a tool of his wife." The rest of his report summarized what his agents had found and his conclusion that the

activities of the Phillipses did not violate current law but likely would be covered under the Sedition Bill that was wending its way through Congress:

> Some information concerning these people had come to us prior to this time.
> Investigation showed that Phillips—an employee of a large department store—
> is very pro-German. He made such statements as, "Wilson had bitten off a big-
> ger bite than he could chew," that the German army was superior to ours, that
> the men we were sending over were "cannon fodder," etc. He has visited Ger-
> many where his daughter is said to have been educated. It does not appear, how-
> ever, that his statements were of a character which can be reached under any
> statute now in force.
>
> It appears that both Mrs. Phillips and her daughter are "fast." [Bielaski ap-
> parently missed the correction about Isabelle and the assignation house]. Phillips
> receives a salary of $5,000 a year and the family is said to spend considerably more
> money than Mr. Phillips earns. It is reported about four years ago Mrs. Phillips
> and Senator Harding were found in a compromising position in a hotel in Mar-
> ion, Ohio. It is common gossip that she is furnishing funds to Senator Harding.
> [He had this backward.] It is notoriously known that when Mr. Phillips leaves
> town Senator Harding comes to Marion, and it is said that Mrs. Phillips spends
> considerable time with Senator Harding in Washington, New York, and else-
> where; that Mrs. Phillips is exceedingly pro-German.
>
> Miss Phillips is said to be engaged to a navy officer who is the brother of
> the Baroness Zollner, arrested some time ago for a violation of the espionage act,
> but released because there was little or no evidence against her. The possibility
> of information being wrongfully obtained in this manner is being investigated.
>
> There does not seem to me to be anything especially serious in the activi-
> ties of Mr. and Mrs. Phillips insofar as the Government is concerned, although
> it may be that it would be possible to reach Phillips after the new espionage
> statute is passed, should he continue in his talk. It has occurred to me that the
> persons behind this investigation may have hoped that it would develop some
> facts concerning Senator Harding's relations with Mrs. Phillips.
>
> The investigation will be continued after the new espionage act is passed.
>
> Respectfully
> Chief[6]

On the same day, Bielaski wrote to Agent Weakley in Cincinnati asking him
to continue the investigation against Jim Phillips once the new espionage act
was passed and to "see whether or not some of his statements cannot be made
the basis of a prosecution of him."[7] For whatever reason, the Bureau of Investigation completely missed the evidence that Isabelle and Carrie had spent
almost a month outside Camp Upton when it first opened. In addition,
Bielaski dismissed all the evidence against the baroness, even though the magistrate who heard the evidence found probable cause to hold her for trial on
espionage charges. Bielaski, a trained lawyer, had to know that the mere grant-

ing of bail did not dismiss charges pending against a criminal defendant, yet he acted as if her release on bail had been an exoneration. Similarly, he failed to see reason to investigate the activities of Carrie and Isabelle further, focusing only on Jim Phillips—the family member his own agents told him was the least dangerous.

But not everyone was ignoring Isabelle and Carrie's extended stay outside the federal cantonment. In a letter Harding wrote just two days after Bielaski's memo, he mentioned that suspicions were raised by Carrie and Isabelle's long vacation at Port Jefferson. He does not say who provided him this information—it could have been military intelligence or the APL—but someone advised him that this activity had been watched. And he had been watched, too. Possibly Harding finally was putting things together. His note to Jim makes it sound like Harding himself was questioned as a suspect.

May 1
My Dear Jim:

I was glad to get your letter. It interested me very much. Of course, I know most of the stuff said about Carrie is all rot; in the main, an echo of prejudices excited before we entered the war. I know she is no German informer—couldn't be. Yet these things have been reported. I never doubted her ability to square herself with a reasoning government agent, but I haven't wished her to undergo the annoyance of such a visit. The greater peril is some unheeding, impassioned, self-appointed sponsors of justice and patriotism, who might humiliate or harm her. It is a pity that there can be such danger, but war is hell, and sanity does not always prevail. Hence the need of extreme prudence, caution, wisdom and tact. I am delighted she is working as she is. Of course, she excels—she always does. Hope it is kept up. The "hostess" appointment would be fine, and she would do that well. I think it is under Red Cross auspices. Go to Judge Mouser. It ought not originate from me. It would be impolitic for me to ask him. But I feel sure he can suggest a way—then let me know and I will help at Ohio headquarters or at national headquarters. I am pretty sure Mouser could do it very quickly. Go to him, tell him she wants to do it, and you wish it, and the way will open. It will be fine and will help clear that up the whole situation. I would rejoice over it myself, and Carrie would do it so well and find joy in the doing. Call on me for any needed help.

Now, about Washington. I must not, cannot say it to Carrie, and I had rather she did not know I am saying it to you, because she could misconstrue it, but she and Isabelle ought not to come to Washington now. Nor ought they go to New York. I had some inquiry made about things said, and the Washington

trip last year led to suspicion about acting as an informer (ridiculous, of course)
and the suspicion was confirmed by the long stay at the naval base at Port Jef-
ferson. It is best now to avoid adding to these impressions. It is disgusting, but
the necessity of the case looms big. More I should not want Carrie and Isabelle
to come here unless I could show them some attention. Any call I made, any call
they made would be watched, and it would be not only unpleasant but add to
the talk. Truly, seriously, I think it would be a tremendous mistake to come now.
I am sure you will understand. I would delight to have them enjoy a visit. I
could find pleasure in showing them attention but I am thinking of their good.
You asked, I am answering frankly. It makes me very disgusted that we must con-
sider these things, but my conviction is very solemn. Really, this war problem has
distressed me infinitely more than you can guess. I believe I know Carrie is loyal
and helpful. But passions and prejudices are not at my command. A difficult sit-
uation can't be defied, it has to be met with tact and prudence until the mists
are cleared away. Glad your bond week turned out so well.

Sincerely,
W.G.H.[8]

The whole affair was making him ill. The strains of the war, now turning deadly
for Americans, the duty of national leadership, the constant calls to speak, and
now the threat of a serious investigation that could ruin him—all these matters
were crashing down on Harding. The day after writing Jim, he wrote a revealing letter to Carrie on Senate Chamber stationery. He began cautiously, thanking her for her letter. "You certainly write very sensibly and calmly about the
serious matter in my letter," he wrote her on Thursday, May 3. She complained
that she sensed that he was walking away from her, failing to shield her from the
government's unwarranted investigation. "It is difficult to recall any thing I
wrote," he responded, "which you could construe as an inclination on my part
to avoid the protection one owes a friend. I only wrote to aid in such protection. I know your attitude, I know that your pre-war utterances have left a prejudice, and I know the unreasoning character of popular prejudices amid the
passions of war—so I wrote, impelled by anxiety and a sense of duty."[9]

He was apprehensive about the letters he wrote to her, which some aggressive investigator might stumble on should she be arrested. "I have no semblance of a wish to harass you," he wrote. "I did think you might have letters
and a diary that you might not want to come to the attention of eyes that
could not understand, in case the embarrassing thing happened. I hope it will
not happen. I am fairly sure it will not if you are prudent at all times. Anyhow, please credit me with good instinct, with reluctance to intrude or advise,
but impelled by an anxiety I could not ignore."[10]

"Frankly, I am in the depths," he wrote. "I am half-sick, and blue, and
half sensible, stupid, glum, depressed. I can't sleep. I can't get it right." He

knew he had to get away from it all. "On Dr.'s advice I am going to lay off for a week or ten days and go to the woods. On Monday I start for the Adirondacks, going with a friend to a club camp. No party, just two of us to loaf and fish and get far away from the stress and strain." The depression he describes sounds as profound as some of the worst times he experienced when she was in Europe. "At this moment I hope it helps. Sometimes I do not care. The one remaining string seems nearly broken, I can't even hope as I ought. Maybe it is physical. Maybe it is mental—or both. Anyway I am about all in, no good. If I could be accepted, I'd go to war." He could not get over the feeling that something terrible was about to happen. "Maybe I am only reaping as I have sown and deserve it all. I am pretty much a failure and fizzle, with confidence gone, hope dimmed, and some impending misfortune seemingly hanging with me."

He let her know that he was telling no one else of his feelings. "Enough of this, I know it is rotten of me to confess it. I haven't confessed to any but you. *No one* knows the doctor tells me to go. Please don't mention it, I am discussed enough already. I want to be free from it all. If you think you can write me a line that will help me out of the hole, I'll welcome it."[11]

He wrote to Scobey that he was going to the Adirondacks with his friend Senator Joseph S. Frelinghuysen. When he became president, Harding would sign the resolution ending American involvement in the First World War at Frelinghuysen's estate in Raritan, New Jersey. Harding's letters to Scobey during this period reflect his keen attention to the political situation in Ohio. With the 1918 general election looming, Frank Willis, who had lost the governorship to James Cox in 1916, wanted another shot. Scobey tried to convince Harding to oppose him, mainly because he saw Willis as a threat, both to Harding's Senate seat in 1920 and a formidable presidential aspirant should he take back the governor's seat. Harding correctly saw that Willis would not beat Cox, so he saw no reason to attack the man and possibly divide the party in Ohio. He wrote Scobey that the better tack would be to let him be nominated, and let him lose—"it is therefore the very thing to renominate him and get rid of him."[12]

Forces in Ohio were lining up that would compel Warren Harding to make a decision he did not necessarily want to make: He would have to declare for the presidency as a defensive move to protect his Senate seat.

He went off to the Adirondack League Club at Old Forge for ten days with Frelinghuysen, but not before voting against the Sedition Act, which made it a crime to speak, when the United States was at war, in a disloyal or profane way about the form of government of the United States, its military, its uniform, or the flag. The bill was passed and became law on May 16. It also became illegal to willfully obstruct or attempt to obstruct the recruiting or enlistment services of the United States. Twenty-six senators voted against the conference report in the Senate, and only two Democrats.[13] The chairman of the Senate Military Affairs Committee wanted military courts to try cases under the Sedition Act by court-martial instead of civil criminal courts.[14] With the passage of the Sedition Act, the First Amendment was under siege. German newspapers would be put out of business; the teaching of German would be banned in schools. Most members who passed the Sedition Act wanted it applied especially to members of the International Workers of the World for their criticisms of the war and the draft.

If the act had been in force when Jim Phillips spoke to the agents at the Sinton Hotel in Cincinnati, he could have gone to jail.

In June, Eugene Debs, three-time Socialist candidate for president, was arrested after giving a guarded speech in Canton, Ohio, in which he praised a woman who had been jailed for aiding and abetting a man in failing to register for the draft. He also told the young men in his audience that "you need to know you are fit for something better than slavery and cannon fodder." He ridiculed the aims of the Allies, saying they were the same as those of the Central Powers: to plunder.[15] He was tried and convicted of obstructing the draft, and sentenced to ten years in prison.[16] Debs acted as one of his own lawyers in his trial in Cleveland. He famously said to the court before being sentenced: "Your Honor, years ago I recognized my kinship with all living beings, and I made up my mind that I was not one bit better than the meanest on earth. I said then, and I say now, that while there is a lower class, I am in it, and while there is a criminal element, I am of it, and while there is a soul in prison, I am not free."[17]

His conviction was upheld by the U.S. Supreme Court, Justice Oliver Wendell Holmes, Jr., writing for the unanimous Court.[18] Wilson would deny a presidential pardon for Debs drafted by his attorney general, Mitchell Palmer, when it appeared Debs would die in prison from ill health.[19] "Denied," Wilson brusquely wrote across the document. Harding, a few days before his first Christmas in the White House, commuted Debs's sentence and those of twenty-three other political prisoners jailed during the war.[20]

Harding decided during the spring of 1918 that he needed to spend some significant time away from Washington and that he needed to go back to his roots—speaking at Chautauqua meetings in pleasant locales during the summer. He signed up for two extended tours, one in June and the other beginning at the end of July, to speak in northeastern New York, Vermont, and New Hampshire.[21] He was in desperate need of regeneration.

Perhaps Carrie recognized how much he needed her. Despite all the danger now attendant to their meetings with each other, they started to see each other again, and some of the old intimacy returned. In June they rendezvoused twice, but not in Washington or New York where they might be shadowed. The first time was Marion. "I am to speak briefly at Camp Sherman on Friday night," he wrote Carrie of his plans on June 12, "and will not get away from there before 10 p. m." The next day he was to be at a Republican advisory committee meeting in Columbus.[22] Knowing how busy he would be, he suggested to Carrie that she meet him at a train stop outside Marion (the Union Station stop at Hocking Valley cross) on Saturday night at nine at night. If she could not pick him up in her car, he wrote that he could take a taxi from Union Station to her home, away from prying eyes. "If it is agreeable I will stop over night and breakfast there," he wrote, obviously knowing Jim would not be home. "I am anticipating a good and helpful visit." He again was signing his letters *Constant*.

The second meeting came during the first leg of his Chautauqua tour, sometime between June 27 and July 5. "I am leaving to-night for New York State to deliver half a dozen Chautauqua addresses with my plans adjusted to return to Washington on the 5th," he wrote Scobey on June 27.[23] Carrie and Warren met during this speaking excursion in New York, in a town or village on a lake.

In July he wrote fondly of these June "interviews." "I went to write yesterday," he wrote on July 14, "because it was just four weeks ago that I enjoyed the perfection of hospitality as your guest, unspeakably favored, and only two weeks ago we visited the sights, and enjoyed the walks, and explored the Angler's retreat, and later worshipped together across the lake. It was all so superb. I find myself recalling every detail and dwelling in the incomparable things."[24]

In this letter, he wrote about the obvious scrutiny they both continued to face. The passage was written in the context of responding about a record he had made—a novelty at the time—that someone had played for Carrie. She wondered why she had not known about it from him. The phonographic recording (made in a hotel, not the engineers' "laboratory") was "a patriotic record," which he thought was not of very high quality. But the reason he did not send it was not because of his uneven delivery, but because of its patriotic theme. "I really wished to send you one, I wished you to have my voice, even though not recognizable to me, but you can understand why I never sent it. It is a war record. We are not in accord. I did not wish to irritate you with my vices."[25] At this point in the letter he more fully described the surveillance they were both under:

I have always respected your capacity to think for yourself. I know of your intelligence, your wide reading and your familiarity with affairs abroad. I have never insisted you should agree with me, nor that you should surrender your own views. So much as possible I have deliberately avoided discussion, because it is not pleasant to be in debate with you, and though you are brilliant, you are not in your greatest charm when earnest in argument. But I have deplored the lack of concord. It has spoiled so many things. The sending of a record is only a very minor instance. You have never guessed what concern it has given me. I don't think you ever stopt to realize. I am not complaining, I merely want you to understand. Your attitude became conspicuous. You know how it was not only discussed at home and echoed in forty directions but you know it was reported to the departments here, and we both know my name was coupled with yours, not discreditably, but coupled. People said you influenced my votes—and you were right on national issues. You and I know better, but the embarrassment abided just the same. You wrote about my having said we would see more than ever of each other after my coming here. I did expect it, and believed it. But you can understand why now it is not so. The war situation, your attitude, my responsibility, all these lead to close observance. No one knows how many watchful eyes are following. You never leave home that it is not noted. When you recently came here I knew of your presence in the city from home before I had a chance to see you. It was factual information, too. When I came to M—every move is observed. I can not call or dine with you that it is not noted. I think much of this meddlesome watchfulness is aimed at me rather than you, but the point is that it exists, and we have to be governed accordingly. It has interfered with the realization of a hundred beautiful dreams. It will continue to interfere until conditions change, because duty makes its calls to both, and no one can be defiant just now. Enough of this. It grew out of the record inquiry.[26]

His earnest hope was that they would see a day when "the world is somewhere near normal again." In the meantime, they somehow had reached a point of respectful disagreement, and much to Harding's relief, Carrie finally seemed to be accepting things. For the first time in years, they wrote like concerned spouses to one another. She advised him to watch out for his health and promised to knit him a sweater, which he dearly wanted as the product of her hands, but he told her not to rush it—he would not need it until October. "I am observing your advice on tobacco," he wrote, "and keeping up golf as best I can." Things almost felt back to normal. "It is good to want you—the big desire of living and loving," he wrote.[27]

Things were anything but normal in Europe, however. The Germans had struck hard in the Ludendorff Offensive, resulting in spectacular losses on all sides, and they almost broke through the enemies' defenses, advancing to the Marne River and threatening Paris. But, with significant American help, the German attacks were turned back, and eventually the great German spring offensive ground to a halt.[28] The final German offensive was launched on July 15, the day after Harding's letter to Carrie.[29] By July 18, a dramatic counterblow by Allied troops under the French marshal Ferdinand Foch ended the German offensive for good and had the Germans in retreat.[30] The Germans were exhausted, their morale shattered. In August, the Allies would begin what would become known as the Hundred Days Offensive, starting with the Battles of Amiens and Somme. The end of the war was in sight.

The Americans had arrived just in time.

CHAPTER 50

"You Are the Wonder Woman of the World"

The New Jersey shore in late July was warm but refreshing. "Came over here Saturday, machine and family, will golf and enjoy the surf a few days, then go to N. Y. to attend to some matters there, then motor up to Cooperstown, my first engagement, on July 29," Harding wrote Carrie from the Hotel Traymore in Atlantic City, on Tuesday, July 23.[1] He was starting the second leg of his Chautauqua tour. He rarely referred to Florence by name in his letters, generally calling her "the Mrs." or "Mrs. H.," but in this one, he employed the even more distant-sounding "family" to describe her. From Cooperstown, he wrote, "the machine and family will return to Washington or go on to Ohio. I am going to do the tour alone."

Thus began what would be an idyllic month for him, the last stretch of tranquility and beauty that he would ever know. He was scheduled to travel through the pristine northern parts of New York State, beyond Rochester but west of the Adirondacks, a wooded stretch of land that slopes down to the banks of Lake Ontario. Once there, he would turn farther north, winding his way up through the country that was nestled alongside the St. Lawrence River with Canada visible on the other side. He would speak in small, picturesque towns: Oneida, Fulton, Wolcott, Oswego, Camden, Antwerp, and Gouverneur. Then he would take a boat on the St. Lawrence through the Thousand Islands and up for a day in Montreal. He would circle north of the

Adirondacks and back down, finishing in Plattsburgh, New York, and Montpelier, Vermont.

He cherished the idea of the time alone and vowed to spend much of it studying and writing in between his speaking engagements. "I am hoping to take up warfare and international relationships again, in greater detail and thoroughness," he wrote to Carrie.

But he also wished that she would join him. "I am hoping the Poutersons will be able to help me," he wrote. If she could come for a day, a weekend, a week or more, any or all would be welcomed. But she had to be discreet. "Select prudently," he implored. "Let no one at M—know about plans, because there may be inquiries there. But you must come. There are grand possibilities. Plan for a full week or more. *Grand!*"[2] Irrespective of whether she could make the trip, he pleaded with her for letters. "Don't disappoint me," he begged. "Send one like a fellow looks at the second and third and fourth times because he likes to linger on a sentence."

He wrote: "I love you. I need you. I want you."[3]

On the day he was in Cooperstown, he got a letter from her in response to his invitation. "Glad to hear from you and sorry you had to be ill," he wrote. He provided her with his detailed itinerary and again asked for letters, sent two days in advance to ensure timely delivery, and for a wire telling him if and when she could join him.[4] He tried to contact her over the next week, sending telegrams to the Statler Hotel in Cleveland, where she seemed to be a frequent guest.[5] He was disappointed when she did not respond, though he hoped she would simply appear at one of the cities on his itinerary.

She still had not shown up by the second week of August, but he kept up his stream of letters and telegrams to her, beseeching her to come. His letters, though, sound almost blissful, even in her absence—he was enchanted by his spectacular surroundings. "I wish you could have seen the tented grounds," he wrote of his time in Ogdensburg. "The tent was pitched on the banks of the St. Lawrence (I love that river) and it was simply delightful. I must tell you. I had a bully good week last week."

He described his trip through the Thousand Islands to Montreal over one weekend. That Sunday in particular, August 11, left him breathless but serene. "It was heavenly and so beautiful, so satisfying, if that term fits. There are rapids in the river, the boat takes them, and I had a series of wonderful thrills," he wrote. "I wish you might enjoy it as I did." He had difficulty putting it into words. "It was a weekend of combined charm and content, of thrills and restfulness, of placid waters and splashing rapids, and so much that was beautiful to behold and feel in nearness," he wrote touchingly of the glorious days. "You will find difficulty in understanding my enthusiasm, but it was a day divine."[6]

His time in Montreal was almost sacred to him, reminding him of their trip there as the new year of 1912 opened. Yet even in this state of delight, he still worried about her, given her penchant for rashness. From Malone, New York, on August 16, he wrote a letter that recorded his fire for her—"I am wild for you"—but also contained a warning. "May I write your worst fault?" he asked. "*Defiance!*" He wrote that in his opinion she needlessly stirred controversy and alienated those who otherwise wanted to respect and love her. "Wisdom must rule for us rather than hate," he reproved her. Moreover, he reminded her that her attitude was dangerous to both of them. Exposure would bring him ruin, leave him vulnerable and helpless—and he would be unable to protect her. He would lose his ability to earn money to help support her. "We would be on the rocks in a hurry, if all were turned to upheaval," he wrote. He wanted to avoid it. He would even retire from public service if she wished at the end of his Senate term, he wrote. "I want to quit in honor," he insisted. "I have sought to serve in honor and keep a trust I prize, but I'll retire willingly."

"Don't stir contention," he lectured. "If you can't agree, think but don't speak. Don't write! Period. I beg you."[7]

On Saturday, August 17, Harding wrote to Carrie from the Hotel Witherill in Plattsburgh, New York, situated on Lake Champlain. Before the U.S. entered the war, Plattsburgh was the place where friends of Theodore Roosevelt and his Rough Rider compatriot, General Leonard Wood, had constructed a preparedness summer camp for potential army officers. Opened in the summer of 1915, it was populated mainly with blueblood volunteers, young men from Harvard and Yale, or young professionals and businessmen from New York City and Chicago—gentlemen soldiers. They all paid for their own travel, food, and uniforms. The name "Plattsburgh" became synonymous with "preparedness" and universal conscription.[8]

Nan Britton claims that Warren Harding asked her to join him in Plattsburgh on Saturday, August 17. "He stopped at a hotel I recognized recently in a post card picture as the New Witherill," she wrote.[9] Britton recounted a beautiful morning in which she and Harding strolled into the countryside outside Plattsburgh to spend the entire time together in a lovely meadow. "A red letter day in our calendar of happiness," she dubbed it. She was specific about the timing. She arrived at 8 AM and he greeted her. "Gee, Nan, I'm s' glad t' see you!" she had him say. He then explained that they could spend "the whole blessed morning together" but that he would be tied up speaking at the Plattsburgh training ground all afternoon.

Britton's choice of this as one of a dozen specific dates provided in the book, along with the name of an obscure hotel, continues to beg the question of whether she had seen Carrie Phillips's collection before writing her book. The particular letter that Harding wrote to Carrie from Plattsburgh was one of the easiest to identify among those kept by Carrie because it was one of the few Carrie kept with its postmarked envelope. Both the letter and the envelope prominently display the Hotel Witherill name with a photo of the hotel. It would have been easy to pick out from the collection.

Another fact to consider: The postmark shows that Harding mailed his letter to Carrie at 3:30 in the afternoon—exactly the time Ms. Britton says Harding was speaking to a crowd that would monopolize his afternoon. When, then, did he write the letter? In the meadow with Nan? As he spoke to the people of Plattsburgh? Is it believable that he would write a note to Carrie Phillips while Nan Britton was with him? That he would mail it right under her nose?

Further, Britton's account does not square with two things he wrote about in his letter to Carrie. One was that he was feeling a little sick that morning from the night before. "Had a grand audience last night," he wrote to Carrie of his talk in Malone, New York. "Nearly keeled over once while speaking. Don't know what was wrong. It couldn't be the heat, for it was rather cool." If he was lightheaded and worried about his health, it would seem inconsistent for him to be in such a chipper mood with Nan, even stopping at a store to buy cigarettes on the way to the meadow, as Britton described him in her book. Second, he noted in his letter to Carrie that he had received a "big bundle of mail" at his hotel in Plattsburgh and that he was working hard to "clean it up." These are not the kinds of details he needed to make up—they have a ring of truth, especially since he had been away from his Senate office for so long. Working through a mass of correspondence would not leave time for an all-morning gallivant with Nan.

Moreover, Britton seems to have cribbed something Harding wrote to Carrie in the Plattsburgh letter, though she provided her spin to make the story more entertaining to her 1927 audience. She embellished her story with a slighting (literally and figuratively) reference to Senator La Follette.

Harding wrote to Carrie that he had just received word that morning that he was being called back to Washington for a Senate vote, so he was likely to cut his speaking tour short and leave for Washington after his talk in Lancaster, New Hampshire, on the twenty-first. In addition, he needed to get back to Washington to try to convince some senators to do him a favor by making speeches in Ohio on August 27 at the Ohio Republican State convention. (The state convention in fact was held at Columbus on August 27–28.)[10] "Not only is the call to vote impelling, but I am in a tangle about getting a couple of speaking senators to go to Ohio for the 27th," he wrote Carrie. "I simply must have them, and it is evidently going to require personal contact."[11]

Compare what Harding wrote to Carrie in his letter to her from Plattsburgh with Nan Britton's account of her supposed conversation with Senator Harding in the meadow:

> We were both full of loving reminiscences and future plans, and Mr. Harding included in his musings certain things bearing upon his position as senator. . . . Right then he was up against a problem which was causing him considerable anxiety: the folks back home had scheduled him for a speech in December, I think he said, and he was supposed to call upon some fellow senator to accompany him to Marion and make an address also.
>
> "La Follette would be fine," he mused with emphasis as he chewed thoughtfully on a stalk of timothy, "but he doesn't want to do it."
>
> "Why?" I inquired.
>
> "Oh, principally because he is small of stature compared with me and a bit sensitive on that score; I can understand perfectly, although he is a convincing speaker and I think it would make a sensation in Marion."[12]

The story, though amusing, has an obvious flaw. La Follette, at the time, was one of the most reviled men in the United States; many were still clamoring for his removal from the Senate and/or his deportation to Germany. No one with the slightest political sense or ambition would have suggested him as a possible speaker at the height of the war in the summer of 1918.

The statements Harding made in his letter to Carrie, by contrast to Britton's story, are historically verifiable. The Senate was debating a highly controversial draft bill at the time, known as the Man Power Bill, which would significantly expand the draft age to include all healthy males from eighteen years of age to forty-five.[13] Moreover, Harding was required to be in Ohio on August 27–28 for the state Republican convention where he did participate as one of the principal speakers, and it is likely that he would have tried to get other senators to speak given that the proposed platform dealt with important and controversial national issues, such as prohibition.[14]

A few days after writing from Plattsburgh, Harding penned a six-page missive to Carrie from Montpelier, Vermont. Its tone does not hint that he had been recently with another woman. To the contrary: It is full of teasing and earnest wishing for her to be with him. "It would have been grand if you could have been east for Sunday—Saturday and Sunday at Plattsburgh and Monday at Burlington," he wrote on August 20. "Lake Champlain beautiful, from either side." He even kidded her sexually, providing further proof that this was a time of harmony between them. "Tomorrow is a dream of a little town with the White Mountains in clear view and Mt. Washington in splendid outline against the sky," he wrote. "My friend's home is on Mt. Pleasant and is an adorable place. He owns the mountain. It is not big, but it is alone, and so attractive. Wish I could take you to Mt. Jerry. Wonderful spot. Not in the geographies, but a heavenly place, and I have seen some passing views there and reveled in them. Gee! How I wish you might be along."[15]

After traveling back to Washington and then to Ohio for the state convention, Harding stole away to see Carrie in Marion. He then returned to Maine to finish his Chautauqua duties. Writing to Carrie on the train en route from Boston to Laconia, New Hampshire, Harding apologized for the all the running around, but the promoters of his speaking engagements only found a substitute for him for a week and he was obliged to return to conclude his engagements. "I left Col— in a rush, after a very rushing time there, with little sleep, no moments alone, no time to see friends, almost none to see kinfolk," he wrote on Thursday, August 29. "I saw so little of you, and I wished to see so much of you. But it was good to look into your wonderful face and hear your voice and be near for a little while."[16] They had a cherished farewell. Asking for a letter, he wrote: "I wanted one as pleasing and cordial as our little exchange of greetings at the door, just as I left." He was enraptured. "You are the wonder woman of the world." He was so engrossed in their parting, he wrote, that he missed a train connection, but used the time to see his sister. He provided Carrie with his detailed itinerary for the remainder of his tour, hoping to meet up with her in New York or Boston once he finished his obligations in Maine on September 5.

That September and October, he spent time speaking on behalf of the Liberty Loan campaign—he had learned his lesson about opposing it—traveling in Ohio and to Chicago. He also participated in Ohio's general election, supporting Willis, who would lose to James Cox. As the war was speeding toward an armistice, with everything collapsing in Germany, the kaiser abdicated on November 9.[17] The Bavarian royal family tried to claim the imperial throne, without success.[18] Across the United States and then the world, a great flu pandemic broke out, eventually killing people by the tens of millions. Everywhere in the United States meetings and campaign rallies were canceled; entire towns were quarantined. Most of the flu's victims were healthy young adults, not the weak, young, or old who usually succumb to influenza. Harding himself was injected with some sort of "antitoxin" vaccine in Marion. He wrote Scobey that the vaccine strengthened his confidence that he could avoid the deadly disease, but no one was sure how or when the epidemic would subside.[19]

In New York, Baroness Zollner was arrested in October for violating the conditions of her bail and ordered to Fort Oglethorpe to be interned for the remainder of the war. She stayed in New York, however, because of the influenza raging in the camp. She was supposed to be transferred when the epidemic ebbed.[20] The war ended before that could happen. She was never incarcerated.

Nor did she ever stand trial.

CHAPTER 51

"We Have Blundered"

"City Grieves for Colonel," the *New York Times* headline read on the morning of January 7, 1919.[1] It seemed impossible: the indomitable Theodore Roosevelt was dead. He was sixty-one. He died in his sleep, apparently of an embolism.[2] In the Senate, the Reverend Forest J. Prettyman, standing at the vice president's desk, offered a eulogistic prayer. "Almighty God, as we meet today to represent this mighty nation, the shadow of a great loss falls upon us," he solemnly intoned. "One of the men of might, a leader of men, a patriot and scholar, has passed from us." Senator Lodge, T.R.'s long and cherished friend, began to speak but faltered. He gripped his desk, his voice trembling with emotion, and simply sat down, dazed and stricken. Pursuant to a resolution tendered by Senator Thomas Staples Martin of Virginia, the vice president, Thomas Marshall, appointed fifteen senators to attend the funeral on behalf of the Senate—Warren Harding was one of them.[3] On January 8, Harding was in Oyster Bay witnessing the simple funeral at an Episcopal Church. He walked with the Senate delegation to the gravesite on a snowy hill, where grown men, including former president Taft, sobbed like children.[4]

On the day Roosevelt died, Woodrow Wilson was in Italy responding to immense crowds that had come out to cheer him in Turin. No American president had visited Europe while in office. Heavy rain and an early hour did not dampen the enthusiasm for the American president.[5] "Viva Wilson, god of peace!" the people shouted. It was a scene that would be repeated over and over, from Rome to Paris, where Wilson hoped to broker the peace of the world. In Berlin, fighting broke out in the streets, German against German.[6] The Allies began to tighten their food embargo, seeking to further weaken Germany and any sentiment within its population to restart the war should the tenuous agreement to end it fall apart. Germany would be forced to accept whatever peace terms the Allies meted out. Some within the Allied camp did not want to allow Germany to use its remaining gold reserve to purchase food; they wanted it saved to pay reparations. Starvation loomed, especially in the countryside.[7] A Bolshevik-style revolution in Germany was widely feared.

Back in Ohio, Carrie Phillips brooded over the disastrous end for the Germans. She had seen Harding prior to the election, when he was in Ohio canvassing for the Liberty Bonds, but these had been only short encounters, and one was unhappy. "It was good to see you," he wrote on November 18 back in Washington, "good to have some little visits, little glimpses of content. You grew in my regard—if that were possible—and all interviews *save one* were happy," he wrote. "We will forget that one, though I'll remember your injunction."[8] He wrote that he might have stayed in Marion for another week after the election because the Armistice on November 11 "altered the program to be met here." Yet he felt things souring with her, likely in response to the deteriorating situation in Germany, so he knew it was better to be "removed from disappointing situations." He still wrote words of love and wished for her to come to Washington to visit, but their relationship, like the chilly late autumn weather, was cooling from its summer warmth.

On December 5, Carrie penned a letter to Warren, keeping a draft for her collection. "SOME VICTORY!" she sneered about the end to the war. "Our 'great victory' will level us," she wrote. "35 billions of debt and a hubbub of crap heaps, for instance just aeroplanes alone, not mentioning the four pounds of [poison] gas that each of these twenty thousand planes were to drop on Germany to extinguish the race." She wondered if he got "the import of the 'forced' laugh as yet, no?" Her defiance was up. "Well I didn't think our 'victory' would mean enough to the U. S. A. to go into it," she observed. "I do not now. I still think I *never* shall." She reminded him that she told him that his "yes" vote on war meant betrayal of the country. "La Follette etc— cleared—quite a joke—there never was a case against him. How queer you all must feel who talked so against him." She derisively wrote of newspaper reports that the kaiser might be arrested in Holland, where he was in exile.[9] Putting the kaiser on trial? "Where is [British Foreign Secretary Sir Edward] Grey?" she asked. "Where the Serbian murderers?" What about the two hundred million "hungry souls"? she railed.[10]

"So nothing from nothing leaves nothing," she wrote abjectly. As she had done all along, she was projecting her feelings about the world onto their relationship. "It's appearances, *not love.* I'd dearly love to write of love if love could write—no one in this world today can read the language if any one in the world could write it."

"Your polite little frigid note received," Harding wrote back on December 8. "It is all right. I had no reason to expect more. Probably it is all I deserve. Let it go at that. I am always disappointing everybody and you in particular, even when I do the best that I know how."[11] He had grown suspicious by her recent behavior and he inquired: "Say do you mind telling me where you spent Sunday, Nov. 17?" Later in the letter he asked her if Robinson had been back to Marion. "Glad you had adorable company," he wrote sarcastically. He told her that things had not been going smoothly or happily for him. "But it all goes in the sum total, and there is a law of averages." In fact, Florence was again very sick. "As a result," Harding wrote Ed Scobey around this time, "her kidney is swollen to eight or ten times its normal size and is far more painful than you can imagine."[12]

Despite it all, he wrote Carrie a very affectionate Christmas note. He regretted that the current situation made it impossible to celebrate Christmas with her as in years past, when they found stolen moments. "I am thinking of the library," he wrote of one of their Christmas revelries. "How beautiful and wonderful you were to me. I wish it might be again." He still maintained that theirs was no mistaken love. It grew stronger over the years, "in spite of trials, misunderstandings, disappointments and discouragements." Referring back to their start in 1905, he wrote: "Thirteen years declared, ten years experienced, ten years since the sublime sacrament."[13]

Harding had some reason to cheer that fall as a result of the outcome of the 1918 elections. The Republicans had scored major victories across the country, presaging what was to come in 1920. The electorate were war-weary, tired of big government and all the sacrifices and bombast about saving the world. The Republicans seized control of the Senate, a bad development for Woodrow Wilson since the Senate would need to approve any treaty he brought back from Paris. Partisan lines were already being drawn over the reconstruction of Europe and the proposed League of Nations championed by the president. Wilson did not help his cause by snubbing powerful senators when he planned his peace delegation. He took with him a career diplomat and Republican, Henry White, and General Tasker Bliss, along with Colonel

House and Secretary of State Lansing, but he rarely consulted with anyone other than House.[14] Even Lansing felt ignored. Harding wrote to Scobey that "a good many fellows on our side of the Chamber seem to be interested in making utterances against the President because of his trip abroad." He would not join them. "I think myself the trip is a mistake but I do not see anything to be gained by hammering at Wilson." Wilson would find his own way to self-destruct, Harding believed. "The public has a fairly just appraisal of him at this time but if we will only let him go on his egotistical way," he observed in his prescient way, "I think he will cease to be a strong factor in American political life."[15]

At the time of the 1918 elections, both he and Scobey had seen Roosevelt as the sure nominee in 1920. Scobey worried that with the large Republican victories in taking both the House and the Senate, Republicans might overstep their bounds. "The House is too much of a victory," he warned Harding, "because if we get too much of a majority there we are liable to do some foolish things ourselves."[16]

With Roosevelt's death a few months later, a new picture emerged for Harding. Scobey was right on it. "It looks to me like if you want to be President now, here is you opportunity," he wrote on the day Harding was in Oyster Bay attending T.R.'s funeral.[17] Scobey was not alone. That same day he was in New York the *New York Times* ran a piece about the likely Republican nominee now that Roosevelt was dead—the subhead of the article was "Talk Most of Harding": "[T]here was insistent talk of Senator Harding, and everywhere that his name was mentioned at the Capitol Senators appeared to be satisfied with the idea of his being put forth as the 1920 candidate." In one day, the paper observed, he "appeared to have jumped into a prominent place in the consideration of the possibilities."[18]

Harding obviously had little to do with this press. He had no time to influence opinion or gather in supporters. The feelings about him were spontaneous and genuine. His fellow senators held him in high esteem, recognized his hard work and his ability to conciliate and bridge-build while still standing on principle when compromise would not do. Contrary to biographers who have claimed Harding was a do-nothing senator, his colleagues knew better. "He has supported legislation of a pronounced advanced character and has, in doing it, won the confidence of the progressive element," the *New York Times* reporter wrote based on his interviews in Washington.[19] He pointed out that Harding recently came out in favor of women's suffrage, further winning support from the Progressive element. He was seen as a statesman. More, he had the benefit of being from Ohio, known as the maker of presidents. "The Republican Party more than once has been obliged in a crisis to turn to Ohio," the *Times* reported.

Harding brought his usual self-effacing outlook to all the hype. "I expect it is very possible that I would make as good a President as a great many men who are talked of for that position and I would be almost willing to make a bet that I would be a more 'common sensible' President than the man who now occupies the White House," he wrote Scobey. "At the same time I have such a sure understanding of my own inefficiency that I should really be ashamed to presume myself fitted to reach out for a place of such responsibility." He preferred to stay in the Senate, recognizing that if he ran for president he would be "unhappy every hour from the time I entered the race until the thing were settled."[20]

He continued to duck becoming a candidate even after he received a stirring reception when he spoke to a joint session of the Ohio General Assembly on January 29. Scobey told him to "ride along easy" without committing himself, but that he should start building his machinery behind the scenes. "Of course, if you should announce your candidacy, everybody else who has a candidate would commence to throw rocks at you," Scobey observed.[21] But even aside from this political wisdom, Harding seemed to be truly reluctant. He told Scobey the burden of running would exhaust him.[22]

His relations with Carrie turned frigid. On February 7, he wrote her a desultory note responding to a letter she had sent and one sent by Isabelle, apparently complaining about continuing surveillance. He wrote that she and Isabelle could hardly expect less in a world in turmoil. "No matter how irritating things are here, like irritations have attended Americans in Germany," he wrote dismissively. "I am sorry." He said he would be in Marion to discuss the reckoning of accounts between them around the eleventh or twelfth, making reference to what seems to be the beginning of her demands for money. If she had been on the German payroll, as some in Marion suspected, those funds would have ceased as the war was lost. As Carrie's anger shifted now, it appears she began to ask Harding to supplement her income. He thought her demands excessive, even "socialistic."[23]

A few weeks later, he wrote to her that he was aware of her plans, apparently, to extract more money from him. "I know you have plans, big plans, and you mean to carry them out," he wrote on March 3, his nerves on edge, his worries oppressing him. "They are important. I hope you have pondered well." He wrote that her "suggestion of an appropriation" was not "lost on me." He did not believe it possible to comply, he ventured. "While I can't appropriate as you suggest, I am ever ready to respond to any request within my power." He asked her to meet in person, "for a needed long talk." He was on his way to St. Augustine and Augusta that week with fellow senators to get away from the incredible tensions building in Washington and to play some golf with his colleagues. "I crave tranquility and freedom from care," he wrote Carrie.[24] Pressure had reached the boiling point as the Senate signaled its intention to oppose the League of Nations as it was proposed. "My own judgment is that President Wilson is such a bullhead that he will have no hesitancy in risking ruin of this country to carry his points in Paris," Harding wrote Scobey on March 5.[25]

Warren began writing Carrie letters that anyone could read, and signing them "Gov," and what letters he sent were few and far between. Clearly, he was starting to distrust her every move and motive, hoping to keep her from exploding the bombshell that he said would ruin them all. At times he wrote in homilies, getting his point across in story, but his meaning was apparent. On April 7, for example, he scratched out a six-page open letter that appears on its face to be a breezy note concerning his work and news about Isabelle. But when he wrote about golf, the warning to her to be prudent was evident: "Golf is a great thing to develop self-control," he wrote, back from Augusta. "One must ever keep his eye on the ball, and never press. To take the eye off the ball is fatal—a sure fizzle shot, and pressing in eagerness or blindly striking out in anger is worse than futile. Real life is much the same way."[26] In a similar fashion, his writing seemed to indicate he was already beginning to pay her bills. "I wish you would enclose to me the printed slip on your Phil. Ledger [the newspaper *Philadelphia Ledger*], so I can attend to its renewal," he wrote. The meaning appears to be that he wanted her to update her own personal ledger of expenses so he could pay them. "The Ledger is a paper really worth while," he wrote in seeming misdirection. "Always glad to hear from you."

The news on Isabelle was real, though. She was engaged, but not to Adolf Pickhardt. Her betrothed was William H. Mathee, Jr., an American soldier who had been born in Aachen, Germany, when his father was acting U.S. consul there. The letters provide no explanation of what became of Isabelle's relationship with Pickhardt. One can speculate that it was a disfavored relationship from the Pickhardt side from the start and that it became too risky once the baroness was arrested. Isabelle and Mathee would marry in September of 1919, and though Harding did not attend, he did send a telegram of congratulations.[27]

Meanwhile a true dilemma was taking shape for Harding in Ohio politics. The old Progressives with whom he fought in the past were looking to push him out of the Senate seat for one of their own, and they hoped to make that happen by forcing him to declare his candidacy for the presidency.[28] Harding wrote to Carrie that he would not run for president. "You need not be concerned about my ambitions," he wrote in his April 7 letter. "I know how you feel about them, but you need not think of them—for there are none. I know myself pretty well, I know my insufficiencies, my incapacities and alas! My transgressions."[29]

On July 10, Wilson appeared before the Senate to personally deliver the peace treaty with Germany that he had negotiated in Paris. The Democrats gave him a warm reception; the Republicans were cold. Wilson, exhausted and sick, performed poorly. He read from his speech and was not interrupted once by applause. "Several times during the first half of the address," the *Times* reported, "he dropped a word in reading the typewritten copy, on small cardboards, which he held in his hand, and then reread these sentences." He set aside his notes only at the very end and then delivered a stirring conclusion: "The stage is set, the destiny disclosed. It has come about by no plan of our conceiving, but by the hand of God, who led us into this way," he said, sounding more like his minister father than realpolitik statesman. "We can only go forward, with lifted eyes and freshened spirit, to follow the vision. It was this that we dreamed at our birth. America shall in truth show the way. The light streams upon the path ahead, and nowhere else."

But Henry Cabot Lodge and his fellow Republicans were not buying. As submitted, the peace treaty would fail.

Wilson took his case to the people, engaging in a cross-country speaking tour, but he was stricken with a serious cerebral event, likely a stroke, in September outside Wichita, Kansas, just as his supporters in the Senate seemed to turning the tide in the administration's favor.[30] His physician, Dr. Cary Grayson, canceled the rest of Wilson's trip on September 26.[31] He had a massive stroke once back in the White House. He would never be the same again. He became a shut-in, with only a few people, principally his wife, having access.

Carrie and Warren's relationship was devolving into one of money. In August, it appears she decided to purchase an expensive new car and called him to insist he provide the funds. By then Jim Phillips was in deep debt, Isabelle was about to be married, and Carrie seemed to be acting out of anger over the looming prospect that Harding would run for president. She probably felt deeply betrayed, and just as probably needed money to maintain her lifestyle. She threatened him with his letters, knowing that this was always a sure way to extract money. He wrote that he could not pay directly for a car because such an amount would be noticed, likely by Florence, perhaps even by snooping authorities. He begged her to cancel the car purchase and he would pay any damages to the car dealer. If she insisted, he asked her to send Jim to Washington to work out a payment arrangement through him. The tenor of the letter is near panic. He used loaded phrases like, "It is little less than madness . . ."

It appears that Carrie also began to plan a trip to Europe that fall—an unlikely destination given the devastation and economic and political chaos that prevailed, especially in Germany.[32] But he knew she would need funds for that trip.

On August 18, he wrote another letter, this time referring to a specific demand for him to pay her $10,000 by the following March. It is not clear what this money was for, but he tied it to her willingness to return his letters. "I do not wish to be penalized for the tribute I have paid you all these years [in his letters]. I use the word tribute in the highest and most beautiful sense. I'd like the papers—for your sake as well as my own." He offered to pay her $5,000 at once and $5,000 in March, but he insisted she remove the threat posed by her continuing possession of his letters. He asked her to be fair. In "wiping out embarrassments," he wrote, "let's play 50–50."[33]

The Progressives finally made their move to pin him down on his intentions in October, passing a resolution in the state Republican advisory committee that asked him to answer the question: Would he run for Senate or president? He knew if he announced for president, his enemies would take his Senate seat. If he announced for the Senate, the Progressives would throw their support behind General Leonard Wood, and if Wood won, the Progressives would control the state party and the dispensing of federal patronage jobs in Ohio. Harding initially declined to be pushed into making an announcement.[34] But then Copper Proctor, of the famous Cincinnati soap company family, declared for General Wood in mid-November, leaving Harding with no choice but to announce his candidacy. If he let the Wood boom grow, Wood's backers in the state could take over the state party and then even oppose Harding's renomination to the Senate. He was in jeopardy. Thus, to protect his Senate seat, Harding declared his candidacy for president on December 16, 1919. "You know how reluctant I was to take this step," he wrote Ed Scobey, "but it seemed like I needed to do it to preserve my political life and influence in Ohio."[35]

He justified his decision in a letter to Carrie in February 1920. They recently had had an interview in person. He told her he had not been lying to her about his intentions when it came to the presidential race. He did not "intend to be an aspirant in the big way," he maintained, it had been forced upon him. "I had not such preference, from personal inclinations, and I had had intonations of your hostility," he wrote on February 2. "I yielded to pressure. I was being undermined in my own state, and my good friends urged it to be a desertion of them to deny them such influence and cooperation as I could command."[36]

There had been so many misunderstandings, so much hurt. He responded to a charge Carrie had made that Florence was trying to cause her annoyance behind the scenes: "Mrs. H. has not mentioned your name in two years." If truth be told, he wrote, it was Carrie who had "offended and estranged, and stirred hostility that no personal quarrel could engender." As a result of her own conduct, she had been close to "serious embarrassment," he wrote, likely referring to how near she had been to being arrested.

"Enough of this," he wrote, signaling his change of subject. "Now to more intimate matters," he began. "We have blundered. We will not talk about blame. I accept my full share of it. We did blunder." He wrote that he gave her the most tribute he could and there was no cheating, but they had erred. "We both understood. We were both married. No lies were told. We felt the sense of family obligations. Happily there has been no irreparable damage." So now it was time to make decisions. He had been so distressed over what she might do that he had contemplated his own death. "I have often wished the final end for myself. In remorse, worry and distress I would welcome the great sleep. But normal beings cannot command it. We must live to make the best amends we can."

He therefore made his proposal—she could choose. He would, if she desired it, retire from public life altogether and never go back to Marion to reside. He would end his term in the Senate and find a way out of the presidential race, though he would need to do it in a way that did not involve simply quitting the race. "You must let me choose the process, but I will retire fully, utterly, finally after next March 4." Or he could continue his public life and remain influential and pay her $5,000 each year he was still in public office. It was not the large sum she had demanded, "but it will add to your comfort and make you independent to a reasonable degree."[37]

He awaited her reply.

Two weeks later, he was still waiting. She wrote a vague letter but not a direct response. "Will you be good enough to write precisely what is expected, precisely what must be—precisely what I must do to save you and yours and my own?" he wrote on February 15. "There is much at stake that you can help me and help yourself by specifying."[38]

The letters do not show what she finally said, but by late March and April the tone in his letters suggests that they had reached an accord. He wrote that he was looking forward to seeing her in Marion, he wrote, and he noted that the tenor of her most recent letter from New York seemed rational. "It was more like you than any in a long time," he wrote on April 5.[39]

The final letter that he wrote to her was after his nomination in the summer of 1920. On July 2 in Washington, Harding wrote that Jim Phillips had come to Washington to obtain what appears to be a written apology from Florence for some affront to Carrie. Harding said he could secure the "signed paper," but it would be at a cost—"it will be the end of friendly relations with the Phillipses." For this reason he was reluctant, and asked Carrie to rethink it. If she still insisted, he would obtain the document and send it forthwith. He said he would be glad to meet her to discuss in person if this did not suffice—in New York, Baltimore, or Atlantic City.[40]

There is no record of how this dispute was resolved.

Exactly four months later, on November 2, Warren Harding was elected the twenty-ninth president of the United States, by an unprecedented margin of victory.[41] It was his fifty-fifth birthday.

What Warren Harding and Carrie Phillips started in the summer of 1905 had implications beyond an illicit love affair. The letters Carrie saved, out of sentiment but also as leverage and protection, tell of the part their love affair played in his decisions to run for the Senate and ultimately the presidency. The world was changed as a result of whatever it was that happened on August 23, 1905.

The frustrating thing about the letters is that there is so little of Carrie's voice. She is heard mainly in her angriest moments, activated by the tumult of a world that seemed so unfair and irrational to her. We do not see the woman Harding clearly loved. We do not feel the loving presence she had to have projected to him.

Harding knew he would pay an exacting price for his relationship with Carrie. He wrote frequently that under a universal law of compensation, he would have to suffer to the same extent that he had known bliss. To him, the price was worth it. Few figures in history have left such a rich record of ecstasy in a romantic relationship, and few have been so unfairly treated in reputation. With these letters now uncovered, and the beauty and blemishes fully known, it is time to get past the charges of scandal and look anew at Harding as a real person and to judge his accomplishments in public life, which were many, by objective standards and not by whispering campaigns, or innuendo, or speculation, or through the perpetuation of myth and fiction. Warren Harding was possessed of the unusual gifts of common sense and foresight. His pronouncements of what it means to be an American and what America's role in the world ought to be are worthy of unbiased study. He was president at just the moment he was needed by the United States and his wisdom should be honored.

Epilogue

Elden Groves read in the summer of 1964 about all the fuss over love letters that had been discovered from Warren G. Harding to a woman named Carrie Phillips, and he smiled to himself. Groves wrote a column for the *Ohio Farmer* magazine called "Over the Back Fence." He knew Carrie Phillips, he wrote for his readers. They were business partners, of a fashion, in the raising of German shepherd dogs. The newspaper stories about the love letters brought back some fond and sad recollections to Elden Groves.

He first met Carrie in 1938 when he answered an ad she had placed in a national magazine about her dogs. When he showed up at her home in Marion, no one was there. He waited around a few minutes and a taxi pulled up and she got out, her arms full of bags from a trip to the grocery. Groves explained the reason he was there, as she rummaged through her purse to find her keys. She talked a mile a minute, he remembered, fumbling and poking around in her purse, but could not find her keys. She was still a handsome woman even in her sixties, Groves thought. Then she stopped searching and looked at him.

"But *I* can get in!" she beamed at Groves. "She reached under the porch banister and got an old tire iron tool, and used it to pry up a window," he recalled. He immediately saw this was not the first time she had performed this operation. "The lower part of the sash was all scarred up from past prying, and I commented on it," Groves wrote. She admitted that she usually forgot her keys, and she usually got in this way. "Fortunately it was a low window," he wrote, "and she hopped in and soon had the front door open."[1]

The letters actually had been discovered some years before 1964. As Carrie grew old, she became senile. Eventually her lawyer, Don Williamson, got himself appointed as her guardian and had her placed in a state old-age nursing home in 1956. There had been rumors that Harding had given Carrie some jewelry that was hidden in her house; Williamson looked around to see if there was any sign of it. The house was a mess from dogs that had run undisciplined. When Williamson and his wife broke open a locked closet upstairs, they found not diamonds but letters. Williamson recognized what he had uncovered but was not sure what to do with them, so he took them home and kept them in his basement. His wife and a friend read them over and contemplated writing a novel based on them.[2]

There they remained for the next six years. Carrie died in February 1960 at the Willits Rest Home on North Prospect Street in Marion. She was eighty-seven. Her husband, James Eton Phillips, had predeceased her by two decades, having died in 1939, and her daughter, Isabelle P. Mathee, was living in Wisconsin when her mother died.[3] In the fall of 1963, as the centennial of the birth of Warren Harding approached (November 2, 1965), authors eagerly anticipated the opening of the Harding Papers, which had for so long been under the control of the Harding Memorial Association. The Ohio Historical Society, after years of negotiation, won in a competition for the papers with the Library of Congress in the summer of 1964 and finally secured an agreement for the transfer of the papers from Marion to Columbus, where they would be made available to scholars for the first time. Kenneth Duckett, curator of manuscripts for the Ohio Historical Society, had put the plans in place to accept possession of the papers in the second week of October 1963. He was expecting an uneventful delivery, though the elderly president of the Harding Memorial Association, the aging Dr. Carl Sawyer (son of the Harding physician Doc Sawyer), insisted that the papers have a heavy and loud police escort to dissuade any old Teapot Dome scoundrels who might attempt to hijack them.

Duckett was met by Francis Russell, one of the scholars who had signed up to write a Harding biography, on the day the Harding Papers were being unloaded at the historical society. Russell had uncovered the Harding letters in Marion when he spoke with Don Williamson a few days earlier, and Williamson decided that the time was right to disclose the letters to an outsider. Russell and Duckett eventually entered into a secret deal to keep the letters quiet until Russell published his book. The Harding family found out about the existence of letters and sued. The case dragged on for years and resulted in a settlement in which the parties agreed to deposit the original letters in the Library of Congress and microfilm copies in the Ohio Historical Society.

Russell's book, *The Shadow of Blooming Grove,* published in 1968, became a bestseller. Though Duckett's papers show that Russell had very limited time, likely less than a full day, to review the handwritten documents, he included excerpts in his book from notes he kept, but these passages were redacted due to the lawsuit.

The American Protective League continued to exist for some months after the war ended. Attorney General Gregory issued a call for Leaguers to "Carry On!" in the first weeks after the Armistice to assist the government in the work of postwar reconstruction, but the APL was quietly disbanded some months later when Gregory resigned and was replaced by Mitchell Palmer as Wilson's attorney general.[4] Palmer championed a young man named J. Edgar Hoover within the Department of Justice at the time, and Hoover later assumed the top job in the Bureau of Investigation, where he served as one of the successors to A. Bruce Bielaski. The bureau changed its name to the Federal Bureau of Investigation in 1935. Hoover got his start in the Palmer Raids during the so-called Red Scare immediately after World War I. The raids were aimed at suspected radicals, anarchist, and Bolsheviks. Bielaski left the bureau to go into private law practice and then became an undercover prohibition agent.

Nan Britton published her book, *The President's Daughter,* in 1927. It sold widely and made a significant amount of money. She claimed that she became pregnant with her daughter, Elizabeth Ann, as a result of a sexual encounter with Harding in his Senate office in January 1919, the month T.R. died and Harding was proclaimed a frontrunner for the presidency. As with so many of her claims, there is no proof, and it stretches the bounds of credulity to think Harding would risk being caught in his Senate office just when he had come into the national spotlight as a leading contender for the highest office in the land. Nevertheless, since so many of her dates and "facts" are corroborated by the Phillips letters, her story could be true, though not as she has embellished it. In a small town like Marion, if people wanted to break in and "borrow" letters Carrie Phillips kept in her home—and likely some people knew of their existence—it would not have been hard. Such a temporary theft would have been even more easily accomplished if Carrie and Jim continued their frequent travels, leaving the home empty and unattended for long periods.

In fact, Carrie and Jim did travel to Japan in the fall of 1920. Jim reported on their trip to the Orient to the Marion Chamber of Commerce on February 21, 1921. Francis Russell wrote in his book that the Republican National Committee paid the Phillipses $20,000 to take a trip around the world on the condition they left Marion before the election and stayed away. "Jim and Carrie left for Japan at the summer's end," he wrote.[5] In fact, however, the trip appears to have taken place *after* the election. In the *Marion Star* report of Jim's talk to the Chamber of Commerce, he discussed arriving in Japan and being besieged by newspaper correspondents who believed their traveling party had come to Japan "to secure information for President-Elect Harding."[6]

It is not clear whether Carrie attended the inauguration, but her collection does include a ticket to the inauguration ceremonies on March 4.[7]

The only evidence that Warren and Carrie had contact after he became president comes from two letters from her brother Chester Fulton, which she kept with the Harding collection. Fulton lived in Washington and appears to have acted as a go-between for Harding and Carrie. The first letter from Chester is dated January 10, 1922: "The President called me on phone one minute ago and asked me to advise you that he would be here all this month, and would be able to see you anytime, if you would kindly wire or write me, when you are certain that you will be here, I will telephone Mr. Harding and let him know all about it."[8] In the second letter, dated in June 1923, Chester sent Carrie a ticket to Europe, but his letter does not indicate that the ticket was from President Harding. It is possible he was working as an intermediary and that Harding paid for the ticket. He does state that he saw the president that day and that Harding agreed to see someone named Harris when he returned from his Alaska trip. Chester was pleased Carrie was going to see her "dear ones" in Europe and he wrote that he hoped she would find her friends "all well and happy."[9]

Warren Harding died on August 2, 1923, in the Palace Hotel in San Francisco. His death came unexpectedly near the end of a rigorous cross-country speaking tour, called the "Voyage of Understanding," which took him through the West and up into Alaska. He grew sick on his way from Alaska to California and stopped in San Francisco to recuperate. Though wild rumors were printed in the 1920s and 1930s, there is no evidence of foul play in his death. Gaston Means's book, *The Strange Death of President Harding*, in which he implies that Florence Harding poisoned her husband, appears to be a total fabrication. Likely Harding died from the heart problem that he wrote to Ed Scobey about when Scobey's wife, Evaland, was suffering from heart troubles.

Ed Scobey was appointed by Harding as the director of the U.S. Mint, a position he resigned from not long after Harding's death. Scobey died of "a stroke of apoplexy" on February 7, 1931, at his home in San Antonio. Last rites at Scobey's funeral were performed by (who else?) the Reverend Samuel Capers.[10]

Florence Harding died sixteen months after Warren's death, on November 21, 1924.

Baroness Iona Zollner died on March 12, 1932, in Paris a month after suffering injuries in a car accident. She was fifty-two.[11] Her second husband, Baron Loeffelholz von Colberg, would marry four more times, was financially ruined after 1931, and became a top officer in the Labor Service (RAD) for the Nazis. He died on the first day in April 1945.

Adolf Pickhardt became Commodore Pickhardt and served as the U.S. Naval Attaché for Air at the U.S. Embassy in Berlin from 1940 until war was declared in December 1941. He was exchanged in June 1942 after being held in a concentration center with other diplomats in Germany. He died in 1947.[12] One of his brothers, Dr. Otto C. Pickhardt, tended to Winston Churchill after a taxicab struck him in New York City in December 1931.[13]

When it came time to select an appropriate memorial for Warren Harding in Marion, Carrie Phillips wrote out a long letter to Dr. Carl Sawyer. From the context, she appeared to be writing from Europe. Someone had sent her the memorial address Charles Evans Hughes had delivered to Congress on February 28, 1924, and she thought his remarks showed "a keen appreciation for Gov's wonderful traits." She was surprised. "As a rule such seemingly little things are sometimes overlooked in the biographies of great men. I think it is a mistake in biographies to omit all the slight and seemingly trivial details and give only the big events. Nothing is trivial in the life of great men."

One thing Hughes said caught the spirit of what she was thinking after Harding's death. It was a passage Hughes delivered about the privilege, the power, and the vanity of human life. "There comes a time in a soul's career," she added to what Hughes said, "when vanity is burned out of him and he becomes a perfected self conscious center in the universal consciousness impersonally working for the whole of mankind according to a Divine Plan."

That was Warren Harding, she thought. "He had reached that place," she wrote. "He was ready to go on."[14]

The last time Elden Groves went to see Carrie about her dogs, he really was just checking in to see how she was doing. Writing about it in 1964, he recollected that it must have been not long before she was committed to the nursing home. "After I had knocked a time or two, I heard her call from inside," he wrote. "I had to wait quite a while, and finally the door opened." He was shocked by her condition. "She was quite old and frail looking (and I suppose she was near 80). I decided that she had been in bed when I knocked, and had dressed hastily." Though she was still chatty, he wrote, her mind wandered. Groves was not sure she remembered who he was. "The house and her clothing had deteriorated seriously, and behind a locked kitchen door, a dog barked madly."

She couldn't show him in because the dog was spoiled and she couldn't control him.

He never went back, and he felt guilty and sad about it years later when he read all the publicity about the love letters.

Carrie Phillips only spoke once for the record about her relationship with Warren Harding and the charge that she was a spy. In 1931, Warren's two letters to Jim Phillips in the spring of 1918 warning that Carrie was under investigation somehow showed up at A. S. W. Rosenbach's in New York. Rosenbach, a noted collector of rare books and manuscripts, refused to say how he got the letters. The *New York Times* carried a story: "Harding as Senator Befriended Woman Suspected as a Spy."[15] The next day, after Harding's old secretary, George Christian, identified the woman in the letters as Carrie Phillips, she took a call from a *Times* reporter and laughed off as gossip the notion that she was a German spy. "Marion, you know, is a small city and people like to talk," she said. "I considered it a huge joke that I was reported to have entertained German nobility."[16]

To another reported at another paper, she was quoted as saying the whole matter was silly. "Mrs. Phillips said," the *Cleveland Plain Dealer* reported, "the then-Senator Harding's letters were written out of 'neighborly interest.'"[17]

Afterword

In September 1927, just after Nan Britton published *The President's Daughter,* my grandfather, Francis Durbin, wrote a letter to James M. Cox, then a private citizen at the *Dayton Daily News.*[1] Francis Durbin's father, William W. Durbin, had been Cox's campaign manager when he ran for governor of Ohio in 1918, and both he and Francis were closely involved in Cox's run for the presidency against Warren Harding in 1920. I have detailed that involvement in *Linking Rings, William W. Durbin and the Magic and Mystery of America* (Kent State University Press, 2004).

Francis married my grandmother, Nora Agnes Kelly, in May 1915, the month the *Lusitania* was sunk. My grandmother, known as Agnes or "Ag," grew up in Marion, Ohio. Ag would have been about five or six years older than Isabelle Phillips and Nan Britton, having been born in 1890. The Kellys ran a grocery store in Marion and knew everybody in town.

Francis wrote to Jim Cox that he had just finished reading Nan Britton's book. He reported that his sources in Marion thought the account was true. "I was in Marion yesterday," Francis wrote to Cox, "and there is no question but that the facts in this book are absolutley true." After my work, I think my grandfather may have gotten it wrong.

But he did provide an intriguing answer to my question of why the Democrats in 1920 did not use as a campaign issue the information the Bureau of Investigation had uncovered about Carrie Phillips and her affair with Warren Harding. "The only regret I have," Francis wrote to Cox, "is that in the 1920 campaign, when a few of us had the goods in regard to Mrs. Phillips and other disreputable things about the then candidate for President, the mask was not torn off and the American people told what kind of a man the Republicans had foisted upon them."

His explanation about why the information was not used is as follows: "I blame a few selfish individuals like Joe Tumulty [Wilson's personal secretary] and various other Democrats who had the goods and who felt like we were going to lose for not telling the truth as they knew it to be," Francis wrote. "But they wanted to practice law in Washington and did not want to have the ill-feeling of the administration."

I have pondered about what my grandfather meant when he wrote that the Democrats "had the goods in regard to Mrs. Phillips." Did they know what the Bureau of Investigation discovered about her German spy connections? Did they know only that Harding was having an affair with her? Did they have possession of copies of her letters?

Since Francis died before I was born, he and I never had a chance to talk about it. What is clear, though, is some people within the Wilson administration made the conscious decision not to bring up the Harding affair and some people, like my grandfather, were bitter about it.

So part of the mystery is solved but so much more remains. That is as it should be. History would be no fun if we didn't have puzzles to solve and questions to ponder.

NOTES

SHORT FORMS USED IN NOTES

The Harding/Phillips letters have been assigned numbers based on an early ordering of the letters by archivist Kenneth W. Duckett. Each time a letter is cited, the number will be used, with the page reference. For example, in the citation WGH to Carrie Phillips, November 11–15, 1913, 16.18, the number "16.18" refers to the sixteenth letter in the collection, page 18. The letters are on a microfilm located at the Western Reserve Historical Society, Cleveland, Ohio. In addition, the Kenneth W. Duckett Papers 1963-2003, Manuscript Collection No. 4938, records and files of Kenneth W. Duckett relating to the letters and the Harding lawsuit are also located at the Western Reserve Historical Society, Cleveland, Ohio (hereafter Duckett Papers).

Investigative Case Files of the Bureau of Investigation, 1908–1922, Record Group 65, "Old German Files," File OG 107702, RG 65, National Archives and Records Administration, College Park, Maryland (containing the transcript of *United States v. Baroness Ione W. Sutton Zollner,* Espionage Proceedings before United States Commissioner Samuel J. McAllester, Chattanooga, Tennessee, December 22–24, 1917)(hereafter National Archives, Zollner Tr).

Investigative Case Files of the Bureau of Investigation, 1908–1922, Record Group 65, "Old German Files," File OG 143708, RG 65, National Archives and Records Administration, College Park, Maryland (Mrs. J.E. Phillips file) (hereafter National Archives, File OG 143708).

Investigative Case Files of the Bureau of Investigation, 1908–1922, Record Group 65, "Old German Files," File OG 145984, RG 65, National Archives and Records Administration, College Park, Maryland (Ione Zollner file) (hereafter National Archives, File OG 145984).

Investigative Case Files of the Bureau of Investigation, 1908–1922, Record Group 65, "Old German Files," File OG 186369, RG 65, National Archives and Records Administration, College Park, Maryland (Lt. Adolf Pickhardt) (hereafter National Archives, File OG 186369).

Investigative Case Files of the Bureau of Investigation, 1908–1922, Record Group 65, "Old German Files," File OG 115006, RG 65, National Archives and Records Administration, College Park, Maryland (Lt. James W. Spaulding) (hereafter National Archives, File OG 115006).

Investigative Case Files of the Bureau of Investigation, 1908–1922, Record Group 65, "Old German Files," File OG 103, RG 65, National Archives and Records Administration, College Park, Maryland (Pickhardt & Kuttroff Company file) (hereafter National Archives, File OG 103).

Warren G. Harding Papers, Ohio Historical Society, Columbus, Ohio (hereafter WGH Papers).

Ray Baker Harris Papers, Ohio Historical Society, Columbus, Ohio (hereafter Harris Papers).

Malcolm Jennings Papers, Ohio Historical Society, Columbus, Ohio (hereafter Jennings Papers).

Frank E. Scobey Papers, Ohio Historical Society, Columbus, Ohio (hereafter Scobey Papers).

PROLOGUE

1. WGH to Carrie Phillips, November 11–15, 1913, 16.18.
2. "Hughes Eulogizes Harding In Congress," *New York Times,* February 28, 1924; Secretary Hughes's Memorial Tribute Delivered February 27, 1924, before a joint session of Congress, reprinted in Joe

Mitchell Chapple, *Life and Times of Warren G. Harding: Our After-War President* (Boston: Chapple Publishing, 1924), 310.

3. WGH to Carrie Phillips, May 28, 1917, 55.1–2.
4. Ibid., 55.7.
5. Robert K. Murray, *The Harding Era, Warren Harding and His Administration* (Minneapolis: University of Minnesota Press, 1969), 398.
6. "Harding Says Negro Must Have Equality In Political Life," *New York Times,* October 27, 1921.
7. "Debs Sees Harding; Not Asked, He Says, To Alter His Views," *New York Times,* December 27, 1921.
8. *Congressional Record,* 65 Congress, 1st Session, April 3, 1917, pp. 253–254, Harris Papers.
9. WGH to Theodore Roosevelt, June 12, 1917, Harris Papers.
10. Francis Russell, "The Shadow of Warren Harding," *Antioch Review* 36 (Winter 1978), 57–76.
11. *Time Magazine,* January 10, 1972.
12. Chapple, *Life and Times of Warren G. Harding,* 312–313.

CHAPTER 1: ESPIONAGE IN CHATTANOOGA

1. National Archives, Zollner Tr. 86-89 (Thomas Stiff testimony), and Zollner Tr. 90-91 (D. G. Grant testimony).
2. Ibid.
3. National Archives, Zollner Tr. 179–180 (Baroness testimony).

CHAPTER 2: THE AMERICAN PROTECTIVE LEAGUE AND LOVE TRICKS OF WOMEN SPIES

1. "Baroness Zollner Held on Spy Charges," *New York Times,* December 25, 1917.
2. "Love Tricks of a Woman Spy," Sunday magazine, *Cleveland Plain Dealer,* February 10, 1918.
3. National Archives, File OG 143708. (The *Plain Dealer* article is mentioned in the report of Bureau of Investigation agent Howard M. Stern, Cincinnati, Ohio, dated March 29, 1918. Stern interviewed Frank Campbell and others, including Ralph Lewis, who later married Warren Harding's sister Abigail.)
4. National Archives, File OG 143708 (Frank Campbell to Calvin Weakley, Special Agent in Charge of the Bureau of Investigation in Cincinnati, OH, February 20, 1918).
5. Joan M. Jensen, *The Price of Vigilance* (New York: Rand McNally, 1968), 17–31.
6. Emerson Hough, "The Web, The Authorized Story of the American Protective League," extracts reprinted in the *Cleveland Plain Dealer,* June 1, 1919.
7. Jensen, *The Price of Vigilance,* 130.
8. Ibid., 188–218.
9. National Archives, File OG 143708 (Report of Charles Jenkins, Bureau of Investigation, Cleveland, Ohio, August 15, 1917, reciting a telegram from Mr. Queen, Marion Branch of APL to Mr. Charles De Woody, Bureau of Investigation, dated August 13, 1917).
10. National Archives, File OG 143708 (Chief, Marion Branch APL, to Charles D. Frey, APL, Washington, D.C., February 14, 1918).
11. National Archives, File OG 143708 (Report of Howard M. Stern, Bureau of Investigation, Cincinnati, Ohio, March 29, 1918).

CHAPTER 3: "THE SWEETEST, DEAREST LITTLE BROTHER YOU EVER SAW"

1. "Harding Recalls Mother as Source of Inspiration," Philadelphia *Public Ledger,* May 12, 1923.
2. Ray Baker Harris, "Background and Youth of the Seventh Ohio President," *Ohio History* 52, no. 3 (July–September 1943): 260, 262–264.
3. George T. Harding, "Reminiscences of Abraham Lincoln," *Ohio State Archaeological and Historical Quarterly* 32, no. 1 (January 1923): 282–283. "Little did Private George T. Harding dream that in the distant future he would see his own son in the White House, an honored successor of President Abraham Lincoln."

4. George T. Harding autograph of a photo from *Manuscript Magazine* 7, no. 3 (spring 1955): 163, Harris Papers.
5. Phoebe Harding to her Brother and Sister, n.d. (1866), Harris Papers.
6. "World's End Near, Says Dr. Harding," unidentified newspaper clipping May 17, 1922, Harris Papers.
7. Carolyn Harding Votaw to WGH, June 29, 1912, WGH Papers.
8. Charity Harding Remsberg to Ray Baker Harris, June 6, 1928, Harris Papers.
9. C. W. Post to Warren Harding, February 6, 1913, WGH Papers.
10. Charles E. Stewart, M. D., associate director of the Battle Creek Sanitarium, to Ray Baker Harris, June 9, 1939, Harris Papers.
11. Charity Harding Remsberg to Ray Baker Harris, July 19, 1938, Harris Papers.
12. Herrick's historical claim to fame is that he greeted Charles Lindberg in Paris after his 1927 historic flight across the Atlantic. Herrick was the U.S. ambassador to France at the time, having been appointed by Warren Harding in 1921.
13. W. H. Riley to WGH, May 2, 1905, WGH Papers.
14. WGH to Carrie Phillips, December 1918, 19.2.
15. Charity Harding Remsberg to Ray Baker Harris, June 6, 1938, Harris Papers.

CHAPTER 4: SATURDAY, DECEMBER 22, 1917: AN ESPIONAGE HEARING BEGINS

1. "No Company For Baroness," *Daily Times* (Chattanooga, TN), December 24, 1917.
2. James B. Jones, Jr., "The Baroness and the Lieutenant: Love and Espionage in War-Time Chattanooga, 1917–1918," Every Day in Tennessee History, http://netowne.com/historical/tennessee/baroness.htm
3. Ibid.
4. "Baroness Zollner Now Charged with Being a Spy in the Service of the German Empire," *Sunday Times* (Chattanooga, TN), December 23, 1917.
5. National Archives, Zollner Tr. 1 (Commissioner Samuel J. McAllester).
6. National Archives, Zollner Tr. 1–70 (Thompson's testimony).
7. National Archives, Zollner Tr. 74–75 (Lieutenant M. E. Sullivan testimony).
8. National Archives, Zollner Tr. 125 (Deputy Marshal McMahon testimony).
9. National Archives, Zollner Tr. 130 (Deputy Marshal McMahon testimony).

CHAPTER 5: CARRIE

1. WGH to Carrie Phillips, January 6, 1913, 9.33–34.
2. WGH to Carrie Phillips, September 15, 1913, 15.17–18.
3. "Matthew H. Fulton Passes Away Today," *Marion Star,* December 1, 1906.
4. Carl Sferrazza Anthony, *Florence Harding, The First Lady, The Jazz Age, and the Death of America's Most Scandalous President* (New York: William Morrow,1998), 70; Francis Russell, *The Shadow of Blooming Grove: Warren G. Harding in His Times* (New York: McGraw-Hill Book Company, 1968), 167.
5. Anthony, *Florence Harding,* 70.
6. "Matthew H. Fulton Passes Away Today," *Marion Star,* December 1, 1906.
7. "Death Claims Mrs. Phillips," *Marion Star,* February 5, 1960.
8. Uhler-Phillips Letterhead, August 18, 1906, WGH Papers.
9. WGH to Carrie Phillips, March 25, 1913, 11.1.
10. J. E. Phillips to WGH, August 18, 1906, WGH Papers.
11. In 1905, Amos sent Florence a telegram from his winter home in Daytona, Florida, at the start of her long recovery from emergency kidney surgery: "Be calm, cheerful and full of hope for you will surely be well again. Papa." Amos Kling to Florence Harding, March 1, 1905, WGH Papers. That winter, Warren took Florence to Cuba to assist in her recovery and then the two visited Amos in Florida before returning to Marion.
12. Anthony, *Florence Harding,* 24–27.
13. WGH to Carrie Phillips, November 18, 1913, 17.3–4.
14. WGH to Carrie Votaw, August 4, 1907, Harris Papers.

15. Ibid.
16. Ibid.
17. Ibid.
18. "Alexander Hamilton," 1908, Speeches, WGH Papers.
19. Ibid.
20. WGH to Mrs. Christian, February 14, 1909, WGH Papers.
21. Ibid.
22. WGH to Carrie Phillips, September 15, 1913, 15.10–11.
23. WGH to H. R. Kemerer, Carrolton, Ohio, July 22, 1909, Harris Papers.
24. WGH to Carrie Phillips, March 25, 1913, 11.3.

CHAPTER 6: BARON KURT LOEFFELHOLZ VON COLBERG

1. National Archives, Zollner Tr. 128 (McMahon testimony).
2. "Baroness Zollner Now Charged With Being A Spy in the Service of the German Empire," *Sunday Times* (Chattanooga, TN), December 23, 1917.
3. "Back to Jail Without Bond," *Daily Times* (Chattanooga, TN), December 25, 1917.
4. National Archives, Zollner Tr. 136 (Baroness testimony).
5. National Archives, Zollner Tr. 136-145, 188-221 (Baroness testimony).
6. Information on family tree provided to author by Gordon Dawson, son of Beresford Shope and grandson of the baroness. Dawson lives in New Zealand. Gordon Dawson to author, April 29, 2009, author's collection.
7. "American and German Deer, An Effort to be Made To Cross the Two Breeds By Mr. Pickhardt," *New York Times,* January 5, 1884.
8. "Streetscapes/Reader's Questions," *New York Times,* February 1, 2004.
9. "The Pickhardt Mansion on Fifth Avenue Sold," *New York Times,* February 6, 1895; "Mr. A. Duane Pell The Buyer of the Pickhardt Mansion," *New York Times,* February 20, 1895.
10. "Wilhelm Pickhardt," *New York Times,* June 28, 1895.
11. "Married in Hoboken," *New York Times,* January 23, 1896. $10 million would be about $238 million in 2009.
12. Ibid.
13. "Sydney Beresford Pickhardt," *New York Times,* July 17, 1896.
14. National Archives, Zollner Tr. 164-168 (Baroness testimony).
15. "Shope—Pickhardt," *New York Times,* April 20, 1897. The Church of Heavenly Rest was built by Civil War veterans as a memorial to those who served and died in the war. It was built at Fifth Avenue and Forty-fifth Street in 1868, but the parish moved to Fifth Avenue and Ninetieth Street in 1925.
16. "Society at Home and Abroad," *New York Times,* October 19, 1902 ("Among those who sailed yesterday were Mrs. Charles Warner Shope and her children. Mrs. Shope is the widow of Charles Warner Shope, who died last year. She was Miss Pickhardt, and her father built the great house on Fifth Avenue which is occupied now my Mr. and Mrs. Alfred Duane Pell. Mrs. Shope will live abroad."). William Krebs, Shope's uncle and a bachelor, died in 1905 in Paris, "where he had lived with a sister since his retirement." "William Krebs," *New York Times,* April 29, 1905. Krebs was "one of the best known insurance adjusters" in New York, but had been an invalid for eight or nine years before his death. Ibid.
17. The baroness testified she met the Oppenheims through their daughter, Mrs. Parkinson Sharp. They met in Nice, France, when the baroness visited there with the Krebses. She then visited with Mrs. Parkinson Sharp in London at her home and met Baroness Flossie Oppenheim there. National Archives, Zollner Tr[0]. 218 (Baroness testimony).
18. "Baroness Arranges Her Third Wedding," *New York Times,* April 9, 1910.
19. National Archives, Zollner Tr. 139-141, 214-216 (Baroness testimony).

CHAPTER 7: "IT FLAMES LIKE THE FIRE AND CONSUMES"

1. Mark Sullivan, *Our Times, The War Begins, 1909–1914* (New York: Charles Scribner's Sons, 1932), 428.

2. Randolph C. Downes, *The Rise of Warren Gamaliel Harding, 1865-1920* (Columbus: Ohio State University Press, 1970), 166–167.

3. James D. Robenalt, *Linking Rings, William Warner Durbin and the Magic and Mystery of America* (Kent, Ohio: Kent State University Press, 2004), 129-155; Landon Warner, "Judson Harmon," in *The Governors of Ohio* (Columbus: Ohio Historical Society, 1954), 153.

4. WGH to Charles D. Norton, Secretary to the President, August 3, 1910, WGH Papers; Francis Russell, *The Shadow of Blooming Grove: Warren G. Harding in His Times* (New York: McGraw-Hill Book Company, 1968), 209.

5. James E. Phillips to WHG, September 1, 1910, WGH Papers.

6. Malcolm Jennings to WGH, August 15, 1910, WGH Papers. Jennings's letter confirms the Phillipses were on the trip with the Hardings. "Tell the Phillips [*sic*] that everything is reported lovely on the hill [referring to the neighborhood where the Phillipses had a house, known as Gospel Hill] and at the store [referring to Uhler-Phillips, the dry good store]."

7. Ed Scobey to WGH, September 15, 1910 (Hollenden House, Cleveland, Ohio), WGH Papers.

8. WGH to Charles D. Hilles, November 15, 1910, WGH Papers.

9. Russell, *Shadow of Blooming Grove,* 201–202.

10. Charles Scribner's Sons to The Harding Publishing Co., December 7, 1910, WGH Papers.

CHAPTER 8: CHRISTMAS EVE, 1910

1. Nepenthe is a substance that people supposedly took in ancient times to forget their sadness or troubles, or the plant that produced the substance; something that eases pain or makes people forget their troubles. "Respite and nepenthe from thy memories of Lenore," Edgar Allen Poe, *The Raven* (1845).

2. WGH to Carrie Phillips, December 24, 1910, 1.1.

CHAPTER 9: A GERMAN CAVALRY OFFICER NAMED ZOLLNER

1. National Archives, Zollner Tr. 141-142 (Baroness testimony).

2. Raymond E. Spinzia, "Those Other Roosevelts: The Fortescues," The Oyster Bay Historical Society *Freeholder Magazine Online,* http://www.oysterbayhistory.org/freeres.html (2006).

3. "What Is Doing In Society," *New York Times,* June 9, 1900; "Some Happenings In Good Society," *New York Times,* June 17, 1900.

4. Joao Paulo Nunes, "Writing Dialogues, Reading Myths: Ezra Pound, William Carlos Williams, and the Publication of *Kora in Hell," Journal of American Studies of Turkey* 11 (2000): 63–72.

5. "Drug Kills E.W.S. Pickhardt, Took Overdose for Insomnia—Married Stepdaughter of R. B. Roosevelt," *New York Times,* July 8, 1909.

6. National Archives, Zollner Tr. 142 (Baroness testimony).

7. Ibid.

8. "Baroness Arranges Her Third Wedding," *New York Times,* April 9, 1910.

CHAPTER 10: "CONSTANT"

1. WGH to Carrie Phillips, January 28, 1912, 4.1. Other references to "exile" include: WGH to Carrie Phillips, January 2, 1913, 9.3 ("lonely, weary stay in exile"); and WGH to Carrie Phillips, September 17, 1913, 13.22 ("surely your exile is not wholly in vain").

2. WGH to Carrie Phillips, January 2, 1913, 9.16.

3. WGH to Carrie Phillips, November 14, 1913, 16.19–20.

4. George M. Quigley, cashier of the Agnes Memorial Sanatorium, to WGH, December 27, 1909, WGH Papers. The letter shows that Harding, not Florence's father, guaranteed Marshall's stay in the sanitarium.

5. Carl Sferrazza Anthony, *Florence Harding, The First Lady, The Jazz Age, and the Death of America's Most Scandalous President* (New York: William Morrow, 1998), 86.

6. Marshall DeWolfe to WGH, February 1, 1911, WGH Papers.

7. James E. Phillips to WGH, February 21, 1911, WGH Papers. This Western Union "night letter" is one of a handful of writings extant between Harding and Jim Phillips. It shows they had a fond relationship. Jim referred to Harding as "Gov," and a contemporaneous telegram refers to Carrie as "Sis." "Go ahead bermuda plan if agreeable to sis all keep mum till my letter received." Jim Phillips to WGH, February 21, 1911 (Western Union Night Message), WGH Papers.

8. E. P. Shaffner to WGH, February 21, 1911, WGH Papers. "I am the man whom he leased the 'Enterprise' from," Shaffner wrote.

9. Jim Phillips to WGH, April 25, 1911, WGH Papers.

10. WGH to Carrie Phillips, September 15, 1913, 15.1.

11. Anthony, *Florence Harding,* 112.

12. Marshall DeWolfe to WGH and Florence Harding, March 22, 1914, WGH Papers.

13. Ed Scobey to WGH, June 3, 1911, WGH Papers.

14. Invitation, The President and Mrs. Taft at the White House, for Monday evening, June 19, 1911, celebrating marriage from 1886 to 1911, WGH Papers.

15. Ed Scobey to WGH, June 23, 1911, WGH Papers.

16. Ed Scobey to WGH, July 1, 1911, WGH Papers.

17. Ed Scobey to WGH, July 22, 1911, WGH Papers.

18. Brooks Fletcher to WGH, August 5, 191, WGH Papers ("As you are not leaving until August 8th this letter will reach you one day before your departure").

19. References to this rendezvous are scattered throughout the letters, but pieced together, they reveal the exact date and place they met. His letter of August 14, 1916, dates the encounter: "I recalled the joy I knew with you on Aug. 18, 1911, and wanted to make them live again." WGH to Carrie Phillips, August 14, 1916, 49.2.

20. WGH to Carrie Phillips, November 29, 1913, 18.10–11.

21. WGH to Carrie Phillips, August 16–19, 1916, 50.6.

22. WGH to Carrie Phillips, September 15, 1913, 15.12.

23. WGH to Carrie Phillips, November 13–15, 1913, 16.4–5.

24. Although no mention is made of the name, Harding did write a letter of recommendation for a soprano to the Redpath-Slayton Lyceum Bureau in November 1911. L. B. Crotty to WGH, November 22, 1911, WGH Papers.

25. As the code refers to their Boston and Montreal experiences, which happened at the end of 1911 and the beginning of 1912, it has to have been written after January 1912.

26. Code, undated, 3.1–3. He discussed the code in a January 1913 letter. "I wanted to cable you from [Grand Rapids, Michigan, where he was speaking for a fee to the Chamber of Commerce] but I hadn't the code, and could not trust my memory to pick out words I felt so much like sending." WGH to Carrie Phillips, January 16–18, 1913, 10.5.

27. WGH to Carrie Phillips, September 21, 1913, 14.7.

28. Ibid.

29. WGH to Carrie Phillips, April 4, 1915, 31.13

30. WGH to Carrie Phillips, February 17, 1916, 42.4.

31. WGH to Christians, Christmas Eve, 1907, George C. Christian, Sr. Papers, WGH Papers (he signs as "Jerry").

CHAPTER 11: "I GOT THE FEVER"

1. National Archives, Zollner Tr. 145-146 (Baroness testimony).

CHAPTER 12: "FATE TIMED THAT MARVELOUS COINCIDENCE"

1. WGH to Carrie Phillips, January 2, 1913, 9.2.

2. Jim Phillips to WGH, November 22, 1911, WGH Papers ("Dear Governor, A belated birthday present—*for your office.* Yours J. E. Phillips.")

3. L. F. Williams to WGH, October 30, 1911, WGH Papers.

4. WGH to Carrie Phillips, April 1917, 81.12–13.

5. WGH to Carrie Phillips, September 15, 1913, 15.17.

6.   WGH to Carrie Phillips, January 28, 1912 4.8.
7.   WGH to Carrie Phillips, January 5, 1913, 9.22; WGH to Carrie Phillips, May 13, 1912, 6.11.
8.   WGH to Carrie Phillips, September 15, 1913, 15.13.
9.   William S. Hawk to WGH, January 12, 1912, WGH Papers.
10. WGH to Carrie Phillips, January 28, 1912, 4.5-12.
11. "Ohioans Here Show Loyalty to Taft," *New York Times,* January 28, 1912.
12. "Brands Recall as 'Nostrum Reform,'" *Cleveland Plain Dealer,* January 28, 1912.
13. WGH to Carrie Phillips, January 28, 1912, 4.12.

CHAPTER 13: "I'D RATHER BE A LICKED WARRIOR AND SURVIVE, THAN A HEALTHY COWARD"

1.   Randolph C. Downes, *The Rise of Warren Gamaliel Harding, 1865-1920* (Columbus: Ohio State University Press, 1970), 176.
2.   Ibid., 176–177. *Marion Star,* February 18 and June 20, 1912.
3.   WGH to Carrie Phillips, May 13, 1912, 6.1–8.
4.   James Chace, *1912, Wilson, Roosevelt, Taft and Debs—the Election That Changed the Country* (New York: Simon & Shuster, 2004), 95–99, 105–106.
5.   Downes, *The Rise of Warren Gamaliel Harding,* 179.
6.   Ibid., 180–181.
7.   Ibid., 181.
8.   William Howard Taft to WGH, June 5, 1912, WGH Papers. The telegram is dated June 4 from the White House to the Southern Hotel in Columbus, also in WGH Papers.
9.   "Harding to Nominate Taft," *New York Times,* June 8, 1912. William Howard Taft to WGH, June 10, 1912, WGH Papers. ("I have yours of June 7th, and thank you sincerely for your kind agreement to nominate me at Chicago.")
10. William Howard Taft to WGH, June 15, 1912, WGH Papers.
11. WGH to Carrie Phillips, May 13, 1912, 6.8.
12. See letters and telegrams from Brentano's to WGH, dated May 29, June 1, and June 3, 1912, and a letter from the Hamburg-American line, dated June 3, 1912, WGH Papers. The books he sent were the *A Hoosier Chronicle,* a bestselling novel by Meredith Nicholson about Indiana life and politics at the turn of the century ("It is always morning and all the days are long in Indiana"); the *Lonely Queen,* by H. C. Bailey, a novel about the Tudor queen Elizabeth; and *Oscanana.*
13. WGH to Carrie Phillips, January 6, 1913, 9.28.
14. Downes, *The Rise of Warren Gamaliel Harding,* 183.
15. "Harding Nominates Taft," *New York Times,* June 23, 1912.
16. "Taft Nomination Speech" [at GOP National Convention], June 22, 1912, Chicago, Illinois, Speeches, WGH Papers.
17. Logan was the running mate of James Blaine.
18. Alice Roosevelt Longworth, *Crowded Hours* (New York: Charles Scribner's Sons, 1933), 202–203. This quote has been widely used by historians, but usually with a twist that drops the reference to the delegates-at-large political dispute. Historians make it sound as if she thought Harding was a crook in its traditional sense, as opposed to her obvious political meaning.
19. In Warren Harding's 1912 papers is a poet's spoof, in Mr. Dooley style, on the Armageddon speech, entitled "Armygiddin." The poem, by F. F. D. Albery, ends:

     So ye'll sthand at Armygiddin an' ye'll battle fer the Lord,
     An' ye'll sthrike down ivery evil wid that great big flamin' sword;
     But the throuble wid yer schame, me bye, is plainly fer to see—
     Ye're the Lord himself an' Evil is whatever aint fer ye.

20. "Mr. Roosevelt's Speech," *New York Times,* June 18, 1912.
21. Carrie Votaw to WGH, June 29, 1912, WGH Papers.
22. William R. Timken to WGH, June 29, 1912, WGH Papers.
23. Ibid.
24. William R. Timken to WGH, July 30, 1912, WGH Papers.

25. H. H. Timken to WGH, November 13, 1912, WGH Papers.

26. Carrie Votaw to WGH, September 14, 1912, WGH Papers. "Daisy will be here now in six weeks more," Carolyn wrote to her brother. "She is coming from China."

27. Assistant Secretary of Department of the Interior [name indecipherable] to WGH, November 14, 1912, WGH Papers.

28. Henry L. Borden to WGH, October 28, 1912, WGH Papers.

29. Ed Scobey to WGH, November 12, 1912, WGH Papers.

30. H. H. Timken to WGH, November 13, 1912, WGH Papers.

31. H. H. Timken to WGH, November 15, 1912, WGH Papers.

CHAPTER 14: "EVERYBODY WOULD BE ABLE TO GET THE BETTER OF ME"

1. National Archives, Zollner Tr. 147–148 (Baroness Zollner testimony).

2. The P&O is the Peninsular & Oriental Steam Navigation Company. The *Muldavia* became an escort ship for convoys in the North Atlantic and was torpedoed and sunk off the Isle of Wight in the spring of 1918. *Snyder County Annals* (Middleburgh, PA: Middleburgh Post, 1919), 342–343 (sketch of First Lieut. Chas. N. Brosius, M.C., Shamokin Dam, PA).

CHAPTER 15: "MY CARRIE, BELOVED AND ADORED"

1. "Maniac in Milwaukee Shoots Col. Roosevelt: He Ignores Wound, Speaks An Hour, Goes to Hospital," *New York Times,* October 15, 1912.

2. Kathleen Dalton, *Theodore Roosevelt: A Strenuous Life* (New York: Alfred A. Knopf, 2002), 404–407.

3. Invoice from Vogue Company to the Harding Publishing Co., October 25, 1912, WGH Papers.

4. David B. Day (a Canton attorney and Timken friend) to WGH, January 25, 1913, WGH Papers ("We were all very sorry that your business engagements denied us the pleasure of your continued presence with the party. Mr. W. R. Timken is now in Bermuda and Mr. H. H. in California. I learned from Mr. W. R. Timken that Judge Borden succeeded in making a satisfactory sale of his interest in the ranch to the St. Louis parties that were connected with him in the transaction.") For other letters confirming Warren's departure from the hunting trip, see William R. Timken to WGH, December 31, 1912, and H. H. Timken to WGH, January 2, 1913, WGH Papers. Both men described a fairly miserable time after Harding left. Harry developed a bad case of bronchitis, W. R. a bad cold, and someone nicknamed "Pops" came down with the grippe. "It seems the exposure during that rainy spell was too much for us," W.R. Timken wrote. "We were not used to it." Even Florence's daughter-in-law Esther DeWolfe wrote about the Texas hunting trip. "Mother tells me you've been in Texas on a hunting trip—you must have had a wonderful time." Esther DeWolfe to WGH, December 29, 1912, WGH Papers.

5. This five-day trip can be dated exactly from his letters. He refers to December 13 to 17 in a letter he wrote on January 3, 1912. WGH to Carrie Phillips, January 3, 1912, 9.12. He also confirms that the *Mauritania* arrived on a Friday, December 13, in a January 16, 1913, letter. WGH to Carrie Phillips, January 16, 1913, 10.5–6. Finally, he wrote that his Texas letters arrived on a Monday and he returned to Marion on a Wednesday after seeing Carrie, which would have been Tuesday, December 17, 1912. WGH to Carrie Phillips, January 4, 1913, 9.27.

6. WGH to Carrie Phillips, January 4, 1913, 9.27–28.

7. Ibid.

8. WGH to Carrie Phillips, September 15, 1913, 15.11.

9. WGH to Carrie Phillips, January 3, 1913, 9.9–10.

10. WGH to Carrie Phillips, January 5, 1913, 9.17–18.

11. WGH to Carrie Phillips, January 6, 1913, 9.25–26 ("You express disappointment that we didn't visit more. *I rather expected that.* I am not sorry, except that it disappointed you. There was not a dull or disappointing moment *to me.* You see, Dearie, our time was so short, and I am so crazy about you, that I would choose to love even more, rather than less, but we did visit a lot and rather enjoyably and helpfully, I thought.")

12. WGH to Carrie Phillips, September 15, 1913, 15.12.

13. WGH to Carrie Phillips, January 6, 1913, 9.25.

14. WGH to Carrie Phillips, September 15, 1913, 15.6.
15. WGH to Carrie Phillips, January 16–18, 1913, 10.8.
16. Ibid.
17. WGH to Carrie Phillips, January 2, 1913, 9.4–5.
18. WGH to Carrie Phillips, January 2, 1913, 9.1.
19. Ibid., 9.11.
20. Ibid., 9.4.
21. Ibid., 9.5.
22. WGH to Carrie Phillips, January 5, 1913, 9.18–19.
23. Ibid., 9.5.
24. Ibid., 9.6.
25. Ibid.
26. Ibid., 9.6–7.
27. Ibid., 9.8.
28. Ibid., 9.28.
29. Ibid., 9.12.
30. Ibid., 9.19.
31. Ibid., 9.20–21.
32. Ibid., 9.21.
33. In a subsequent letter, he sent Carrie the two letters that Isabelle wrote. Her mother's trip to see Harding in the United States in December 1912 appears to have been called a "Paris" trip— Carrie must have told Isabelle she was taking a trip to Paris for those weeks. "I could not convey her tact and diplomacy without sending the complete letters," Warren wrote to Carrie on January 18. "Note that she never alludes to your 'Paris' or your Russia trips at all. I do not think you ever need fear her telling anything. If she were a man she would make a perfect diplomat." WGH to Carrie Phillips, January 16–18, 1913, 10.2.
34. Ibid., 9.23.
35. Ibid., 9.31.
36. Ibid., 9.34.

Chapter 16: "Mrs. H Is an Invalid"

1. WGH to Carrie Phillips, January 16–18, 1913, 10.7.
2. Ibid., 10.2.
3. Ibid., 10.3.
4. Perhaps it was because of his strong feelings, but every time Warren wrote his rival's name, his handwriting is hard to decipher. It looks like Ginger—but it is hard to make out. "Gregor" or some such name would make more sense, but the best I can come up with consistently is Ginger. It is not clear if this is the same man who later is referred to as Robinson.
5. WGH to Carrie Phillips, January 16–18, 1913, 10.3.Harding refers to the Allens in his September 21–24, 1913 letter: "I think I have already spoken of Mrs. Allen. Yes, I'd like to see her houses. She is so good a friend of you , but I have no other curiosity. J—spoke of her spurning my message [of "esteemed respect"]. Should I have sent my love? Honestly the term is too sacred to me to fling it around indiscriminately." WGH to Carrie Phillips, September 21–24, 1913, 14.8.
6. WGH to Carrie Phillips, January 16–18, 1913, 10.9.
7. Ibid., 10.6.
8. WGH to Carrie Phillips, March 25, 1913, 11.3.
9. WGH to Carrie Phillips, March 29, 1913, 12.1.
10. Andrew Cayton, *Ohio: The History of a People* (Columbus: Ohio State University Press, 2002).
11. WGH to Carrie Phillips, March 29, 1913, 12.2.
12. WGH to Carrie Phillips, March 25, 1913, 11.2.
13. Ibid., 12.3.
14. Brentano's bill, dated March 22, 1913, WGH Papers.
15. Brentano's bill, September 16, 1913, WGH Papers (misaddressed to Mrs. Charles F. Phillips). This was the second time that Brentano's got her name wrong. "I seem to have a messy time with books

from Brentano's meant for you, except when I call at the store in person." WGH to Carrie Phillips, September 21, 1913, 14.2.

16. Keith Vawter to WGH, April 14, 1913, WGH Papers.

17. WGH to Carrie Phillips, August 18, 1913, 8.4.

18. Mary Harding to WGH, April 15, 1913, WGH Papers.

19. Mary Harding to WGH, June 7, 1913, WGH Papers.

20. WGH to Carrie Phillips, August 18, 1913, 8.5.

21. WGH to Carrie Phillips, September 15, 1913, 15.8–9.

22. WGH to Carrie Phillips, August 18, 1913, 8.5.

23. Ibid., 8.5–6.

24. Ibid., 8.2.

25. WGH to Carrie Phillips, September 16, 1913, 13.8.

26. William H. Miller, Jr., *The First Great Ocean Liners In Photograhs* (New York: Dover Publications, Inc., 1984), 63–64. For Harding's pronunciation of *Imperator,* see WGH to Carrie Phillips, September 16–17, 1913, 13.20.

27. WGH to Carrie Phillips, September 15, 1913, 15.9–10.

28. Jim returned to Marion on September 20, 1913. WGH to Carrie Phillips, September 21, 1913, 14.1. That means his trip from England to Marion took eighteen days (he wrote Harding that he was leaving England on September 6). He likely spent some time in New York on his way back.

29. The letter written on September 15 and the composite one of September 16–19 both start at page 5. WGH to Carrie Phillips, September 15, 1913, 15; WGH to Carrie Phillips, September 16–19, 1913, 13. The letter written September 21 starts on page 1 and notes that Jim returned to Marion the day before. WGH to Carrie Phillips, September 21–24, 1913.

30. WGH to Carrie Phillips, September 15, 1913, 15.19–20.

31. Ibid., 15.5.

32. Ibid., 15.6.

33. WGH to Carrie Phillips, September 16–19, 1913, 13.11–12.

34. WGH to Carrie Phillips, September 21–24, 1913, 14.1.

35. Ibid., 14.5.

36. Ibid., 14.11.

CHAPTER 17: "I HAVE HAD MY FIRST LARK SINCE YOU WENT ABROAD"

1. WGH to Carrie Phillips, November 11–15, 1913, 16.1.

2. Ibid., 16.7.

3. WGH to Carrie Phillips, November 18, 1913, 17.3-4.

4. WGH to Carrie Phillips, November 11–15, 1913, 16.15.

5. Ibid., 16.14.

6. Dr. George T. Harding, Jr. to WGH, November 6, 1913, WGH Papers.

7. WGH to Carrie Phillips, November 11–15, 1913, 16.14.

8. Francis Russell, *The Shadow of Blooming Grove: Warren G. Harding in His Times* (New York: Mc-Graw-Hill Book Company, 1968), 240.

9. WGH to Carrie Phillips, November 11–15, 1913, 16.7.

10. Ibid., 16.12.

11. WGH to Carrie Phillips, November 29, 1913, 18.9.

12. The Big Four Railroad was the Cleveland, Cincinnati, Chicago, and St. Louis Railway. Its biggest roundhouse was located in Bellefontaine, Ohio, not far from Marion. The railroad operated from 1889 to 1922.

13. WGH to Carrie Phillips, November 29, 1913, 18.5–6.

14. WGH to Carrie Phillips, November 11–15, 1913, 16.5–6.

15. Ibid., 16.3.

16. Ibid., 16.9–10.

17. Ibid., 16.9–10.

18. Ibid., 16.2.

19. Ibid., 16.16.

20. Ibid., 16.13.
21. On rumors about Mrs. F.: ibid., 16.13.
22. WGH to Carrie Phillips, September 16, 1913, 13.5.
23. Ibid., 13.13.
24. WGH to Carrie Phillips, November 18, 1913, 17.15 ("Perhaps we shall meet, but not till I can come to you. I have felt the shame of my selfishness again and again over asking you to come to me. But there was no other way.")
25. WGH to Carrie Phillips, September 16, 1913, 13.18.
26. Ibid., 15.11–14.
27. WGH to Carrie Phillips, November 11–15, 1913, 16.16–17.
28. WGH to Carrie Phillips, November 18, 1913, 17.6–7, 13.
29. Ibid.,17.14.
30. WGH to Carrie Phillips, November 11–15, 1913, 16.21.
31. WGH to Carrie Phillips, November 18, 1913, 17.14.
32. WGH to Carrie Phillips, November 11–15, 1913, 16.4.

CHAPTER 18: "I WAS LITERALLY SEDUCED AND URGED INTO THE STEP"

1. WGH to Carrie Phillips, June 4, 1914, 23.3–4.
2. Charity Remsberg to WGH, January 19, 1914, WGH Papers.
3. Ed Scobey to WGH, January 19, 1914, WGH Papers.
4. WGH to Carrie Phillips, April 11, 1914, 22.1.
5. WGH to Carrie Phillips, June 4, 1914, 23.2.
6. Ibid., 23.4.
7. Harry Daugherty to WGH, November 16, 1912, WGH Papers.
8. Carl Sferrazza Anthony, *Florence Harding, The First Lady, The Jazz Age, and the Death of America's Most Scandalous President* (New York: William Morrow,1998), 109. Andrew Sinclair, *The Available Man, Warren Gamaliel Harding* (New York: The MacMillan Company, 1965), 52.
9. Malcolm Jennings to WGH, April 11, 1914, WGH Papers.
10. Randolph C. Downes, *The Rise of Warren Gamaliel Harding, 1865-1920* (Columbus: Ohio State University Press, 1970), 198.
11. Ibid., 199.
12. "Joseph B. Foraker, Ex-Senator, Dead," *New York Times,* May 11, 1917.
13. WGH to Carrie Phillips, June 4, 1914, 23.5.
14. Ibid., 23.2.
15. Ibid., 23.1.
16. Ibid., 23.8.
17. Ibid., 23.7.
18. Ibid., 23.8.
19. WGH to Ed Scobey, June 18, 1914, Scobey Papers.

CHAPTER 19: "SOPHIE! SOPHIE! DON'T DIE! STAY ALIVE FOR THE CHILDREN!"

1. Robert K. Massie, *Dreadnought* (New York: Ballantine, 1991), 858–859.
2. "Heir to Austria's Throne Is Slain with His Wife by a Bosnian Youth to Avenge Seizure of His Country," *New York Times,* June 29, 1914.
3. Robert J. Donia, *Sarajevo: A Biography* (Ann Arbor: University of Michigan Press, 2005), 120–124.

CHAPTER 20: "I AM BUSIER THAN AN OLD HEN WITH A BROOD FULL OF CHICKS"

1. WGH to Carrie Phillips, July 19, 1914, 24.1.
2. Ibid., 24.3.
3. Mark Sullivan, *Our Times, Over Here, 1914-1918* (New York: Charles Scribner's Sons, 1933), 1–8.

4. Arthur S. Link, *Wilson: The Struggle for Neutrality* (Princeton, NJ: Princeton University Press, 1960), 2 (quoting E. M. House to Woodrow Wilson, May 29, 1914).

5. See Marion County Chautauqua Program for Thursday, July 30, 1914, WGH Papers. The afternoon included a full concert by the Chicago Operatic Co. The evening was a music prelude by the Chicago Operatic Co. and then the "Famous Debate" between Bede and Seidel.

6. WGH to Carrie Phillips, July 19, 1914, 24.4–5.

7. Ibid., 24.5–6.

CHAPTER 21: "YOU ARE AN ENEMY ALIEN"

1. National Archives, Zollner Tr. 148–150 (Baroness testimony).

2. Reginald L. Poole, ed., *The English Historical Review,* vol. 28 (London: Longmans, Green and Co., 1913), 409. Major-General Sir Alfred E. Turner, *Sixty Years of a Soldier's Life* (London: Methuen & Co., 1912).

CHAPTER 22: "THIS WAS SURELY A GREAT VICTORY"

1. Robert K. Massie, *Dreadnought* (New York: Ballantine, 1991), 907.

2. Wilson Link, *The New Freedom,* 462–463.

3. Randolph C. Downes, *The Rise of Warren Gamaliel Harding, 1865-1920* (Columbus: Ohio State University Press, 1970), 205.

4. WGH to Joseph Foraker, August 20, 1914, WGH Papers; see also Francis Russell, *The Shadow of Blooming Grove: Warren G. Harding in His Times* (New York: McGraw-Hill Book Company, 1968), 247.

5. WGH to Ed Scobey, August 22, 1914, Scobey Papers.

6. Malcolm Jennings to WGH, August 14, 1914, WGH Papers.

7. John D. Weaver, *The Brownsville Raid* (Austin: Texas A&M University Press, 1992); "Tale that Foraker Will See Roosevelt," *New York Times,* April 20, 1915; "Foraker Men Are Angry," *New York Times,* May 9, 1908.

8. Weaver, *The Brownsville Raid,* 2.

9. *Marion Star,* September 27, 1914; Downes, *The Rise of Warren Gamaliel Harding,* 220–211.

10. Ibid.

11. WGH to Ed Scobey, September 12, 1914, Scobey Papers.

12. Ed Scobey to WGH, September 22, 1914, Scobey Papers.

13. Ibid.

14. WGH to Ed Scobey, September 28, 1914, Scobey Papers.

15. Downes makes fairly weak arguments that Harding encouraged others in anti-Catholic rhetoric in 1914. Downes, *The Rise of Warren Gamaliel Harding,* 213–215.

16. Malcolm Jennings to Ed Scobey, October 24, 1914, Scobey Papers.

17. Ed Scobey to WGH, November 9, 1914, Scobey Papers.

18. WGH to Ed Scobey, November 25, 1914, Scobey Papers.

19. Ed Scobey to WGH, November 9, 1914, Scobey Papers.

20. WGH to Ed Scobey, November 25, 1914, Scobey Papers.

21. Ibid.

22. Ibid.

23. Ed Scobey to WGH, undated, Scobey Papers.

24. Kathleen Dalton, *Theodore Roosevelt, A Strenuous Life* (New York: Alfred A. Knopf, 2002), 425–442.

25. Ibid.

CHAPTER 23: "I EXPECTED MY HUSBAND TO STAY IN AMERICA"

1. National Archives, Zollner Tr. 150–154 (Baroness testimony).

2. Kathleen Dalton, *Theodore Roosevelt, A Strenuous Life* (New York: Alfred A. Knopf, 2002), 444.

3. "Calls on Germans to Go into Politics," *New York Times,* August 17, 1915 ("Even if you could silence twenty million Americans of German birth or descent"); "The German-American's Halluci-

nation," *New York Times,* May 13, 1916 (University of Michigan professor claims the 20 million German Americans includes "vast number of the descendants of pre-Revolutionary Germans, who are as old in American sentiment and American tradition as the Declaration of Independence"). "There was . . . a substantial population of German-Americans, nearly 10 percent of the nation's total, by far the largest non-English ethnic minority. The U.S. Census of 1910 listed 8,262,618 people in the United States who had checked off Germany as their country of origin." Stewart Halsey Ross, *Propaganda for War: How the United States Was Conditioned to Fight the Great War of 1914–1918* (New York: McFarland & Company, 1996), 100.

4. Arthur S. Link, *Wilson: The Struggle for Neutrality, 1914–1915* (Princeton, New Jersey: Princeton University Press 1960), 34.

5. Carrie Phillips Notes, May 1917, 87.1.

6. Ibid., 87.2–3.

7. Link, *Wilson: The Struggle for Neutrality,* 31.

8. WGH to Carrie Phillips, March 23, 1917, 62.1.

9. Neil M. Johnson, *George Sylvester Viereck, Books at Iowa* 9 (University of Iowa, November 1968) (www.lib.uiowa.edu/spec-coll/Bai/johnson2.htm); Tom Reis, "The First Conservative: How Peter Viereck Inspired—and Lost—a Movement," *The New Yorker,* October 24, 2005.

10. Reis, "The First Conservative."

11. "Calls Germans to Go into Politics," *New York Times,* August 17, 1915.

12. "Lays Bare German Plots," *New York Times,* December 7, 1918.

13. "U. S. Looks into Spy Propaganda," *New York Times,* August 16, 1915; "Two Admit Stegler Named Capt. Boy-Ed," *New York Times,* February 28, 1915.

14. "Viereck Got $100,000 from the Germans," *New York Times,* July 26, 1918.

15. "Says Germany Paid $140,00 to Viereck," *New York Times,* February 11, 1922.

16. National Archives, Zollner Tr. 238 (Baroness testimony).

CHAPTER 24: "WHY DIDN'T YOU SAY WHAT YOU WROTE?"

1. WGH to Carrie Phillips, January 26, 1915, 28.1 (on Palace Hotel stationery, San Francisco).

2. Ibid., 28.1–2.

3. Ibid., 28.3.

4. Ibid., 28.9.

5. Ibid., 28.10.

6. Ibid., 28.4.

7. Ibid., 28.5.

8. Unfortunately, though Carrie kept some of Robinson's letters, they were destroyed by Ken Duckett when he had control of the collection at the Ohio Historical Society. Duckett was advised by his lawyer to destroy the letters because he had his hands full with the Harding suit and did not need heirs of Robinson also coming forth. Duckett regretted following his attorney's advice but did so believing that the letters were not of significance since Robinson was not a figure in history like Harding. Duckett transcript of tapes of his recollection, dictated September 4, 1969, Duckett Papers.

9. Ibid., 28.7.

10. Ibid., 28.6.

11. Ed Scobey to WGH, February 17, 1915, Scobey Papers.

12. WGH to Ed Scobey, March 26, 1915, Scobey Papers.

13. WGH to Carrie Phillips, February 19, 1915, 29.1–3.

14. "Favorite Sons," *New York Times,* March 12, 1915.

15. Ed Scobey to WGH, March 30, 1915, Scobey Papers.

16. Ed Scobey to George B. Christian, Jr., April 19, 1915, Scobey Papers.

CHAPTER 25: "APPARENTLY CONSIDERABLE PANIC"

1. U.S. Department of State, George Clack, executive ed., *Outline of U. S. History* (2005), 202, http://www.america.gov/st/educ-english/2008/April/20080407122445Seaifas0.64362.html.

2.   Arthur S. Link, *Wilson: The Struggle for Neutrality 1914–1915* (Princeton, New Jersey: Princeton University Press 1960), 106–136; C. Paul Vincent, *The Politics of Hunger: The Allied Blockade of Germany, 1915–1919* (Athens: Ohio University Press, 1985), 30–38; Edwin J. Clapp, *Economic Aspects of the War, Neutral Rights, Belligerent Claims and American Commerce in the Years 1914–1915* (New Haven, CT: Yale University Press, 1915). Author Stewart Halsey Ross points out that Professor Clapp's book was funded by the German government, through Dr. Heinrich Albert. Stewart Halsey Ross, *Propaganda for War, How the United States Conditioned to Fight the Great War of 1914–1918* (Jefferson, North Carolina: McFarland & Company, Inc., Publishers), 106; Patrick O'Sullivan, *The Lusitania, Unraveling the Mysteries* (Dublin: Collins Press, 1998), 22; Diane Preston, *Lusitania: An Epic Tragedy* (New York: Walker, 2002), 40–43.
3.   Link, *Wilson, The Struggle for Neutrality,* 312–316.
4.   Clapp, *Economic Aspects of the War,* 6; Link, *Wilson, The Struggle for Neutrality,* 187–190.
5.   Link, *Wilson, The Struggle for Neutrality,* 323.
6.   Vincent, *The Politics of Hunger,* 42.
7.   Clapp, *Economic Aspects of the War,* 6.
8.   Link, *Wilson, The Struggle for Neutrality,* 162–170.
9.   Ibid., 91–118.
10.   Ibid., 134.
11.   "Lusitania Warning Sent from Berlin," *New York Times,* January 31, 1918.
12.   Preston, *Lusitania,* 166–171.
13.   Ibid., 240.
14.   "Berlin Hails New Triumph," *New York Times,* May 9, 1915.
15.   "Impeach Bryan, Says Viereck," *New York Times,* May 9, 1915.
16.   Ross, *Propaganda for War,* 124.
17.   Link, *Wilson, The Struggle for Neutrality,* 379–382.
18.   Link, *Wilson, The Struggle for Neutrality,* 383.
19.   Ibid., 407.
20.   Preston, *Lusitania,* 345.

CHAPTER 26: "BERNSTORFF USED DYES AS WAR CLUB"

1.   "Bernstorff Used Dyes as War Club," *New York Times,* June 16, 1919.
2.   *1918 Year Book of the Oil, Paint and Drug Reporter* (New York: Oil, Paint and Drug Reporter, 1919) (Alien Property Custodian Report of A. Mitchell Palmer on Chemicals and Dyes), 5–16; Stanley Frost, *Germany's New War Against America* (New York: E.P. Dutton and Company, 1919), 82-105.
3.   A. Mitchell Palmer and Francis P. Garvan, *Aims and Purposes of the Chemical Foundation and the Reasons for Its Organization* (New York: De Vinne Press, 1919), 3-70. Garvan was identified as the president of the Chemical Foundation in the *Times* article and as the successor to Mitchell Palmer as the Alien Property Custodian in this book. (By the time of this publication, Palmer was the attorney general of the United States).

CHAPTER 27: "IT IS MY INTENTION TO WORK AT MY JOB INSTEAD OF HARANGUING DINNER PARTIES"

1.   William Gibbs McAdoo, *Crowded Years* (New York: Houghton Mifflin, 1931), 324–327.
2.   Stewart Halsey Ross, *Propaganda for War, How the United States Conditioned to Fight the Great War of 1914–1918* (Jefferson, North Carolina: McFarland & Company, Inc., Publishers), 130.
3.   Arthur S. Link, *Wilson: The Struggle for Neutrality, 1914–1915* (Princeton, New Jersey: Princeton University Press 1960), 555.
4.   Joan M. Jensen, *The Price of Vigilance* (New York: Rand McNally, 1968), 13–14.
5.   "U.S. Looks into Spy Propaganda," *New York Times,* August 16, 1915.
6.   "Says Propaganda Cost Forty Millions," *New York Times,* November 15, 1915.
7.   "How Germany Has Worked in U. S. to Shape Opinion, Block the Allies and Get Munitions for Herself, Told in Secret Agents' Letters, *New York World,* August 15, 1915; Ross, *Propaganda for War,* 131.

8. Kathleen Dalton, *Theodore Roosevelt, A Strenuous Life* (New York: Alfred A. Knopf, 2002), 485.

9. Francis Russell, *The Shadow of Blooming Grove: Warren G. Harding in His Times* (New York: McGraw-Hill Book Company, 1968), 259–260.

10. WGH to Ed Scobey, July 12, 1915, Scobey Papers.

11. WGH to Ed Scobey, September 6, 1915, Scobey Papers.

12. George B. Christian, Jr., to Ed Scobey, October 18, 1915, Scobey Papers.

13. Carl Sferrazza Anthony, *Florence Harding, The First Lady, The Jazz Age, and the Death of America's Most Scandalous President* (New York: William Morrow, 1998), 116.

14. WGH to Ed Scobey, December 13, 1915, Scobey Papers.

15. Evalyn Walsh McLean, *Queen of Diamonds* (Franklin, TN: Hillsboro Press, 2000) (a commemorative edition of *Father Struck It Rich,* first published in 1936).

16. Ibid., 213–215.

17. WGH to Carrie Phillips, December 11, 1915, 34.1.

18. Ibid., 34.2.

19. Ibid.

20. Ibid., 34.3.

21. McLean, *Queen of Diamonds,* 216–217.

22. Gene Smith, *When the Cheering Stopped* (New York: William Morrow, 1964), 20–21.

23. Russell, *Shadow of Blooming Grove,* 249; Sargent's *Handbook Series, The Best Private Schools of the United States and Canada* (Boston: Porter E Sargent, 1915), 128.

24. WGH to Carrie Phillips, December 11, 1915, 34.3.

25. "Kaiser Recalls Boy-Ed and Papen," *New York Times,* December 11, 1915. The kaiser later rewarded Boy-Ed for his service by decorating him with the Order of the Red Eagle, third class, with swords. "Kaiser Decorates Boy-Ed," *New York Times,* May 13, 1916.

26. "Statements by Boy-Ed and Von Papen; Both Say They Have Merely Done Their Duty; Other Important Dismissals May Follow," *New York Times,* December 4, 1915.

27. Ibid.

28. "Says Burleson Pleaded with Him," *New York Times,* February 7, 1922.

29. WGH to Carrie Phillips, December 22, 1915, 35.1.

CHAPTER 28: "HE WAS AN AMERICAN FROM THE WORD GO"

1. National Archives, Zollner Tr. 153-154 (Baroness testimony). She testified that Beresford entered the Naval Academy on September 30, 1917. Ibid., 197.

2. Ibid., 198.

3. Ibid., 199.

4. "President Roosevelt Gives the Bride Away," *New York Times,* March 18, 1905.

5. National Archives, Zollner Tr. 334-335 (Bedford S. Shope testimony).

CHAPTER 29: "SO ROBINSON CAME!"

1. WGH to Ed Scobey, February 1, 1916, Scobey Papers.

2. Randolph C. Downes, *The Rise of Warren Gamaliel Harding, 1865-1920* (Columbus: Ohio State University Press, 1970), 262–263.

3. Ibid.

4. WGH to Ed Scobey, January 20, 1916, Scobey Papers.

5. WGH to Carrie Phillips, January 24, 1916, 40.2–4.

6. Ibid., 40.4.

7. WGH to Ed Scobey, January 20, 1916, Scobey Papers.

8. WGH to Carrie Phillips, January 30, 1916, 41.1.

9. WGH to Carrie Phillips, February 22, 1916, 43.1.

10. WGH to Carrie Phillips, February 17, 1916, 42.4.

11. Ibid., 43.1–2. This is an unusual use of his pseudonym "Jerry." Usually it had a sexual connotation.

12. "Candidates Grilled by Gridiron Club," *New York Times,* February 27, 1916.

13. WGH to Carrie Phillips, February 17, 1916, 42.1. This sentence seems to tie her "thrilling to another man" in Europe to Robinson. If so, he and the man identified as Ginger, whom Carrie knew in Berlin, are the same person.

14. WGH to Carrie Phillips, February 22, 1916, 43.6. This letter further solidifies that she came back from Europe having known and thrilled to Robinson's attention.

15. Randolph C. Downes, *The Rise of Warren Gamaliel Harding,* 239.

16. "Wilson Will Decide on Sussex Soon," *New York Times,* April 9, 1916; "Some Concessions Made," *New York Times,* May 5, 1916; "Diplomatic Break Averted," *New York Times,* May 6, 1916.

17. Diane Preston, *Lusitania: An Epic Tragedy* (New York: Walker, 2002), 361.

18. WGH to Carrie Phillips, March 4, 1916, 46.1.

19. WGH to Carrie Phillips, February 22, 1916, 43.2, 10.

20. Ibid.

21. "Fail to Pick Chairman," *New York Times,* March 22, 1916; "Roosevelt Confers with G.O.P. Leaders," *New York Times,* April 8, 1916.

22. "All Rests with the House," *New York Times,* March 4, 1916.

23. "Roosevelt Confers with G.O.P. Leaders," *New York Times,* April 8, 1916.

24. Ibid.

25. WGH to Carrie Phillips, May 17, 1916, 48. In writing about this letter, Ken Duckett connected the Baltimore visit to the Republican State Convention in Baltimore, which was reported to be concluded the previous day, Tuesday, May 9. "Regulars Win in Maryland," *New York Times,* May 10, 1916. Since the regulars won in Maryland and the delegation was "uninstructed," with some leaning toward Hughes and some toward Roosevelt, it seems like this would be an ideal scenario for a candidate who wished to make a "dark horse" bid. Thus, it appears unlikely the Maryland state convention was the thing that persuaded him of the "futility of such pursuit."

26. WGH to Carrie Phillips, May 17, 1916, 48.2.

CHAPTER 30: "THE STRENGTH OF THE WARRIOR AND THE SKILL OF THE ENGINEER"

1. "Third Day of Pouring Rain," *New York Times,* June 9, 1916.

2. "Colonel to Stay in Race to Finish," *New York Times,* June 7, 1916.

3. "Republicans Lack Fire," *New York Times,* June 8, 1916.

4. Ibid.

5. "Harding Defines Issues," *New York Times,* April 9, 1916.

6. Randolph C. Downes, *The Rise of Warren Gamaliel Harding, 1865-1920* (Columbus: Ohio State University Press, 1970), 242–243.

7. Ibid., 243.

8. George B. Christian, Jr., to Ed Scobey, May 17, 1916, Scobey Papers.

9. "Can't Deliver Convention," *New York Times,* June 7, 1916.

10. WGH to Carrie Phillips, August 16–19, 1916, 50.3.

11. Kathleen Dalton, *Theodore Roosevelt, A Strenuous Life* (New York: Alfred A. Knopf, 2002), 467.

12. Ibid.

13. WGH to Theodore Roosevelt, June 28, 1916, WGH Papers.

14. "Giant U-Boat Held to Be a Trader," *New York Times,* July 11, 1916.

15. Paul Konig, *Voyage of the Deutschland, the First Merchant Submarine* (New York: Hearst's International Library Co., 1916), 25. The book was reprinted with an editorial note by Dwight R. Messimer, *Classics of Naval Literature* (Annapolis, MD: United States Naval Institute, 2001).

16. "German U-Boat Reaches Baltimore, Having Crossed Atlantic in 16 Days; Has Letter from Kaiser to Wilson," *New York Times,* July 10, 1916.

17. "Giant U-Boat Held to Be a Trader," *New York Times,* July 11, 1916.

18. Ibid.

19. Ibid.

20. "German Editors Rejoice," *New York Times,* July 11, 1916.

21. "Zeppelin Here Soon, Says Captain," *New York Times,* July 13, 1916.

22. "Many German Firms Expect to Benefit by U-boat's Trip," *New York Times,* July 10, 1916; Stanley Frost, *Germany's New War against America* (New York: E. P. Dutton, 1919), 89–101.

23. Jules Witcover, *Sabotage at Black Tom: Imperial Germany's Secret War in America, 1914–1917* (Chapel Hill, NC: Algonquin Books, 1989).

24. "Glass Damage Exceeds a Million; Few Downtown Buildings Escape," *New York Times,* July 31, 1916.

25. "N. Y. Firemen Work in Rain of Bullets," *New York Times,* July 31, 1916.

26. "Ellis Island Like War-Swept Town," *New York Times,* July 31, 1916.

27. WGH to Ed Scobey, July 22, 1916, Scobey Papers.

28. "Hughes Acceptance Tonight," *New York Times,* July 31, 1916.

29. "Many Explosions Since War Began," *New York Times,* August 31, 1916.

30. "Washington Starts Explosion Inquiry," *New York Times,* July 31, 1916.

31. Witcover, *Sabotage at Black Tom,* 3–6.

32. "Hughes Motors Bareheaded," *New York Times,* July 31, 1916.

33. "Year's Hottest Day Cause of 3 Deaths," *New York Times,* August 1, 1916.

34. "Hughes Accepts, Attacks Record of His Opponent," *New York Times,* August 1, 1916.

35. National Archives, File OG 143708 (Chief of the Marion Branch of the American Protective League to Charles D. Frey, February 14, 1918).

CHAPTER 31: "I LEARNED TO LOVE *WITH* YOU"

1. WGH to Ed Scobey, August 15, 1916, Scobey Papers.

2. WGH to Ed Scobey, July 22, 1916, Scobey Papers.

3. Jules Witcover, *Sabotage at Black Tom: Imperial Germany's Secret War in America, 1914–1917* (Chapel Hill, NC: Algonquin Books, 1989), 176.

4. WGH to Carrie Phillips, August 14, 1916, 49.1.

5. Ibid., 49.4. It is interesting that he wrote that he wished her to be in New York with him on August 23, since he wrote to Scobey contemporaneously that he expected to be in New York with Florence and that they might be able to see Mrs. Scobey, who was vacationing in the North for the summer and about to go to Canada, "out of the wicked environment of Manhattan Island," he joked. WGH to Ed Scobey, August 15, 1916, Scobey Papers.

6. WGH to Carrie Phillips, August 19, 1916, 51.

7. Ibid., 51.1.

8. WGH to Carrie Phillips, August 15-19, 1916, 50.15 (sent on August 22).

9. Ibid., 50.3–4.

10. Ibid., 50.4.

11. Ibid., 50.4–5.

12. Ibid., 50.9.

13. Ibid., 50.17–18.

14. Ibid., 50.16.

15. Ibid., 50.17.

16. Ibid., 50.21.

17. Ibid., 50.26.

18. Ibid.

19. Ibid., 50.24–25.

20. Ibid., 50.26.

21. Ibid., 50.39.

22. Ed Scobey to Warren Harding, September 16, 1916, Scobey Papers.

CHAPTER 32: "NO, THIS MAKES ME TOO PROMISCUOUS"

1. "Kaiser's Last Trump," *New York Times,* August 31, 1916.

2. "Allies See Victory Nearer," *New York Times,* August 29, 1916; Jules Witcover, *Sabotage at Black Tom: Imperial Germany's Secret War in America, 1914–1917* (Chapel Hill, NC: Algonquin Books, 1989), 178–179.

3. Witcover, *Sabotage at Black Tom,* 179.
4. Arthur S. Link, *Wilson: Campaigns for Progressivism and Peace* (Princeton, NJ: Princeton University Press, 1965), 164–170.
5. Ibid., 153–155.
6. Ibid., 155.
7. Randolph C. Downes, *The Rise of Warren Gamaliel Harding, 1865-1920* (Columbus: Ohio State University Press, 1970), 249.
8. WGH to Carrie Phillips, undated, 36.5–6 (on stationery The Plains Hotel, Cheyenne, Wyoming).
9. Link, *Wilson,* 156–160.
10. Downes, *The Rise of Warren Gamaliel Harding,* 249.
11. WGH to Ed Scobey, November 21, 1916, Scobey Papers.
12. Ibid.
13. Ibid.
14. Unidentified attorney to Carrie Phillips, November 18, 1916, 53.
15. WGH to Carrie Phillips, December 1, 1916, 54.7.
16. Ibid. He wrote Scobey on November 21 from Marion that he and Florence were "expecting to go into our new shack" when they returned to Washington. WGH to Ed Scobey, November 21, 1916, Scobey Papers.
17. WGH to Carrie Phillips, December 1, 1916, 54.8.
18. Ibid.
19. WGH to Carrie Phillips, February 22, 1916, 43.7. Isabelle's remark is referenced twice in the letters, once in the February 22, 1916 letter (43), and again in this December 1, 1916, letter. WGH to Carrie Phillips, December 1, 1916, 54.1-2.
20. WGH to Carrie Phillips, December 1, 1916, 54.3.
21. Ibid., 54.7.
22. Ibid., 54.11.
23. Ibid., 54.10.

CHAPTER 33: "TODAY WE RAISE THE QUESTION OF PEACE"

1. Arthur S. Link, *Wilson, Campaigns for Progressivism and Peace, 1916–1917* (Princeton, New Jersey: Princeton University Press, 1965), 184–191; "British Advocate Doubly Armed Ships," *New York Times,* November 20, 1916.
2. Link, *Wilson,* 192.
3. Ibid.
4. Ibid., 193. The remarks were reminiscent to Lenin's "power was laying in the streets, we just picked it up."
5. Ibid., 209–210.
6. Ibid., 213–214.
7. "Colonel Attacks Wilson for Note," *New York Times,* January 4, 1917.
8. "Mr. Roosevelt at His Worst," *New York Times,* January 5, 1917.
9. "Lansing Explains Notes," *New York Times,* December 22, 1916.
10. Link, *Wilson,* 222–223.
11. "Secretary Lansing's Two Statements Regarding Peace Note to Belligerents," *New York Times,* December 22, 1916.
12. Link, *Wilson,* 223–234.
13. Ibid., 225.
14. "Senators Skeptical as to Peace Outlook," *New York Times,* December 13, 1916.
15. *Cleveland Leader,* December 13, 1916.
16. WGH to Ed Scobey, January 23, 1917, Scobey Papers. See also WGH to Malcolm Jennings, January 10, 1917, WGH Papers (references Roosevelt meeting).
17. WGH to Ed Scobey, January 1, 1917, Scobey Papers.
18. WGH to Carrie Phillips, January 11, 1917, 37.1–2.
19. Ibid., 37.3.
20. Ibid., 37.8.

21. Ibid., 37.9.

22. Ibid., 37.10.

23. Link, *Wilson*, 239–247.

24. Ibid., 251.

25. Ibid.,, 250–251.

26. Ibid., 265–266.

27. Ibid., 284.

28. Ed Scobey to WGH, February 2, 1917, Scobey Papers.

29. *Marion Star*, January 22 and 23, 1917.

30. WGH to Carrie Phillips, January 20, 1917, 39.2.

CHAPTER 34: "I KNOW YOU ARE IN REBELLION"

1. Arthur S. Link, *Wilson, Campaigns for Progressivism and Peace, 1916–1917* (Princeton, New Jersey: Princeton University Press, 1965), 290.

2. Ibid., 291.

3. Ibid., 296.

4. Ibid., 299–301.

5. WGH to Carrie Phillips, February 4, 1917, 58. The public letter is not in the Phillips collection. It is quoted in part by Francis Russell, "The Shadow of Warren Harding," *Antioch Review* (Winter 1978): 65. The complete letter is reprinted in Russell's papers maintained at the University of Wyoming.

6. WGH to Carrie Phillips, February 4, 1917, 58.1–2.

7. Ibid., 58.2.

8. Ibid.,58.3.

9. Ibid., 58.4.

10. "Senate Indorses Wilson," *New York Times*, February 8, 1917.

11. WGH to Carrie Phillips, February 8, 1917, 82.1.

12. Ibid., 82.2–3.

13. Ibid., 82.4.

14. Ibid., 82.7.

15. WGH to Carrie Phillips, February 10, 1917, 65.1.

16. WGH to Carrie Phillips, February 11, 1917, noon, 60.1–2.

17. Ibid., 60.2.

18. Ibid., 60.6.

19. "Sir Gilbert Parker Here," *New York Times*, January 22, 1917. "Publishers in Khaki, Office 'Boys' in Skirts," *New York Times*, February 11, 1917. (Charles F. G. Masterman at Wellington House was in charge of propaganda in England. "Sir Gilbert Parker has been there with him, in charge of all propaganda work in the United States.")

20. WGH to Carrie Phillips, February 12, 1917, 117.8.

21. Ibid., 117.9.

22. Ibid., 117.9–10.

23. WGH to Carrie Phillips, February 16, 1917, 61.1.

24. Ibid., 61.2–3.

25. Ibid., 61.3–4.

26. Ibid., 61.7–8.

27. WGH to Malcolm Jennings, February 21, 1917, WGH Papers.

28. WGH to Carrie Phillips, eve of March 4, 1917, 85.1.

29. "Bitter Wrangle as Senate Closes," *New York Times*, March 5, 1917.

30. "President Wilson's Address to Congress," *New York Times*, February 27, 1917.

31. "Extra Session Fight in Senate," *New York Times*, February 24, 1917.

32. Link, *Wilson*, 345–348; "Senators at Night in Fiery Debate; Filibuster Ends," *New York Times*, February 25, 1917.

33. Link, *Wilson*, 342. The Senate can consider treaties and nominations—things within the Senate's exclusive jurisdiction—without the entire Congress in session. Wilson called the Senate to special

session to consider a treaty issue involving the payment of reparations by the United States to Columbia over the separation of Panama in 1903.

34. "Extra Session Fight in Senate," *New York Times,* February 24, 1917.
35. "President Wilson's Address to Congress," *New York Times,* February 27, 1917.
36. Ibid.

CHAPTER 35: "WE SHALL MAKE WAR TOGETHER AND TOGETHER MAKE PEACE"

1. "Text of Germany's Proposal to Form an Alliance with Mexico and Japan Against the United States," *New York Times,* March 1, 1917.

CHAPTER 36: "A LITTLE GROUP OF WILLFUL MEN,
REPRESENTING NO OPINION BUT THEIR OWN"

1. Arthur S. Link, *Wilson, Campaigns for Progressivism and Peace, 1916–1917* (Princeton, New Jersey: Princeton University Press, 1965), 351.
2. "Laconia Case 'Clear-Cut,'" *New York Times,* February 28, 1917.
3. Link, *Wilson,* 353–356.
4. Ibid., 342–345.
5. "Bitter Wrangle as Senate Closes," *New York Times,* March 5, 1917.
6. "Text of Manifesto Signed by 68 Senators," *New York Times,* March 4, 1917.
7. WGH to Carrie Phillips, eve of March 3, 1917, 85.1.
8. "No Lusitania if T. R. Ruled," *Marion Star,* February 27, 1917.
9. Theodore Roosevelt to WGH, March 2, 1917, WGH Papers.
10. WGH to Carrie Phillips, eve of March 3, 1917, 85.2–3.
11. Ibid., 85.4–5.
12. "Bitter Wrangle as Senate Closes."
13. "President Takes Oath," *New York Times,* March 5, 1917.
14. Ibid.
15. Ibid.
16. "Statement of the President to the Public," *New York Times,* March 5, 1917.
17. "Great Mass Meeting Here," *New York Times,* March 6, 1917. The Special Session of the Senate only had been called by Wilson on February 23, to start on March 5 at noon. "Extra Session Fight in Senate," *New York Times,* February 24, 1917.
18. "Alters Rule of 100 Years," *New York Times,* March 9, 1917.
19. "Admits He Has Full Power," *New York Times,* March 10, 1917.
20. WGH to Carrie Phillips, eve of March 3, 1917, 85.4.

CHAPTER 37: "MY COUNTRYMEN, THE REPUBLIC IS ON TRIAL"

1. WGH to Ed Scobey, March 12, 1917, Scobey Papers.
2. Malcolm Jennings to WGH, March 13, 1917, WGH Papers.
3. WGH to Malcolm Jennings, March 19, 1917, WGH Papers.
4. "Revolution in Russia," *New York Times,* March 16, 1917.
5. "Manifesto of the Czar and Son's Abdication," *New York Times,* March 18, 1918.
6. "Pledge if Reform," *New York Times,* March 17, 1918.
7. "America First to Recognize the New Russia," *New York Times,* March 23, 1917.
8. Arthur S. Link, *Wilson, Campaigns for Progressivism and Peace, 1916–1917* (Princeton, New Jersey: Princeton University Press, 1965), 397.
9. "Patrols Pick Up Survivors," *New York Times,* March 19, 1917.
10. Link, *Wilson,* 405.
11. "All Rests with Congress," *New York Times,* March 22, 1917.
12. WGH to Carrie Phillips, March 23, 1917, 62.
13. WGH to Carrie Phillips, March 23, 1917, 62.2.
14. WGH to Carrie Phillips, March 25, 1917, 63.2–3.

15. Ibid., 63.3.
16. WGH to Carrie Phillips, March 28, 1917, 64.1-2.
17. "Address to the Cincinnati Business Men's Club," March 31, 1917, Cincinnati, Ohio, Speeches, WGH Papers.
18. "Our Republic Now on Trial," *Marion Star,* April 2, 1917.
19. "Arbitrament" is defined as the act of arbitrating or the judgment of an arbitrator. Here Harding meant the judgment of arms.
20. Link, *Wilson,* 421–426; "Must Exert All Power," *New York Times,* April 3, 1917.
21. "War Address," April 4, 1917, Speeches, WGH Papers.
22. "Keen Debate for 13 Hours," *New York Times,* April 5, 1917.
23. WGH to Ed Scobey, April 16, 1917, Scobey Papers.
24. "Aliens a Problem Here, Says Gerard," *New York Times,* March 20, 1917.
25. "Red Cross Bandages Poisoned by Spies," *New York Times,* March 29, 1917.
26. Jensen, *The Price of Vigilance,* 17–24.
27. "German Intrigue Is Still Kept Up," *New York Times,* November 22, 1918.
28. Ibid., 25–26.

CHAPTER 38: "FIRST MET HIM AT A HOP"

1. National Archives, Zollner Tr. 346–348 (Spalding testimony).
2. National Archives, Zollner Tr. 155–156 (Baroness testimony), 303 (Bedford Shope testimony).
3. National Archives, Zollner Tr. 303–304 (Bedford Shope testimony).
4. WGH to Carrie Phillips, December 1, 1916, 54.8.
5. National Archives, Zollner Tr. 169 (Baroness testimony).
6. Ibid., 163.
7. Ibid., 160–161.
8. "President's Proclamation of a State of War, and Regulations Governing Alien Enemies," *New York Times,* April 7, 1917.
9. Ibid.
10. National Archives, Zollner Tr. 161–126 (Baroness testimony).
11. Ibid., 163.
12. Ibid., 170–172.

CHAPTER 39: "YOU SUDDENLY THREATENED ME WITH EXPOSURE TO THE GERMANS"

1. "Roosevelt Exhorts West to Join in War," *New York Times,* April 29, 1917.
2. "Officials Oppose Early Expedition," *New York Times,* April 11, 1917.
3. "Col. Roosevelt Sees President," *New York Times,* April 11, 1917.
4. "Mr. Roosevelt at the White House," *New York Times,* April 12, 1917.
5. Randolph C. Downes, *The Rise of Warren Gamaliel Harding, 1865-1920* (Columbus: Ohio State University Press, 1970), 262–263.
6. "Senate Debate Spirited," *New York Times,* April 29, 1917.
7. "Enlisted Pay Is Doubled," *New York Times,* April 29, 1917; Downes, *The Rise of Warren Gamaliel Harding,* 263.
8. "Roosevelt Exhorts West to Join in War," *New York Times,* April 29, 1917.
9. "Will Not Send Roosevelt," *New York Times,* May 18, 1917.
10. Henry Cabot Lodge to Theodore Roosevelt, April 30, 1917, WGH Papers.
11. WGH to Theodore Roosevelt, May 7, 1917, WGH Papers.
12. Ed Scobey to WGH, May 2, 1917, Scobey Papers.
13. WGH to Ed Scobey, May 7, 1917, Scobey Papers.
14. *Marion Star,* May 3, 1917.
15. WGH to Ed Scobey, May 7, 1917, Scobey Papers.
16. The letter is undated, but it discusses his March 31, 1917, Cincinnati speech and also makes reference to his vote for war, which was in the first week of April. Carrie wrote notes about this letter

on an envelope from a New York shoe store, Cammeyer, that has a postmark of May 2, 1917 (Letter 65). So it would seem the letter had to have been written after war was declared and sometime around or after May 2. The letter appears to have been referred to in a letter he did date on May 28. WGH to Carrie Phillips, May 28, 1917, 55.6 ("I sent you a long, frank, heart revealing letter"). Carrie sent a note on Wednesday, May 23, from Cleveland (55.2), which would seem to correspond with notes she made about the topics in this undated letter, on hotel stationery, the Cleveland Statler.

17. WGH to Carrie Phillips, undated, 81.2.
18. "Address to the Cincinnati Business Men's Club," March 31, 1917, Cincinnati, Ohio, Speeches, WGH Papers.
19. WGH to Carrie Phillips, undated, 81.3.
20. Ibid., 81.8.
21. Ibid., 81.11–12.
22. Ibid., 81.18–19.
23. Carrie Phillips Notes, undated, 87.
24. Two facts support this dating of the Hotel Statler notes. First, his letter of May 28, 1917, records that she sent him a note from Cleveland on Wednesday, May 23, where the Hotel Statler is located. WGH to Carrie Phillips, May 27, 1917, 55.2. Second, she references a "negro lynching" the day before she wrote her notes, and the *Marion Star* carried a story "Negro Burned at Stake Today," on May 22, 1917.
25. Ibid.
26. Ibid.
27. Uhler-Phillips ad, *Marion Star,* May 11, 1917.
28. "Over $3,000 for Red Cross Fund," *Marion Star,* May 14, 1917.
29. Carrie Phillips Notes, undated, 87.
30. "Negro Burned at Stake Today," *Marion Star,* May 22, 1917.
31. For a full description of the lynching and its circumstances, see Phillip Dray, *At the Hands of Persons Unknown: The Lynching of Black America* (New York: Random House, 2002), 231–236.
32. Robert Ferrell, *The Strange Deaths of President Harding* (Columbia: University of Missouri Press, 1996), 50.
33. Nan Britton, *The President's Daughter* (New York: Elizabeth Ann Guild, 1927), 25–27.

CHAPTER 40: "I GUESS MY SPIRIT IS BROKEN"

1. Nan Britton, *The President's Daughter* (New York: Elizabeth Ann Guild, 1927), 29–30.
2. Ibid., 30–31.
3. Ibid., 32–37.
4. Ibid.
5. WGH to Carrie Phillips, May 28, 1917, 55.3.
6. Ibid., 55.1–2.
7. WGH to Carrie Phillips, June 30, 1917, 68.2–3.
8. Britton, *The President's Daughter,* 12–14. "There was in Marion a very attractive and extravagant woman whose name, let us say, was Mrs. Henry Arnold. Gossip had it that Mrs. Arnold and Warren Harding were very friendly, and gossip-mongers wondered how Mrs. Harding could be so blind to such a mutual infatuation." She also references "Mrs. Arnold's" age being closer to Harding's age, and mentions her envy over "Mrs. Arnold's" travel to Europe—all Carrie identifiers.
9. Ibid., 13–14.
10. "Patriotism of 1917 to Endure," *Marion Star,* May 31, 1917. See also "Harding Warns of Crisis," *New York Times,* May 31, 1917.
11. Ibid.
12. Randolph C. Downes, *The Rise of Warren Gamaliel Harding, 1865-1920* (Columbus: Ohio State University Press, 1970), 266–267.
13. "Harding under Fire for Hit at War Loan," *New York Times,* June 9, 1917.
14. "McAdoo Ignores Harding," *New York Times,* June 10, 1917.
15. WGH to Malcolm Jennings, June 14, 1917, WGH Papers.

16. WGH to Carrie Phillips, June 7, 1917, 66.
17. Ibid., 66.4.
18. WGH to Carrie Phillips, June 30, 1917, 68.1.
19. Britton, *The President's Daughter,* 39–43.
20. Ibid., 39.
21. WGH to Carrie Phillips, June 30, 1917, 68.1.
22. Ibid., 68.3–4.
23. Ibid., 68.5.
24. "General Pershing in Europe," *New York Times,* June 9, 1917.
25. "Spy Bill Passes; No Censorship," *New York Times,* May 15, 1917; "Says Censorship Will Be Defeated," *New York Times,* May 25, 1917.
26. Malcolm Jennings to WGH, June 18, 1917, WGH Papers.

CHAPTER 41: "SECRETS OF THE HOHENZOLLERNS"

1. "The Secrets of the Hohenzollerns," *Marion Star,* June 23, 1917. The series ran every Saturday for five weeks. William Le Queux, *The Secrets of Potsdam* (London: London Mail, 1917).
2. Compilation of Carrie Phillips Notes, undated, 87.1–4.
3. Ibid., 87.3–4.
4. "The Tragedy of the Leutenbergs," *Marion Star,* June 23, 1917. In *Florence Harding,* Carl Anthony describes an answer filed by DeWolfe in response to Florence's petition for divorce in 1886 in which he made some of these same allegations described by Carrie—that Florence lived a flagrant lifestyle; that she became "acquainted" with many men, including Harding; that DeWolfe at times disputed the paternity of her son, Marshall, though he was clear he did not believe that Harding was Marshall's father. Carl Sferrazza Anthony, *Florence Harding, The First Lady, The Jazz Age, and the Death of America's Most Scandalous President* (New York: William Morrow, 1998), 34. There is no suggestion, though, that Florence was pregnant when she married Harding or that any pregnancy was terminated. Anthony does contend that Florence and DeWolfe never were officially married.
5. WGH to Carrie Phillips, June 30, 1917, 68.5.
6. Carrie Phillips to WGH, July 7, 1917, 52.1.
7. Ibid., 52.2.
8. Ibid., 52.3.
9. Ibid., 52.1.
10. "Mrs. Harding Pictured by One of Her Lifelong Friends," *New York Herald,* February 20, 1921.
11. WGH to Carrie Phillips, July 11, 1917, 69.1.
12. Ibid., 69.1.
13. WGH to Carrie Phillips, July 22, 1917, 70.1.
14. Nan Britton, *The President's Daughter* (New York: Elizabeth Ann Guild, 1927), 47–48.
15. WGH to Carrie Phillips, July 22, 1917, 70.1.
16. WGH to Carrie Phillips, July 22, 1917, 70.2.
17. "Resolution on Peace Passes by 214 to 116," *New York Times,* July 21, 1917.
18. Ibid.; "Berlin Crisis Very Acute," *New York Times,* July 14, 1917.
19. "Berlin Crisis Very Acute," *New York Times,* July 14, 1917
20. "Kerensky Made Russian Premier as Lvoff Quits," *New York Times,* July 21, 1917.
21. "Russians Mutiny as Germans Attack," *New York Times,* July 21, 1917; "Mutiny on Russian Front Spreads," *New York Times,* July 23, 1917.
22. "German Spies Ever Watchful," *Marion Star,* July 23, 1917.
23. WGH to Carrie Phillips, July 22, 1917, 70.2.

CHAPTER 42: "THE CHICKENS HAD SCRAPS FROM THE TABLE"

1. National Archives, Zollner Tr. 170 (Baroness testimony).
2. National Archives, Zollner Tr. 354 (Spalding Testimony).
3. National Archives, Zollner Tr. 144, 164 (Bedford Shope testimony).
4. National Archives, Zollner Tr. 228 (Baroness testimony).

5.   National Archives, Zollner Tr. 164, 228 (Baroness testimony).
6.   National Archives, Zollner Tr., 305 (Bedford Shope testimony).
7.   National Archives, Zollner Tr., 192, 386 (Baroness testimony).
8.   National Archives, Zollner Tr. 195 (Baroness testimony).
9.   National Archives, Zollner Tr., 41–44 (Thompson testimony).
10. National Archives, Zollner Tr.B 202–203 (Baroness testimony).
11. National Archives, Zollner Tr. 170–172 (Baroness testimony).
12. National Archives, Zollner Tr., 40 (Spalding testimony).

CHAPTER 43: "NEED OF DICTATOR URGED BY HARDING"

1.   "Need of Dictator Urged by Harding," *New York Times,* Sunday magazine, August 12, 1917.
2.   "Food Bill Passed by Senate, 81 to 6; War Board Added," *New York Times,* July 22, 1917.
3.   WGH to Malcolm Jennings, July 6, 1917, WGH Papers.
4.   "Senate for Food Board," *New York Times,* July 20, 1917; Downes, *The Rise of Warren Gamaliel Harding, 1865–1920* (Columbus: Ohio State University Press, 1970), 269.
5.   "Need of Dictator Urged by Harding," *New York Times.*
6.   Ibid.
7.   Ibid.
8.   "Service for U. S. Held First Duty at G.O.P. Picnic," *Cleveland Plain Dealer,* July 29, 1917.
9.   WGH to Carrie Phillips, August 4, 1917, 70.2.
10. "Personal," *Marion Star,* July 30, 1917.
11. "Harding Likely to Vote with Drys," *Cleveland Plain Dealer,* August 1, 1917.
12. "Prohibition Wins Victory in Senate; Vote Is 65 to 20," *New York Times,* August 2, 1917.
13. "Harding Amendment Adopted by Senate," *Marion Star,* August 1, 1917; "Prohibition Wins Victory in Senate," *New York Times.*
14. Nan Britton, *The President's Daughter* (New York: Elizabeth Ann Guild, 1927), 48–49.
15. Robert Ferrell, *The Strange Deaths of President Harding* (Columbia: University of Missouri Press, 1996), 72–73, 103.
16. Britton, *The President's Daughter,* 48.
17. Ibid., 49.
18. Ibid., 50.
19. "Senate Poll Shows 66 for Prohibition," *New York Times,* July 31, 1917. John Dean checked the *Congressional Record* for July 30 and did not find Harding responding to a quorum on that day. However, over forty senators did not answer the quorum, and the *New York Times* article characterized action of the Senate floor as minimal. "Debate on the resolution today was desultory, only a half a dozen Senators, including Senators Sheppard, Underwood and Shafroth, speaking on it."
20. WGH to Carrie Phillips, August 4, 1917, 71.1–2.
21. Ibid., 71.2.
22. Ibid., 71.2–3.
23. Britton, *The President's Daughter,* 51–53.
24. Robert J. Laplander, *Finding the Lost Battalion* (Waterford, WI: Lulu Press, 2006), 37.
25. National Archives, File OG 143708 (Charles Jenkins report, August 15, 1917, Cleveland, Ohio).

CHAPTER 44: "NO WOMEN ARE INSENSIBLE TO THE
COURTLY ATTENTIONS OF ARMY OR NAVY MEN"

1.   "Draft Camps Open," *New York Times,* September 9, 1917.
2.   "All Draft Camps Chosen," *New York Times,* June 15, 1917.
3.   "Yaphank Camp: First Description in Detail," *New York Times,* August 12, 1917.
4.   "Draft Camps Open."
5.   "Draft Camp Opens."
6.   "President Would Like to Be in the Trenches, He Says, in Message to National Draft Army," *New York Times,* September 5, 1917.
7:   WGH to Carrie Phillips, August 25, 1917, 72.1.

8.   Ibid., 72.3.
9.   WGH to Carrie Phillips, August 25, 1917, 72.5–6.
10. WGH to Carrie Phillips, August 31, 1917, 73.2.
11. Ibid., 73.1–2.
12. Ibid., 73.3.
13. Ibid., 73.5.
14. WGH to Carrie Phillips, September 11, 1917, 74.1–2.
15. National Archives, File OG 143708 (Charles Jenkins report, August 15, 1917, Cleveland, Ohio).
16. "Death Takes Asa C. Queen," *Marion Star,* February 18, 1917.
17. "Former Postmaster F. T. Campbell Dies," *Marion Star,* September 11, 1938.
18. National Archives, File 143708.
19. Ibid.
20. "Harding as Senator Befriended Woman Suspected as a Spy," *New York Times,* April 13, 1917;
     "'Carrie' Identified as Marion Woman," *New York Times,* April 14, 1931; "Lays Marion 'Spy Talk'
     to Gossip," *Cleveland Plain Dealer,* April 14, 1931.
21. WGH to Carrie Phillips, September 14, 1917, 75.3.
22. WGH to Carrie Phillips, September 17 and 27, 1917, 76 and 77. His next letter in the collection
     is dated December 22, 1917. WHG to Carrie Phillips, December 22, 1917, 79.
23. WGH to Carrie Phillips, October 3, 1917, 78 (On Raleigh Hotel stationery).
24. Nan Britton, *The President's Daughter* (New York: Elizabeth Ann Guild, 1927), 51–61.
25. 75.4.

CHAPTER 45: "ISABELLE, YOU ARE A SUDDEN CHILD"

1.   WGH to Ed Scobey, September 13, 1917, Scobey Papers.
2.   "Kaiser at Riga Extols Victory as Step to Peace," *New York Times,* September 9, 1917.
3.   WGH to Ed Scobey, September 13, 1917, Scobey Papers.
4.   "Peace Move Made in Senate; Met By Call to Fight On," *New York Times,* August 12, 1917.
5.   "La Follette Faces a Threat of Arrest," *New York Times,* September 22, 1917.
6.   "Seeks Expulsion of La Follette," *New York Times,* September 30, 1917.
7.   "Deluge of Demands to Oust La Follette," *New York Times,* October 5, 1917.
8.   "La Follette Says He Will Continue to Oppose the War," *New York Times,* October 7, 1917.
9.   Ibid.
10. "La Follette Asks Right to Be Heard," *New York Times,* October 12, 1917.
11. Joan M. Jensen, *The Price of Vigilance* (New York: Rand McNally, 1968), 63–64.
12. "Deported I.W.W.'s Fed by the Army," *New York Times,* July 14, 1917.
13. Joan M. Jensen, *The Price of Vigilance,* 64.
14. "Government May End Outrages by I.W.W.," *New York Times,* August 2, 1917.
15. "I.W.W. Strike Chief Lynched at Butte," *New York Times,* August 2, 1917.
16. *The Price of Vigilance,* 62–63.
17. WGH to Ed Scobey, October 6, 1917, Scobey Papers.
18. "The Record of Congress," *New York Times,* October 7, 1917.
19. WGH to Ed Scobey, October 6, 1917.
20. WGH to Carrie Phillips, September 17, 1917, 76.1–2.
21. Undated notes of Carrie Phillips, 87.
22. "Carl Pickhardt, 87, Merchant, Is Dead," *New York Times,* April 17, 1939 ("On Feb. 5 Mr.
     Pickhardt and his wife, Mrs. Paula von Scheven Pickhardt, celebrated their fifty-ninth wedding
     anniversary").
23. Draft Letter, undated, in Carrie Phillips's handwriting, 56.
24. National Archives, File OG 143708 (Frank Campbell to Calvin Weakley, Special Agent in Charge,
     Bureau of Investigation, February 20, 1918).
25. WGH to Ed Scobey, October 19, 1917, Scobey Papers.
26. "In War, Says T.R., Not for Democracy," *New York Times,* October 1, 1917.
27. WGH to Ed Scobey, October 19, 1917.
28. WGH to Ed Scobey, October 20, 1917, Scobey Papers.

29. WGH to Ed Scobey, December 6, 1917, Scobey Papers.
30. "Lenine Heads New Cabinet," *New York Times,* November 11, 1917.
31. "To Bare Ship Row," *New York Times,* December 19, 1917.
32. WGH to Malcolm Jennings, December 31, 1917, WGH Papers.
33. WGH to Carrie Phillips, December 22, 1917, 79.3.

CHAPTER 46: "I'M TALKING TO THE WIFE
OF A GERMAN OFFICER, NOW AIN'T I?"

1. National Archives, Zollner Tr. 40–41(Thompson testimony).
2. National Archives, Zollner Tr. 46–47 (Thompson).
3. National Archives, Zollner Tr. 356 (Spalding).
4. National Archives, Zollner Tr. 267–268 (Baroness Zollner).
5. Ibid., 188.
6. National Archives, Zollner Tr. 35–38 (Thompson); 188 (Baroness Zollner).
7. National Archives, Zollner Tr. 36–37 (Thompson).
8. National Archives, Zollner Tr. 305–306 (Bedford Shope).
9. National Archives, Zollner Tr. 279–290 (Baroness Zollner).
10. National Archives, Zollner Tr. 306 (Bedford Shope).
11. National Archives, Zollner Tr. 45–46 (Thompson testimony).
12. "Victor Beutner Drops Dead," *Daily Times* (Chattanooga, TN), December 25, 1917.
13. Ibid.
14. National Archives, Zollner Tr. 176 (Baroness Zollner).
15. National Archives, Zollner Tr. 94 (Parker).
16. Ibid.
17. National Archives, Zollner Tr. 351 (Spalding).
18. National Archives, Zollner Tr. 274–278 (Baroness Zollner).
19. Ibid.
20. National Archives, Zollner Tr. 83 (Lieutenant W. B. Oliver).
21. National Archives, Zollner Tr., 70–84 (Lieutenants M. E. Sullivan, R. G. Carter, W. B. Oliver).
22. National Archives, Zollner Tr. 44 (Thompson).
23. National Archives, Zollner Tr. 85–91 (Stiff and Grant).
24. National Archives, Zollner Tr. 179 (Baroness Zollner).
25. Ibid.,179–180.
26. National Archives, Zollner Tr. 71–72 (Sullivan).
27. National Archives, Zollner Tr. 181 (Baroness Zollner).
28. National Archives, Zollner Tr. 18 (Thompson).
29. National Archives, Zollner Tr. 125 (McMahon).
30. Ibid., 130.
31. National Archives, Zollner Tr. 9–1, 31–34 (Thompson); 128 (McMahon).
32. National Archives, Zollner Tr. 23–25, 35–49 (Thompson).
33. National Archives, Zollner Tr. 40–41(Thompson).
34. National Archives, Zollner Tr. 157–158 (Baroness Zollner).
35. National Archives, Zollner Tr. 116–122 (Agent Edward Finlay, Bureau of Investigation).
36. Ibid., 120.
37. "All Draft Camps Chosen," *New York Times,* June 15, 1917.
38. National Archives, Zollner Tr. 165–167 (Baroness Zollner).
39. "Sunday in Fist Fight with Pro-German," *New York Times,* December 21, 1917.
40. "Back to Jail without Bond," *Daily Times* (Chattanooga, TN), December 25, 1917.
41. "Love Tricks of a Woman Spy," *Cleveland Plain Dealer,* February 10, 1918.

CHAPTER 47: "IT THRILLS ME, MERELY TO LIVE IT OVER IN RECOLLECTION"

1. WGH to Carrie Phillips, January 1, 1918, 80.1–4.

CHAPTER 48: "LET ME LECTURE YOU A BIT"

1. WGH to Ed and Evaland Scobey, January 3, 1918, Scobey Papers.
2. Ibid.
3. "War Problems Shifting," *New York Times,* January 29, 1918.
4. "Baker Must Tell of Future Plans to Keep Up Army," *New York Times,* January 30, 1918.
5. "War Problems Shifting."
6. "Baker Hopeful of Getting Ships for 1,500,000 Men," *New York Times,* February 7, 1918.
7. "Capital Expected Transport Attacks," *New York Times,* February 7, 1918.
8. "Ship Was under Convoy," *New York Times,* February 7, 1918.
9. "Allies Blame U. S. for Not Closing Leaks," *Cleveland Plain Dealer,* February 9, 1918.
10. "Death Penalty for Spies," *New York Times,* February 8, 1918.
11. "Love Tricks of a Woman Spy," *Cleveland Plain Dealer,* February 9, 1918.
12. National Archives, File OG143708 (Report of John S. Menefee, February 19, 1918).
13. National Archives, File OG145984 (Report of Albert D. Cash, February 20, 1918).
14. National Archives, File OG143708 (Report of W. H. Valentine, February 15, 1918).
15. National Archives, File OG143708 (Report of John S. Menefee, February 19, 1918).
16. "Weds under Folds of American Flag," *Cleveland Plain Dealer,* June 13, 1917. This trip to Cleveland is mention in Harding's letter to Carrie of June 7, 1917. WGH to Carrie Phillips, June 7, 1917, 66.1.
17. National Archives, File OG145984 (Report of Claude P. Light, February 18, 1918).
18. WGH to Carrie Phillips, February 17, 1918, 84
19. Ibid., 84.1.
20. Ibid., 84.2–4.
21. "Senate Committee Visits Hog Island," *New York Times,* February 26, 1918.
22. National Archives, File OG143708 (Memo, Thomas Watt Gregory to A. Bruce Bielaski, February 23, 1918).
23. James B. Jones, Jr. "The Baroness and the Lieutenant: Love and Espionage in War-Time Chattanooga, 1917–1918," www.geocites.com/Nashville/9475/baroness.htm.
24. "Nominates Sanford for Supreme Court," *New York Times,* January 25, 1923.
25. National Archives, Zollner Tr. 119 (Finlay testimony).
26. National Archives, File OG 145984 (A. Bruce Bielaski to C. S. Weakley, February 28, 1918).
27. National Archives, File OG 110304 (Report of J. F. Alford, January 26, 1918).
28. National Archives, File OG143708 (Frank Campbell to Calvin S. Weakley, February 20, 1918).
29. "Favors Death for Spies," *New York Times,* March 4, 1918.
30. "To Leave Hospital Today," *New York Times,* March 4, 1918.
31. Russia Signs a Peace Treaty," *New York Times,* March 4, 1918.
32. "Baker Sees Signs of Big Offensive," *New York Times,* February 11, 1918.

CHAPTER 49: "WAR IS HELL"

1. National Archives, File OG 143708 (Report of Leonard M. Stern, March 11, 1918).
2. National Archives, File OG 143708 (Bliss Morton to Chas. De Woody, March 18, 1918).
3. "Harding as Senator Befriended Woman Suspected as a Spy," *New York Times,* April 13, 1931.
4. "Declares Germany a World Outlaw," *New York Times,* April 14, 1918.
5. "Overman Bill Passed Senate," *New York Times,* April 30, 1918.
6. National Archives, File OG 143708 (Memorandum for the Attorney General, April 29, 1918).
7. National Archives, File OG 143708 (A. Bruce Bielaski to C. S. Weakley, April 29, 1918).
8. "Harding as Senator Befriended Woman Suspected as a Spy," *New York Times.*
9. WGH to Carrie Phillips, May 2, 1918, 88.1–2.
10. Ibid., 88.4.
11. Ibid., 88.3–4.
12. WGH to Ed Scobey, April 2, 1918, Scobey Papers.
13. "Senate Accepts Sedition Bill," *New York Times,* May 5, 1918.

14. "Spies and Their Congeners," *New York Times*, April 22, 1918.
15. "Allies Seek Plunder, Debs Tells Socialists," *New York Times*, June 17, 1918.
16. "Find Debs Guilty of Disloyal Acts," *New York Times*, September 13, 1918.
17. "Debs Gets 10 Years in Federal Prison," *New York Times*, September 15, 1918.
18. "Debs Loses Appeal; to Serve Ten Years," *New York Times*, March 11, 1919.
19. "Wilson Refuses to Pardon Debs," *New York Times*, February 1, 1921.
20. "Harding Frees Debs and 23 Others Held for War Violations," *New York Times*, December 24, 1921.
21. WGH to Ed Scobey, May 7, 1918, Scobey Papers.
22. Randolph C. Downes, *The Rise of Warren Gamaliel Harding, 1865-1920* (Columbus: Ohio State University Press, 1970), 287.
23. WGH to Ed Scobey, June 27, 1918, Scobey Papers.
24. WGH to Carrie Phillips, July 14, 1918, 57.1.
25. Ibid., 57.4.
26. Ibid., 57.5–7.
27. Ibid., 57.10–12.
28. "American Blow Upsets Foe," *New York Times*, July 16, 1918.
29. "Expected to Reach Epernay in One Day," *New York Times*, July 16, 1918.
30. "British Army on the Alert," *New York Times*, July 19, 1918.

CHAPTER 50: "YOU ARE THE WONDER WOMAN OF THE WORLD"

1. WGH to Carrie Phillips, July 23, 1918, 89.
2. Ibid., 89.4.
3. Ibid., 89.6–7.
4. WGH to Carrie Phillips, July 29, 1918, 90.
5. WGH to Carrie Phillips, August 3–6, 1918, 91; WGH to Carrie Phillips, August 6, 1918, 92.
6. Ibid., 93.3–4.
7. WGH to Carrie Phillips, August 16, 1918, 94.5–7.
8. "City Men Drive at Army Work," *New York Times*, August 11, 1915.
9. Nan Britton, *The President's Daughter* (New York: Elizabeth Ann Guild, 1927), 61–63.
10. Randolph C. Downes, *The Rise of Warren Gamaliel Harding, 1865-1920* (Columbus: Ohio State University Press, 1970), 274.
11. WGH to Carrie Phillips, August 17, 1918, 95.1.
12. Britton, *The President's Daughter*, 63.
13. "18 to 45 Draft to be Adopted by House Today," *New York Times*, August 24, 1918.
14. "Ohio Republicans for Prohibition," *New York Times*, August 29, 1918.
15. WGH to Carrie Phillips, August 20, 1918, 97. 3–4.
16. WGH to Carrie Phillips, August 29, 1918, 98.1.
17. "Socialist as Chancellor," *New York Times*, November 10, 1918.
18. "Bavaria Presents Claim to Throne," *New York Times*, November 3, 1918.
19. WGH to Ed Scobey, December 14, 1918, Scobey Papers.
20. "Baroness' Plan Is Heard Today," *Knoxville Journal and Tribune*, January 16, 1918.

CHAPTER 51: "WE HAVE BLUNDERED"

1. "City Mourns Colonel," *New York Times*, January 7, 1919.
2. "Embolism Caused Death," *New York Times*, January 7, 1919.
3. "Congress Mourns Colonel's Death," *New York Times*, January 7, 1919.
4. "Bury Roosevelt with Simple Rites as Nation Grieves," *New York Times*, January 9, 1919.
5. "Italians Cities Give President Amazing Greeting," *New York Times*, January 7, 1919.
6. "Scattered Firing in Berlin," *New York Times*, January 9, 1919.
7. C. Paul Vincent, *The Politics of Hunger: The Allied Blockade of Germany, 1915–1919* (Athens: Ohio University Press, 1985), 86–109.
8. WGH to Carrie Phillips, November 18, 1918, 99.1–2.

9. "Ex-Kaiser Silent Now through Fear," *New York Times,* December 5, 1918.
10. Carrie Phillips to WGH, December 5, 1918, 100.
11. WGH to Carrie Phillips, December 8, 1918, 101.
12. WGH to Ed Scobey, December 4, 1918, Scobey Papers.
13. WGH to Carrie Phillips, "For Christmas Eve" 1918, 117.1–2.
14. "President Starts Abroad," *New York Times,* December 5, 1918.
15. WGH to Ed Scobey, December 4, 1918, Scobey Papers.
16. Ed Scobey to WGH, November 14, 1918, Scobey Papers.
17. Ed Scobey to WGH, January 7, 1919, Scobey Papers.
18. "Roosevelt's Death Upsets 1920 Plans," *New York Times,* January 7, 1919.
19. Ibid.
20. WGH to Ed Scobey, January 14, 1919, Scobey Papers.
21. Ed Scobey to WGH, February 1, 1919, Scobey Papers.
22. WGH to Ed Scobey, February 7, 1919, Scobey Papers.
23. WGH to Carrie Phillips, February 7, 1919, 102.1–2.
24. Ibid., 102.4.
25. WGH to Ed Scobey, March 5, 1919, Scobey Papers.
26. WGH to Carrie Phillips, April 7, 1919, 103.4-5.
27. WGH to Isabelle Phillips, September 27, 1919, WGH Papers (telegram).
28. Randolph C. Downes, *The Rise of Warren Gamaliel Harding, 1865-1920* (Columbus: Ohio State University Press, 1970), 305.
29. WGH to Carrie Phillips, April 7, 1919, 103.3–4.
30. "Wilson Will Hold Treaty Rejected by Senate Change," *New York Times,* September 26, 1919.
31. "Strains of Years Tells on Wilson," *New York Times,* September 27, 1919.
32. WGH to Carrie Phillips, undated, 104.
33. WGH to Carrie Phillips, August 18, 1919, 105.1–2.
34. WGH to Ed Scobey, November 22, 1919, Scobey Papers.
35. WGH to Ed Scobey, December 8, 1919, Scobey Papers.
36. WGH to Carrie Phillips, February 2, 1920, 112.
37. Ibid., 112.3–7.
38. WGH to Carrie Phillips, February 15, 1920, 101.
39. WGH to Carrie Phillips, April 5, 1920, 109. The other letter is WGH to Carrie Phillips, March 22, 1920, 108.
40. WGH to Carrie Phillips, July 2, 1920, 110.
41. "Gigantic Majorities," *New York Times,* November 3, 1920.

EPILOGUE

1. Eldon Groves "I Knew Her," *Ohio Farmer,* September 5, 1964.
2. Francis Russell, "The Shadow of Warren Harding," *Antioch Review* 36 (Winter 1978).
3. "Death Claims Mrs. Phillips," *Marion Star,* February 5, 1960.
4. "'Carry On!' Attorney General Gregory Urges," *The Spy Glass, A Bulletin of News and Better Methods Issued by the American Protective League,* November 22, 1918.
5. Francis Russell, *The Shadow of Blooming Grove: Warren G. Harding in His Times* (New York: McGraw-Hill Book Company, 1968), 402.
6. "Abolition of Excess Profits Tax Needed," *Marion Star,* February 21, 1921.
7. Inauguration Ceremonies Ticket, March 4, 1921 ("Admit Bearer to the Senate Wing of the Capitol, to the East Galleries and to the East Front"), from Duckett microfilm.
8. Chester Fulton to Carrie Phillips, January 10, 1922, 113.
9. Chester Fulton to Carrie Phillips, June 18, 1923, 114.
10. "Scobey Rites Are Set for Saturday," *San Antonio Light,* February 7, 1931.
11. "Mrs. Sutton-Shope, Once Baroness, Dies," *New York Times,* March 12, 1932.
12. "Adolf Pickhardt, Long Navy Officer," *New York Times,* July 2, 1947.
13. "Churchill to Leave Hospital," *New York Times,* December 20, 1931.
14. Carrie Phillips to Carl Sawyer, undated, 115.4–5.

15. "Harding as Senator Befriended Woman Suspected as a Spy," *New York Times,* April 13, 1931.
16. "Carrie Identified as Marion Woman," *New York Times,* April 14, 1931.
17. "Lays Marion 'Spy Talk' to Gossip," *Cleveland Plain Dealer,* April 14, 1931.

AFTERWORD

1. Francis W. Durbin to James M. Cox, September 30, 1927, James M. Cox Papers, Wright State University, Dayton, Ohio.

Acknowledgments

*T*his book would not have been possible without the help of many people. John Dean has been the most important. It was his agreement to appear at the symposium at the vice presidential debate at Case Western Reserve University in 2004 that sparked my question to the Western Reserve Historical Society about any Harding memorabilia they may have that would be of interest to John when he visited Cleveland. John had recently completed an important biography of Harding at the request of Arthur Schlesinger, Jr., as part of the American Presidents Series. This inquiry is how I came to know of Kenneth Duckett's microfilm. John has been intimately involved with this project from that time through the present. He and I communicated with the Hardings to let them know we were working with the Duckett materials, he introduced me to Airié Stuart at Palgrave, and most importantly, he took endless phone calls and responded to a mountain of emails as I uncovered the material presented in this book and puzzled through all the important historical questions they raised. He had infinite patience, keen insight, and great enthusiasm but was always thoughtful and cautious in his approach to every question. He has a rigorous sense of treating history with as much objectivity as possible and he is widely read and scholarly in his approach. He has a lawyer's demand for proof. No one could ask for a better mentor and friend. As I told him many times, this book would not have come into existence without his help and support.

Kermit Pike of the Western Reserve Historical Society also played a pivotal role in this book. Kermit met and befriended Ken Duckett at archivists' meetings and functions over the years and it was Ken's friendship with Kermit that prompted him to give his materials to the Western Reserve Historical Society. Kermit is a professional's professional. He has great respect for history and his duty to history as an archivist. His work and devotion over the years at his historical society has made it one of the great treasures in the collection and preservation of American history. Ann Sindelar and Stephen Doell at the Western Reserve assisted me in research and in working with the Duckett papers.

Ken Duckett gave me permission to review and use his papers and talked with me a few times on the phone. He read a draft of this book and provided comments.

Dr. Warren G. Harding III of Cincinnati was also an important point of contact for me. He had a tough task, recognizing that his father did not wish these letters to be made public in his belief that the matters contained therein were entirely personal and should be kept that way. But Warren was open to discussion with me about the potential historical significance of the letters. He also has taken a lead role, along with his brother George, in protecting the legacy of his great-uncle's brother. Warren rightly focuses his attention on the important contributions of his ancestor and he never interposed any request or demand about what would appear in this book.

I also need to thank several people who read drafts and listened to my thinking aloud about the evidence I was finding. My readers included Tom Aldrich, Brian Lamb, Susan Belman, Gail Motley, Joanna Connors, and Michael Lindsay. Thanks also to researcher Thomas Huber, Roosevelt historian Harry Lembeck, and to relatives of Baroness Zollner, Gordon Dawson, and historian David Detzer, for their sharing of family geneology. Melinda Gilpin of the Harding Home ran down leads. Allison and Amanda Lansell helped with the transciption of the letters. Thanks to my cousin Jack Miller for picking up the files from the National Archives.

And, finally, I would be remiss if I did not effusively thank Palgrave for its extraordinary work. Airié Stuart, as editor and publisher, took special interest in this project and provided wise counsel and guidance with the manuscript. She has built a staff of extremely capable and loyal associates, including Michelle Fitzgerald, Lauren Dwyer, Donna Cherry, and Airié's executive assistant and great diplomat, Marie Ostby. They all know what they are doing and under Airié's leadership appear to be having fun—likely a rare thing in the stressful publishing world these days. They are an amazing group. Thanks to all.

Index